CASTLES OF EUROPE

CASTLES OF EUROPE

FROM CHARLEMAGNE TO THE RENAISSANCE

William Anderson
Photographs by Wim Swaan

Foreword by Sir John Hackett GCB DSO MA BLitt LLD
Principal of King's College, University of London

B. Mitchell

TORONTO

This edition published 1984 by Omega Books Ltd,
1 West Street, Ware, Hertfordshire, under licence
from the proprietor.

ISBN 0 907853 04 8

Printed and bound in Hong Kong by South China Printing Co.

Above: A trebuchet from an edition of *De Re Militari* by Valturio,
Paris, 1532.
Title page: The brass in Fletchling Church, Sussex, of the builder
of Bodiam castle Sir Edward Dalyngrigge, and of his wife.

Contents

Building the Tower of Babel, from the *Maciejowski Old Testament*; French, thirteenth century. *New York, Pierpont Morgan Library*, M.638, fo 3.

List of Plates

Front end papers
Knights jousting, drawing by Dürer, 1489. *London, British Museum*
Back endpapers
Drawings of machines and fortifications: (top right hand page) a castle
defended by heavy, low towers, the entrance guarded by a bastion.
Perhaps a design for the modernization of a castle in the Romagna;
attributed to Leonardo da Vinci, from the Codex Atlanticus, *Milan,
Biblioteca Ambrosiana*, 41v-*b*; and from Ms. B, fos 24v and 55v, *Paris,
Bibliothèque Nationale*; fo 24v shows (top) studies of the trajectories
of artillery fire at Castello Sforzesco, Milan.
Jacket front
Eltz, W. Germany
Jacket back
Battle at the gates of a city. *London, British Museum*, Stowe Ms. 54,
fo 83.

Maps and Plans

PREFACE

The yoke permitted
Gentle dray horses to build
Coercive castles[1]

This recent *haiku* by W. H. Auden expresses beautifully and succinctly the interconnections of the castle with all sides of medieval life. It is this flavour I have tried to communicate.

A word is necessary on the way this book is arranged. The captions sometimes contain much information that is not in the text. This was intended to avoid breaking the chronological flow of the text as far as possible. Chapter 1 describes how the castle was evolved; Chapter 2 describes the spread of the castle as a means of conquest in the eleventh century. The next three chapters deal with the castle in the twelfth and thirteenth centuries; Chapter 3 is concerned with general considerations, ranging from warfare to social life and literature. From this point onwards the division of Chapters 4, 5, 7 and 8 has a geographical basis. Chapter 4 covers the castles of France, the British Isles, and Spain with a side-look at the Holy Land, and chapter 5 the castles of the Empire (including the present Germany, Switzerland, Austria and Italy). In Chapter 6 (a pendant to Chapter 3) I attempt to distinguish some of the new factors affecting the castle in the fourteenth and fifteenth centuries and the next two chapters follow the same pattern as Chapters 4 and 5. Chapter 9 is concerned with the introduction of firearms, and Chapter 10 acts as an epilogue.

Some readers may complain that their favourite castles or groups of castles receive no mention; the numbers built will help to explain why. Here I could mention only 300 or so out of the tens of thousands that still survive or once stood. Others will complain with greater justice of the castles of whole regions or countries that are treated very shortly or ignored altogether. I can only answer that I have been forced to concentrate on certain important areas and periods and so exclude others in trying to strike a balance between mentioning as many different castles as possible and trying to relate the reasons for their building, and the manner in which they were used, to the political and social life of the Middle Ages. Also the quality of the information available varies widely from country to country and region to region and I have frequently had to depend on a range of sources limited both in depth and detail.

In writing this book I have incurred many debts of gratitude. First I must thank General Sir John Hackett, Principal of King's College, London, for a foreword which makes so many telling points. I had the benefit of conversations with Wim Swaan, the photographer, who is an architect himself and who has shown in the companion volume to this, *The Gothic*

Cathedral, how deep is his appreciation of the art and buildings of the period. Next I would like to thank Professor Donald Bullough of Nottingham University who read two drafts and with kindly patience helped me with advice and corrections. Dr Kenneth Fowler of Edinburgh University read the portions on French and English castles with precision and care. Dr Henry J. Cohn of Warwick University has criticized the manuscript especially where it affects the history of the Empire. My friend Dr Paul Thompson of the University of Essex made several very helpful suggestions. In many ways my chief debt is to a scholar who prefers not to be mentioned but whose caustic and witty pen in fighting error, pretension, and unjustified generalizations, gave me new insight into the demands of the subject and into the many places where, still, I have fallen short. I am, of course, responsible for all the faults that remain. Judith Filson was of the greatest assistance to me both in reading for me and taking notes and in her enthusiasm for the subject spurred on by her great love and wide knowledge of architecture. My acknowledgements to all the scholars and writers whose works I have made use of are given in the bibliography and notes at the back. I must also thank others who have not read the manuscript but who have helped in other ways. I must record my gratitude to Professor M. R. D. Foot who, although in no way responsible for anything in this book, first gave direction to my early and scattered interest in military history. Señor J. F. Finó kindly sent me proofs of the latest edition of his book on French castles. Mr H. J. H. T. Moddermann, Treasurer General of the *Institut des châteaux historiques*, helped me with queries and generously lent me material. The library staff of Chelsea College obtained books from abroad for me that otherwise I should never have read. Gerta Calmann put me in the way of finding other extremely useful books. Mrs Betty Ellis typed the first two drafts of the book for me. My colleagues in the Nuffield Foundation Science Teaching Project were extraordinarily patient with me. My wife read, criticized, and made many useful suggestions. My children helped by keeping out of the way when I was working and by not falling off the battlements when we visited castles. Finally I must express my gratitude to Moira Johnston of Elek Books Limited for helping me in so many ways, in getting me books, allowing me extra time, and for her ingenuity and persistence in obtaining on so many occasions exactly the illustration that was required.

January 1970

FOREWORD

by Sir John Hackett, GCB, DSO, MA, B LITT, LL D
Principal of King's College, University of London

There are many ways of considering castles. They can be looked at first of all from a purely military point of view, and even then have more than one aspect–strategical, for example, or tactical, or technical, or logistical. They also have political interest and importance, as well as social, economic, architectural, romantic, aesthetic. A special inclination to think about them in one of these ways may lead to restlessness or impatience when they are presented in another. Thus an economic historian exploring the effect on a neighbourhood of the pattern of confidence and constraints imposed upon it by the proximity of strong places is likely to find a description of their ruins in purely scenic terms unsatisfactory. A student of political history investigating the part played in dynastic devolution by the tenure of a secure family base may lose patience with romantic stories of seductive troubadours. Yet all these, and more, ways of thinking of castles, and of what went on around and in and because of them, are to be found among us and none deserves to be lightly dismissed. The shaping in much of western Europe of local economic development by the proximity of fortified dwellings is of great importance. So is the relationship between the degree of security offered by a defensible family base and the viability of dynastic succession. All these things deserve–and receive–close attention. But the ruins exist too, in some profusion and often with great beauty. Since the building now in decay was put up almost always for a functional purpose it was usually located on a spot that mattered–a high place, perhaps, or a place that for some reason or another (the nearby canalization or crossing of communications for example) could not be ignored. It tends still to be a noticeable feature of a landscape into which, with the effect of passing time upon local materials, it has often become largely assimilated.

There it stands, an extension of nature under the hand of man, lonely, crumbling, creeper-covered, pleasing to the eye and evocative of thoughts pleasurable or melancholy, feelings of regret or satisfaction, reflections philosophic or sentimental. As for troubadours and castle ladies, these too have their place. The importance for our western European literature and style of life of the concept of courtly love is immense. Every castle romance traces back, whether in form or content or in both, to sources of the highest significance in the growth of the culture in which we are bred.

There is thus no exclusively respectable way of thinking about castles and any book about them, if it aims to be a full and important statement as this one does, must recognize the existence of more than one point of view and the need to satisfy a variety of requirements. A writer of such a book must accept that, apart from questions of hard fact which can usually though not always be judged against the record, his interpretations may not everywhere be equally welcome. His right to say what he likes, however, deserves to be most vigorously defended. This is a book containing much erudition, in which a tremendous mass of material is marshalled, not least in a collection of pictures which must surely be unique. Anyone with any liking for castles at all will find here a vast amount to interest and much to stimulate and where the stimulus is to informed disagreement it is not the less valuable for that.

What distinguishes the castle from other habitable edifices is an essential military purpose of a quite specific kind. This was the denial of entry. Other buildings with other primary purposes–farmhouses, barns, churches, storehouses, for example–have been furnished with the means of denying entry to those whom it was thought better, for more or less pressing reasons, to keep out. This did not necessarily make castles of them. They would only become castles if, being inhabited also as dwellings, the requirement to deny entry to them took precedence over pretty well all other requirements.

Denial of entry created a secure space within which those who disposed of it could not be prevented by others outside from doing as they wished–from surviving, for example, or from making or keeping what they wanted to make or keep. On the security of a space, and the immunity from interference of those who occupied it, is based the military importance of the castle and the enormous influence it has had in the development of a culture whose pattern probably owes more to military factors than to anything else. Between the tenth and fifteenth centuries, for half a millennium, the castle was not only the most important artefact in western Europe: it was possibly even its dominant element.

The chief function of the castle was to furnish, in a military structure, a secure base for offensive action. This is not to say that it was not very often used defensively. It could be used to meet defensive requirement, or in the offensive, or in the counter-offensive and in the pages of this book will be found a wealth of clear examples of each of these applications. But even when its purpose was primarily defensive it fulfilled this purpose only by the possession of a potentiality for offensive action. Without this it could in the military context be safely ignored. The offensive capability lay in the soldiery it harboured and a castle would be quite correctly described as 'commanding' the area over which fighting men, based securely within it, could effectively operate.

The castle could be regarded from another point of view as a protected but (unlike the tank today) immobile weapon platform with certain conceptual similarities to the hardened silo which houses a ballistic missile upon a launching pad in the strategic weapons systems of a superpower. With the introduction of gunpowder the similarity of the castle to the weapon-in-the-silo system grows both more and less; more because the attack is now made by means of a missile weapon, less because the missile weapon from the cannon was projected by an explosion and was no longer self-propelling like the man-at-arms. In this context we should be careful not to make too sharp a distinction between the man-at-arms and the weapons he bore. The man-at-arms together with these instruments and his skill in their use should be regarded, in sum, as a weapon. The military significance of the castle lay in the furnishing of a secure base from which this weapon could be offensively applied at a distance from it.

Herein lay the great advantage of mounted men over dismounted. Not only could the mounted man be more heavily protected, carry heavier and therefore more efficacious tools, use them more effectively than the foot soldier by reason of the elevation of his weapon platform and develop shock action out of the momentum of the moving horse; he could also move much more quickly than the foot soldier and, perhaps most important of all in relation to the castle, his radius of effective action from his base was greater. Three or four miles was in normal times (I exclude campaigning) about the limit of the radius of action of the foot soldier from his base. It would be less in unfavourable terrain. That of a mounted man would be double this and more, while his response time would be much shorter. A foot soldier would scarcely be expected to move at more than three and a half miles in the hour. The quicker response of mounted troops can be judged from the speeds formerly laid down in the British Army in the manual *Cavalry Training*: four miles an hour at the walk, eight at the trot and fifteen at the gallop. We aimed to cover five miles in the hour through the marching day. Our horses were lighter, of course, than the animals bred for remounts in the twelfth century. They were handier and less burdened. In what was called marching order, a troop horse with an average man would be carrying not much less than three hundred and fifty pounds. This would be considerably less than the all-up weight of a fully equipped and protected mounted man-at-arms in, say, 1250.

The importance of the mounted man in the military structure of western Europe in the Middle Ages, with all the immense and still incalculable effect this has had upon the development of our culture, depended above all on the stirrup. The introduction of the stirrup had as important an effect on the development of weapons technology as the introduction of gunpowder, mechanical propulsion or nuclear fission. The system of which the castle is a cardinal feature would have been quite otherwise without the stirrup. The castle is indeed a machine for ruling and fighting, as the author of this book points out. It might best be looked at, however, following a mid-twentieth century mode, as one component (the major component perhaps) in a complete weapons system. Advancement in techniques, developments in design, the availability of new and improved materials all play a part in the development of the system as a whole. The parts of the system can be studied to some degree in isolation but we should never lose sight of the coherence of the system as a whole if we are fully to understand the functioning of the parts. But let us here be careful about overtones in the term 'knight' if what we are seeking to investigate is not an institution, that of knighthood, but the functional significance of the mounted man-at-arms.

However castles are looked at or thought about, there is much in this beautiful book for everyone. Early origins in Europe, in which a good deal must remain speculative, lead to firmer and better-known ground, as we move forward through wooden structures and the motte and bailey to more enduring monuments of stone. Here the restless, questing Normans catch the eye, stern realists with harsh, inquiring minds of seemingly endless adaptability. When they invaded England they brought stone castle building with them but used it now as it had not been used at home, as an instrument for the consolidation of conquest and the stabilization of a foreign subject realm. If the Norman Conquest changed England it also changed the Normans. The very military structure within which they operated underwent a radical change in transplantation. The oath of allegiance now to be taken by sub-tenants directly to the crown diminished in England the opportunity for that armed dissidence on the part of tenants-in-chief which the dukes in Normandy had themselves so profitably exploited. Norman feudalism is based upon the castle and the horse; it was a military structure employing a powerful weapons system to political ends. The Normans in south Italy, Sicily and the Levant, the emperors in Germany and Italy; the relationship in England and on the continent between private crenellation and public order—not always and everywhere an identical relationship—and the huge increase in castle building in stone wherever feudalism ramified and developed; the influence of the Crusades, both in feed-out and feed-back; considerations of siting and construction; spur castles, *Wasserburgen,* concentric fortification, related military techniques, the impact of the development of the whole weapons system on science and literature; the Angevins, the Capetians, the Valois, the Hohenstaufens; the Welsh and Scottish wars in England, the extension of Teutonic control over Slavs beyond the Elbe; Ireland, Spain, Portugal; Bohemia, Hungary, Scandinavia; the growth of mercenary military service and the new professionalism of the late fourteenth and fifteenth centuries; the decline of the dominance of the mounted man-at-arms with the rediscovery of infantry and the impact on the system as a whole of the introduction of gunpowder; the brief revival in military importance of the fortified dwelling in the seventeenth century, during the Thirty Years War in Germany, the Wars of Religion in France and the Civil War in England; the final separation of fortress and dwelling once more to develop independently; these and many other strands are here woven into a fabric which it would be quite impossible to reduce into the compass of what can be described in a page or two. This is a large topic and not at all an easy one to manage. But we have here a notable and beautiful book upon it, with the most splendid pictures, by reason of which a central theme in the growth of western society will now be better understood. It is important that this better understanding should spread. For in whatever one of many different ways these fortified dwellings may be regarded, or in whatever combination of several, there can be few things in the background of the western European more important, or commanding wider interest, than the castle.

Fig. 1 Map of Europe and part of the Middle East showing principal sites.

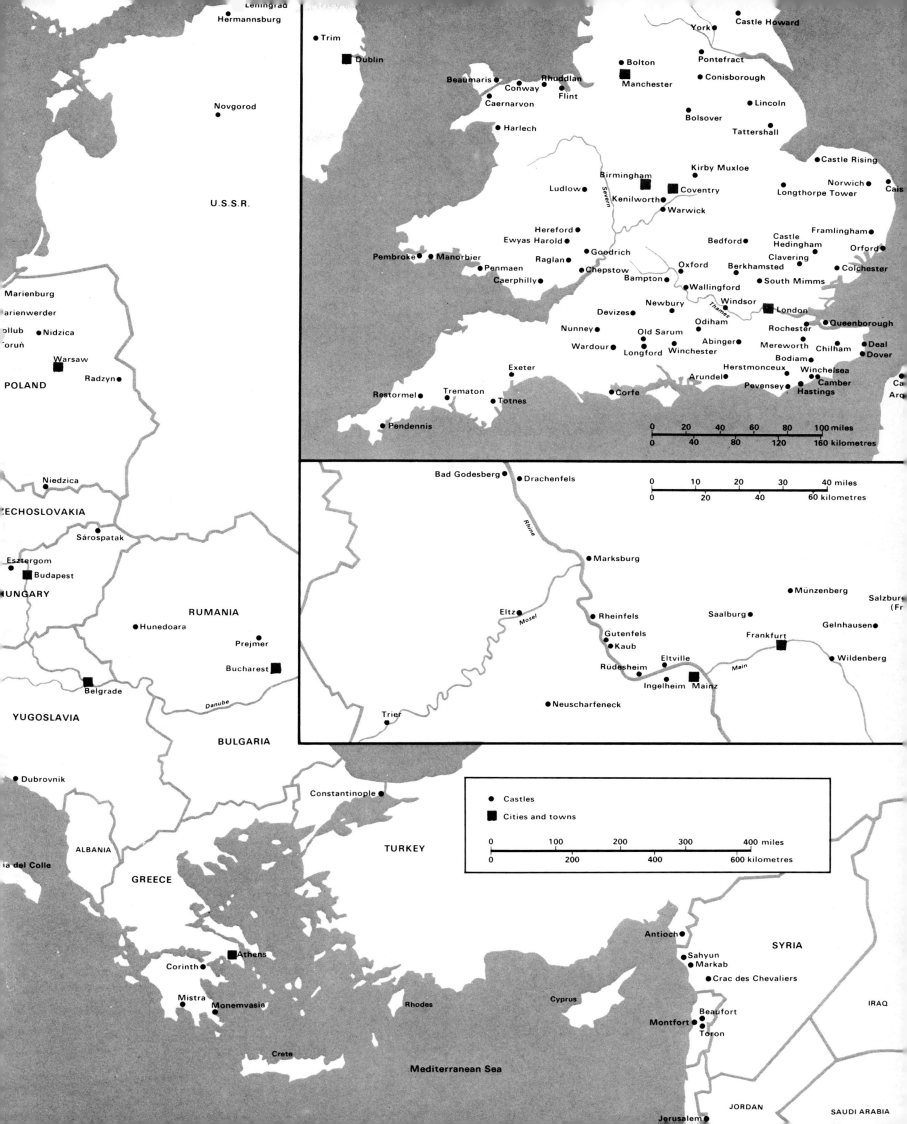

Leningrad
Hermannsburg
Trim
Dublin
Novgorod

York
Castle Howard
Bolton
Pontefract
Beaumaris
Conway
Rhuddlan
Manchester
Conisborough
Caernarvon
Flint
Lincoln
Harlech
Bolsover
Tattershall

U.S.S.R.

Castle Rising
Birmingham
Kirby Muxloe
Ludlow
Coventry
Norwich
Kenilworth
Longthorpe Tower
Cais
Warwick
Framlingham
Hereford
Bedford
Ewyas Harold
Castle Hedingham
Orford
Pembroke
Manorbier
Goodrich
Clavering
Penmaen
Raglan
Chepstow
Oxford
Berkhamsted
Colchester
Caerphilly
Bampton
Wallingford
South Mimms
Marienburg
Windsor
London
arienwerder
Newbury
Thames
ollub
Nidzica
Devizes
Odiham
Queenborough
oruń
Nunney
Old Sarum
Rochester
Warsaw
Wardour
Abinger
Mereworth
Chilham
Deal
Radzyn
Longford
Winchester
Bodiam
Dover
POLAND
Exeter
Herstmonceux
Winchelsea
Arundel
Camber
Restormel
Trematon
Pevensey
Hastings
Ca
Corfe
Arc
Totnes
Pendennis

0   20   40   60   80   100 miles
0   40   80   120   160 kilometres

Bad Godesberg
Drachenfels
0   10   20   30   40 miles
0   20   40   60 kilometres

Niedzica

Rhine

ECHOSLOVAKIA

Marksburg

Sárospatak

Münzenberg
Esztergom
Salzbur
Budapest
Eltz
Rheinfels
Saalburg
(Fr
UNGARY
Mosel
Gutenfels
Gelnhausen
RUMANIA
Kaub
Frankfurt
Hunedoara
Eltville
Wildenberg
Prejmer
Rüdesheim
Main
Ingelheim
Mainz
Bucharest
Belgrade
Neuscharfeneck
Danube
Trier
YUGOSLAVIA

BULGARIA

Dubrovnik

Constantinople
● Castles
■ Cities and towns

ALBANIA
TURKEY
0   100   200   300   400 miles
0   200   400   600 kilometres
ia del Colle

GREECE
Antioch
SYRIA
Athens
Sahyun
Corinth
Markab
Crac des Chevaliers
Mistra
Monemvasia
Rhodes
Cyprus
IRAQ
Beaufort
Montfort
Toron
Crete
JORDAN
SAUDI ARABIA
Mediterranean Sea
Jerusalem

INTRODUCTION

Throughout history man has sought permanent security by building fortifications, and every variation of landscape that Europe has to offer reveals evidence of this desire: lake villages, Bronze- or Iron-Age encampments dense with bracken and gorse, Roman town and frontier walls, a Norman motte standing like a large inverted pudding-basin, a castle on a mountain peak, a fortified monastery, a town still cramped within its star-shaped bastions of the seventeenth century, or a gun emplacement of the last war, its concrete now brown with rust. All these examples tell a story of men's need to guard their families, their land, their cattle, their crops, their factories, their way of life, and their local or national pride. This book deals with only a short part of the long history of defensive building, from the times of Charlemagne and of the Vikings to the French invasion of Italy in 1494, but to the fortifications of no other period does there attach the romance and fascination that draws us to the castles built and lived in during these few hundred years.

Why do castles still exercise this fascination over us? It is not only the still powerful effect of Walter Scott and his fellow Romantic novelists and poets who taught Europe to admire them again, nor the childhood fairy stories, nursery rhymes, films and television serials about Robin Hood or King Arthur and his knights that steep us in the atmosphere of crenellated walls, blue-tiled towers, flapping banners, trumpets sounding, and the rattle of a drawbridge being lowered for a party of knights in gleaming armour to pass over the moat on their way to battle. There are deeper reasons for this fascination, connected with the fact that society today is still deeply affected by the political and social rules evolved by the men and women who built and resided in the castles. These distant people who bequeathed us language, laws, literature, and nationhood are our ancestors, whether by blood or by the spirit, and in studying the castle we are brought nearer to their time. Their society, frequently based on the castle, gave us Magna Carta; one of the most important influences in European secular literature in the poems of the troubadours and the minnesingers; and new ideals in romantic love and in personal honour and liberty, to offer only a few examples. The special attraction of the castle which makes it stand out from earlier and from later fortifications in our imagination draws on traditions that are alive today. These traditions would never have been so strong

1 Josselin, France. The frontage on the Breton River Oust of the former home of the great constable of France, Olivier de Clisson, who bought the castle in 1370 and made it a weapon of royal power against the dukes of Brittany.

had the castle not provided one of the stabilizing factors in their early development and had it not played a notable part in the recovery of secular civilized life in Europe. Napoleon once said that fortifications are necessary if only to gain time; this is true of the castle in our period, not merely for military reasons but because the presence of castles gained time also for the tranquillity, the sense of ease, and the reflection that are necessary to civilization.

What is a castle? *The Shorter Oxford English Dictionary* wisely keeps its first definition very loose: 'a large building or group of buildings protected by fortifications'. This covers both the royal castles which acted as military bases or as garrisoned forts and the royal and baronial castles which were fortified residences. In the latter sense the castle has a double nature: it is both a home and a fortress. These two elements were forced into marriage by necessity; it was rarely a comfortable or an equal partnership and in most European countries the marriage had ended in divorce by the seventeenth century when the partners could only develop if separated. It is, however, this double nature which makes the castle so different from the dwellings and the fortifications of other periods. Throughout this book the reader will be aware of the constant swing between the castle built chiefly as a residence and the castle built chiefly as a military base or fortress. Whichever element is dominant depends on the political climate of the period and the country at the time of building; it is because of this sensitivity to social and political influences that one cannot tell the story of the castle simply as a matter of architectural or military history. In this comparatively short study I have tried to set each main area and period of castle building against the general historical background, charting the variations of this double nature in the castle as it responded to these influences. At the same time, by descriptions of the buildings, by stories from contemporary chroniclers, or with biographical details I have tried to give an impression of the diversity of roles that castles played. These roles were exceedingly varied, whether as a means of terrorizing a conquered population, or as toll stations on a river or a mountain pass, or as a military arsenal, or as a shrine for relics, or, as in the case of some of the Hussites, a fortress devoted for a time to Christian communism. Some castles never had to withstand a single siege and for the whole of their existence were calm country houses. Others had short and violent lives and were constantly under attack. Some were the centres of administration for their districts and were more busy with the sharpening of pens than of arrows. Others, like the Swiss

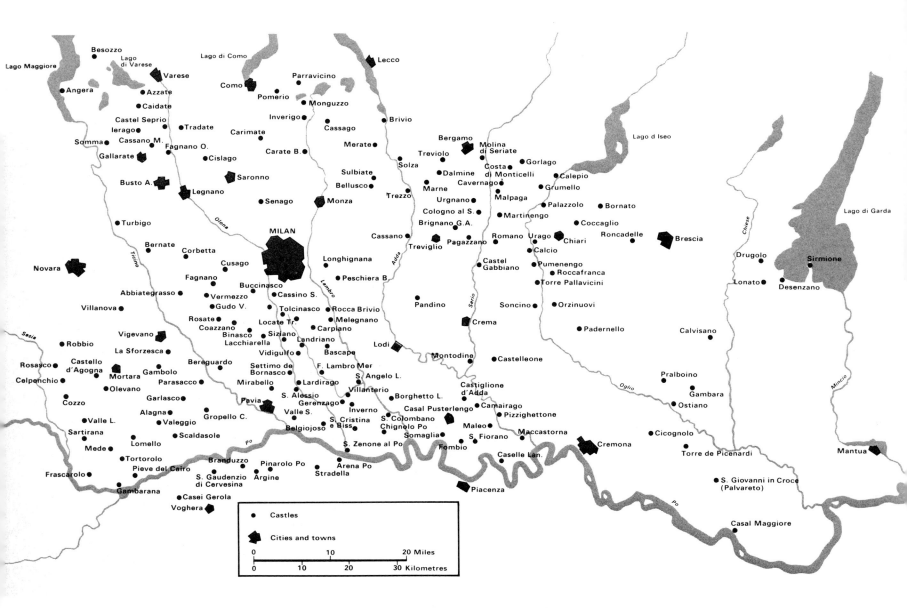

Fig. 2 The distribution of the principal castles in part of the plain of Lombardy within a 50-km (30-mile) radius of Milan and extending south-east towards Mantua. There are 170 marked here but many other less important ones existed or still exist. (After Perogalli, C. *Castelli della pianura Lombarda*)

grotto fortresses, were barely fortified mountain caves, acting as the holds of robbers and brigands. Some were the palaces of kings and princes ablaze with colour, fashion, life, and intrigue; and some were dour outposts for down-at-heel mercenaries with never the sight of a woman.

The forms the castle took and the purposes it served varied, of course, from country to country, but one of the rewards of looking at castles on the scale of Europe as a whole is to be reminded of the international nature of medieval life at its best: the great pilgrimages, the Crusades, the common bonds of religion and chivalry, and the exchange of ideas, artistic influences, and techniques. Castles were the post-stages in this international exchange and it may give some idea of their importance in medieval society to quote estimates of the numbers that were built. According to one, there were 10,000 castles in Germany alone. For France some estimates give more than twice that number, though they are probably

exaggerated. In Aquitaine there was a castle every eight miles along important routes (four miles being considered the effective range of sortie from each). In Spain, there still exist more than 2,500 castles, a number which reaches 10,000 if fortified works of all kinds in the post-Roman period are included.[1] Even a country as far east as Poland has 450 castles surviving in various states of repair. In Belgium there are more than 900. In Italy, the province of Verona alone contains over 100 fortresses and the map on this page shows the density of castles over part of the plain of Lombardy. The achievement of small populations in building a few hundred cathedrals is astonishing but the much larger numbers of castles built during the same period makes the energy of medieval communities even more amazing.

At least as early as King Alfred of England, it was said that men are divided into three kinds: those who pray, those who fight, and those who work. Castles are the architectural remains of those who fight. The remains of those who pray, the cathedrals, abbeys, and churches, have retained their original purpose longest. The labour of the peasant, which cleared the great forests, drained the marshes, and tilled and marled infertile soil, created the country landscape of Europe. Castles,

2 A grotto fortress as shown by Merian the elder in *Topographia Austriacarum*, 1649. In present-day Italy, the River Brenta is shown in the foreground and the town of Cismon d'Grappa on the right.

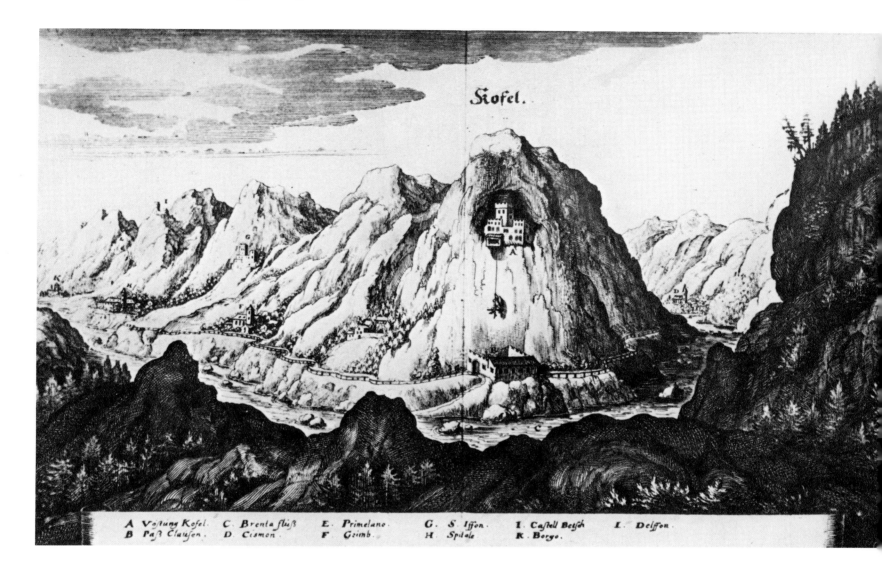

however, have had the shortest lives in terms of fulfilling the functions for which they were built. Many are still lived in; some are used as barracks. But it needs now a great effort of the imagination to understand their dominating role in stabilizing medieval society or the part they played in the growth of Europe and in the fixing of its political geography and in the foundation of many of its cities and towns. Castles were essential to the political structure of the society which built and lived in them. It was because of this that so many thousands of castles were built. In a time when the very metal needed to mint money was physically scarce, castles represented an enormous investment and although they may now seem merely romantic ruins or military curiosities they were to medieval monarchs what the provision of rocket bases and early-warning systems are to modern governments. And it was not only kings and rulers who wanted castles, because to possess many castles was the desire of great numbers of ambitious princelings and feudal lords. The strong castle was the great landowner's token of success in the eyes of the world; dining in his hall he was surrounded by dependants who were ingrained with a lifelong devotion to his person and his advancement. Going to war he attacked other castles and, if

he were a keen builder, tried to learn everything he could of the latest methods in making his home impregnable. The heroes he hoped to emulate, Roland, Oliver, the Cid, Arthur, Lancelot, all were given magnificent castles in the imagination of the poets, and even the Holy Grail, the ultimate desire of every true knight, had its home in the Castle of Carbonek.

Castles, therefore, touch every side of medieval life from the basest to the most sublime: the aim of this book is to give an impression of their rich diversity and the world they defended and nurtured.

THE ORIGINS OF THE EUROPEAN CASTLE

The monks of the Dark Ages built their monasteries to save their souls and in the process to help preserve civilization. The first castle builders had a more primitive compulsion – to defend life itself from the Norsemen and the Magyars. Out of the troubles of the ninth century grew feudalism, a political and social system whereby land and rights are held by a vassal of his lord, not in outright ownership, but in exchange for specified military assistance and for a number of other duties, including making payments on great occasions or crises in the career of the lord. The vassal in return expected protection, largesse, and security in his tenure.

Historians have noted the appearance of this system in other countries at various periods, notably in Japan from the twelfth century onwards where the *daimyo,* or land-holding magnates, built castles for their private wars, especially in the sixteenth century.[1] The history of the European castle, with its twin aspects of home and fortress, is inextricably linked with the rise and flowering of this new social order. Wherever in north-western Europe there was anarchy, feudalism appeared to counteract it and with feudalism came the castle. What makes the castle so different from the fortifications of the classical world is that it derives from the new non-Roman society that

first appeared in a civilized form in the age of Charlemagne. This society was under pressures either of invasion or of social change that, in the ninth century, forced together the formerly separate elements of home and fortress: the ancient German and Scandinavian way of life, based on the open hall and on scattered settlements, had to be concentrated within fortifications whose designs derived from either the classical world or the ring-works which had earlier sheltered camps of refuge or protected religious centres. These pressures created the first castles.

One way of understanding the original features of the castle and how these were dependent upon new social and military forces is to contrast them with the fortifications of the ancient world. From this contrast certain unchanging principles of attack and defence become evident.

Classical fortifications and siegeworks

Military architecture is probably as old an art as religious architecture and in some of the temples and citadels of ancient Egypt and Mesopotamia the two are found combined. The great gateways, or pylons, of an Egyptian temple such as Medinet Habu (1200 BC) are fortresses in their own right.

3 The siege of a city from the palace of Ashurnasirpal II (883–59 BC) at Nimrud. The wheeled siege-engine is equipped with a ram for battering the walls while archers in its tower rake the wall-walks of the city with arrowfire. Note the flanking towers in the city walls.

The Hittite citadels provide some of the earliest examples of flanking (ensuring that no part of one's own defences provides a cover for the enemy to attack unobserved or out of range). Even the form of defence known as crenellation, the up-and-down edging to battlements which is to us one of the chief identifying signs of the castle, may have originated in Mesopotamia–not as a military device to protect defending archers but as an architectural expression of a holy snake symbol to signify the sacred character of the building it crowned.[2] If this were so, a good commander would still be quick to realize its advantages and the famous bas-reliefs of Ashurnasirpal II show in other ways how advanced the Assyrians were in siegecraft by the ninth century BC (plate 3).

So much experience of fortifications and sieges had been gained by the ancient world, in Egypt, Mesopotamia, Asia Minor, and Greece, that by 200 BC a school devoted to military architecture was founded on the island of Rhodes. The subject was studied at other schools as well and the results were published in manuscripts such as those of Pyrrhus of Macedonia, Diades, Agesistratus, Aeneas, and Philo of Byzantium. The last was writing in about 120 BC, and he moved to Alexandria where he became a pupil of the great engineer, Ctesibius. The ideas these men evolved were preserved in Byzantium and the Arab world and reached the western world through the writings of Vitruvius and Vegetius. The Romans came across this highly developed siegecraft during their conquests of the Greek world. No more sophisticated devices were used than at the siege of Syracuse, for example, during which Archimedes, using one of his numerous inventions, was said to have burned the Roman fleet by training great mirrors on to the ships. After their final conquest in the east, and in the course of extending their Empire northwards through Gaul, the Rhine valley, and Britain, the Romans adapted this experience to new uses.

The Romans invented a simple plan for fortifications–the *castrum* or camp, devised in the first place as a base for taking by siege an enemy town or fort. This camp was generally rectangular in form, surrounded by a rampart or a wall and protected beyond that by a ditch or a series of ditches. Four gates, one in the centre of each wall, straddled the roads that led to the centre of the camp, where stood the tent of the legionary commander. This simple plan, from which seasoned troops could construct a *castrum* in a matter of days, was gradually adopted for permanent camps or barracks, such as the Castra Praetoria built at Rome by Tiberius for the Praetorian guard in AD 23 (see also plate 4), and it even came to be used in some cases for the founding of new cities. As settlements became permanent, so towers carrying weapons and other sophistications were added. Even in its simplest form, however, it provided a Roman army with a fortified base which was always difficult to take. It can be compared with the Normans' use of the rapidly built motte and bailey described in Chapter 2, which was also a means of consolidating a position on ground already conquered.

The Romans' skill in building their army camps was naturally applied also to the defences of the towns upon which the trade of the Empire depended. Many of them survived, despite neglect, for so long that they could be repaired for defence against the Vikings in the ninth century, and even later incorporated into medieval fortifications, as with the multi-angular tower at York. In their building techniques, as in other matters, the Romans drew upon the experience of the Greeks,

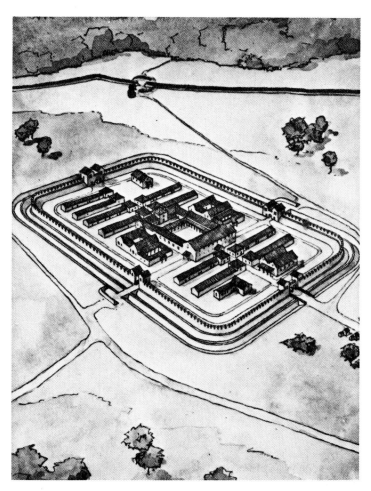

4 Saalburg, near Bad Homburg, W. Germany. A water-colour reconstruction of a Roman frontier fortress of the second century AD. Its regular plan derives from the *castrum*, the Roman army camp.

using timber bonding in the very walls, which made these walls far more resistant to the action of a ram. They were also, of course, admirable masons and built with such permanence that, to take one example of the enduring quality of their work, even today builders' contracts for work in the City of London provide for extra payment should the Roman wall be encountered. Great care and experience were used in the placing of towers–the avoidance of sharp angles that could be attacked by bores, the provision of further defences on the wall rampart, and the burying in soft soil of large pots in the outworks that would cause siege engines to sink.

These defences were, of course, planned with certain well-established means of attack in mind. The methods of siegecraft used by the Romans, which were to be the same in the Middle Ages, were of four main types–mining, ramming, escalade, and the use of projectile weapons such as the *petraria* and *balista*.[3]

In mining, the object was to take away enough of the foundations of a tower or a wall to cause the superstructure to collapse either by subsidence or by setting fire to the pit-props. This method could be opposed by counter-mining by which the defenders tried to cut through to the attackers' gallery and to drive them off either by fighting or by smoking them out like wasps with foul-smelling substances.

In the case of ramming, the largest tree to be found in the neighbourhood was felled, stripped, and furnished with a heavy metal head, sometimes actually in the shape of a ram's

head – hence its name. To protect the men working it the ram was sheltered by a penthouse. This penthouse, moving upon wheels or rollers, had a roof composed of several layers, including mortared tiles, covered by heavy mattresses, to make it proof against missiles dropped from the walls, and it was topped with hides to prevent it catching fire. The ram was hung on chains from the roof of the penthouse and the men inside would swing it against the walls. The penthouse also acted as a protection for the bore or *musculus* whose action was to pick away, stone by stone, at the walls – a technique more effective against Roman timber-bonded walls than the ram.

Escalade meant the use of ladders (a very dangerous procedure), or the building of great siege-towers constructed to the height of the wall they were designed to attack. The defenders on the ramparts could be raked with fire while a drawbridge was lowered to the wall-walk and the besiegers then rushed out to fight hand-to-hand. These towers were extremely cumbersome to move; they were in constant danger of overturning or of catching fire, or of being battered to pieces by the artillery of the besieged.

Into this last category came the *petraria* and the *balista* – weapons for hurling large stones or javelins.[4] The Romans had developed them to a considerable degree of power and accuracy but it is possible that medieval military engineers produced many improvements on Roman artillery, including the use of counterpoises in the trebuchet, a device unknown to the Romans who depended on such weapons as great bows worked by tension or stone-throwing machines worked by the torsion of human or animal hairs and fibres.

There was, therefore, scarcely a method of fortification or siegecraft known to the Middle Ages that had not been employed by the Romans or their predecessors. The one great difference between the methods of fortification lay in the purpose for which they were used. The communications of the Roman Empire were set by the great trade routes – for the import of grain from North Africa to southern Europe, spices and cloth from the East, pottery and soap from Gaul, or metals from Spain. The transport of goods, sped on well-tended roads and freighted on pirate-free seas, went from fortified town to fortified town – those towns into which it was the Roman policy to concentrate the population. The boundaries of this Empire were guarded by professional soldiers, often recruited hundreds or thousands of miles from the provinces in which they served. The camps they built and the walls they manned had a solely military purpose: to defend the Roman roads and the *Limes*. These fortifications, far more effective and thorough than most works of the Middle Ages, were related to an international strategy. Except for the Danevirke, built between *c* 810 and *c* 1160 to protect Denmark from the south, we can find nothing in the Middle Ages conceived on the scale of Hadrian's Wall or the defences of the *Limes*, the borders of Germany with the Empire, or, to seek an example from another continent, with the Great Wall of China

5 *Above left* A ram in its penthouse, sometimes called a 'sow' or a 'cat'; a woodcut from the 1585 edition of Vegetius' *De Re Militari*, published in Antwerp.

6 *Left* The 'tortoise', a detachment of Roman soldiers attacking under cover of their shields; another woodcut from the same edition of Vegetius.

7 *Right* The Lateran Gate, Rome. The impressive brickwork of this ancient part of the defences of Rome.

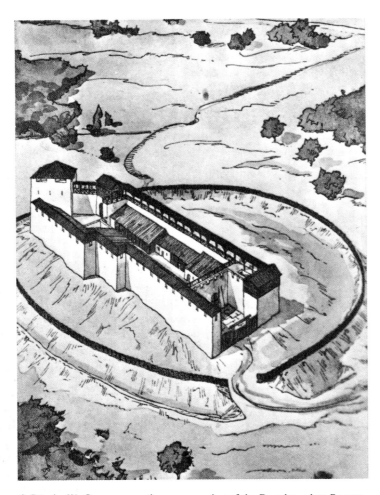

8 Bürgle, W. Germany, on the upper reaches of the Danube; a late Roman fortress of the fourth century AD; a water-colour reconstruction.
The spacious and regular layout of the camp in plate 4 has been rejected in favour of a system of defending the fortress sector by sector.

which stretches over a distance as far as that from Calais to Istanbul. In contrast, the first castles of the early Middle Ages were centres of rural and local administration. In many of their functions they were the heirs of the Roman villa rather than of the Roman town.

The villa, the centre of Roman rural life whether in Italy or in the provinces, was rarely a fortified building. There was more to be feared from uprisings of the slaves by whose labour the great estates (or *latifundia*) were tilled, than from outside attacks. The problem therefore was to keep the slaves *in* rather than marauders *out*. The system can be compared to that of the brick slave houses which stood alongside the wooden mansions of the southern slave states before the Civil War in America.

Not all Roman fortifications depended on the *castrum* plan. An introduction in the time of Antoninus Pius (138-161 AD) was the *burgus,* or watchtower, which was probably the fore-runner of the *Bergfried,* the nucleus of many later German castles. Even the rigid ground-plan of the *castrum* became modified, as in the fourth century fortress of the Bürgle near Gundremmingen in which the *burgus* acts as a sort of keep (plate 8). This plan conforms with the principle of defence according to which most early castles were to be built–the defence of a fortress sector by sector, and it is a sign of a lack of confidence. The Roman *castrum* like Saalburg near Hom-burg (plate 4), on the other hand, could deal with attack from

sides all of equal strength. The adoption of a system of piece-meal defence points to a much less assured spirit in the builder, as though when fighting he is only trying to gain time–not to drive off the attackers once and for all. By the fourth century there is another sign of decaying confidence: the frontier defences could no longer keep out the barbarians and between 306 and 337 Constantine adopted a policy of defence in depth in Gaul by providing the towns with fortified walls, traces of which remain to this day.

But the fortification of towns did little to arrest the decline of the Empire's trade in the fourth and the fifth centuries AD and this was followed by a corresponding decline in the towns. Richer citizens removed to the country where they tried to make themselves entirely self-supporting except for luxuries. Other factors contributing to the break-up were the extreme decrease in the population and the barbarization of the Empire. Society lacked cohesion, a lack caused by the dwelling together of so many races that remained separate in language, law, and customs.

This meant, in effect, a return to the form of defence that had prevailed in most of Europe before the establishment of the Roman Empire: the provision of local centres of refuge–a system that had perhaps never been interrupted in lands such as Scandinavia and the territories of the Slavs and those regions of Germany which had avoided Roman rule. The most sophisticated non-Roman fortifications had been the stone brochs with double walls built in the north and west of Scotland, possibly by settlers from south-west Britain, largely in the first century AD as a refuge from slavers. The most famous of these is the Broch of Mousa in the Shetlands.

The recent excavations on South Cadbury Hill in Somerset[5], which some identify with the site of King Arthur's Camelot, show what happened in one case after the Roman withdrawal. The hill, which has a record of settlement going back to the Neolithic Age, was a pagan cult centre in the fourth century AD. By the end of the next century–traditionally the period of Arthur–it was fortified by a stone wall pinned through with timbers at right angles to the wall, running to the stone embankment which acted as a wall-walk. The timber-pinning was a Roman practice. There were many similar sites of refuge, especially in Germany and Poland, but these either show a decline from the scientifically designed fortifications of the classical world or else were never in a position to be influenced by them. By the fifth century series of forts were built on the Baltic islands, on the west coast of Sweden, and in many parts of Norway and Finland.[6]

The medieval castle builders were fascinated by Roman methods. Later Roman writers on military affairs, such as Vegetius, were studied avidly by many notable commanders in the twelfth century. The memory of Rome's greatness was

9 Chillon, Switzerland. Standing on an island site on Lake Geneva fortified from antiquity, the castle of Chillon owes its present form to the architect Pierre Mainier working for Peter II of Savoy in the middle of the thirteenth century. He brought earlier constructions, such as the central tower or *Bergfried* (known as the Tower of Alinge), into a coherent system of defence which, because of the strength of the site, demanded the use of flanking towers only on the land side (right). The castle's most important function, because it occupied a site on a vital trade route, was the control of water traffic on the lake. Although it still contains many notable medieval interiors, dating from its use by the counts of Savoy as a residence (plates 10 & 52) it was used later as a prison, notably for François Bonnivard, a hero of the Swiss reformation who inspired Byron to his poem *The Prisoner of Chillon.*

not preserved solely by the Church, with its Latin and its claims to have inherited the western Empire. It was preserved also by structures as enduring as the Porta Nigra at Trier (plate 11), Hadrian's Wall, the walls of Rome itself, and Constantine's Gallo-Roman town walls. The first Crusaders must have been well accustomed to the sight of Roman fortifications but when, in 1096, they came to Byzantium, they found a city where the great Roman military skills had not only been preserved but improved.

The walls of Byzantium

The construction of the land walls of Byzantium began in 413 AD against the threat of the Ostrogoths and the Huns. Three years before, Alaric the Visigoth had sacked Rome. The western Empire was in dissolution and the inhabitants of Gaul and Italy were forced to acknowledge that they would have to live with their conquerors. Why were the Byzantines so much more effective than the Romans against the barbarians? One answer is that they had kept their civilization at a higher general level and therefore defended it more vigorously. Another is that, unlike Rome, Byzantium's population was still growing and the eastern Empire was still very rich. The building of the walls was followed over several centuries by a strengthening of military organization, according to rules attributed to the Emperors Maurice (562-602) and

10 *Left* Chillon, Switzerland. An interior of the castle with traces of wall-paintings surviving above some of the many windows overlooking the lake.

11 *Above* The Porta Nigra at Trier (*Augusta Trevirorum*), W. Germany, a Roman gateway, *c* 300 AD; a nineteenth-century engraving.

Leo the Wise (886-911) in the *Strategicon* and the *Tactica*. Where in the west the leaders of society were warriors and chieftains hungry for fighting, the Greeks sought to avoid battle as much as possible and to conserve their power. By the early fifth century, Rome had shrunk far within the walls of Aurelian. But in the same period, Byzantium had spread far beyond the confines of the Emperor Constantine's original defences, thus making a new wall necessary.

This wall, strengthened every sixty yards by great towers (see fig. 3), ran across the west side of the promontory on which the city stands. Built of stone with a concrete core and bonded with brick lacing courses five bricks in depth, the inner wall is 15 ft (4.6 m) thick at the base. This great wall is preceded by a lower wall, 6 ft 6 in (2 m) thick, again supplied with protruding towers, which sheltered a road running the extent of the city walls. The third line of defence was provided by the moat, which was crossed by bridges to the five main gates, which in their turn led to the centre of the city.

This placing of the lower and the higher walls enabled a new defensive tactic to be employed: two lines of archers, one firing over the head of the other. This device was to be repeated in thirteenth-century Europe, especially by Edward I in some of his concentric castles in Wales. The towers were capable of carrying the great weight of the Byzantine missile-throwing engines and also their machines for throwing Greek fire. Greek fire was invented about 670 AD. Many have tried to guess at its contents. Professor Partington describes it as 'a distilled petroleum fraction combined with other specified ingredients, but not containing saltpetre'. It could be extinguished only with great difficulty and was particularly effective in naval

12 Istanbul, Turkey. The land walls of Byzantium from the Tekfursaray. They were begun in 413 AD as a defence against the Ostrogoths and the Huns.

battles. Kallinikos of Heliopolis invented a method of projecting Greek fire through siphons in the prows of ships. It was probably used against the Arabs in their first attempts to seize Byzantium and later against the Russians whose fleet was destroyed by it in 941.

In the time of Justinian (527-65), before the rise of Islam, there was an attempt to regain the lost possessions in Italy and North Africa. For a short period under the generalship of Belisarius this was successful and to consolidate these gains Justinian launched a vast programme of building fortresses and city walls–a policy celebrated by the historian Procopius in *On the Buildings*. Many of these fortresses, especially in the Holy Land, were to be taken over and added to by, first, the Arabs and, later, the Crusaders who were to learn from their example. Although this expansive movement was to be thrown back by Islam, the inhabitants of Byzantium remained proud of their technical superiority in weapons and their knowledge of the science of fortifications. So much so that, later, in the tenth century, in an exchange of insults between the Emperor Nicephorus and Liutprand of Cremona, the ambassador of Otto the Great, one of the Byzantine charges was that the Franks were ignorant savages who knew nothing of how to besiege a city.[7]

The walls of Byzantium played a vital part in European civilization. Earlier writers, taking their cue from Gibbon[8], have poured scorn on Byzantine armies, ignoring the firm military policy with its insistence on the avoidance of direct conflict and its devious and subtle stratagems which is far more comprehensible to us today. But walls are designed to keep enemies out and for a thousand years those walls preserved Greek civilization until the time came when western Europe was sufficiently mature to comprehend it.

The efficiency of a defensive system must be related to the intelligence and value of the society it is meant to defend and, although for too many historians Byzantium seems to have been in a state of advanced decadence from its very foundation, there was an astonishing vitality that survived even the conquest of the city by the Crusaders in 1204. On that occasion a breach was made in the walls but it was later repaired, and even when the walls finally crumbled, before the cannon of Mehmet II in 1453, they had defied both him and his new weapons for many months with far too few soldiers and with almost no help from the West.

Three great invasions
Although the early castle builders were the heirs of a great tradition in the arts of fortification from the ancient world and although this tradition still survived undiminished in Byzantium, the general form of the medieval castle was decided by other forces–the forces, in fact, that made feudalism necessary, that drove free men to surrender their land and their liberty to gain the protection of a strong man and his castle.

All Europe was affected by invasions, whether by the Saracens, the Magyars, or the Vikings, each of which left their mark upon some part of the continent; the abbey of Luxeuil in Burgundy, for example, was plundered by all three. The first of

13 Almería, Spain. Part of the great complex of Moorish and Christian fortifications. Almería was founded in the eighth century on the site of a Phoenician fortress. It fell to the Christians in 1147, but was recaptured after ten years and they did not gain it finally until 1489. The round towers form part of the additions built by Ferdinand and Isabella.

these invasions and the one that probably did much to destroy the international exchange and the old trading organization of the Roman Empire was that of the Saracens.

The Saracens

Beaten back from Byzantium in 675, the Saracens were able to devote their main energies to North Africa, which they conquered by 695. Sixteen years later they invaded Spain, then under Visigothic rule, and in nine years they possessed nearly the whole peninsula except for the northern province of Galicia. Great builders, they constructed powerful fortifications and citadels, and the history of castle building in Spain was to be largely connected with the slow process of reconquest by Christian kings. By the tenth century the Saracens had built many hundreds of strongholds on the coast and in the interior of Spain. These are known as *alcazabas* among which Málaga and Almería (plates 13 and 14) survive. Many of these strongholds remained in constant use throughout our period and of Almería one Spanish writer says, 'the union formed by the *alcazaba,* the castle of San Cristóbal, and the important flanking wall constitute without doubt the most important medieval work of fortification in Spain'.[9] These *alcazabas* consisted of irregular walls of enceinte, generally following the contours of a defensible hill and made stronger by square or polygonal towers. Their chief building material consisted of

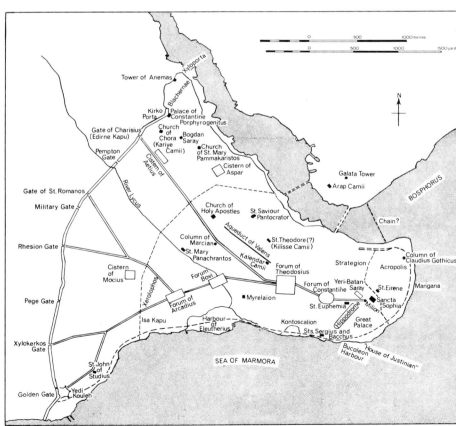

Fig. 3 Map showing the disposition of the land walls of Byzantium and the rest of the city. (After Talbot Rice, D. *Constantinople*)

tapia, a mixture of cement and pebbles poured between boards and left to dry in the sun. It produced an extremely strong wall and as the material was not suitable for round towers the Moors kept to their square or polygonal construction as at Baños de la Encina in southern Spain (plates 15, 16 and 17).

From Spain the Saracens entered France, only to be thrown back by Charles Martel at the battle of Poitiers in 732 or 733. They still remained a threat to Europe, however, and a hundred years later had begun the long drawn-out conquest of Sicily. In 846, they laid siege to Rome when Leo IV converted the tomb of Hadrian into the great fortress now known as the Castel Sant'Angelo (see plate 18). They also established a permanent fort at Garde-Frainet in Provence from which they raided travellers between France and Italy. They were only driven out after they had captured an abbot of Cluny in 972, and thus provoked rather too powerful enemies. There were to be many contacts with the Saracens which had a pronounced effect on the building of castles. Here we are concerned with them as a force that helped to create the new society in Europe which appeared under the Emperor Charlemagne.

The knights of Charlemagne

The new man of this new society was the knight or professional cavalryman, and he was a very expensive necessity. His equipment was equal in value to that of twenty oxen. He needed a hauberk (a leather jerkin faced with metal plates), or later a shirt of mail, a helmet, a shield, a lance, an axe, and at least one horse. The horse had to be a destrier, that is virtually a carthorse, strong enough to carry the knight and his weight of metal in a charge. These horses were expensive to train and to keep. The knight needed a squire to look after his armour because it was always rusting and a groom to guard the horses, literally with his life. The Byzantine emperors had for some centuries maintained armies of cavalry, but they still possessed gold from a rich trading society to pay for them. The Franks had no such resources; their leaders had either to maintain a company of knights as part of their households, or else they gave the knights landed estates, in return for which the knights

had to be ready to come to the lords' defence when required and to maintain their own armour and mounts. This was the beginning of what is called Carolingian feudalism. The knightly class at this period was not hereditary, although every knight would have been sure to want his son to become a knight. The system was to lead to great changes in men's view of society and to the ways in which land was held.

Charles Martel was the mayor of the palace in the Merovingian kingdoms of Austrasia, Neustria, and Burgundy in the early eighth century. His family had come to power first in Austrasia where, by the grants of newly cleared land to nobles who were anxious to 'commend' themselves, they established their power on a basis of feudal patronage. With the backing of this military and political support, Charles Martel's son Pepin brought an end to the Merovingian dynasty and was made king with the Pope's approval. By this act a new form of society was recognized; the king was still the leader but he never acted without the advice and counsel of his vassals. Unlike the Merovingian kings, the Carolingian monarchs were held responsible to their people, and this attitude of duty and dependence was one of the most potent forces in the making of the Middle Ages.

14 *On previous pages, left* Almería, Spain. Eleventh-century Moorish flanking walls and towers built down the hill dominating the town and port.

15 *Previous page* Baños de la Encina, Spain. Moorish walls and flanking towers of the tenth century built of *tapia,* a mixture of pebbles and mortar sun-dried to great hardness. The early date of this castle (967 AD) shows how advanced the Moorish conquerors were in the art of fortification when compared with most of contemporary Christian Europe.

16 *Left* Baños de la Encina, Spain. The superb lines of the tenth-century Moorish double horseshoe gateway.

17 *Above* Baños de la Encina, Spain. Built to defend the line of the Guadalquivir before Jaèn, this castle was captured from the Moors by the Christians in 1212 just before the battle of Las Navas de Tolosa. After their victory they then built the *torre del homenaje* on the north (just visible left of centre) as an extra defence and as a symbol of their victory.

Charlemagne, the first western Emperor since 476, needed horsemen even more than his father Pepin; his conquests extended from Hamburg to Barcelona, and much can be learned of his military organization from the capitularies he issued. For example, in the *Capitulare de Exercitu Promovendo* of 803, the great vassals are ordered to take to the field as many retainers as possible. A count could leave only two men behind to look after his wife but he was allowed another two to discharge his business for him. A bishop was only allowed to leave two. Every holder of land had to provide something for the army, even if it were only a quarter part of a soldier's equipment. Thus Charlemagne procured for himself a large and efficient army for the building of his empire.

According to the *Capitulare Aquisgranense* of 813, he organized what appear to be trains for siegeworks, and for supplying the army. The supply train was equipped with rations for three months and clothing for six. He took great care to record the supplies of armour in his empire and he forbade their export even though steel swords made in Carinthia and Styria from the eighth century by the cementation process were in great demand all over Europe. Writing about a hundred years after the event, the Monk of St Gall

18 *Above A sporting contest on the Tiber at Rome* by Claude-Joseph Vernet, 1750, showing the Castel Sant' Angelo. Originally the mausoleum of the Emperor Hadrian, it was converted into a fortress in the middle of the ninth century by Pope Leo IV as a defence against the Saracen attacks on Rome. It continued to receive further embellishments and defences especially at the end of the fifteenth century. Its most famous siege was in 1527 when Pope Clement VII was attacked there by the forces of the Emperor Charles V, an event described by Benvenuto Cellini in his *Autobiography*.

20 *Right* Richmond, England. The great square keep of the middle twelfth century, built in the tradition of the White Tower at London. Scolland's Hall is one of the few stone castle buildings that can be dated to the years immediately following the Norman Conquest of England in 1066. Richmond is an example of a castle acting not only as the residence of a great lord but also as an administrative centre for the hundreds of manors held of him in vassaldom.

19 Carolingian cavalry and footsoldiers attacking fortifications; end of the ninth century. This particular manuscript illustration from the St Gall 'Golden Psalter' shows the stirrup in use, one of its earliest western representations. The lance is held lightly in the hand and is not couched. *St Gall, Stiftsbibliothek*, cod. 22, p. 141.

provides a dramatic description of the advance of Charlemagne's army on Pavia in 773.

'Then approached the iron king, crowned with his iron helm, with sleeves of iron mail on his arms, his broad breast protected by an iron byrnie, an iron lance in his left hand, his right free to grasp his unconquered sword. His thighs were guarded with iron mail, though other men are wont to leave them unprotected that they may spring the more lightly on their steeds. And his legs, like those of all his host, were protected by iron greaves. His shield was plain iron, without device or colour, and round him and before and behind him rode all his men, armed as nearly like as they could fashion themselves; so iron filled the fields and the ways and the sun's rays were in every quarter reflected from iron. "Iron, iron everywhere", cried in their dismay the terrified citizens of Pavia.'[10]

Charlemagne's chief enemies in the east, the Saxons, still had their giant encampments such as the Eresburg, now the site of the town of Obermarsburg, the Hohensyburg, and the Skidroburg. As Charlemagne advanced into their territory, he seems to have built rectangular fortresses or *curtes* in West Saxony as far as the Weser. After his truce with the Saxons in 785, however, he gave up the ambition to conquer them entirely and came to an arrangement whereby he was accepted as their overlord. East of the Weser he seems to have constructed oval or round-shaped camps of earthworks and palisades, much smaller in size than the old Saxon encampments but resembling them in ground-plan with an irregular distribution of buildings within the palisade. These round fortresses seem to have played the same part as administrative centres and rallying points for troops as those further west. Sometimes they were built in close proximity to the Saxon camps as, for instance, the Hunenring built near the Grotenburg and the Bomhof near the Skidroburg.

In other ways the building of fortifications does not seem to have played a large part in Charlemagne's military system. The size of the army he was able to collect and the astonishing obedience he commanded in his wide territories perhaps made it unnecessary. His palaces were built in various parts of his lands to provide lodging and centres for administration and, as at Aachen or Ingelheim, were undefended, but these buildings were to have a profound effect upon the later design of castles because of their regular, rectangular ground plan. Dorestad in Holland (plate 24), for example, is typical with its division into two enclosures, the *curtis* and the *curticula,* and

outside these, the *pomerium*. Another effect, though long delayed, was that, by introducing Italian craftsmen and by encouraging the use of stone for secular buildings, he set a standard of living and a style of design that was not to be forgotten.

It is from the period of struggle between the Franks and the Saxons that the noted German scholar Carl Schuchhardt[11] dates the dualism that runs through the design of German castles. On the one hand there were regular plans based on the Roman remains and the Carolingian palaces and, on the other, the inheritance from the Saxons: round walls or walls dictated by the lie of the land enclosing an irregular distribution of buildings without particular regard for the part they should play in the total system of defence.

Another legacy of the age of Charlemagne to the castle was an indirect one. It lay in the effect his memory exercised on the

21 *Above left* La Cuba, Sicily. The exterior of the latest of the Norman palaces to be built, *c* 1180. It was surrounded on three sides by a lake and was probably used for official receptions. An inscription round the top of the buildings bade the visitor 'pause and admire the illustrious dwelling of the most illustrious King of the Earth, William the Good'.

22 *Left* Volterra, Italy. The fortress begun by Lorenzo de' Medici after an uprising in the town against Florentine rule had been put down by a massacre in 1472. The fortress compelled the submission of Volterra which was vital to Florence because of the nearby mines, the chief product of which was alum. Alum was needed for fulling the cloth made in Florence, her main source of wealth.

23 *Above right* A suggested reconstruction of the palace at Ingelheim, based on excavations. *Landesbildstelle Rheinland Pfalz.*

24 *Right* Dorestad, Holland. A water-colour reconstruction of the Frankish eighth-century *curtis* clearly showing the regular ground-plan which was to have a strong influence later on the design of castles.

25 The Rock of Cashel, Eire. The round tower, here grouped with ruins of buildings of a later date, is one of a series of similar towers probably built by the Irish in the ninth century and later as centres of refuge from the Viking invaders. An engraving from Hearne's *Antiquities of Ireland*, 1791.

society living in the castles. The continued inspiration of the legends and myths that surrounded him and his paladins gave rise, long after his death, to the *chansons de geste*, the poems chanted and sung in the castle halls of the eleventh and twelfth centuries. Just as the Hohenstaufen Emperors were consciously to emulate the splendour of his palaces in their own architecture, so the imagination of the youth of Europe was stirred with the visions of heroism, of Roland and of Oliver, of the battles against the Moors. An obscure skirmish in the Pyrenees became the heroic last stand of Roland at Roncesvalles, and in setting off for the Holy Land the Crusaders had a precedent, they believed, in the struggles of the paladins against the infidel. If, therefore, Charlemagne can be said to have contributed little to the visible form of the castle as it first appeared two hundred years later, his memory helped to give it something equally important: high ideals of courage and faith which deeply affected later generations who were to live in the castles and thereby created the atmosphere which draws us to them today.

Charlemagne's empire did not long survive his death. With his great armies so well supplied and armed, and with the rumours of invincibility flying ahead of their approaches, Charlemagne had not only created a new unity in Europe, but also brought lands into his realms that the Romans had preferred to leave untouched. His was, however, entirely a land power and it was under his weaker successors that the importance of seapower was felt for the first time since the loss of the Mediterranean – when the Viking invasions began in force.

The Viking invasions

One of the most frightening talents of the Vikings was their speed of movement so that they constantly attacked with the advantage of surprise. They were able to cross far greater distances than Charlemagne's armies, for all their efficiency and their range of action, ever managed, travelling from Scandinavia, past Gibraltar to Italy, or across Russia by the portages on the Dnieper or the Volga at a much faster rate simply because they were the only seapower. It is thought that Charlemagne had crushed the sole possible rivals to the Vikings when he put down the Frisians, and although late in his reign he had based a navy on the Channel it did not survive long under his successors.

The Viking invasions are important in the development of the castle for several reasons. They broke up Carolingian society, which meant in effect western Christian society, to such an extent that a new local feudal society arose. The local warrior who could lead, arm, and protect his followers became an increasingly free agent. The Viking forced his victims to defend themselves by fortifications. He introduced a new speed into warfare and therefore provoked, by reaction, the need for a military device that could delay that speed. Coming from a divided and unruly society, Viking warriors already knew the value of strong defensive camps that could be erected rapidly. And it was their descendants, the Normans, who were to become the masters of castle building in north-west Europe, Sicily, and the near East.

It took a long time for this reaction to gather force. After Charlemagne's death, his descendants were at first more concerned with their quarrels of succession than with reports of distant marauding bands. The centres of government, whether imperial, royal, or comital, as we have seen, were not generally fortified. They consisted of groups of halls, such as the imperial palaces at Aachen or Ingelheim. Apart from the few trading towns, such as Duurstede and Quentovic, the only other centres of population were the abbeys, rich in gold and vestments, which again were not fortified. The wide estuaries of Europe were open to the Norse ships with their shallow draught, and the settlements they found up the Thames, the Seine, the Loire, and the Rhine were almost totally unprepared to defend themselves.

In Ireland, the strange round towers, like that on the Rock of Cashel (plate 25), were probably built at this time as a refuge from the Vikings. A large part of the country itself became a Viking kingdom. In England, the temporary and partial unification achieved by Offa of Mercia collapsed completely under the weight of disaster. On the continent, the system of building fortifications or *Burgen*, which would appear to have been successful under Charlemagne in keeping hold of his eastern conquests, was allowed to lapse.

Three entries in the *History of the Church of Rheims* by Flodoard[12] show the change that overtook the peace of the Empire. The first tells how Ebo, the bishop of Rheims, asked Charlemagne's son, Louis the Pious, to grant him the Gallo-Roman walls of the town to use as a quarry for the rebuilding and aggrandizement of his church of Notre-Dame. Louis, then enjoying a period of great calm, granted him not only the walls but also the gates of the town. Ebo's successor as bishop, Hincmar, was allowed to continue with the demolition. The third entry, however, shows Hincmar's successor, Fulk, having the church of St Denis knocked down to make walls to shelter the town from the ravages of the pagans.

26 Gravensteen, Ghent, Belgium. The famous Castle of the Counts, seen here in its present twelfth and fourteenth-century form with its keep (centre) and palace (left) behind its extensive roughly circular perimeter walls, is built on the site probably once occupied by a Viking fortress. It later became a comital castle and remains of tenth- or eleventh-century stone buildings are incorporated in the late twelfth-century keep.

There is some evidence that the Vikings had already developed their own style of fortification at home. It may be, however, that the camps they built overseas were a response to their immediate military needs or that they learned the value of these camps from their contacts with Russia. Whatever the influences, they always guarded their longer halts inland with effective and hurriedly constructed camps of earth and wood, preferably on islands. The first permanent fortress the Vikings built in the west was at Dublin. In the Netherlands they made Asseult, Louvain, Ghent, and Courtrai into fortified sites which proved very hard to take. They established winter camps controlling the mouths of the Thames, the Loire, the Garonne, the Charente, the Seine, and the Somme. In the Slav world to the east, however, they came across lands covered in *grody*, or fortresses, to which the population fled from attack. It has been suggested[13] that the etymology of their name for Russia, *Gardarike*, is 'land of the *grody*', although it is more likely that it is 'land of the fortified homestead' from *gård*, the Swedish word for homestead. The vast stretch of land which is now Poland and Russia then resembled later medieval Europe in its density of fortified places far more than the open and undefended settlements of the Carolingian empire. In the east the Viking rulers built more permanent

fortifications to guard their trade routes and their great cities of Kiev and Novgorod.

Slowly it was realized that even if the Vikings could not be defeated at sea, it might be possible to impede their progress on land by building fortifications along their most usual routes. By the second Edict of Pitres (864) Charles the Bald ordered the construction of fortified bridges up the Seine. These fortifications were mainly of wood but showed their effectiveness in the great siege of Paris in 885–6. The Vikings had first to overcome the bridges further down the river to make sure of a safe retreat. When they reached Paris, they had to besiege, not the undefended town they had sacked with ease twenty years earlier, but an island city joined to the mainland by two fortified bridges with stone towers at their landward gates. According to the writer Abbo,[14] if he did not embellish his poem by borrowing from his classical reading to make the siege more dramatic, the Vikings assaulted the fortifications with every device of siegecraft they had learned. They used the bore to pick away stones, until they were foiled by a shower of boiling oil on the operators. They mined the tower and were succeeding until they were driven back by the darts and bolts of the *balistae* on the walls. They brought up three great rams under the shelter of penthouses, an operation spoilt by the defenders letting down large forked beams which gripped the rams and stopped them swinging. They sent fire-ships against the bridge and these were caught aground on stones in the river bed. The attackers promised their lives to the defenders of a beleaguered tower if they surrendered and murdered them the moment they laid down their arms. The defence stood up to all these terrors and the siege was finally raised by the appearance of an army of the Emperor Charles the Fat who bought off the Vikings by a danegeld of silver and the free offer to sack Burgundy, then in revolt against him. There they laid siege in vain at Sens which was still defended by its Roman walls. Many other settlements were provided with walls by or at this time. Local lords were building castles in the Charente region in about 868. Walls like those at Paris were built at Bruges in 879, Cambrai after 881, Tournai in 898, and Huy in 895.[15] The castles at Ghent (plate 26) and Antwerp seem to have been adapted at this time from fortifications actually built by the Vikings. These were trading centres but it is probable that wherever there was a group of population large enough a castle or some sort of fortification was constructed, whether as the residence of a count or a bishop, as at Utrecht, or an abbey, as at Montreuil-sur-mer.

In Wessex, King Alfred adopted the same procedure of fortification. After he had defeated Guthrum at Ethandun in 878 and re-established his rule, he set out to defend the limits of his kingdom by the construction of fortified towns or *burhs*. Each *burh* was made the responsibility of a certain number of hides, whose thegns had to supply materials and men for its building and upkeep. By the beginning of the tenth century, there were thirty of these *burhs* in existence and they functioned well at this time as defences and scarcely any were successfully besieged by the Danes. One example of their use was in 896 when a party of Vikings had gone up the river Lea. Alfred constructed two *burhs* on either side of the river, joined them with a boom, and so sealed off the enemy, who had to abandon their ships which were borne off to London in triumph. The work of building *burhs* was carried on by Alfred's successors after his death and the construction of these fortresses played an essential part in the eventual Danish collapse.

Thus the men of western Europe were learning to defend themselves against the Vikings. A new terror, however, had sprung from the east, a race who seemed as swift in attack as the Vikings and as impossible to pursue – the Magyars.

27 Werla, near Goslar, W. Germany. A water-colour reconstruction showing what one of the series of fortresses originally devised by Henry the Fowler looked like in about 950 AD.

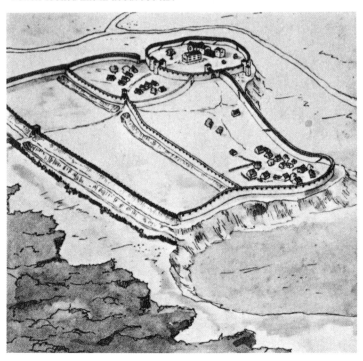

28 Gniezno, Poland. Part of the wall of the tenth-century fortress showing the method of construction using layers of logs arranged in cross patterns to achieve the greatest possible stability. The base of the wall-walk is made of giant crates of logs filled with stones and sand.

The Magyar invasions

The Magyars attacked in small bands of horsemen. They first appeared as a serious threat at the end of the ninth century and they were not finally crushed until Otto the Great's victory at the battle of the Lech in 955. Their raids extended as far as Lombardy, Provence, and Burgundy, and they dealt a final blow to the Carolingian kingdoms.

It may well have been in the hope that he would be able to repel these invaders that in 919 Henry the Fowler was made king of Germany, the first of the Saxon dynasty. He had to deal with Slav attacks as well as those of the Magyars and he gave a fresh impetus to the building of fortifications by the system of fortress-towns he devised for the defence of Saxony and Thuringia. He gained time for their construction by buying off the Magyars. All his knights were formed into groups of nine. One of these nine men was selected to live in a fortress-town and build houses there for the other eight, who in return were to cultivate his land. A third of the produce from the land was stored in the fortress-town as provision against a siege. On Henry's orders, the building of these towns continued day and night until they were finished. By decreeing that all festivals and holidays should be celebrated in these fortress-towns, he built up their importance in the minds of the population whom they were meant to protect. Surviving Roman works, like those at Strasbourg and Trier, were used where possible and elsewhere new settlements arose, as at Brunabor (the future Brandenburg) and Magdeburg. A reconstruction of one of these fortresses in about 950, Werla near Goslar[16], is shown in plate 27 and it is remarkable for its extent of stone walls, the division of the bailey (see page 51) into sectors and the strong towers with which the gates are defended. Thus Saxony and other parts of Germany were well defended not only against the Magyars but also against the Slavs. By 950 the Bavarians had recovered to such an extent that it was they who invaded and plundered Magyar territory.

Henry also ordered the monasteries to fortify themselves and to provide a refuge for the people of the neighbouring *Gau*, or administrative district. These arrangements were recorded by the monk Widukind at the monastery of Corvey. The monks of the famous abbey of St Gall, which suffered from raiding by the Magyars, even built a *Wassirburc* or water castle in the early tenth century.

Early fortresses and castles

Recent excavations in many countries have added to the numbers of other fortifications in Europe of the early Middle Ages which were already known. Work at Gniezno[17] in present-day Poland has revealed a notable ring-work fortress of the tenth century where the walls were constructed not mainly of earth but of logs used with great prodigality (plate 28). The spaces between the logs were filled in with stones and sand and the outer side was coated with clay. Earlier examples of this style of building exist in Poland and they were to remain in use far into our period.

Another fortress, excavated comparatively recently, is the vast camp of the late tenth century at Trelleborg in West Zeeland (plate 29). The plan was laid out with astonishing exactitude; basically sixteen great wooden halls, all 100 ft (30.5 m) long, built in elliptical shapes like upturned boats, stood in squares of four each within the earthern ramparts and another fifteen houses stood outside the walls. An even bigger site, on the Lim Fjord at Aggersborg, contained forty-eight houses each 110 ft (33.5 m) long. These and two other encampments appear to date from the early years of the reign of Sweyn Forkbeard and they were used as barracks for the soldiers whom he and his son Canute led to the conquest of England. The money financing their construction probably came from the danegeld or tribute money paid in huge sums by Ethelred the Unready in a vain attempt to stave off the conquest. Built at a time when the old highly individual free-

29 *Right* Trelleborg, Denmark. A model reconstruction of the giant encampment or barracks probably built by Sweyn Forkbeard in the late tenth century, as a base for the terrorizing of England and later for its conquest. *Copenhagen, Nationalmuseet.*

30 *Below* The Husterknupp, W. Germany. A fortified site occupied from before 900 AD up to the fourteenth century. The three reconstruction drawings show (*a*) the late Carolingian fortified farmstead; (*b*) the transitional motte or artificial hillock made in the second half of the tenth century; and (*c*) the motte-and-bailey form converted in the twelfth century. (After Herrnbrodt)

continuously from before 900 AD till some time in the fourteenth century. The excavations [19] show that it was almost certainly chosen in the first instance as a place of refuge from the Vikings. The swampy surroundings and its position in a loop of the River Erft would have attracted fugitives. Although its defences, consisting only of ditches and palisades without mounding, were small, it contained several wooden buildings, and it is interesting that people in the country – for this was a fortified farmstead – were now prepared to live within their defences, instead of keeping nearby encampments to which they could flee. This settlement remained in much the same form till the middle of the tenth century, and it is of great importance for showing in one case how a motte-and-bailey castle developed from earlier forms of fortification.

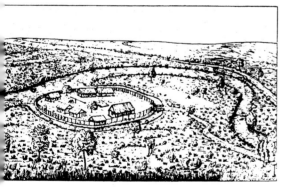

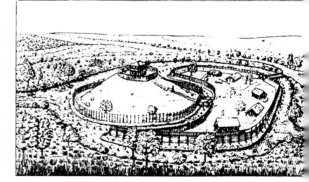

booting spirit of the past was in decline before the new power of the kings, Trelleborg and the other camps reveal a previously unsuspected power of organization possessed by the Danish monarchy at this period.[18]

Neither Gniezno nor Trelleborg are strictly castles, and to find early examples of the true combination of home and fortress one must at this period go further west to France and the Rhineland. Plate 30 shows the development of the Huster-knupp in the area of the lower Rhine, a site occupied

Most castles and fortresses of this period were constructed like the Husterknupp, of earth works and wooden palisades. Building in stone was largely the prerogative of the Church. Nevertheless there remain a few stone castles dating from the beginning of the eleventh century or the end of the tenth. Among these are the castles and watchtowers in the Roussillon designed for border defence on the Pyrenees. Many castles in the south of France which originated in this period, Quéribus, Peyrepertuse, and those of Lastours, were built in

31 *Right* Peyrepertuse, France. This extraordinary castle built on a mountain crest in the extreme south of the department of Aude is mentioned in a document of 1020 as one of a series of castles belonging to the count of Besalu. The remaining buildings of this early date are incorporated in the complex (centre right). In the thirteenth century another castle, the Château Saint Jordy, was built at the other end (top left) of the crest and additions were made to the older defences. St Louis used it as a border castle against Roussillon, and in the fourteenth century Henry of Trastamara took refuge there after the battle of Nájera in which the Black Prince and Pedro the Cruel triumphed and took prisoner Bertrand du Guesclin.

32 *Below* Chinon, France. A view from across the River Vienne showing part of this great military complex which consisted of three castles: (left to right) the Château du Coudray, the Château du Milieu, and the Fort St Georges (out of the picture). The site was earlier occupied by the Gauls and the Romans. Remains of a tenth-century stone castle are to be seen in the Château du Coudray. Henry II died in the Fort St Georges and the castle fell to Philip Augustus in 1205 after a siege of eight months. He strengthened the Château du Coudray with a keep built at its most vulnerable point and among the prisoners at a later date were Templars (1308). Here also in 1429 Joan of Arc resided.

extremely mountainous country and, with their later additions, are superb adornments to the landscape.[20] At Chinon part of a curtain-wall in the Château du Coudray (plate 32) can not only be dated by its masonry to the tenth century but also provides evidence that hoarding (wooden galleries built out over the walls with holes in the floor through which to drop missiles on the enemy below) and crenellation were known in Europe long before the first Crusade.[21] Two important early German stone castles were built at Rüdesheim on the Rhine.[22] Both have as their nuclei stone towers which were enclosed at a later date by stone enceintes. The Niederburg or Brömserburg (plate 35) was probably built on Roman foundations and was in use in about 1000 by an archbishop of Mainz as a toll station on the river. The other, known as the

Oberburg or Boosenburg (plate 34), has a stepped tower that may be of the tenth century. The earliest parts of Chillon in Switzerland (plate 33), including the central tower of Alinge and the tower of the Duke, are of this period also.

The area of Europe that would appear in this period to have had the densest concentration of castles was in north-west and central France and in Flanders, significantly the area that suffered most from the Viking invasions and where a new society grew up to deal with the anarchy of the times.

The society of the early castles
Certain strong monarchs such as Charlemagne, Alfred the Great, and Henry the Fowler, had understood the importance of strong fortifications, and had provided them as part of

imperial or royal policy. Such a strategy, however, depended upon a powerful and respected ruler. Weaker rulers, like the descendants of Charlemagne, were incapable of the swift military movements needed to deal with the Vikings and could not maintain at a distance of several hundred miles the morale and discipline necessary for keeping a fortress in repair, and also for seeing that garrison duties were properly carried out.

Nonetheless the population needed protection, and from this need grew the political and military system known as feudalism. The system of commendation, whereby the great leaders became vassals of the emperor or king, spread downwards through society as lesser men increasingly felt it better to resign their freedom and their land in return for the protection of a strong local landowner or monastery. The seigneuries that had grown up as grants of land from the royal or comital authority, especially in northern France and Flanders, became more and more autonomous and self-dependent defensive and economic units. Monasteries or bishoprics had to find laymen who were capable of leading their serfs in battle, and so the posts of the *vidame* (vicedominus) in France and the *Vogt* in Germany became established. The power of these new leaders became established in the manner described by Richard Koebner:[23]

'The professional fighting man wished to live as a noble man; and that implied not only service to his lord but economic independence as a resident landowner. So the increase of the knightly class led to its endowment with halls, dependent peasants' holdings, rights of jurisdiction and claims to services previously owed to the state. The number of "noble" residences associated with village settlements grew. In France, as early as the ninth century, they became the fortresses of knights. Royal control over fortifications weakened: nobles built their own strong-houses on the land—their *châteaux* and *firmités*, at first mere blockhouses. Dependent peasants were obliged to group their homes about the lord's strong place, and the village was often named after it—*firmitas castrum*: *La Ferté Vidame*. In Normandy, it is true, strong dukes, though they gave hundreds of villages to single noblemen, forbade them to build their own castles. Such building was always the sign of a weak central government.'

34 The Boosenburg, Rüdesheim, W. Germany. The stepped tower, possibly tenth century or earlier, rises from an enceinte of later date; a steel engraving dated 1840.

In Merovingian and Carolingian times rich landowners had helped the royal or imperial governments as little as possible, although they could employ their wealth and social position to their own advantage. As the power of the central government to protect declined, so they were in danger of losing everything. Especially in France north of the Loire and in Flanders, the duty to govern was forced upon the local lord: effective government was at the level of the local military leader and, therefore, it was he who had to provide defence for his land in the form of castles, police it with his vassal knights and men-at-arms, hold a court for his tenants, and make them build roads and bridges. Under the crisis that followed the Viking invasions in the ninth and tenth centuries these men who had privileges now had to accept responsibility.[24]

33 *Left* Chillon, Switzerland. Two of the oldest parts of this famous castle are to be seen in this photograph: (top left) the central Tower of Alinge (perhaps tenth century, altered in the thirteenth), and the eleventh-century Duke's Tower (top centre) incorporated in later buildings.

35 *Above* The Brömserburg, Rüdesheim, W. Germany. An early lithograph of this eleventh-century Rhine castle. Additions were made in the twelfth century.

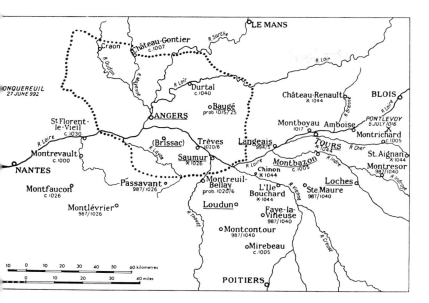

The test was too strong for many of the old leaders of society and in the tenth century large numbers of new men often of obscure origins rose to the forefront. Their power came to be based on the *mesnie,* the extended family relationships of blood, interest, commendation, and vassaldom. Each private castle provided a centre where its lord could live surrounded by his large family to whom he was a father. The sense of loyalty, the strongest emotional element in feudalism, derives from this intense family love of the *mesnie* and the fiery local patriotism that was focused on the castle. The few hints we have of life in these castles show a dull and brutish existence composed of heavy labour in the fields interrupted by savage private wars, with little trade or travel and with winters confined to the fireside. It is only from poems written down at a later date that we feel the intensity of their passions, as when in *Raoul de Cambrai* Guerri the Red sees his men killed with heavy spears and he weeps over them, his tears running down to his breeches.[25] The danger of the times and this new sense of the family explain more than anything else the reason why the castle came to be the centre of early medieval secular society. The home became a fortress and the fortress a home because society was enmeshed in war and the wars were between family groups at enmity.

These new men held the key position in the feudalism of the Middle Ages, because they were first and foremost warriors. But they had not gained their positions simply for the reason that they were able to protect their followers; they could also draw on the old hero magic of their Frankish and Teutonic forebears. They were admired for their violence, their fertility, their physical prowess, and their toughness. Their peasantry was as superstitious as themselves and the history of feudalism is contained in folklore as well as in charters of grants and commendations.[26] Many of the curious duties owed later by

36 *Left* Fougères, France. The Tour Guibé and the Tour Mélusine, carrying the flag-post, a fourteenth-century tower whose name shows the enduring power of the fairy legend specially connected with the Lusignan family.

Fig. 4 *Above* Map of Anjou in the time of Fulk Nerra. The dotted line encloses the Carolingian county of Anjou. Names show sites of castles in Fulk Nerra's hands or dependent on him. Dates indicate castles built by him. Undated sites mean they were built before his time. An asterisk indicates capture by Fulk Nerra in the year mentioned. (After Southern)

serfs to their lords, quite apart from work in his fields, payments in produce and kind, labour in building his castle, must be traced to this magical source. These were often called love-duties and from them probably derived the later legends of the *ius primae noctis,* which gave the lord the right to deflower any girl married on his demesne, or the even less comprehensible duty of beating the lord's moats and ponds with long sticks to prevent the mating calls of the frogs from disturbing his sleep at night.

Some families cherished legends specially concerned with their origin, telling of fairy or devilish blood. These legends, working on superstitious minds, could be embroidered and used for propaganda purposes, as in the case of the great family of Lusignan who claimed descent from the Fairy Melusine who was half beautiful woman and half fish. Many castle towers are named after her, as at Fougères (plate 36). A similar legend lay behind Richard Coeur-de-Lion's outburst: 'From the devil we came; to the devil we return'. He was referring to a legendary countess of Anjou of great beauty and mysterious charm who would never stay at mass for the elevation of the host. When one day her husband tried to force her to remain, she floated out through the window with two of her sons in the folds of her dress, never to return and thus proving her devilish origin.

A nearer relative of this lady is one of the most important figures in the early history of the castle and he was Fulk Nerra, count of Anjou.[27]

Fulk Nerra and Langeais

The family of the counts of Anjou first came to prominence in the period of Fulk the Good (941-60), a time when the exceptional fertility of the area–caused by lying fallow in long years of depopulation after wars and invasions–attracted wealth and settlers. Anjou was one of several counties and duchies that owned the nominal suzerainty of the kings of France, and whose rulers acted virtually as independent princes at this time. Fulk Nerra succeeded his father, Geoffrey Greymantle, as count at about the age of sixteen in 987. He was to rule until 1040. His first victory was to defeat and kill Conan of Rennes at the battle of Conquereuil in 992 and thus secure his possessions from attack from the west. The rest of his long fighting life was devoted to the encirclement of the city of Tours, a prize won after his death by his son, but as a consequence of Fulk Nerra's efforts.

Whenever he gained land, he built a fortress, constructing a strategic chain (see map on this page) intended to cut in two the lands of his chief rivals, the counts of Blois. His castle of Langeais[28] (plate 37), one of the earliest stone castles which is known to have been standing before 995, was built to threaten Tours.

It is generally agreed that Langeais is the earliest known example of the rectangular donjon or keep, an architectural form which the Normans were to scatter over England and parts of the Mediterranean lands, and which was to play a continually recurring part throughout the Middle Ages. As, in much of the rest of Europe–Germany, southern France, Italy– the castle was already developing or was to develop from the nucleus of the tall but more slender tower, Langeais, being basically a hall but made of stone, shows clearly the different line of development to be followed by the castle in central and northern France and in the British Isles. Its importance, therefore, is immense. The keep of Langeais stands on the narrow crest of a long spur between the River Loire and the River Roumer.

37 Langeais, France. The earliest datable example of the rectangular donjon or keep, Fulk Nerra's castle as it now remains. Later castles were built at Langeais, including one belonging to Pierre de Brosse, adviser to St Louis and later to Philip the Bold who had him hanged for accusing his queen of poisoning her own son. English troops of Henry VI captured the castle and sold it for 2,500 gold écus in 1427 on the condition that all the buildings except for Fulk Nerra's keep should be torn down. A new castle begun in 1465, one of the grandest fifteenth-century French castles, still stands.

Its ground measurements are 55 ft 5 in by 23 ft (16 m by 7 m) and its masonry consists of small, roughly cut stones, regularly coursed. The walls vary in thickness according to the direction from which attack was feared and they are strengthened by buttresses. Only the north and east walls, both damaged, still stand but much can be told from these and other remains. The floors were wooden, but that of the first storey seems to have been supported by a stone pillar. As with later examples of this style the great hall was on the first floor and the entrance seems to have been on this level, by a staircase in a small tower with its door set at right angles to the east wall of the keep. If this were so, it shows that considerations of flanking were already being taken into account and this adds to the originality and interest of the design.

Why did Fulk use stone for a castle in which he would not live continuously, and when for a hundred years and more the timbered motte-and-bailey castle was still to be used as a thoroughly efficient means of defence? This and others of his castles were besieged many times in the course of his life, sometimes to be taken and sometimes to be recaptured, and the stone castle, apart from its resistance to fire, would not seem to have proved obviously superior to the wooden castle at this time. Perhaps his ambition and rapacity, which were to remain an awful memory for many centuries, demanded permanent and ostentatious evidence. Murder, treachery, and plunder were nothing in the pursuit of his aims, or where his pride was affronted. He was especially attracted by the bones of saints which he wanted to possess in his own lands. According to one legend, in the year 1000, the date set for the ending of the world, he murdered his wife Elizabeth for

unfaithfulness, and set fire to his own city of Angers. After he had crushed a rebellion by his own son he made him crawl in the dust for miles wearing an ass's saddle. He enforced the acknowledgement of his suzerainty over the county of Maine from its ageing count, Hugh, on his deathbed. And he rewarded Hugh's successor, Herbert of Maine, who helped him overcome the gravest crisis of his reign at the battle of Pontlevoy against Odo of Blois, by inviting him to Saintes for the declared purpose of investing him with the city. Once there, Herbert was flung into prison for two years until he had been reduced to recognizing Fulk's suzerainty. The story that best conveys the terror Fulk inspired concerns his second wife, Hildegarde, whom he cherished dearly. One day while returning to one of his castles he entered a potter's shop and amused himself by making a cup of clay. He then entered the castle and went to his wife in the hall on the first floor. There he offered her the cup, saying: 'This was made for you by the man you love best.' Hildegarde started up, convinced he was accusing her of infidelity, denied everything, offered to go through the test by water, and before he could stop her leaped from a window of the hall into the river below from which she was rescued from drowning only with difficulty.[29]

Fulk's sins would provoke long bouts of remorse. He made the journey to Jerusalem on at least three occasions, returning home to commit more outrages, and dying at Metz in 1040 on his return from the last visit. During this last pilgrimage, two servants, sworn before setting out to obey his every command, led him round the city, one dragging him by a halter, the other lashing his back, all before the eyes of the Moslems. If no social or moral scruples deterred him from his crimes of violence neither did pride alter his determination to repent.[30] He built two great abbey churches, one at Angers and one near his castle of Loches (which was later to be rebuilt with one of the finest of French keeps).

This wild and extraordinary man provokes thought, partly through his originality and partly through his immense energy. With him and men like him in mind (he was not atypical) we can sense the driving force that was necessary to build a castle and see in the castle the stored and vital power of his time. So many strands important to the history of castles are to be found in his career. He not only built stone castles to threaten and terrify; he placed them in a strategic chain. He had close connections with the Church, which, in the beginnings of the Romanesque period, had a virtual monopoly of architects building in stone. He was rich—another essential for building in stone. He went to the Holy Land on pilgrimage, a journey to be followed by the Crusaders, who brought back techniques which had wide effects on castle building in the twelfth century. But, above all, he bequeathed to the Plantagenets not only his outrageous temper but the military sense which made of them the dynasty whose exploits in castle building in Europe were to be rivalled only by the Capetian and Valois kings—who also counted him among their ancestors.

CASTLES IN AN AGE OF CONQUEST

The energy of the north had shown its power once under Charlemagne and then because of the pressure of great invasions and of the resulting anarchy it had been forced to contract. In the eleventh century Europe was about to expand in every possible way. Through the gradual development of feudalism in the north-west and the accompanying spread of a number of technological improvements and inventions, the chief of them being the castle, this great flood of energy found new channels of expression and a new realization of power.

In northern and central France and Flanders the castle gradually became the focal point of feudal society. As the lord of the castle made it a miniature capital, as self-dependent as possible, gaining control of all the means of power, whether the labour of his serfs, the mills, the toll stations, the smithy, the horses, or the exaction of reliefs and other dues, so the castle drew together all the separate innovations in order that they functioned as part of a common whole. Many of these improvements predate the castle, in some cases by several centuries, but it is their gearing together that is important. Among them were the introduction of the heavy plough, improved harness for haulage animals, the stirrup and the horseshoe, all adopted during the Dark Ages[1], but it needed the new feudal society to give them their full impact and to synthesize them into the social structure. The introduction of the heavy plough, the strip system, and the rotational system of crops, had led to the growth of the manorial economy. Every knight and, therefore, every castle depended for upkeep on the basis of the manor.[2] New peasant communities collected in villages, rather than in scattered hamlets, because various parts of the plough and the oxen were owned by several people. But large groups of humans offer richer plunder to attackers than a scattered population and the new co-operation in the village was to lead to a new readiness in defence. The use of the heavy plough opened up fertile but hitherto untilled land which meant an additional surplus of fodder to support an ever-growing population of horses. The process of clearing new land and the foundation of new villages, which was to be one of the greatest achievements of the Middle Ages in the making of Europe, was already under way. The manor was established. The castle as the centre of local political power came to dominate all these changes and activities.

With the expansion of the feudal system in the eleventh century, however, the castle was given a new and more aggressive character as a base for subjugating newly conquered territory and imposing on the surrounding country new political and social systems. This new role profoundly affected the ways in which castles were designed and made them more sophisticated. A new social class had arisen out of the specialist mounted rider, the knight. As the principle of primogeniture had gained ground in the course of the eleventh century and as the military and political status of the knight had hardened into a sense of an ordained social superiority, so there arose the problem of land hunger, especially for younger sons who could not or would not go into the Church. The answer lay in conquest—and foremost among the conquerors were the Normans. By 1066 they had assimilated and refined all the techniques on which feudalism depended. Their near neighbours, the counties of Flanders and of Anjou, had also reached a high stage of feudal development and the Normans had learned much from them. They were now ready to transform yet more of Europe with the codes and practice of their particular forms of feudalism in a movement of expansion that won for them either the outright possession of, or positions of great power in, England, Scotland, Ireland, Spain, Sicily and southern Italy, and the Holy Land.

The Normans

Wherever the Normans went, they built castles and, therefore, to the military, economic, and historical reasons for the extraordinary development of the castle in the early Middle Ages is added a new factor—the Norman character. Men as different as William the Conqueror, Robert Guiscard, or Bohemond of Antioch, combined a genius for organization, a hardness, and an ability to channel the native savagery of the Norse character into means of gaining political advantage through systematic terrorism, with an instantaneous ability to adapt to new ideas and techniques, and they possessed, above all, an overriding self-confidence. This genius gave to feudalism its harshest expression.

The Normans had settled around the mouth of the Seine in about 911 under their leader Rollo, who took the land as a nominal vassal of Charles the Simple. Gradually they were christianized and they adopted the speech of their new country. The dukes consolidated their authority through their vassals, the *vicomtes,* and by adopting feudal relationships for their duchy. In times of strong overlords the *vicomtes* kept their castles as centres of ducal power, but, equally, would use them to defy their masters in periods of unrest. Troubled times were the more usual, whether from civil war, or because of the need to defend frontiers against encroachment from Paris, Maine, or Anjou, or because of the private warfare which was almost continuous in that society.

Normandy, England, and the Conquest

The youthful William the Conqueror (1027?-87), only nine when he succeeded to his father's dukedom, was forced constantly to fight his unruly vassals whose castles stretched across Normandy. From 1037 to 1047, the date of the battle of Val-ès-Dunes when William first crushed his vassals, there seems to have been continuous anarchy and warfare. Even after his victory William was again obliged to fight his own subjects in alliance with the French crown and its other fiefs, and it was not until 1060 that he was able finally to establish his power. But his natural talent for war had been increased in that period and the experience of his newly loyal vassals in fighting, slaughtering, and besieging one another could now be turned to their mutual advantage in the conquest of England.

How far these conditions were fulfilled remain to be seen from current diggings and investigations. The castle was not totally unknown because, under Edward the Confessor, his Norman favourites had constructed castles but these were few. The only ones known are those at Hereford, Ewyas Harold, and Richard's Castle and probably the one at Clavering in Essex. Early this century a great debate broke out between historians as to whether or not the Anglo-Saxons had built castles. The question seemed settled by Mrs Armitage with the publication in 1912 of her exhaustive work which proved, on the basis of the evidence then available, that the Anglo-Saxons had possessed no castles and that they were an introduction of the Norman Conquest, the pre-Conquest examples also being the work of Normans in any case.

38 Incidents from the Bayeux Tapestry during Harold's enforced stay with the Normans: the surrender of Dinan by Conan, duke of Brittany, who hands over the keys of the motte-and-bailey castle to William (on the left)— and William giving Harold armour.

The effect of the Vikings on France had been to weaken and almost destroy the power of the central government thus allowing the growth of private fortifications. On England their effect had been completely opposite: there it was the royal power that increased under Alfred and his successors.[3] The building of *burhs* had been under direct royal control and although, as the recent excavations at South Cadbury Hill of the gatehouse of the time of Ethelred the Unready show, their builders were capable of great sophistication, it would seem that the Anglo-Saxon nobility had not had the responsibilities of their counterparts across the Channel forced on them and therefore they did not build private fortresses. Also, England did not have feudalism. A thegn, receiving land from the king, would have it permanently. He might have performed an act of commendation to the king, acknowledging him as his lord, but his rights of possession were not subject to his performance of his public duties. The Anglo-Saxon aristocracy seems to have preferred the old Germanic and Norse halls for its dwellings, although the stipulations conferring thegn-hood in an early eleventh century code include the possession of a certain amount of land, a private chapel, and a *burhgeat*. The *burh* was the ring-work, either surrounding a town or a smaller encampment, and the *geat* was probably a gate-tower.

William in England

What William gained by Hastings, he held on to with his castles. Just as he had defeated the Anglo-Saxons drawn up in their old-fashioned shield-wall formation with his modern combination of cavalry charges and highly efficient onslaughts of arrows, so he used the equally modern device of the castle to keep his conquest. Unlike the Normans, the Anglo-Saxons had not grasped the implications of the new technical innovations–even though they knew of them– and, therefore, did not remodel their military organization. Ordericus Vitalis, one of the most important chroniclers of the Normans and himself partly of English birth, noted the lack of castles in England as a significant reason for the Norman victory. 'In the English districts there were very few fortresses, which the Normans call castles [*castella*]–so that although the English were warlike and brave, they were little able to make a determined resistance.'[4] In this connection it is interesting to note that the next two important invasions of England from the continent, those of the future Henry II during the Anarchy and of Louis VIII of France during the reign of King John, both ended in stalemate partly because of the large numbers of castles held by their opponents.

The Normans, forced at home to fight over small distances, hedged in by fortifications, all of which had to be taken to secure retreat, were able to travel across England with great speed after the battle of Hastings. The only place to make a notable defence was the walled city of Exeter, holding out in

idea are that there is nothing in writing to suggest the existence of such a plan and that the poor knowledge then current of the geography of the country would have ruled out its application, had it been thought of. There are some factors which have been brought as evidence, however, to support the idea of strategic planning. Professor Beeler[6] has drawn attention to the large number of castles in the interior, suggesting that William followed a policy of defence in depth, and also to those surrounding London and Coventry, the two most important centres of communication. There were, for example, over 100 castles from which guard could be kept on the approaches to London at distances of between twenty-five and fifty-nine miles. The thickest concentration of castles, however, lies along the Welsh marches, where the intensity of warfare with the

1068 for eighteen days, but it surrendered when William undermined the walls. Wherever the Normans reached an important strategic point, they immediately started digging – and yet another great palisaded mound would rise above the town or village to depress the natives into subjugation.

William had started the pattern, even before fighting Harold, by building a castle at Pevensey, where he landed, within the Roman fortress of Anderida. Then on reaching Hastings he ordered the construction of a motte (plate 39). After Hastings he seized the Anglo-Saxon *burh* at Dover, built a castle there and moved in a circuitous route to London. After his coronation on Christmas Day 1066 he ordered the construction of ramparts and a ditch on the site soon to be occupied by the Tower of London. Two months later he had gone back to Normandy, leaving behind Odo of Bayeux and William fitz Osbern, who, according to the *Anglo-Saxon Chronicle*, 'built castles far and wide throughout the land, oppressing the unhappy people: and things went from bad to worse'.[5] The construction of castles in towns was carried out quite ruthlessly. In Lincoln, 166 houses were destroyed because they stood on the land intended for the castle; in Norwich, 113 houses were similarly demolished. As William and his followers introduced castles, they also brought in feudalism. With every castle that was built came an accompanying string of dues and duties which increased the feudalizing of the country. Each of these castles, to a greater or lesser degree, depending on whether it was a royal or a baronial fortification, called for the feudal service of castle-guard – a duty by which a vassal served a certain period in garrisoning his lord's estate. This concerned the knights and men capable of or trained to bear arms. The building of castles also demanded the service of castle-work from the peasants – a duty made familiar in Anglo-Saxon times from work on the *burhs* or ring-works but infinitely more onerous under their new masters. As the castle was often the most obvious centre of a baronial domain, so one finds the term *castellaria* being used to denote a barony or honor. Thus the area of 199 manors surrounding Richmond Castle (plate 40) is described in *Domesday Book* as the *castellaria* of Richmond.

By 1100 (thirty-four years after the Conquest) a great number of castles had been built in England. It may have been as many as 500 or so. The intensity of castle building in this period has suggested to some writers that William was fulfilling a plan of national defence in their construction; he had to fear not only uprisings of the native population but also an invasion from Denmark. The objections put forward to this

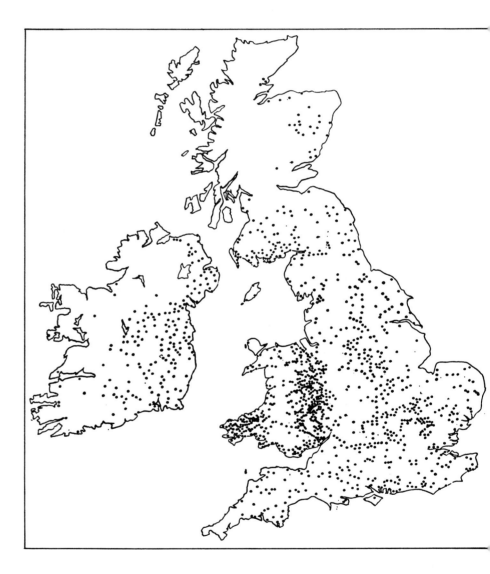

39 *Top left* The construction of a motte at Hastings before the battle took place, from the Bayeux Tapestry. Note the method of suggesting layers of earth. On the right a messenger tells William news of Harold.

Fig. 5 *Above* The distribution of motte castles in the British Isles. Many of these, especially in Ireland, were built in the twelfth century. Note the density of sites in the Welsh Marches, extending along the south Wales coast into Pembrokeshire. (After Renn)

Welsh made life much more difficult to live in peace and security (see fig. 5).[7]

Whether William had such a plan or not, the success of castle building in his reign is shown by the important part his garrisons played in resisting the rebellion of 1069, the most serious crisis of his reign. In this revolt the navy of King Sweyn of Denmark was beaten off by the garrisons at Dover, Sandwich, and Norwich before it reached the mouth of the Humber in 1070. By this time William had established a series of royal castles along the main roads of southern England with terminal points at Exeter, York, Lincoln, and Norwich. Herefordshire, under William fitz Osbern, and Kent, under Odo of Bayeux, were made military commands and in Sussex the old organizations of rapes were turned directly into feudal castleries. The type of castle which enabled these reforms to be enforced was, in general, what is called a motte-and-bailey castle, but the design could be very varied.

The motte-and-bailey castle

The motte-and-bailey castle as usually shown in reconstruction drawings consists of an artificial hillock (the motte), palisaded round the summit and the base, carrying a wooden tower on top, and surrounded by a ditch formed by the excavation of earth. The motte is connected by a bridge to the bailey, a larger, lower area enclosed by an earth wall and walk strengthened with palisades on the outer side. The bailey, too, has a surrounding ditch and the whole complex forms a figure of eight. Two assumptions were generally made about these castles: that the motte was constructed first of all; and that the Normans had already fully evolved the technique of building motte-and-bailey castles before they landed in England. The last point was challenged as a result of recent fieldwork in Normandy showing that there are very few motte-and-bailey sites which can be dated to before the Norman Conquest. From this arises the fascinating suggestion that it was in the actual throes of the Conquest that the Normans learned to develop the form to its greatest effect. This would mean, as Brian Davison says, that 'the Conquest brought about a radical change not only in the habits of the English but in the habits of their conquerors as well.'[8]

The theory that the motte was the first part of the castle to be constructed has been proved wrong in certain cases; excavations in Germany and Ireland show that the motte was a later addition to an already existing ring-work. The site of the Husterknupp (plate 30, see page 41) was transformed in the late tenth century from a palisaded encampment into a far more effective defensive site, with what Herrnbrodt calls a *Kernmotte* or transitional motte. Its full transformation into a motte-and-bailey castle, with a high motte surmounted by a wooden tower, did not come until the beginning of the twelfth century. Here the defences of the castle were improved by the gradual rising of the water level in this period. Again at Castle Neroche in Somerset the motte was added to a gigantic earthwork complex of earlier date. But it should also be said that recent fieldwork has shown the great diversity of forms and adaptations of forms amongst castles of the motte-and-bailey type (see below).

Although, as was shown by the example of Fulk Nerra,

40 Richmond, England. A view of the great twelfth-century keep of this castle which in the previous century had played an important part in enforcing the success of the Conquest in Yorkshire.

stone castles were being built in France in the late tenth century, the wooden castle, often further protected by a palisaded bailey, remained typical of eleventh-century fortification for several reasons. First, the building of stone castles involved the employment of masons, and, therefore, was expensive. Money was scarce, but wood was plentiful, and every able-bodied peasant could act as a woodcutter if not as a carpenter. The lord of a district could impress his local labour into constructing a fortification that could withstand all but the most determined attacks. Second, the dukes of Normandy, when firmly in command, tried to prevent their vassals from fortifying their dwelling places. But a wooden fortification could be erected in a matter of weeks, almost before the overlord could hear of it and prevent its building, whereas a stone

41 Berkhamsted, England. An aerial view of this Norman motte-and-bailey castle. The later stone buildings have largely fallen down and winter flooding leaves the earthwork pattern plain, showing clearly the separation of motte from bailey. The castle guarded the road to London from the Midlands across the Chilterns. Not far from here William received the submission of the English Church and nobles.

castle might take several seasons to build. Even if the palisades and towers were destroyed, the earthworks would often remain and could be refurbished very quickly, as appears from a story from the next century told by Lambert of Ardres. In about 1139 Henry of Bourbourg, at war with Arnold of Ardres, arranged for the site of an old destroyed castle which stood within sight of Arnold's castle to be surveyed in secret. He then had a wooden castle prefabricated, its parts were conveyed at night to the earthworks, and one morning Arnold and his astonished people saw menacing them a completed wooden castle which they only took after a violent siege.[9]

In flat country the motte or hillock was artificially raised and surrounded by a ditch formed by excavation of the earth, but in hilly country the builder naturally chose to construct on a rocky base. One method of raising an artificial mound is shown in the Bayeux Tapestry (plate 39), where William the Conqueror's camp is in the process of construction. The earth was raised in layers which were then rammed down. The Bayeux Tapestry also shows finished mottes at Dinan, Dol (plate 42), and Rennes, and suggests in its stylized way a familiar military technique. At the base of the mound the ditch was provided with a counterscarp or bank surrounding the exterior of the construction. From the tower on the motte, watch could be kept over the countryside and the bailey, again protected with its own palisade and ditch, provided refuge for the local population and its farm animals in time of trouble. The difficulty of keeping cattle alive through the winter in the Middle Ages made it even more important to preserve stock during adversity. Again, the peasants who had built the castle would have to serve as part of the defending force in an emergency and it was in such circumstances that the mutual

42 An attack on the motte at Dol—from the Bayeux Tapestry. Duke Conan of Brittany is fleeing on the other side.

responsibilities in feudal society were tested to the full. Here then in the bailey were the barns, shippons, and storehouses where the peasants gathered. Also in the bailey was the cook-house, kept well away from the motte for fear of fire.

The wooden tower which often surmounted the motte might vary in size from a construction almost rivalling one of the new stone keeps to a simple hall. Nothing remains of these wooden towers, although from the evidence of the Bayeux Tapestry they may have been highly decorated and carved rather like the Norwegian wooden stave-churches (plate 43). The red sandstone dragon heads that project from the Norman chapel at Kilpeck in Herefordshire, which seem to be inspired by wooden gable-ends, may give a clue to the forms this decoration took. Some towers seem to have consisted of storeys raised on timber pillars above the ground which left the first floor open and gave the defenders greater ease of movement within the palisade surrounding the crest of the motte. They were perhaps faced with tiles or hides as a protection against fire and the entrance might have been by a bridge or staircase leading to the first storey. It has been suggested, from the evidence found at excavations of the motte at Abinger which revealed the post-holes of the timber tower, that here it was in fact the tower which was built first and that the mound was heaped about its massive pillars; in this case the tower would have been built before the defensive ditch was dug. At South Mimms in Hertfordshire, excavated by Dr John Kent, the motte was similarly designed as a base for a great wooden tower over sixty foot high and the entry to the tower was through a timber-lined tunnel. Scarcely any part of the motte was visible from the outside because its sides were revetted with a palisade and its summit was covered with mortar. A totally different use of the motte appears at Penmaen in Glamorgan where the summit of the motte served as a bailey and the chief strength of the castle lay in its gate

tower. These few examples show something of the variety of forms to which the motte-and-bailey castle could be adapted.

What were these wooden towers like to live in? A passage in the *Miracles of St Benedict* (end of the eleventh century) describes the large room on the first floor where 'the powerful man . . . together with his household, lived, conversed, ate, slept'.[10] In fact all life was public, as in a permanent military bivouac. A rather grander house built for Arnold of Ardres in the Pas de Calais (see page 99) at the beginning of the twelfth century by the carpenter, Lodewijck of Bourbourg, is described thus:

'Arnold, lord of Ardres, built on the motte of Ardres a wooden house, excelling all the houses of Flanders of that period both in material and in carpenter's work. The first storey was on the surface of the ground, where were cellars and granaries, and great boxes, tuns, casks, and other domestic utensils. In the storey above were the dwelling and common livingrooms of the residents, in which were the larders, the rooms of the bakers and butlers, and the great chamber in which the lord and his wife slept. Adjoining this was a private room, the dormitory of the waiting maids and children. In the inner part of the great chamber was a certain private room, where at early dawn or in the evening or during sickness or at time of blood-letting, or for warming the maids and weaned children, they used to have a fire . . . In the upper storey of the house were great garret rooms, in which on the one side the sons (when they wished it), on the other side the daughters (because they were obliged), of the lord of the house used to sleep. In this storey also the watchman and the servants appointed to keep the house took their sleep at some time or other. High up on the east side of the house, in a convenient place, was the chapel which was made like unto the tabernacle of Solomon in its ceiling and painting. There were stairs and passages from storey to storey, from the house into the kitchen, from room to room, and again from the house into

43 *Below left* The thirteenth-century wooden stave church at Fantoft in Norway. Compare the roof decoration with that on the wooden motte-tower at Dinan from the Bayeux Tapestry shown in plate 38.

44 *Below right* Crocodile or dragon heads projecting from the south wall of the early twelfth-century church at Kilpeck, Herefordshire, built close to an earlier motte-and-bailey castle.

the loggia where they used to sit in conversation for recreation, and again from the loggia into the oratory.'[11]

This passage describes a tower built in 1117 but households of a similar complexity must have existed in the previous century. Such organization must have depended upon the proper fulfilment of an immense number of rules–something to be discussed in Chapter 3.

Another description of the motte appears in the life of Bishop John of Thérouanne by John of Colmieu written about 1130:

'Bishop Jean used to stay frequently at Merchem when he was going round his diocese. Near the churchyard was an exceedingly high fortification, which might be called a castle or *municipium* built according to the fashion of the country by the lord of the manor many years before. For it is the custom of the nobles of that region, who spend their time for the most part in private war, in order to defend themselves from their enemies, to make a hill of earth as high as they can, and encircle it with a ditch as broad and deep as possible. They surround the upper edge of this hill with a very strong wall of hewn logs, placing towers on the circuit, according to their means. Inside this wall they plant their houses or keep, which overlooks the whole thing. The entrance to this fortress is only by a bridge which rises from the counterscarp of the ditch, supported on double or even triple columns, till it reaches the upper edge of the *motte*.'

The motte-and-bailey castle was to continue in use for a long time and it spread under Anglo-Norman influence in the twelfth century to Scotland and Ireland. William, however, by building in stone, launched a movement that was to render the motte-and-bailey completely obsolete. His White Tower or Tower of London, one of the most famous castles ever built, was a powerful expression of his desire to display his new kingly estate and the permanence of the conquest he had made.

45 The Tower of London. A view looking eastward into the Chapel of St John showing the gallery walk.

The Tower of London

To see the White Tower as it appeared to Londoners of the late eleventh century one must wipe a veil of blood from one's eyes. Admittedly it was a fortress built to subjugate London, but it was not a prison, it was not a storehouse of tilting armour, it was not made less significant by big surrounding buildings.

46 A messenger informs William of Harold's capture. The building on the right symbolizes a palace or castle, presumably Rouen—from the Bayeux Tapestry.

When the king and his chief vassals were present it was a court, garnished with rich hangings and wall paintings, lit at night with torches that shone on the splendour of gold and rich cloths. There the bishops and the clerks of the administration would scurry with their missives, the ladies of the court would converse and walk, and the crowds of lords and their knights would gather. Henry III was to order its exterior to be white-washed in the thirteenth century, and perhaps it was painted in this manner from its earliest days. Washing the walls with lime had in any case a practical as well as a decorative purpose; it preserved the mortar. The banners of William would have floated from its corner towers and its high walls stood in defiance of foolhardy rebels or to greet its owner as he returned by the Thames from some expedition or journey.

Construction began in the 1070s under the direction of Gundulf of Bec, later bishop of Rochester.[12] It has been suggested that this and Colchester, another stone keep constructed by William in England, were inspired by the ducal palace at Rouen, long since destroyed. The palace shown in the Bayeux Tapestry (plate 46) may be that at Rouen, and it is known that it possessed not only a hall but also a donjon built by Duke Richard I (942-96). This may, in its turn, have owed its design to the fortified palaces of late-Carolingian northern France. The White Tower, whatever its precursors, was certainly a palace as much as a castle. The only part that

47 *Overleaf* Rochester, England. The square keep built 1126–39, one of the several buildings built in the tradition of the Tower of London. The entrance was through the forebuilding on the left.

48 *Overleaf, right* Rochester, England. The thirteenth-century round tower at the south-east corner of the keep built to replace the square corner tower brought down by King John's miners from the Forest of Dean in 1215. The mine was filled with the carcasses of forty fat pigs which were then set alight.

monastics whom he encouraged. For although it is difficult now to see the Norman Conquest as anything but a successful war for gain, it was accompanied by a papal blessing and was seen by the Normans as a rightful crusade against a usurper who had retracted his oath over holy relics, against a schismatic and uncanonical archbishop, and against a degenerate English Church which obstinately sang the wrong tunes. The chapel reminds us of this crusading zeal.

The Tower is built of Kentish rag stone. Although from some angles it looks a square construction (plate 49), it is of an irregular shape. The chapel and its undercroft butt out in an apsidal projection to the south-east. The original entrance (now destroyed) was by steps to the first floor from the south, the direction of the river. The basement, which was kept for stores and sometimes for prisoners, had no entrance from the outside – as was usual with stone keeps of this period. The height of the walls is about 90ft (27.4m), decreasing in

49 *Above* The Tower of London, a seventeenth-century view by Hollar showing the White Tower and Traitor's Gate, the river entrance. In the later thirteenth century it was converted by Edward I into one of the most impressive concentric castles in Europe.

50 *Above left* Berkeley, England. An aerial view showing the shell keep which in this case had masonry built up from the base of the mound on which it was formed. Frequently added to at later dates, this castle was the scene of the murder of Edward II.

51 *Right* Château Gaillard, France. The remains of one of the most famous castles of the Middle Ages. Built by Richard Coeur-de-Lion, between 1195 and his death in 1199, its capture by Philip Augustus from King John in 1204 marked the end of Angevin rule in Normandy.

52 *Overleaf* Chillon, Switzerland. The thirteenth-century room of the Chatelaine showing a simple chevron wall pattern and wall hangings. The wooden columns copy contemporary masonry work. The furniture is, for the most part, of later date and untypical.

now retains its palatial flavour is the chapel (plate 45), with its gallery where the members of the royal family could conduct their devotions without being disturbed by soldiers or members of the household in the main body. The plain severity of the chapel has always aroused admiration. Most castle chapels have the air of being yet another necessary office of the whole complex of buildings; here, it strikes one as the most important part of the castle. This is perhaps what Gundulf was really setting out to defend in building the Tower for William. Its puritan calm accords well with William's deep attachment to the Church and to the new reforming zeal of the Norman

thickness from 15 ft (4.6 m) at the base to 11 ft (3.4 m) in the upper storey – a massiveness typical of Romanesque building though increased by the desire for military security. Some of the original windows, which must have been much smaller, were replaced by Sir Christopher Wren in the early eighteenth century. Inside there is a great cross wall which served several purposes: it gave added strength to the whole building, it simplified the roofing, it helped to support the wooden floors, and it gave the garrison the chance, if ever the keep should be infiltrated, of containing the attackers in one half while they defended the other.

The square keep and the shell keep
Square keeps of this type possessed obvious advantages over the wooden motte. They could not catch fire, they could be built to a much greater height, and because of their height they did not demand the same concentration of soldiers as was needed for the defence of the lower earth-and-timber walls. The disadvantages were that their square corner towers could be attacked quite easily with the bore and the square shape narrowed the field of fire from the flanks. In the next century, the evolution of the polygonal keep and the round tower offset these faults but square keeps continued to be built throughout our period. It should, by the way, be remembered that nearly a hundred years might pass after the building of a castle before its defensive qualities would be severely tested – by which time siege techniques would have improved and the defenders would have to contend with skills the builders had not taken into account. One example of this is the siege in 1215 of Rochester Castle (plate 47) which was built in the 1130s. There, King John's supporters managed to undermine one of the square corner towers and break into the keep. The defenders retreated behind the crosswall inside the keep and held out there until forced to surrender. The broken corner tower was then replaced in that century by a round tower so constructed that it was more difficult to bore (plate 48).

William's other great stone castle in England was built at Colchester, possibly as a centre of defence against the Danes for East Anglia, then, according to *Domesday Book,* the richest area in the country. The keep at Colchester – built partly on the podium of a Roman temple dedicated to a deified earlier conqueror of the country, the Emperor Claudius – covers an even larger area than the Tower of London although now it has lost its upper storeys. Other stone castles built in the eleventh century probably include Pevensey, parts of Richmond (plate 40), and the Peak but stone castles were certainly rare at this time. The motte-and-bailey served its purpose and stone was introduced only gradually – first of all probably for the chapel, such as that in the episcopal castle of Durham. The other feature of the castle to invite rebuilding was the gate, always one of the chief sources of concern. By the beginning of the twelfth century the wooden surround on top of the

53 *Left* Dover, England. The upper chapel of this powerful and important fortress built by Henry II on a vital route connecting the two parts of the Angevin empire. This chapel is a small but fine example of the transitional style that preceded the change to the Gothic.

54 *Top right* Colchester, England. An eighteenth-century view of what was William the Conqueror's most magnificent stone keep.

55 *Right* Restormel, England. The late eleventh or early twelfth-century shell keep of this Cornish castle; an engraving dated 1809.

motte was beginning to be replaced with a stone wall, thus making what is called a shell keep; examples can still be seen on their mottes at Arundel, Windsor (much altered, plate 56), Totnes, Restormel (plate 55), and Trematon. But more impressive than these are the square keeps built throughout the twelfth century in the tradition of the Tower, such as Richmond (plate 40), Castle Rising (plate 128), Hedingham (plate 129), Middleham (plate 132), and Newcastle (plate 141). In all cases, they were smaller than their model but, unlike it, they occupied the sites of earlier castles. They took over the function of the motte as the last defence in war and the home of the lord in peace. The bailey with its wooden palisade probably remained much as before. A construction such as Richmond or Castle Rising, built not by the king but by a magnate, revealed a considerable change of attitude and a deeper sense of security; the Norman barons had come to stay, and were no longer quite so dependent on the king as they had been when they were invaders co-operating out of necessity.

The Normans in Sicily
The other great Norman conquest in the eleventh century was of southern Italy and Sicily. Invited to serve as mercenaries in 1016, by 1046 the Normans had conquered the greater part of Apulia and Calabria. In 1061 they seized Sicily from the Moslems in an amazing series of battles and sieges. Once established there, and on the mainland, they built cathedrals, monasteries, palaces, and castles. Adranò, one of the earliest castles (plate 57), built before 1100 by Roger I (1031-1101), is

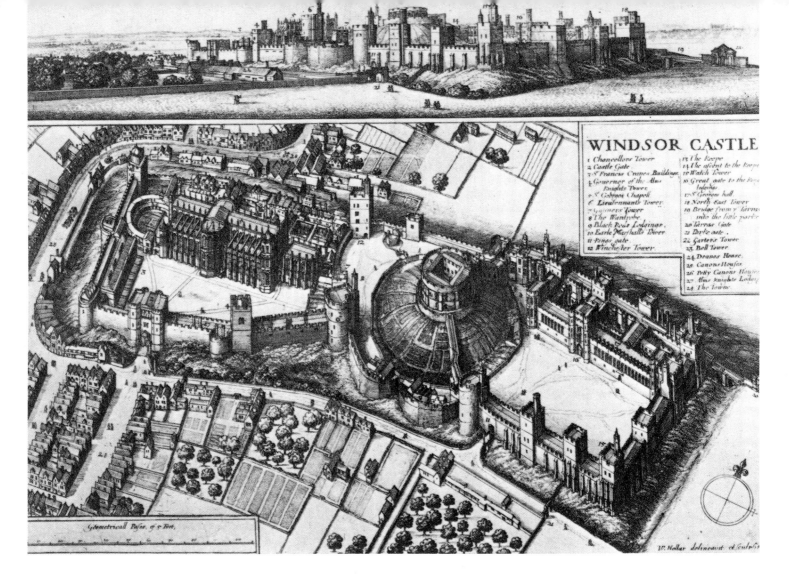

WINDSOR CASTLE
1 Chancellors Tower
2 Castle Gate
3 S. Frances Cranes Buildings
4 Governor of the Alms
Knights Tower
5 S. Gorges Chapell
6 Lieutenants Tower
7 Squiers Tower
8 The Wardrope
9 Black Rods Lodeinas
10 Earle Marshalls Tower
11 Kings gate
12 Winchester Tower
13 The Keepe
14 The ascent to the Keep
15 Watch Tower
16 Great gate to the Kings
lodaines
17 S. Gorges hall
18 North East Tower
19 Bridge from y' Kings
into the little parke
20 Tarrace Gate
21 Darke gate
22 Garterre Tower
23 Bell Tower
24 Deanes House
25 Canons Houses
26 Petty Canons Houses
27 Alms knights Lodaing
28 The Towne

Geometricall Paces of 5 Feet.

W. Hollar delineavit et sculpsit

the ideal Norman keep constructed before the full assimilation of Islamic culture. This assimilation is seen in the surviving portions of the two twelfth-century palaces of La Zisa (plate 58) and La Cuba (plate 21) in both of which the rectangular Norman form is adapted to a luxurious mode of living and to contain strong Islamic and Byzantine elements in the design.

The strength of the Normans' power in Sicily led to their special connection with the papacy in the investiture contest, but only after the quarrel had broken out. The events in Germany were among the few major political struggles of eleventh-century Europe in which the Normans were not directly implicated from the beginning. In Germany, however, there was a very different society and the growth of castle building in the Empire bears little relation to the processes seen so far in the west.

56 *Above* Windsor, England. A bird's-eye view of this castle by Hollar showing the appearance it largely retained until Wyatville's reconstruction for George IV. The round tower derives from a shell keep.

57 *Left* Adranò, Sicily. An example of the Norman keep in Sicily built prior to 1100 by Roger I of Sicily before the full assimilation of Islamic influences which are to be seen so strongly in La Zisa and La Cuba.

58 *Right* La Zisa, Sicily. A fountain in the central hall of this twelfth-century Norman palace. Strong Islamic influences are obvious in the honeycombed recess like the *mihrab* of a mosque and the use of geometrical patterns. It was begun by William I. William the Good II (1166–89), who completed the palace, patronized Arabic poets, kept a harem of Moslem women, and was protected by a bodyguard of negroes.

German castles of the eleventh century

Every powerful ruler in Germany from Charlemagne to Henry the Fowler had used a system of fortresses to repel invaders and to settle newly-won land to the east. The construction of these fortresses had, however, always been under imperial control and to build an adulterine castle was to invite terrible penalties and the destruction of the castle. The strength of the Emperors, the part played by free colonists in the immense effort of clearing and settling vast stretches of land that brought civilization to large parts of Germany, and the close relationship between the Church and central government had all delayed the full arrival of feudalism – and therefore the building of private castles. Gradually in the eleventh century French influence creeping in from Lorraine caused many nobles to pay more attention to the fortification of their manor houses. Apart from those which incorporated Roman masonry, or consisted of a single defensive tower, the *Bergfried*[13] (itself probably a descendant of the Roman frontier watchtower), most of these early German castles seem to have been made of wood; a fortress as important as the Wartburg, for example, had two wooden towers in 1080. The motte-and-bailey castle was not adopted generally, although there remain a few examples, such as the Husterknupp, already described. More typical is the tower such as that shown in plate 61, the castle from which the Habsburgs take their name, now in Switzerland. But the fact that the Germans had built few castles and knew little of siegecraft is no sign of backwardness; it contrasts well with the anarchy of France and is evidence of a higher general degree of order.

Germany differed in many ways from France. There was a large number of free peasants, especially in Saxony, and land was frequently owned outright as an *allodium* or patrimonial estate (this in fact applied to parts of Aquitaine). There were also different answers to the problem of overpopulation; one was the large tracts of land within Christian Germany that, until the eleventh century, remained uncleared and which now provided settlements for energetic peasants. Another was the prize to be won of the Slav and pagan lands to the east, an objective which was to be increasingly pursued in the next century but which had already begun with successes such as that of Bishop Burchard of Halberstadt when in 1066 he captured and destroyed the great fortified temple of the Slavs at Rethra. The political importance of the Church was much greater than in France. The Church worked extremely closely with the Emperors, the authority of the bishops deriving from the vast ecclesiastical estates for which they did homage to the Emperor on consecration. It was this last point that caused the quarrel between Henry IV and Pope Gregory VII and it was during the resulting anarchy that the German-speaking lands, from possessing few castles, became thickly populated with them.

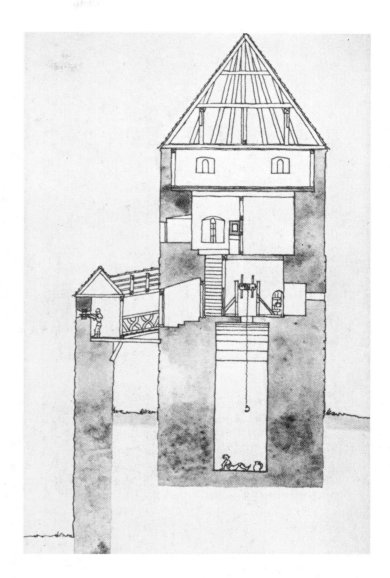

59 *Left* The crowned eagle; a mosaic in the fountain recess shown in plate 58. Byzantine influences, as in these mosaics, combined with Islamic to make the interior of the palace exceptionally luxurious.

60 *Top right* A reconstruction drawing of the *Bergfried* of Harburg, W. Germany. The chief functions of the *Bergfried*, a special characteristic of the castle in German-speaking lands, were as a watchtower and as a final refuge, rarely as permanent living quarters. Like the contemporary Anglo-Norman keeps, its entrance was on the first floor.

61 *Right* Habsburg, Switzerland. The castle from which the Habsburg Emperors took their family name, it was begun in the early eleventh century and added to at later periods.

Henry IV

Henry IV (1056-1106) had already dealt with serious unrest in Saxony before the investiture contest broke out in 1075. Determined to extend the royal demesnes in Saxony and to secure control of the silver mines of the Rammelsberg, he had increased and enforced the dues owed him by the free peasants there, sent commissioners to determine his rights, and built castles which he garrisoned with Swabians, Bavarians, and Franconians. He was able to build these castles all the more easily because one of his most faithful servants was an architect of obviously exceptional talent, Benno II, Bishop of Osnabrück. St Norbert of Magdeburg's *Life*[14] shows Benno a man of humble origins rising by his abilities to act as churchman, administrator, judge, expert on agricultural improvements, and pacifier. Just as William the Conqueror had his ecclesiastical expert on fortifications in Gundulf of Bec, so Henry had his in Benno. The link between secular and ecclesiastical building is shown by the fact that Benno not only superintended the building of the castles of the Harz but was also responsible for drawing the plans and laying the foundations of the Romanesque cathedral of Speyer. He was a man of remarkable character who managed to remain friends with Henry, with Pope Gregory VII and with the anti-Pope Clement III until his death in 1088, and succeeded in this with typical subtlety. On one occasion when a vote was being taken by the bishops on whether to support Emperor or Pope, he was unwilling to commit himself to either party, and, being a small man, he hid himself in a hollow altar, praying while the debate raged. After the vote had been taken, he reappeared and on being challenged was able to swear that he had never left the church. His fellow bishops, therefore, believed he had been made invisible by a miracle and did not press him for his opinion. This shows something of the practical ingenuity that marked the good castle builder.

The greatest and most dreaded of Benno's fortresses was the Harzburg. In 1073, incited by a noble named Otto of Nordheim, the Saxons rose in rebellion. The chronicler Bruno gives Otto's manifesto to the rebels–fascinating for the prominence it accords to the castles. Speaking of Henry, Otto says:

'He has built as you know, strong castles in places that are naturally strong, and there he has collected no small multitude of his henchmen [*fideles*], equipped with arms of all sorts. These castles could not possibly have been built against the heathen [Slavs], who have in the past devastated our whole country which is adjacent to theirs: for it is in the very middle of our land (where no heathen have ever tried to carry on war) that they have been built with such vigour. What they portend– and there are already many of you who know it from experience–you are all about to experience shortly, unless God's mercy and your valour prevent it. Your goods and those who live with you will be carried off in those castles against your will, they will use your daughters and wives for their desire as much as they want. They will take command of your serfs and your beasts of burden–yes, and you yourselves they will force to carry all sorts of burdens on your backs, even dung.'[15]

The rebellion was serious. Henry fled from the Harzburg and met the rebels the next year in an attempt at settlement. He cleverly alienated the Saxon nobles from the peasants by offering to dismantle his castles if the nobles dismantled theirs. The peasants in a fury exacerbated by a Slav raid, attacked the Harzburg, destroying the tombs of Henry's son and his brother Conrad, and flung their bones, together with the venerated skull of a saint, into a ditch. Henry revenged himself by the

62 Rethra, E. Germany. The fortified temple of the Slavs, the destruction of which in 1066 marked an important point in the reconquest of the pagan lands to the east; a water-colour reconstruction.

slaughter of the Saxon peasantry at the battle of Homburg on the Unstrut in 1075. The royal castles were rebuilt and Henry seemed, at the diet of Goslar, on the point of bringing Saxony completely into his power. It was then that Gregory VII re-awoke all the violence of Germany by his letter of December 1075, urging Henry to absolute obedience. At the same time a papal legate threatened him with the possibility of excommunication and, by implication, the loss of his throne.

The investiture contest

The investiture contest was one of the most important causes of the spread of castle building in Europe. During the anarchy let loose by the quarrel, castles sprang up throughout the lands that are now Germany, Austria, Switzerland and Italy, and castles were to be the principal scenes of the most dramatic events of the contest. Since the time of Charlemagne the chief permanent strength of the imperial and royal government had been its close alliance with the Church. The bishops, in return for their power and the vast possessions they controlled, were confirmed in their election by the imperial government. In opposing Gregory, Henry believed he was defending his ancient and quasi-divine rights, while Gregory believed he was the instrument of God in redeeming the purity of the Church. The quarrel went deeper than the form of the investiture of bishops: it was a fundamental struggle between Pope and Emperor over who should have supremacy in Christendom. In 1076 Gregory excommunicated and deposed Henry and released his subjects from their obedience. The Saxons joined with the dissatisfied princes of the south, and rose against him. The princes made preparations at the diet of Tribur and Oppenheim to depose him and called him to answer before the Pope at a diet to be held at Augsburg in February 1077. They kept constant guard from castles lining the routes to the Alpine passes to prevent any communication between Henry and the Pope. The great castle of Hohensalzburg (plate 63), built by a bishop of the papal party, first comes to prominence at this time. Henry, however, managed to leave Germany by way of Burgundy and reached Italy via the Mont Cenis pass, eluding his enemies in a remarkable mid-winter journey through the Alpine ice and snow; Lambert of Hersfeld describes how the queen and her ladies sat on ox hides on which they sledged down from the pass.[16] Once in Italy Henry safely reached the castle of Canossa (fig. 6) in the Emilian Apennines where Gregory was waiting for his escort over the Alps. This castle, which recent excavations have shown was unusually complex for an Italian fortification of the period[17], possessed three circuits of walls. Before the Pope would receive the king he demanded that Henry should surrender his crown and do penance. Henry agreed and was admitted to the second circuit of the walls. There, as Gregory himself wrote:

'On three successive days, standing before the castle gate, laying aside all royal insignia, barefooted and in coarse attire, he ceased not with many tears to beseech the apostolic help and comfort, until all who were present or who had heard the story were so moved by pity and compassion that they pleaded his cause with tears and prayer. All marvelled at our unwonted severity, and some cried out that we were showing not the seriousness of apostolic authority, but rather the cruelty of a savage tyrant. At last, overcome by his persistent show of penitence and the urgency of all present, we released him from the bonds of anathema, and received him into the grace of the Holy Mother Church.'[18]

Gregory, by his duty as a priest, was forced to betray the rebels in Germany whom he had incited to revolt. The rebels, even so, deposed Henry and elected the Swabian Rudolf of Rheinfelden king in his stead. The civil war continued, Henry being finally and irrevocably deposed in 1080 by the Pope. Henry's answer was to invade Italy the next year and by 1084 he had taken most of Rome, while Gregory resisted in the Castel Sant' Angelo (plate 18). The Normans under Robert Guiscard came to Gregory's assistance, looting and burning a great part of the city, and they bore him off to Salerno where he died in 1085. It took Henry IV another six years to put down the opposition in Germany and he then had to struggle until 1097 with the forces of Matilda of Tuscany in Lombardy; when he died in 1106 he was in the midst of a rebellion led by his own son, the future Henry V. He died still excommunicate, his authority weakened by constant papal propaganda against his claims to rule by divine right, the crown lands diminished by grants to supporters, and areas of his Empire depopulated

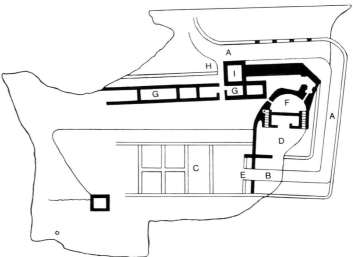

63 *Left* Hohensalzburg, Austria. Added to continuously up to the seventeenth century, the original castle was built in 1077 by Archbishop Gebhard, a supporter of the Pope in the investiture contest, who hoped by building castles, here and elsewhere at Werfen and Friesach, to secure one of the highways across the Alps.

Fig. 6 *Above* Plan of Canossa, Italy, in the early twelfth century. This castle in the Emilian Apennines, owned by Matilda, countess of Tuscany and supporter of Pope Gregory VII, was the scene of the submission of the Emperor Henry IV to the Pope in January 1078 during the investiture contest. *A*. Street leading from the town to the fortress. *B*. Entrance. *C*. Palace of Matilda. *D*. Chapel of St Apollonius. *E*. Castle gateway. *F*. Crypt. *G*. Underground cellars. *H*. Doorway to cellars. *I*. Tower. (After Bertolani del Rio)

and gone to waste in the misery and anarchy of war. One effect was an intensification of feudal institutions already existing in Germany.

The new German society

Those who benefited most from the investiture contest were the great princes who exacted every obedience from their vassals but denied that they themselves owed any similar duties to the Emperor they elected. The other gainers were the burghers, especially those of the Rhineland towns, who had supported Henry IV and had been able to defend themselves behind their city walls against the papal forces. The chief losers were many of the freemen who formerly had recognized no superior but the Emperor but who were now forced to positions of feudal subordination becoming, at worst, serfs. An increasingly important part was to be played by the *ministeriales,* a rank unknown in the rest of Europe but producing in Germany many notable warriors and families. They were administrators and soldiers who first appear in the royal service and whose uses were soon apparent to the princes and bishops. Often they were of low rank, even serfs, in origin but, as will be seen, they sometimes rose to be more powerful than members of the free aristocracy. As in ninth and tenth-century France, the very insecurity of society at this time drove the smaller landowner to surrender his freedom and land to a more powerful neighbour because he could no longer support the direct burden of military service. The more powerful neighbour was in turn subject to a greater lord whose own rivalries often impelled him to increase the number of his vassals continually. The same military reforms that had changed France, and more recently England, hastened the process; the Saxon freemen in their rebellions had fought on foot and had rarely been a match for mounted knights. Every bishop or great landowner needed mounted soldiers for his defence and for establishing what frequently came to be hereditary garrisons in his ever-growing numbers of castles.

The sudden importance of the castle by the beginning of the twelfth century is shown in the way that powerful families adopted the names of their castles, rather than of their *Gau* or old territorial district from which the Carolingian counts had drawn their titles. For example, Frederick of Büren built his castle at Staufen (plate 64), thus naming the most famous imperial house of the Middle Ages, the Hohenstaufen. An Emperor of another family, Lothar II (1125-37), was known after his castle of Supplinburg. The family of Bertold took its ducal title from the castle of Zähringen. Lesser families naturally followed this fashion, edging their way into greater independence as a result. Thus, with the breakdown of central

65 Karlstein bei Reichenhall, W. Germany. A water-colour reconstruction of a castle built on a mountain peak in about 1100.

64 Reconstruction and plan of Staufen, W. Germany, as it appeared in 1090, based on excavations in 1936 and 1938. This was the castle from which the imperial family of the Hohenstaufens took their name.
1. Keep. 2. Palace. 3. Chapel with cellar. 4. Well. 5. Houses.
6. Walk along the battlements. (After Munz)

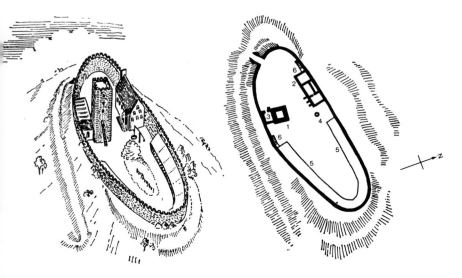

power, in the course of the twelfth century the castle became the pivot of local government, and throughout Germany the *Burgbezirk* or castellany denoted an administrative district. These castles were not generally built on land held of another man but on allodial estates – unlike, for example, the English practice after the Norman Conquest. Built in civil war without authority, they were as adulterine as any baron's motte in the contemporary England of Stephen. However, no figure comparable to Henry II Plantagenet appeared before Frederick Barbarossa, and he found it politic to recognize in retrospect the titles and rights to castellate which the new nobility had already appropriated to themselves.

The motte-and-bailey castle and the Anglo-French keep only reached full development when they were employed as a means of conquest. Although Henry IV in quelling the Saxons used much the same methods as William – the building of fortresses and the use of cavalry against footsoldiers – the military pressures on the German castle builder were not the same. When he built a castle, it was often on land that had been in his family for centuries, and he still wanted it to be a home. He was not building a military outpost in a foreign land, and he generally trusted to his knowledge of the country and his selection of a naturally strong site, often a mountain peak such as Karlstein bei Reichenhall in Bavaria (plate 65).[19] Others might be on a spur cutting into a river, such as Rothenburg (plate 66). This meant not only that the science of flanking did not develop till a later date in Germany, but also that the domestic buildings did not have to be forced into the defensive

network but could be placed more for the owner's comfort than for his defence. Thus even the *Bergfried*, whose chief function was as a watchtower, is frequently not made full use of in the outer defences. The main emphasis in defence was on the gates and the roads leading to them. Defences on the approach could sometimes reach a ludicrous extent, as with the castle of Hochosterwitz in Carinthia, which very much later came to have fourteen successive gates and three great ditches.

From stressing the differences between the French and Anglo-Norman castles and those of Germany we must now turn to a country totally dissimilar in its development and use of fortifications from either–Spain.

Spain

The struggle of the Christians in Spain to win back land from the Moors led them at an early stage to build castles. In the last chapter mention was made of the Moors' exceptional skill in fortification and many lessons were well learned by the Christians. The very name of Castile reminds us of its origins as a mark, or borderland, established between León and the Moors and guarded by a line of castles. Towns such as Burgos (again another castle name) slowly grew up around the protection of a castle and even the monasteries have been described as 'fortified ranch houses'. At the same time a large number of Iberian, Roman, and Visigothic stone buildings were restored and adapted to the needs of the Reconquest.

It was in the eleventh century that the Christian north gained its first great successes. Here the native rulers were greatly aided by Norman and French adventurers, many of whom were to settle in Spain and later to win high positions for themselves. One of the most important events of this period was the siege of Barbastro in the north-east in 1064.[20] Under the command of William VIII, duke of Aquitaine, an army of Normans and Frenchmen, blessed by the Pope, besieged and took the city. They captured thousands of prisoners, sending some to France, some to Rome, and some to Byzantium. It has even been suggested that these prisoners included a Moorish corps of engineers, who had been involved in the siege, and a number of craftsmen superior in technical skill to any in northern Europe. This movement of craftsmen may have had a bearing on the new grandeur shown in religious and secular architecture in England and Normandy at the period of the Conquest. International exchange of ideas must have occurred

66 *Top* Rothenburg, W. Germany. A castle built on a spur cutting into the River Tauber, as it might have appeared in about 1100.

67 *Above* Karlstein, W. Germany. A steel engraving of the Romantic period by Würthle showing the ruins.

68 *Top right* Rothenburg, W. Germany. The ruins of the castle in 1823; an engraving by J. G. Martini.

but rather because he had just taken one of the daughters as his wife, pointing out that the Moslems had done the same with Christian women when they conquered the country. In his broken Arabic the count then asked another girl to sing and he pleased and surprised the Jew by the enthusiasm he showed for the music and verses.[21]

Other successes followed. Toledo surrendered to Alfonso VI in 1085 and there he took the castle of San Servando (plate 70 shows it in its present fifteenth-century form). Alfonso refurbished the castle, which had originally been built by the Arabs in 866 on Roman foundations to protect the bridge of Alcántara, and made it a Benedictine monastery with monks from Cluny and Sahagún. It was burned in the Almoravide

69 *Above left* Clavijo, Spain. The ruins of the castle dominating the scene of the battle in 844 where St James the Apostle of Spain is said to have appeared and inspired the Christian forces to their first great victory over the Saracens.

70 *Left* San Servando, Toledo, Spain. Built on a site occupied by a Roman *castrum* and, after the conquest of Toledo in 1085, a Benedictine monastery where the Cid once stayed, this castle is now wholly fifteenth century, the work of Pedro Tenorio, archbishop of Toledo, who rebuilt a Templar castle which had succeeded the monastery. The pointed merlons are typical of *Mudéjar* work (see page 237) and the design of the balconies in the *torre del homenaje* is also clearly Moorish.

71 *Above* Avila, Spain. Masonry in the city walls, obviously used from older buildings. One stone resembles an altar slab or stone for draining liquid, and the inscription on another is upside down.

72 *Right* Avila, Spain. The San Vicente gate, the most impressive of the nine gates of this walled city, controlling the road to Segovia.

and a more certain story of these exchanges concerns a French count who, in common with the other victorious knights, had been granted a house in Barbastro with all its occupants and contents. The Moorish former owner sent a Jew to the count as an intermediary to ransom his daughters at any price. The count refused, partly because he was now quite rich enough

73 Avila, Spain. Some of the eighty-eight towers of the walls of Avila built between 1090 and 1099 probably making use of already existing Roman walls. The original purpose of the builder, Raymond of Burgundy, son-in-law of Alfonso VII of Castile, seems to have been to provide a huge military base from which to control the lands north of the recently conquered city of Toledo. Eastern and Byzantine influences have been seen in the walls which were constructed by Moslem, Jewish, and Christian workmen. The use of rounded towers in curtain walls seems to have been most exceptional in Europe at this early date.

attack on Toledo in 1099 and Alfonso rebuilt it with curtain walls and a moat. San Servando is mentioned in the *Cantar del Mio Cid* several times and the Cid himself stayed there.

To help control the lands north of Toledo, in 1090, Alfonso's son-in-law, Raymond of Burgundy, brought in twenty French masons to work on the walls of Avila (plate 73).[22] The site was ancient but uninhabited owing to the border strife. For the success of his operations to the south, Alfonso needed a base much larger than could be provided by a castle, so this extraordinary stone encampment with eighty-eight towers came into existence. The traditional theory is that the walls were designed by two masters of geometry, an Italian, Cassandro, and a Frenchman, Florian de Ponthieu, but there is some reason for thinking that Raymond of Burgundy reconstructed existing walls dating from Roman times. Jewish, Moslem, and Christian masons, reputedly nearly 2,000 in number, worked on the walls for nine years till their completion in 1099. When in the next century the cathedral was built and included in the defences of the east wall, Avila quickly revived as a town. The use of stone in curtain walls (see Glossary) on such a scale has no parallel in the Christian west at this time. Moreover the towers possess rounded faces, a shape that was not to become general for at least another hundred years. Avila precedes the other great walled towns of Europe, such as Carcassonne, Aigues-Mortes, Conway, Dubrovnik, and Visby, but is not excelled by them.

The struggle with the Moors caused the development of the castle in Spain to differ greatly from that in England and France, on the one hand, and the Empire, on the other. This difference had many causes: one was the fact that the Christians often took over Moorish castles and adapted them. For example, after seizing an *alcazaba* they would add a keep of their own, the *torre del homenaje*, provided for reasons of safety with a single entrance on the second floor, to act not only as the final point of refuge but as a symbol of their newly-acquired dominion (see plate 17 of Baños de la Enciña at Jaén). Another reason for their difference is because feudalism never gained a deep hold in León and Castile, so the castle was not primarily the residence of a feudal lord. More often it was intended to house garrisons, such as those of the knightly orders of Calatrava and Santiago, founded in the twelfth century, in this function resembling the Moorish practice. The power of the towns was maintained by the granting of *fueros* or charters which defined their rights and duties to the local overlords—this power was naturally supported by the kings, particularly in the case of towns such as Avila which had been reconquered and needed to attract new settlers. Only in Italy and southern France were towns as important a factor in politics at this date.

Spain was, however, teaching the rest of Europe. The interest of the Popes and the monks of Cluny in the progress of the Reconquest and the successes of proclaiming a holy war in the peninsula provided the model for an even greater military adventure—the Crusades.

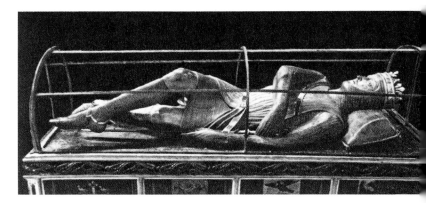

74 The tomb of Duke Robert of Normandy, in Gloucester Cathedral, member of the first Crusade, eldest son of William the Conqueror, defeated at Tinchebrai in 1106 by his younger brother Henry I to whom he lost his dukedom. He died in prison in Cardiff Castle in 1134 where his last years were spent in learning Welsh. The wooden effigy was carved *c* 1250.

The first Crusade

It is a curious fact that many of the finest and most original castles are set at the edges of medieval Europe—in Wales, and Scotland, in Spain, and in the regions belonging to the Teutonic Knights known as the Ordensland. In many cases this is largely because of the expansion of the Normans and their northern French neighbours across the continent and beyond its bounds. Those castles which many consider to be the finest of all, the fortresses built by the Crusaders, resulted from the farthest flung effort of this expansion, an effort so pushed to its limit that the attempt to make the Holy Land part of Europe was doomed to eventual failure—but so rich in cultural and civilizing exchanges that one can still be grateful that it happened.

Pope Urban II (1088-99), in his famous speech at Clermont-Ferrand in 1095 promulgating the first Crusade, had pointed out how small a part of the known world was under the influence of the Western Church and commented bitterly upon the shame of this fact. By doing so he gave hope and a mission to all the numerous landless knights and free men of Europe whose only means of maintaining their rank in society was to travel and fight for possessions elsewhere. The example of the Normans in Sicily and of the French knights in Spain was an added spur. The Holy Land was to be as fully feudalized in the twelfth century as England had been in the eleventh. The castle may have arisen in response to invasions and anarchy and, as the differing examples of Avila and the Tower of London show, had reached a high state of sophistication by the time of the first Crusade; but it was through the experience of the Crusades that the ingenuity of the castle builders of the West was taxed to the full. Monarchs such as Richard Coeur-de-Lion, Philip Augustus, and the Emperor Frederick II went to the land of Outremer and returned brimming with new ideas and techniques they urgently wished to put into practice. Their richer followers came back with the same ambitions. They also returned having discovered that many luxuries were in fact necessities.

Even the first Crusaders, taking four years to reach Jerusalem, must have learned much on that terrible journey. The route followed by those under the command of Godfrey of Bouillon took them from their own well-castled Lorraine, through a Germany now thick with towers as a result of the investiture contest, across Hungary whose nobles lived in huts of reeds, to enter the Eastern Empire by way of Belgrade and Adrianople. Then at Christmas 1096 they saw for the first time the gigantic walls of Byzantium. They were joined by the Normans of Sicily under Bohemond and the Provençals under Raymond of Toulouse. Thence, to the openly expressed relief of their Byzantine hosts, they set out for Jerusalem, a journey that was to take them two and a half years. After taking Nicaea from the Turks with the help of the Byzantines and after a near defeat at the battle of Dorylaeum, the route was open to the great city of Antioch on the River Orontes, seemingly impregnable with its curtain walls and towers. There they built fortifications which were designed to prevent sorties from the city and to cut off reinforcements and supplies and they even built a castle, suitably named Malregard, a form of *Gegenburg* or anti-castle. Antioch fell to them eventually through the treachery of an Armenian in the employ of the Turks. Only the citadel held out for a few weeks but this, too, surrendered after the Crusaders had beaten off a strong Turkish relieving army. After a delay of fifteen months they set out for Jerusalem.

Until the siege of Jerusalem, which began on June 7, 1098, the Crusaders had shown themselves better at open battle, in which their heavy cavalry overpowered the more lightly mounted Turks, than at siege warfare. Now, desperation at being so near to losing their prize, the buoyancy of their faith which, with the help of real or pretended miracles, enabled them to recover their spirits even after the most appalling losses, and the considerable military skill they had acquired on the journey, all contributed to their success. Their first assault failed for lack of enough ladders. The scarcity of wood and other materials in the surrounding country seriously delayed them until some Christian ships carrying ropes, nails and bolts put in at Jaffa. The wood was brought from the forests of Samaria on camel-back or dragged by captive Moslems. Now they began to construct siege-towers, two large ones and a smaller one. Of the two large towers, one was

built for Godfrey of Bouillon by Gaston of Béarn and the other for Raymond of Toulouse by William Ricou. The non-combatant pilgrims, the old men, and the women sewed camel-hide and oxhide and nailed it to the towers as a protection against the Greek fire of the Turks. These towers could only be moved over level ground and, therefore, the ditch round the city had to be filled in at a predetermined point of assault before the towers were trundled slowly up to the walls. It took many hours of struggle before Godfrey of Bouillon, commanding from the top storey of his tower, was able to throw a bridge down on to the north wall at midday on July 15. Once they had gained the wall-walk, more knights and footsoldiers climbed up by ladder. Raymond of Toulouse came through on the other side of the city. While the walls rang with the cries

75 Sahyun, Syria. The main entrance to the castle (extreme right) together with the twelfth-century keep overlooking the man-made gorge seen in plate 121.

of the victors, the resistance of the defenders crumbled and nearly all the Moslem and Jewish inhabitants of the city were put to death. The leaders of the first Crusade rode through the corpses and blood in the streets to set their offerings on the altar of the Church of the Holy Sepulchre, treating as their feudal overlord the God who had confirmed them as His vassals by granting them this new land by their victory. Then in the following years they and their heirs consolidated their success by building large numbers of castles from which they could enforce their alien feudalism upon the land.

CASTLES OF THE 12TH AND 13TH CENTURIES - SOLDIERS, MASONS, LADIES, AND LOVERS

One of the most important effects of the conquests of the eleventh century was the creation of an international society, based largely on the customs and modes of behaviour of the land-owning, warrior class in France, known as *'la chevalerie'* from its special connection with the horse. Although the knight himself might be only a small landowner or a poor mercenary or even unfree, like the *ministeriales* of Germany, the values of knighthood came in the twelfth and thirteenth centuries to extend all through the upper classes to the great lords and members of royal families. A northern French or an Anglo-Norman baron travelling to the Crusades across France and taking a ship from Italy, would find himself constantly in the company of men with similar standards and education and with the same language in common. Not infrequently he would be related to some of them and also to the knights settled in the Holy Land. If he were lucky and returned, he would be welcomed at castle after castle on his journey back and his wife in England, who would have ruled his own castle and estates in his absence, would now appear resplendent in the Eastern silks he brought back for her. Partly from such contacts and partly by spreading to yet more countries, in the twelfth and thirteenth centuries the castle acquired new functions and characteristics. It kept those it had already gained – its defensive nature as a fortified enceinte round the hall or tower of its owner and the aggressive character it had acquired as an instrument of conquest in the eleventh century – but certain new factors emerged. With the increasing use of stone the castle became more permanent: it was more expensive to build and it had to justify that expense by its usefulness. With that new permanence, it became a stabilizing influence with effects far beyond the sphere of war. For example in successfully conquered areas, where it had been chiefly a weapon of war, it could now become a centre of administration or the residence of the conquerors' descendants.

Before dealing with some individual castles of these two centuries (see Chapters 4 and 5), we must look at some general considerations affecting the castle – the means and methods of warfare, the part played in this warfare by the castles, the people who built them, the people who lived in them, and their occupations and pastimes. First of all, one must ask 'Who actually owned and lived in castles in this period?' This can be answered roughly by examining the dwelling places of those on the feudal scale, from king to tenant-in-chief, to vassal barons, and then to the various degrees of subvassals above the rank of serfs. In France, the Empire, and England, as we shall see, the royal castles were only one of various types of buildings used by the royal courts in their journeys, the other types ranging from undefended palaces, such as Westminster or Goslar, to hunting lodges, such as Woodstock, or manors, like Vincennes before its transformation into a castle in the fourteenth century. Some of the royal castles came to act as depots for military stores and were looked after by very small garrisons. Others, depending on the needs of a king in wartime or for purposes of justice and administration, were frequently visited and used by the court. Great nobles or territorial rulers, such as the counts of Champagne, would generally have the same diversity of dwelling places but just as the palaces and manor houses would often be the older constructions, so when they had to build afresh they chose to build castles. In Spain at this time few castles seem to have been residential. In Germany, even by the early years of the twelfth century, most of the nobility did not live in castles although it later became common for magnates and ecclesiastical overlords to entrust castles to *ministeriales* or hereditary castellans. This was not the English practice but there are French examples of this happening, as at Vergy in Burgundy. Whether a baron or a member of the lesser nobility built and lived in a castle would depend on whether he needed to protect his estates in this way, on whether he was rich enough, on whether he could raise enough cash on his estates from the local Jewish money lender, on whether he could get permission from his overlord to build, and on whether the example of his neighbours made it a social necessity. A noble living in a peaceful area of East Anglia would not have the same compulsion to build fortifications that a counterpart living on the Welsh border would have. The East Anglian might have a manor house which would be fortified in some respects but nothing to merit the title of castle, whereas the Marcher baron, probably much poorer in terms of income, depended for his and his family's lives on possessing a complete defensive enceinte. Lower down the scale, the knight, whether landed or not, would not have a castle – unless, of course, he could attract such favour at court that he was married to a great heiress or conquered someone else's castle either at home or abroad. In both cases his rank would change respectively, according to that of his bride and according to his new responsibilities.

Although the possession of a castle was largely the prerogative of the royal families and the upper classes, castles affected all the other levels of society in one way or another. As medieval society was organized on the assumption that warfare was a permanent feature of life, so we must look first at the knight as a soldier, his military education, his arms, his methods of warfare and then at how these factors influenced the castle both tactically and strategically.

The knight

The knight was trained for the cavalry charge and hand-to-hand combat. When he was about seven years of age he was taken away from the society of the women of the castle and frequently he was sent to the castle either of his father's overlord or of a relative and, as in the case of the young William Marshal who, in the middle of the twelfth century, was sent from his father's home in England to an uncle in Normandy, this might mean a very long separation from his family. From then onwards he would be trained in horsemanship, in managing his lance, in becoming accustomed to the weight of armour, and in

wielding the great two-handed swords, axes, and maces then in use. The amusements of his lord in which he would assist, according to his age, were equally physical, being chiefly hunting (a necessity for the provision of fresh meat) and tournaments. He progressed from being a page, during which time he learned to wait at table, to carve meat, a most elaborate and difficult accomplishment, to attend ladies, and to act in

76 Scenes from the life of David: a sheet from the twelfth-century English *Winchester Bible* (*c* 1170) which, apart from its intrinsic beauty, gives much information on civilian and military costume. Note, for example, Goliath's armour (centre top), the double girths and the high pommel and cantle on Absalom's saddle (bottom left). The shields are decorated with simple geometric patterns. *New York, Pierpont Morgan Library*, M. 619, fo 1v.

nearly every way as a personal servant, to become a squire at about the age of fifteen, when he became more actively concerned in learning about the care of arms and of horses and attendance on knights in battle or tournaments. This intense and specialized military training explains how, on the one hand, there was little time left for the acquisition of learning in the clerical sense and also, on the other, how in many areas the sense of social superiority in the nobility fostered by this specialized training depended on this extraordinary form of education.

After being a squire at an age that varied according to the rank of the young man and local custom, he was dubbed a knight. The wealth of Christian associations with which the Church was later to endow this ceremony was absent in the twelfth century. All that was generally needed was a blow from one who was already a knight and then the young man would give a display of his skill in horsemanship and the management of his arms. From then onwards he was part of an international brotherhood, nearly always, whatever his wealth, the recipient of a certain respect and deference.

What caused and ensured the continuance of this form of education? Every holder of land had military obligations either

78 Conical helm with a nasal or nose piece, beaten from one piece of iron. Although this was found in Moravia, it is usually dated to the eleventh or twelfth centuries and bears a strong resemblance to some of the helms in the Bayeux Tapestry. *Vienna, Kunsthistorisches Museum.*

79 *Right* The three Marys are greeted at the Tomb by the angel while the soldiers sleep, their torches doused and using their shields as beds or covers; illumination from a twelfth-century German gospel. *Stuttgart, Landesbildstelle Württemberg*, Bibl. fo 28.

77 Armour in the battle of Hastings; from the Bayeux Tapestry. Note the knee-length hauberks of leather protected with metal rings, the long shields, and the conical helms here made of segments with or without bands.

to the king if he held directly of him or to his overlord. He was expected to bring a certain number of knights and sergeants at his lord's call to serve or fight for a period of forty days, whether in one of the king's wars, to put down rebellions, to engage in private wars or sieges, or to provide garrisons for castles or towns. By keeping under his control the education of his vassal's sons, he not only secured a permanent source of men to fulfil his obligations or defend his own rights, but he also kept alive the personal contact and sense of obligation on which the feudal bond depended. The large households contained in the castles of the greater barons (which we will look at from another aspect later in this chapter) were expressions of this chain of feudal connections, a development of the family group, the *mesnie,* round whom the first private castles had developed and now protected by the arts of

fortification learned during a century of conquest. The positive bond that held this society together was loyalty to one's lord. This was one of the deepest strands in medieval society. To Dante, the worst sinners were Judas Iscariot, Brutus, and Cassius who, for their disloyalty to their lords, are crushed eternally in the mouths of Satan in the bottommost abyss of Hell. In repayment for this loyalty, of course, the vassals expected much in return and some of the most valuable achievements of medieval society arose from the clash of interpretations as to what the mutual obligations of the feudal bond meant.

Arms and armour

The aggressive nature of early medieval warfare and the emphasis on hand-to-hand combat meant that the knight had to be properly fitted with armour if he were to have any chance of survival. The leather hauberks used in earlier days gave way, by the early twelfth century, to body garments of chain-mail which still permitted considerable ease of movement. These had to withstand blows from a couched lance and arrows. The head was protected by the Norman conical helm made familiar by the Bayeux Tapestry (plate 77) fitted with a nose piece. Very few examples of this armour survive (plate 78). Underneath the chain-mail the knight would wear a gambeson or padded garment which would prevent arrows penetrating into the body. But neither mail-shirt nor gambeson could always prevent the damaging effect of bruising and bones breaking. The introduction of the crossbow later in the twelfth century, with a bolt or quarrel of much greater projectile force capable of piercing chain-mail, was another reason for making armour stronger. An introduction of the later twelfth century was the barrel-shaped helm (plate 82) which rested its weight on the shoulders and provided complete protection to the face, unlike the older conical helm which must have been very heavy on the skull.

The knight was further protected by his shield. This grew smaller than the great kite-shaped shields used by the Normans in the Bayeux Tapestry and by the thirteenth century is

80 *Left* A soldier armed with lance, shield, and sword and wearing a scaled hauberk: one of a series of gilt-bronze figures on a chandelier *c* 1140 formerly in the abbey church of St Nicholas, Gross-Comburg. *Stuttgart, Landesbildstelle Württemberg.*

81 *Above* A chainmail hauberk attached to its helm traditionally made for Rudolf IV (1339–65) of Austria and Styria. *Tower of London.*

generally shown with a straight top and a triangular form, an adaptation which probably made for ease of movement on horseback. The shield was one of the first pieces of a knight's equipment to lend itself to the new art of heraldry. As armour hid more and more of the wearer, so it became correspondingly important that he should make himself identifiable by other means. At first the designs were comparatively simple but by the fourteenth century, as the German *Weingärtner Liederbuch* manuscript shows, there was scarcely any part of a knight's equipment that was not emblazoned with his own particular symbols, from the crest on his helm to the cloth trapper of his horse (plate 83).

The knight in the field

When the knight charged at his enemy, he was prevented from falling off by his high, built-up saddle and his stirrups. If he shivered his ash lance, he then drew his sword or used his axe or his mace. A skilful and well-trained knight could obviously be a formidable enemy but the dependence on armour and the extremely stylized training frequently led to an inability to deal with the unexpected and hence to disaster. One example comes from the important battle of Benevento in 1266 which won for Charles of Anjou the Hohenstaufen lands in Italy and Sicily. There, a body of heavily armoured German cavalry stood up to repeated attacks by the invaders until a Frenchman realized that when the Germans raised their weapons to strike their armpits were not protected. The French closed in so tightly that the Germans' long swords were of little avail and using their short daggers they slaughtered the cavalry.[1]

Another disadvantage was the over-dependence on attack in

warfare. Thus when two armies of cavalry met in battle they attacked simultaneously, as in the deadly tournaments with which the knights amused themselves when not fighting in earnest. Defensive strategy of the kind practised so successfully by the Byzantines through long centuries was beyond the capability of the typical western army. Its soldiers never stayed together long enough to learn to stand upon the defensive – that is, until the English victories in Scotland and France in the fourteenth century showed how it might be done. Some great battles, such as Hastings and Dorylaeum, had been won partly by cavalry charges but just as numerous are accounts of defeat where the men could not be restrained from charging at the wrong moment. Attack is the only method open to untrained troops or, as in this case, to troops frequently unused to fighting together. This emphasis on attack was increased by the introduction by the end of the eleventh century, at the latest, of the knight charging with his lance couched. Although the stirrup had been known for several centuries, probably accounting for the greater use of cavalry and therefore the growth in the importance of the knight as a professional cavalryman from Carolingian times onwards, its full value was not extracted until some unknown knight realized that he could combine his own weight with that of his horse when delivering a blow. Thus he had invented a new and powerful military device.[2] Up to the introduction of the stirrup the mounted soldier could have used only the biceps and shoulder muscles in striking a blow; otherwise he would have fallen off, especially if he missed his target. Up to at least the time of the Bayeux Tapestry he used his spear as a throwing or stabbing weapon. Now he could charge with it, and a group of such heavily

82 *Left* Effigy, showing the barrel-shaped helm that succeeded the conical helm, thought to be of Robert, second Lord Tattershall, who died in 1212, now in Kirkstead Church, Lincolnshire.

83 *Above* Armorial devices on shield, pennon, and helm in the form of a crest: Wahsmüt von Künzich, from the fourteenth-century *Weingärtner Liederbuch*. Such decorative use of personal or family devices became increasingly popular from the thirteenth century. *Stuttgart, Landesbildstelle Württemberg, S118, Nr 20.*

mounted soldiers could easily vanquish many times their own number of footsoldiers.

Military historians have in general deplored the paucity of original ideas employed by medieval commanders.[3] Few came up to the standard of William the Conqueror who employed feigned flights at Hastings and a relentless pursuit of his objectives. On the other hand, few had the opportunity of making their names by resounding victories in the field because, compared with later history, not many battles took place at this time. Except in the cases of the great Crusades and Barbarossa's descents into Italy, armies were generally small and concentrations of soldiers would frequently be broken up by the need to besiege numerous troublesome castles. This meant that it was the castle that absorbed much of the available talent amongst thinking military men of the day and just as the ideally equipped knight could attack while remaining completely protected himself, so immense thought and effort went into making a castle that could always let its garrison out to drive off the attackers and always be impregnable to assault.

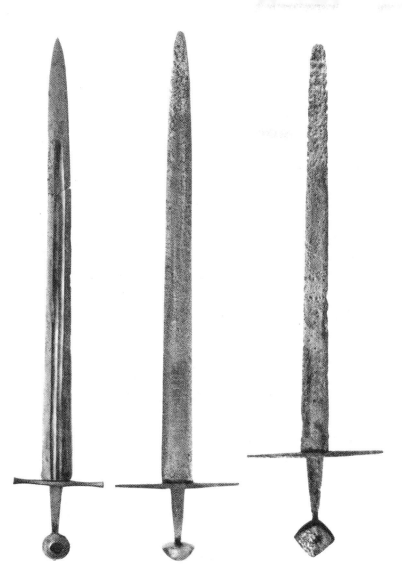

84 *Left* A thirteenth-century English sword from the River Witham. *London, British Museum.*
Centre A sword, thought to be German, 1200–50. *Glasgow, Art Gallery and Museum.*
Right Tenth-century sword; north European. *Glasgow, Art Gallery and Museum.*

The castle in warfare

Whether all these improvements of the twelfth and thirteenth centuries in the defences of castles worked or not depended ultimately on the garrison, on the size of attacking armies, on the stores, and on the morale of the defenders. In some cases well-thought-out defences must have strengthened morale; in others they obviously made the garrison lazy. Small armies summoned only for special purposes in the field had their corollary in small garrisons for castles which were rarely kept on a war basis except in very violent regions such as the Spanish marches, the Holy Land, or Wales. Especially if they were made of earthworks and timber, castles were allowed to fall into desuetude if they were no longer required for their original purpose and no new function could be found for them. Where a monarch or a magnate wished to keep control of a castle without incurring too much expense in maintenance, the answer in Germany and parts of France was to establish hereditary castellans on whom the responsibility for the defence of the castle depended. In England such posts were virtually unknown and the duty of castle guard maintained the royal castles with a changing garrison. But King John had to be prevented by a clause in Magna Carta from forcing knights

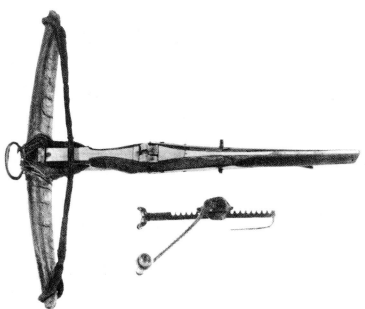

85 *Left* An armorial shield carved in stone, from Steingaden, Swabia. *Munich, Bayerisches Nationalmuseum.*

86 *Above* The crossbow, because of its greater range and projectile force, became increasingly popular from the later twelfth century onwards, both on the field and in siege warfare. It needed, however, considerable skill for its successful use and this favoured the hiring of professional or mercenary crossbowmen by those who could afford them. This example from north Germany is much later, *c* 1475. *Glasgow, Art Gallery and Museum.*

87 *Top* Gisors, France. The chief base of the Anglo-Norman kings in their wars with the Capetians—until its cession to Philip Augustus in 1195 brought about the building of Château Gaillard. The keep, its chemise, and the motte were probably built for William Rufus by Robert of Bellême in 1096–7. Further work was carried out there by Henry I, Henry II, and Philip Augustus; a lithograph by G. Engelmann, 1824.

88 *Above* Odiham, England. An engraving of the ruins of King John's polygonal keep, built in the tradition of the transitional keeps of the twelfth century. A tiny garrison held out for a week here in 1216 against French invaders. From Grose's *Antiquities,* Vol. II, 1772.

89 *Right* Carcassonne, France. The Narbonne Gate, protecting the narrow part of the city joining the spur on which it is built to the neighbouring high ground. Built at the end of the reign of Philip the Bold (1245–85), son of St Louis, its beaked towers, based on an ogival ground-plan, are designed to eliminate absolutely dead ground. Exceptionally well-preserved, Viollet-le-Duc only replaced the roof with slate tiles; subsequently the more suitable clay tiles were substituted. The buildings in front of the gate are part of St Louis's barbican protecting the entrance.

who were willing to undertake their tours of duty to make payments instead, and it is clear that he preferred obtaining money for the hire of professionals rather than depending on eager but not always competent amateurs. Mercenaries had been in demand in England since the time of the Conqueror and Henry I advised his son-in-law, the Emperor Henry V, to solve his difficulties by hiring professional troops. Throughout the twelfth and thirteenth centuries, as warfare became more sophisticated and castles became more difficult in some cases to take and in others to hold, the rulers of many western countries came increasingly to depend upon professional soldiers both for field armies, hiring for example Flemish crossbowmen, and for their castles or siege trains. By the end of the thirteenth century the small permanent garrisons of most English royal castles included a few professional soldiers. Conway, for example, in 1284 had fifteen mercenaries in its garrison of thirty. Then too, kings and those nobles who could afford them would maintain professional soldiers as part of their courts and these would travel with them from castle to palace or manor and back again.

The huge perimeters of many castles would seem to belie the small garrisons known from records to have existed. The need for these great extents is explained by other factors, some of which we come to later, but one of them is that they acted as bases for the gathering together of an army before a campaign. Gisors (plate 87) certainly fulfilled this function in the Anglo-Norman/French wars and it has been calculated that a thousand troops could have encamped within its curtain walls. Lucera (fig. 21), with its huge enceinte, played the same part for Charles of Anjou. One suggestion for the purpose of the outer walls in the concentric castle is that they provided a permanent fortified space for the elements of an army to encamp.[4] The small size of the permanent garrison would mean that in wartime some castles fell because of surprise attacks or because they never received reinforcements. In such cases much would depend on morale and the intelligence of the commander. In 1216 at the siege of Odiham (plate 88) in Hampshire, a castle with a polygonal keep built by King John, three knights and ten sergeants held out for a week against the French invaders before surrendering. Sahyun (plate 75) fell to Saladin in 1188 in spite of its seemingly impregnable position because of the skills of his engineers and the high morale of his attacking forces. Many castles fell to tricks, as Linlithgow did in 1312 when the Scottish soldiers entered the castle hidden in a cart carrying hay and then used the cart to block the gate.

Because the most dramatic individual events in a castle's history are its sieges, the military purpose of the castle is too often thought of as being solely defensive. A description of one of the three sieges of the castle of Le Puiset by Louis the Fat, by Suger in his *Life* of his master, is often quoted as an example of the defence of a motte-and-bailey castle.[5] The first siege, in 1111, was a very fierce engagement in which carts filled with kindling, pork fat, and dried blood were pushed against the gate and set on fire; the motte was only taken after the failure of repeated assaults and a tonsured priest had shown how to break through the palisade. But the use of this example overlooks the reason why Louis the Fat had to go to this effort of enforcing his will. The castle was the base of Hugh of Le Puiset for his offensive attacks on the lands of the Church and his neighbouring lords. At the height of Hugh's power even the count of Chartres did not dare approach within eight or nine miles of Le Puiset. This particular castle was used as

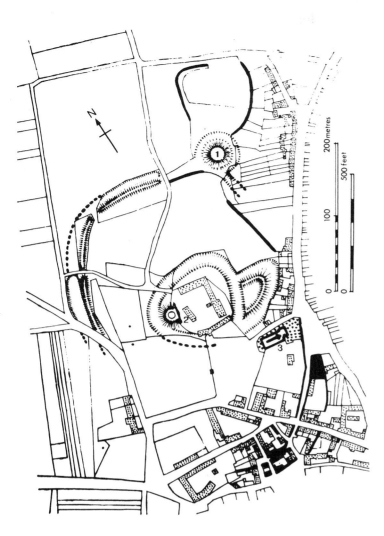

Middle Ages progressed, the design both of armour and of castles became more elaborate, more adapted to keeping what one had than to taking what others possessed. But this was not the attitude of the successful knight of the twelfth century. The warfare to which he was trained depended on attack.

Robin Fedden, writing of the Crusader Castles, has described what he calls 'castle mentality',[6] when the strain of being on the defensive was too much for the nerves of the garrison. This was

91 Ludlow, England. A great Marcher castle and the scene of the twelfth-century story of Fulk FitzWarine (see pages 83 & 84). One of its most unusual surviving features is its round twelfth-century chapel; an eighteenth-century engraving.

a base for offensives for most of its existence, and was on the defensive for only a very short period.

The fact that a great lord encased his body in metal and that he encased his natural home, the hall, in a castle of stone, points to a defensive mentality throughout society. This wariness was proper to a society that was extremely warlike and it was also fostered by the education common to many knights. If, from the age of seven, a boy were brought up almost solely to the business of war and if the only stories he would hear were of great war-chiefs and frightful disasters, there might well be a compensating fear in the back of his mind that he might not come up to the standards of Roland and Oliver, that it would be better to avoid battle behind strong walls rather than be revealed as a coward or a weakling, and that all his wealth should be devoted to personal splendour in apparel and building to conceal an innate lack of strength. So, looking at the armour of these tiny men, one thinks of Andrew Young's musings on a dead crab thrown up by a storm:
'Or does it make for death to be
Oneself a living armoury?'
These reflections contain too much hindsight. Certainly, as the

particularly true of the Crusading kingdom where there were rarely enough men to garrison a fortress properly. He quotes as one example the second siege of El Habis Djaldak, a grotto fortress where the Arabs surrendered after a siege of three weeks, not because they feared the Franks themselves but because they could not endure waiting while they were being dug out 'like badgers'. If the enemy army approaching a castle considerably outnumbered the defenders, naturally the garrison would be wise to keep within the walls – though this is not at all the policy followed by the elder Simon de Montfort at Muret (see page 127). If the forces were better matched, the commander did not mew himself up while his crops were destroyed and his authority over the district diminished. He came rushing out to fight.

An involved story illustrating this and many other aspects of aggressive defence comes from the *Romance of Fulk Fitzwarine*.[7] It concerns not the main hero of the romance, a Robin Hood figure, but his father, Fulk le Brun Fitzwarine, who while a youth was sent as a page to Josse de Dinan at Ludlow Castle, Shropshire (plate 91) in the reign of Henry II. Ludlow at that time was one of the most advanced castles in Britain. It seems to have been unusual in that its enceinte was built of stone, perhaps in the reign of William Rufus. Its stone keep was built later, probably by the time of this story. Josse de Dinan had originally been granted the castle by Stephen. His chief enemies were the Lacys who had claims on Ludlow

Fig. 7 A plan of the defences of Le Puiset, France. 1 and 2 indicate mottes and 3 the church and cemetery. Hatched lines show ramparts or ditches now destroyed. Broken lines indicate twelfth-century enceintes. Dots show buildings erected in 1839. (After Finó)

90 *Left* Aigues-Mortes, France. Part of the walls built for Philip the Bold to protect the port and town originally laid out by St Louis as an arsenal for his crusading expeditions. The moat has been filled in, thus diminishing the apparent height of the walls.

and in about 1160 they attacked it. Josse de Dinan did not hide behind his double walls and hope they would go away; he came out and fought a battle with his enemies. Fulk Fitzwarine, watching from a tower, with Josse's wife and his daughter Hawise, saw that Josse had been cut off by Walter de Lacy and three other knights. Although as a page he had been kept from the fight, he seized an axe and an old helmet, ran down and reached Josse just as he had dismounted. In a prodigy of valour, Fulk killed two of the knights and took prisoner Walter de Lacy and the fourth knight, Arnold de Lisle, who were promptly locked up in the castle. Fulk was naturally considered a hero and arrangements went forward to marry him to Josse's daughter Hawise. But Josse had another ward of good family in his household, Marion de la Bruère, who was being brought up by his wife. Marion fell passionately in love with the captured Arnold de Lisle who persuaded her to provide him with a knotted linen rope. Using this, he and Walter escaped from their prison. Once they were at large a temporary truce was arranged between the Lacys and Josse who now felt free to celebrate the marriage of Fulk to Hawise and to accompany them on a journey away from Ludlow Castle.

Marion de la Bruère sent Arnold de Lisle a message that she could let him in by the same window through which he had escaped and that Josse and his family were away. Arnold informed Walter de Lacy and at the appointed time they came to the castle bringing a hundred men-at-arms. Arnold climbed up the ladder which he left hanging out of the window and went to Marion's room where he made love to her. Meanwhile Walter and his men climbed up the rope and entered the castle. Some opened the castle gates, killing the watchman, and others slaughtered the garrison in their beds. Marion, who was alone with her lover, heard the screams and realized what he had done. She leaped from her bed, seized his sword, ran him through the body where he lay, and then threw herself to her death from the window on to the rocks below.

Walter de Lacy was now in command of Ludlow but Josse and Fulk returned in haste to try and seize it back again. Josse constructed a temporary castle in the British camp at Kaynham, three miles off, as a base for his attack on Ludlow. The siege began. Again, although the roles were reversed, the garrison came out to fight before the walls. This time they were beaten back and Josse's men attacked the outer ward by piling wood against the gate, pouring grease on it and setting fire to it. When the gate was charred through, they burst in and captured the ward. Walter de Lacy, now confined to the inner ward and in desperate straits, sent a secret message to the Welsh Prince of Gwynnedd offering to acknowledge him as his lord if he would come to his assistance. To invite the participation of the Welsh was against all the codes of Marcher behaviour, but the trick worked. The Prince of Gwynnedd arrived with his men and Josse had to fight on two fronts. He was captured in the battle and Fulk, his son-in-law, only escaped after being badly wounded. Fulk then went to court where the Lacys were ordered to release Josse and to dispense with their allies. Josse, however, died soon after (in 1166) and the Lacys kept Ludlow. It took four years to drive the Welsh from Shropshire.

All these events centred on the possession of a castle that is now one of the loveliest ruins of the Marches—where Philip Sidney spent part of his boyhood and Milton's *Comus* was first performed. The weight of association and of later, more civilized behaviour dims our conception of the violence, the fierce passions, the immediate response of aggression to any danger, the state of perpetual warfare. Loyalty to one's lord was the chief law. There was no other action possible for the young Fulk Fitzwarine but to rush to the defence of Josse de Dinan, just as there was no prospect in life left for Marion de la Bruère after she had realized the result of her unwitting betrayal. It was only as a last resort that Fulk went to Henry II to seek legal redress for his wrongs.

The sieges of Ludlow concern a local quarrel between two family groups but in a major war the capture of an enemy's castle was only a secondary aim. The real objective was to capture the enemy himself and as many of his greater vassals as possible. What the attacker wanted, apart from the extortion of land and other concessions, was the ransom. For a great lord this could equal the sum needed to build several castles and, in the case of a monarch such as Coeur-de-Lion, would equal the entire income of the Angevin empire for many years. For this reason, important military commanders were sometimes granted permission to leave a castle entrusted to their care, if it came under threat of attack, and to operate in the open countryside. But as much as to defend its owners or castellan, the role of the castle was to act as a firm military base for the protection of the horses, their forage, the supplies of armour and other warlike stores. Horses were particularly important because they gave the knights their military and social superiority. Jordan Fantosme, in his poem describing the rebellion of the Young King against Henry II of England, says that the loss of a war-horse equals the loss of many soldiers without armour. This is echoed in many places. The young and penniless William Marshal made the beginnings of his fortune from all the horses he captured.

The duties and payments in kind exacted from the peasantry were as much a tax to provide for permanent warfare as a means of enriching their lords. It is difficult, therefore, to separate the strategic considerations that went into the building of a castle from the honor or lordship of which it was the administrative centre. A castle without land or labour to support it was either an extremely expensive military necessity or else it was useless—a point illustrated in the life of William Marshal. In 1199 Richard Coeur-de-Lion and Philip Augustus agreed to a five-year truce on condition that Philip should, while keeping the Norman castles he had already seized, surrender all control of the surrounding castle lands. Richard at first felt he had been tricked into the loss of these castles and shut himself up 'choked with rage like a wounded bear'. The Marshal was the only man who dared go near him and roused him with these words:

'Why be annoyed at such a trifle: you should laugh rather, for you have gained all. The King of France wants peace. Leave him the castles until the next passage to the Holy Land, but keep the land which belongs to us. When he can get nothing from the land and has to keep up the castles at his own cost, he will find that he is carrying a heavier burden than a war. That is what will happen. I wager they will come back tomorrow.'[8]

How did such a castle influence its surroundings? It is often said of a castle that it commands a valley, a river, or a road—a

92 Alter do Chão, Portugal. A stair in the thickness of the wall. This illustration conveys, as do so many castles, the impression of a defensive mentality, a preference for darkness and self-incarceration.

93 *Above* Trifels, W. Germany. The ruins of Hohenstaufen buildings at this important castle. The projection, part of the chapel, is a very early example of a feature much used in German castles; a lithograph dated 1825.

phrase taken from later artillery warfare when it was possible to aim and shoot from a distance. It could have commanded, in that sense, nothing further than the range of a crossbow shot or a lucky cast from a mangonel. The commanding elements were the parties of horsemen which would issue out over a range of from four to eight miles to repel small groups of invaders, to harass larger forces, or merely to patrol. These were the activities that made secure the estates and the administrative area of which the castle was the centre. It was to keep these horsemen in readiness that such large perimeters containing stabling, smithies, armourers, and storehouses had to be provided and, in case of sieges, defended. These areas were necessary for the day-to-day work of the castle–its deep involvement in the life outside. They were often an embarrassment in times of siege simply because of the additional extent of wall that had to be manned, but they were essential: while a siege was often a sudden and not always predictable catastrophe, the quelling of petty disorders, the collection of dues and taxes, and the regulation of lives were immediate and pressing duties that had to be carried out from day to day and it was for those that many royal and baronial castles were built.

The expense and trouble of building a castle often needed the justification of a long-laid plan of attack. One strategic use of the castle was to place it close to the city or territory on which the builder had designs. Fulk Nerra spent much of his life in ringing Tours with fortresses, and there are other examples from the Holy Land. Bohemond of Antioch built castles for his intended siege of Aleppo. In 1103 Raymond of St Gilles began the siege of Tripoli by building a castle within sight of its walls; from this castle, by continually disputing control of the countryside with the Moslems, he induced the surrender of the town after six years. The castles of Toron and Iskandaruna were first built for the subjection of Tyre. Naturally, after Tyre was in Crusader hands, they were turned to its defence but

that was not why the two castles were built in the first place. Between 1136 and 1149 four castles were built in southern Palestine with the object of harrying excursions from Ascalon, which fell finally to the Crusaders in 1153.[9]

The aggressive use of the castle is apparent from its earliest days. To take one example, the illustrious Lusignan family of Poitou, which was to produce monarchs of the Latin Kingdom and of Cyprus, arose from obscurity in the tenth century. By building castles at Lusignan and Couhé in the beginning of the next century and by manipulating their weak ecclesiastical overlords, they forced lesser castellans to become their vassals and extended their power to include numerous other castles.[10] By the end of the twelfth century ten generations of tough and grasping leaders had, by warfare, litigation, and the constant assertion of dubious rights, created a great barony able to play a notable part in Anglo-French affairs. This form of 'creeping aggression' is shown perfectly on a bigger scale by the long history of castle building in Wales, first along the Marches, then along the south coast reaching into Pembrokeshire, and finally by Edward I's containment of Snowdonia. It was not meant to convey to the Welsh at the completion of each stage that the invaders had come so far and intended only to defend these limits, but exactly the opposite: the invaders were coming further. A similar part was to be played by the castles of the Teutonic Knights in the East. A castle on a frontier stands in an architectural posture of defiance and the very building of one such as Château Gaillard was interpreted as a statement of warlike intent and the struggle for its possession ended one of the most important periods in the history of both France and England.

Siting the castle

Considerations of both defence and attack had, therefore, to be taken into account in choosing the general area in which to place a castle and in its actual design. The aim of a great ring of border castles, such as those built or reconstructed by Henry I in Normandy along the edge of the Capetian domains,

was to make the enemy fight at a disadvantage by weakening his initial impulse, and by splitting up his forces. Even if one castle were lost, the effort of defence would often have been worth while in terms of the delay and cost caused to the enemy. The siting of a castle would, therefore, depend not only on its relation to its honor or castellany but on the position from which most damage could be done to an enemy advance. In general the actual choice of site was decided by the tactical advantages of the terrain and the builders would try to make use of geographical accidents which would help defence. Sometimes strategic considerations overruled the choice of what was tactically the best site. For example, the signal towers of the *vicomté* of Conflent are not placed on the hilltops, where they could best be defended, but on the sides of the valleys from which a better watch could be kept on the road.[11] Berkhamsted Castle (plate 41) is placed not on one of the hills around but close to the road to London. The building of a town around a castle might completely change its defensive possibilities and, conversely, when a castle was added to a pre-existing town it could not always be given the best tactical site. The geographical features of which the builders made use are very varied. German castles are generally divided into *Höhenburgen* and *Wasserburgen,* or between those like Trifels (plate 93), high on a mountain near Annweiler, and those at Rüdesheim (plates 34 and 35) on the bank of a river. This division can be broken down further into those castles that stand on rocky peaks, such as the four castles of Lastours, France (plate 96), Loarre, Spain (plate 95), or Rocca Maggiore, Assisi,

95 *Above* Loarre, Spain. One of the chief centres of the Order of the Templars, this castle near Huesca, Aragon, contains elements of the late eleventh century, the twelfth century and later periods, including a particularly fine Romanesque chapel.

96 *Left* Lastours, France. The four castles of this remarkable group not far from Carcassonne: (top to bottom) Cabaret (the earliest and most important), Tour Régine, Fleur d'Espine, and Quertinheux. Simon de Montfort tried in vain to take Cabaret by siege in 1209 and only gained it finally by negotiations. The castles later fell into royal power.

94 *Left* Puylaurens, France. One of the several southern mountain castles such as Lastours and Quéribus, its enceinte closely follows the edge of the summit. Parts of its construction go back to the tenth century. The remains of several lines of forebuildings guarding the entrance can be seen.

Italy (plate 97), and those that stand on spurs of high land, like Langeais, Chepstow, Monmouthshire (plate 98), Château Gaillard on the Seine (plate 51), and many examples from the Holy Land. Again, the builder might choose a site amongst marshes, ponds, or forests, all of which could slow up enemy manoeuvres. One such was Wallingford in Berkshire, which held out from the middle of a marsh for Matilda all through the period of the Anarchy, and later examples include Largoët-en-Elven in Brittany (plate 100) and Pierrefonds, Oise (plate 101). These again differ from those castles which were protected on one or more flanks by rivers, lakes, or streams, such as Ghent, Belgium (plate 106), Chillon, Switzerland (plate 9), or Caerphilly in south Wales.

Applying the principle of delay in defence also affected the design of individual castles from the period of the motte-and-bailey castle up to the development of the concentric design. Here the aim was to present a series of obstacles to the enemy. First the terrain about the castle would be kept clear to deprive him of any cover and there would be special 'killing grounds' where fire could be concentrated. Next would be a moat or a series of ditches, and even if he penetrated the outer ward or bailey he would have to overcome the resistance offered by another ditch filled with stakes, another wall, and finally the stone keep which, sometimes containing a strong interior cross-wall like Rochester, could be divided into two independently defensible parts like watertight bulkheads in a ship. Very often the best stratagem on the part of an attacker was simply to wait until the garrison was starved out or their wells had run dry. Too long a wait, however, would invite other troubles for the attacker – disease through living in an insanitary camp,

97 *Above* Rocca Maggiore, Assisi, Italy. Built on a peak above the town of St Francis, its present form owes most to Cardinal Albornoz in the fourteenth century.

98 *Below* Chepstow, England. Built on a spur cutting into the River Wye, this is one of the great Marcher castles. The rectangular but slightly tapering hall (top centre), built in 1070 with the upper storeys remodelled in the thirteenth century, is thought to have had an influence on the later development of the towerhouse. In the centre foreground is Marten's Tower, built about 1250, with its spurs at the base providing for greater stability and protection from sappers.

99 *Right* Gravensteen, Ghent, Belgium. The remarkable late Romanesque windows of the façade of the castellan's apartments attached to the keep.

or an army come to relieve the defenders, which would mean he had to fight on two fronts or retire. A castle could, therefore, be an extremely effective barrier, especially after the general adoption of stone for its construction.

Masons and builders

The Roman tradition of military engineering was preserved for the Middle Ages in the manuscripts of the works of Vitruvius and Vegetius. Vegetius was a late Roman of uncertain date who wrote *De Re Militari* with the object of restoring the Roman legion. In his fourth book he dealt with siege works and fortifications, especially stressing 'the importance of flanking fire from the towers of curtain walls. From Vitruvius, medieval builders learned the superiority of the round or polygonal tower over the square tower in resisting the blows of battering rams. Vegetius is said to have been the favourite reading of Henry II of England and of Richard,

his son. The popularity of the work is shown in the fact that over 300 manuscripts survive (plate 105) and that other writers, from Hrabanus Maurus in the ninth century onwards, draw copiously from him in writing of military matters. A story that shows well Vegetius' influence comes from John of Marmoutier's life of Geoffrey Plantagenet (the father of Henry II).[12] A group of monks called on him while he was laying siege to the castle of Montreuil-Bellay in 1151. There they found him reading Vegetius and he invited them to return next day to see his new incendiary projectile, based on a description of a weapon in Vegetius, put into action for the first time.

Perhaps the revival of Roman influence can be seen not only in the adaptation of classical techniques to the design of castles and to siege warfare but also over the whole field of Romanesque architecture, especially during and after the second half of the eleventh century when architects and patrons seemed to want to build on a scale that would rival the achievements of the Romans. Here again the importance of the use of stone stands out and here also is a reason for seeing in the increased size and complexity of castles not only an answer to purely military challenges, such as improvements in siege techniques, but a part of the development common to all building in the north, from the time of the construction of the great church of Cluny and of Edward the Confessor's Westminster Abbey onwards. The architect had begun to think in grander dimensions; various new techniques and the improvement of lines of communication hastened him in the fulfilment of his ambitions and it was inevitable that secular buildings, such as the White Tower, should soon be built on the same scale as the many grandiose and recently erected churches of the time. The importance of the architect naturally increased with his new ability to think and plan on a greater scale than ever before. Many influences went to increase his knowledge and the demand for his services.

In dealing with Spain in the last chapter mention was made of the importance to architecture of contacts with the Saracens through such events as the siege of Barbastro (see page 69). Even before the first Crusade the pointed arch, which was to be so vital an element in the Gothic style, had been introduced, perhaps as an Eastern influence. Also before the Crusade the cross-ribbed vault, the other crucial element of Gothic, was introduced to Europe, again perhaps from the East. Saracen architects and engineers captured as prisoners worked in Europe; there is a record of one of them called 'Lalys' who was the builder of Neath Abbey and was perhaps architect to Henry I of England, an inveterate castle builder. The rise of the Gothic style in the first half of the twelfth century did not have a marked effect on the exterior design of castles, except in the use of stone vaulting either for increased safety or in regions like the Holy Land where there was a shortage of timber. The tendency of the Gothic to thinner walls and windows of great size could not be adopted in the castle for

100 *Top* Largoët-en-Elven, France. A lithograph of 1844 showing the great octagonal donjon, built perhaps in the late fourteenth-century for Jean II de Malestroit, partly protected by marshes and water.

101 *Left* Pierrefonds, France. An eighteenth-century view before Viollet-le-Duc's complete restoration of the castle for Napoleon III.

102 *Right* Schönburg, W. Germany. A view of a *Bergfried,* one of two at this Rhine castle founded in the twelfth century.

military reasons and this explains why the external design of the castle continues the Romanesque tradition throughout the Middle Ages. As we shall see, however, when dealing with Coucy and Aigues-Mortes, the Gothic understanding of opposing forces provided a vital insight to future development. The new skills and the answers to new challenges brought about by the Gothic must have had a marked general effect upon the castle simply because the masons who worked on a cathedral one year could have worked on a castle the next.

Many new technical developments came in the twelfth and thirteenth centuries to help the mason. One of the most important was the technique of cutting finely fitting blocks of ashlar for covering the whole surface of a building, thus giving greater permanence and stability. This introduction reached England by about the early years of the twelfth century when Bishop Roger built his new castle and church at Old Sarum in Wiltshire. William of Malmesbury, speaking of his buildings there and at Malmesbury, says, 'he created extensive edifices, at vast cost, and with surpassing beauty; the courses of stone being so correctly laid that the joint deceives the eye, and leads it to imagine that the whole wall is composed of a single block.'[13] Not everyone used such smooth masonry. The Hohenstaufen Emperors, starting with Barbarossa, preferred the use of ashlar with a roughened exterior known as *appareil-à-bossage* or *Buckelquader* in many of their castles. This style, much used in the Holy Land, is thought to have been employed in order to deflect projectiles.

Other factors led to an increased use of stone. The rapid population growth which had started in the tenth century continued; it was a process which is reflected in all the countries mentioned here in the great number of names of towns and castles which have the prefix or suffix, 'new', *'neuf'*, *'neu'*, or *'nuovo'*, and it led to the settlement of mountainous regions where trees were few and where the castle builder was forced to use stone. Also the great forests of the plains were disappearing. Suger described his difficulties in finding oak of the right size for his abbey at St Denis. If one considers that it has been calculated that 8,000 trees (about 200 acres of forest) were necessary to build Trelleborg, one can gain some idea of the devastations caused by the building of hundreds or even thousands of wooden motte-and-bailey castles. In the Midi, where good building stone is rare, building material was composed of brick and pebbles smoothed in river beds and reinforced with courses of ashlar. Wood, of course, continued to be used, especially in hoarding. From the evidence of the

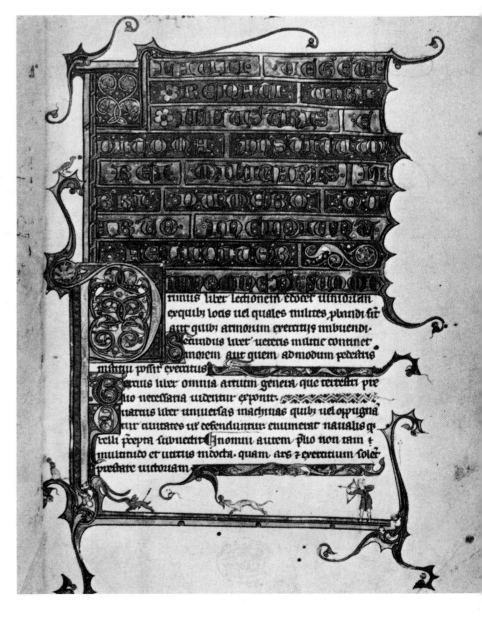

103 *Left* Harlech, Wales. One of the great series of castles such as Caernarvon and Conway built under the supervision of the Savoyard Master James of St George for Edward I as part of his plans for the subjection of north Wales, Harlech has the most eventful history of all these castles. Seized by Owen Glendower in the early fifteenth century, it defied Henry IV's troops until many of its defenders died of starvation. In the Wars of the Roses it was held against Edward IV in a siege lasting over two years. Its most original feature was the gatehouse which combined the residential quarters with a military structure of the greatest strength. Originally the sea came up to the foot of the cliff below and a watergate kept communication open between friendly shipping and the castle.

104 *Top right* Gravensteen, Ghent, Belgium. A stone privy.

105 *Right* A title page from a manuscript of Vegetius' *De Re Militari* dating from the beginning of the fourteenth century. This work was one of the most popular with medieval castle builders and military engineers. *London, British Museum*, Add. ms. 11698, fo 2.

earliest part of the Château du Coudray at Chinon, crenellations and hoarding were in use before the first Crusade, but the example of sieges, such as the first of Le Puiset already mentioned, where the priest was able to work away at the palisade because there was no overhanging projection from which to drop missiles on him, and the experiences of men in the Holy Land, must certainly have led to the much greater provision of these hoardings in the twelfth century. Wood was also used in another way; the Roman method of bonding walls with beams of timber was employed at Gisors and Coucy. An elaboration of this method was adopted in the Sainte Chapelle where iron chains were sunk in the cement core of the crypt walls.

Among the inventions whose wider use affected the building of the castle in the twelfth century was the trebuchet (plate 130), a projectile-throwing weapon worked by counterpoise. One of its first uses was at the siege and capture of Lisbon in 1147 and its importance lies not only in that it was a more accurate and adjustable improvement on the older Roman torsion-worked machines, which would fail in wet weather, but also in that it was one of the earliest inventions of western technology. New scaffolding methods (see Coucy, page 126), the introduction of the wheelbarrow, and a general diffusion of the skills and labours of the masons resulted in more efficient construction. Yet another important introduction in the

106 *Left* Gravensteen, Ghent, Belgium. A view of the keep and the bartizans of the perimeter wall, which could have wooden floors added to their interiors in time of siege to allow defence from two levels. The crenels are defended by restored wooden shutters.

107 *Below* Giant crossbows designed to be shot from all four sides of a tower. Each crossbow could fire three bolts or arrows at a time. This is an illustration to a work on weapons by the Arab writer Murda ben Ali, contemporary with Saladin (1137–93). *Oxford, Bodleian Library*, Ms. Hunt. 264, fo 94.

108 *Right* The death of Louis VIII at the castle of Montpensier in 1226 during the Albigensian crusade. Note the limewashed exterior of the tower. *Paris, Bibliothèque Nationale*, Ms. fr. 6465, fo 251v.

twelfth century was that of the windmill, and building materials could be transported by heavy haulage carts over longer distances with the great improvements made to road systems.

The work of organization was the province of the mason; he had to have considerable practical knowledge and skill in every side of building, and to combine this with international experience in the deployment of labour and materials. Such men were in demand not only for working in stone but also for the construction of earthworks and wooden fortifications.[14] Kings, bishops, great lords, and military engineers, all depended on him for the creation of the perfect castle, one that combined the needs of aggression with the needs of defence, that could let its garrison out to attack but would never let the enemy in. Ordericus Vitalis illustrates this desire to own a completely impregnable castle by telling of Ivri, 'the famous castle, of great size and strongly fortified, which was built by Alberede wife of Ralph, count of Bayeux . . . It is said that Alberede, having completed this fortress and expense, caused Lanfred, whose character as an architect transcended that of all the other French architects at that time, and who after building the castle of Pithiviers was appointed master of these works, to be beheaded, that he might not erect a similar fortress anywhere else.'[15] This is, of course, a variant of a story told long before the end of the eleventh century but the fact of bringing it up to date shows a general respect for the architect's skill at this time.

Later, by the thirteenth century, architects such as St Louis's Eudes de Montreuil and Edward I's James of St George came to have an international renown and occupied the highest places in their masters' esteem. Closely allied to the work of these men was that of the military engineers who were to have a profound effect on the history of Europe.

109 *Below* A thirteenth-century baggage train from the *Maciejowski Old Testament*. Helms, clothes, and chainmail are loaded into the wagons and cooking vessels hang from the side. *New York, Pierpont Morgan Library*, M. 638, fo 27v.

110 *Right* An assault tower with a mobile platform worked on a pulley system; a drawing from Guido da Vigevano's manuscript. *Paris, Bibliothèque Nationale*, Ms. Lat. 11015, fo 47v.

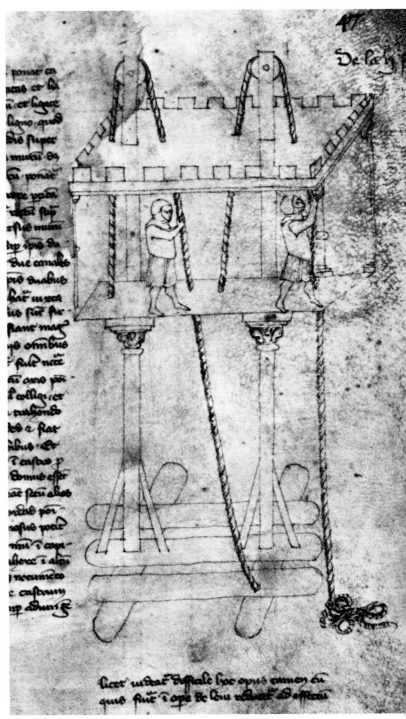

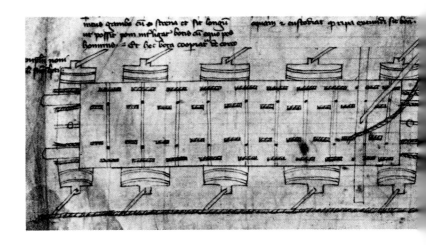

The castle and western science

Contact with the very different Byzantine and Arab societies, where much of the Graeco-Roman technical skills and interest in the natural sciences had been preserved, awoke the dormant scientific interest of the West. To take one example, once they had come across Greek fire and recovered from the shock of seeing it used in action, western travellers made the greatest efforts to find out how it was made. Books of recipes, such as the *Liber Ignium* of Mark the Greek, were copied out and circulated. Through such contacts both Albertus Magnus and Roger Bacon in the thirteenth century first heard of gunpowder and, although there are some accounts of Greek fire being used in action in Europe, probably the greatest effect of this circulation of knowledge was that, however useless many of these recipes were, men began to experiment with materials and so assisted in the beginnings of chemistry.[16]

The chief agent of this diffusion was probably the military engineer. Only he would have both the opportunity to travel and the initial training necessary to understand new and unfamiliar techniques. The complete acceptance of warfare by the society of the Middle Ages as a permanent feature of life probably explains why so many inventions, with later uses of great importance, were the work originally of military engineers, among these inventions being the trebuchet and the fusee (first used in a crossbow and only later in clocks).[17] These military engineers were not only concerned with matters connected with their craft; one of them was the Crusader, Peter of Maricourt, known as Petrus Peregrinus, whom Roger Bacon described in glowing terms as *magister experimentorum* and who gave the West the first full description of magnetism.

This Crusader stands in a line of either soldiers or men interested in military matters, who have made great contributions to the development of western science, men such as

Descartes on service in Germany, Stevinus of Bruges, who developed the science of statics and also wrote a work on fortifications, or the young French engineer officer, Sadi Carnot, who was to formulate the First Law of Thermodynamics. The medieval engineers seem to have come from varied backgrounds and often to have shared their activities

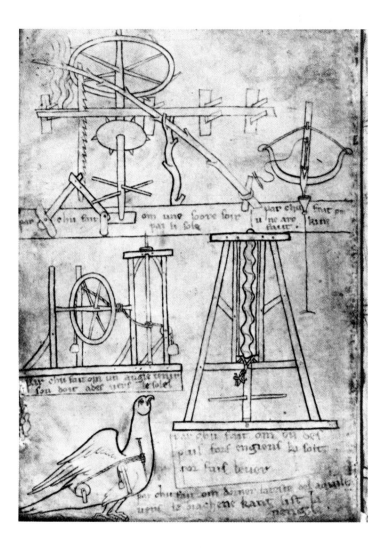

with other professions, such as the French architect, Villard de Honnecourt, who travelled as far as Hungary and left many drawings of military and technical devices, including a trebuchet, in his famous sketchbook (plate 112). Egidio Colonna, who wrote *De Regimine Principum* for Philip the Fair in about 1280, was a churchman and so was the engineer in charge of the siege weapons at the siege of Montségur in 1243-4, Durand, bishop of Albi. At the beginning of the fourteenth century we find the Italian physician, Guido da Vigevano, passionately devising a whole series of prefabricated weapons (plates 110 and 111) which he vainly hoped would

111 *Left* A bridge floating on casks, one of Guido da Vigevano's ideas to persuade Philip V of France to go on Crusade. *Paris, Bibliothèque Nationale,* Ms. Lat. 11015, fo 49v.

112 *Above* A page from the sketchbook of Villard de Honnecourt, *c* 1235, showing various mechanical devices, among them being a hydraulic saw, a crossbow 'that cannot miss', a device for making an angel (on a church roof) turn towards the sun, and a machine for lifting weights. *Paris, Bibliothèque Nationale,* Ms. fr. 19093, fo 22v.

persuade Philip V of France to embark on another Crusade.

There are many more examples of the influence of artists, architects, and scientists upon military affairs, especially in the time of the Renaissance. The castle, together with its related fortifications, remained the chief product of medieval technology and great and undreamed-of consequences were to develop from all the skills devoted to besieging it or to repelling its attackers. Keeping this connection in mind, we turn now to consider the running of the castle, beginning with one of the most valuable twelfth-century descriptions by the English cleric and scientist, Alexander Neckam.

The day-to-day life of a castle

'If a castle is to be decently built, it should be girded by a double moat. Nature must provide the proper site as the motte or mound should be set upon native rock. Where Nature fails, the benefit of skill must take over, and a heavy massive wall, made from stone and cement, has to grow or rise as an arduous task. Outside this a fearsome stockade with squared pales and prickly briars should be well erected. Afterwards a wide ditch in the space in between should be enjoyed. The foundation of the stone wall must be joined with the bowels of the earth. The wall should be supported with pilasters inside and out. The surface of it must be evened by the mason's trowel. Crenels should be separated by proper intervals. Small towers (on this wall) must flank the main keep, or donjon, which is set on the high place in the very centre of everything. [On the wall] let there not be lacking baskets containing huge boulders to be thrown down if the castle is strongly besieged. In order that the defenders may not be obliged to surrender, there should be supplies of spelt and wheat, and haunches and bacon, and other meat put in storage, sausages and entrails, meat puddings, pork, mutton, beef, lamb, and various vegetables. One needs a spring that flows continuously, small posterns, portcullises, and underground passages by which those bringing aid may move about without being seen. One needs also lances and catapults, shields, small light targes, cross bows, clubs, slings and sticks. Balearic slings, pegs of iron, boards, knotty cudgels, and towers hurling fire by which the assaults of the besiegers may be eluded and their purpose foiled. You should have also iron beams, siege mantlets, baskets, heavy slings, and other machines. There should be there palfreys or riding horses, and pacing war horses more suitable for the use of knights. In order that the knights going out may be better cheered, there should sound together trumpets, pipes, flutes, and horns. The divisions and echelons of the fighting men shall be ranged in order by the constables, even when they go forth to a tourney or lance tilting... The castle should have also prudent men, without whose advice nothing should be done in time of hostility, a power which constitutes the greatest strength and highest council of a kingdom—men by whose intercession tortures are applied more mildly, by whose sternness digressors, lawbreakers, violators of ordinances, horse thieves, and murderers may be whipped, punished, or condemned to capital punishment.'[18]

One is left almost breathless from this description at the number and complexity of tasks to be carried out in the daily running of a castle and in maintaining its efficiency, and it must be said that Neckam is writing a Latin vocabulary in which he has to get in as many objects as possible and if his description fitted any castle it would be that of an exceptionally rich English earl or French count. Even in less well-equipped castles the owner would have plenty to do and he could depend upon well-established rules being observed by his miniature court. Like the king, he would have butlers, constables, and marshals, concerned with the provision of his table, the care of his stables, and the feeding of his horses. His vassals' and relations' sons would act as his pages and squires and his wife would be

similarly attended by the daughters of vassals whose education she supervised. The living quarters consisted essentially of the hall with a fireplace which was the centre of social life, and a chamber where the master would withdraw and sleep. The chamber often had a privy or garderobe leading off it. How these rooms were disposed varied from region to region. In German-influenced countries the hall is on the second floor and the living quarters on the first floor. In French and English castles the hall either stands as a separate building, warmed by a central hearth and therefore with a high roof to let the smoke escape through a louver – or else it is placed on the first or second floor of the keep. Here the baron ate in public, conducted his business, held courts, and watched the entertainments. One of the most important features of the castle was the chapel, sometimes dedicated to St Michael who was regarded as the type of the supremely loyal vassal. Here the baron, if he maintained a regular chaplain, would hear daily mass before his usual occupations of hunting or hawking. These pursuits demanded the provision of stables, lodgings for the huntsmen, and mews for the hawks, either in the baileys or wards of the castle or outside the walls.

Open-plan living was the rule and the elaborate social hierarchy, the care taken that everyone should be placed at meals according to his rank, the deference shown to the lord and lady, probably arose as a means of making bearable the pressures of living at such close quarters. Much has been made of how uncomfortable life in a castle must have been, with draughts whistling through the oiled linen window coverings, during freezing nights high up on sites wide open to the winds, but one effect of these large numbers of people living so closely together must have been a considerable generation of animal warmth. Although, from an early time, the baron and his lady had separate quarters and gradually withdrew into greater privacy as the designs of castles such as those of Philip Augustus allowed a more favourable disposition of the residential parts, their male dependants had no such privacy and would sleep together either in dormitories, as described by Lambert of Ardres, or on the bone-strewn rushes of the hall floor.

Again, much has been made of the simple furnishings. The most important piece of furniture was the bed which was placed in the chamber and was used to sit on in the daytime. Kings and barons accustomed to travel would have their beds carried around with them in their baggage. Chairs were few and as they possessed an aura of singular honour they were neither very comfortable nor much in use.

113 *Above* Chessmen from a twelfth-century set found on the island of Lewis, Scotland. Chess is often mentioned in the stories of the period as a favourite pastime and it has been suggested that the influence of the troubadours in exalting the position of women led to the displacement of the king by the queen as the most powerful piece on the board. *London, British Museum.*

114 *Below* A brass aquamanile or ewer in the form of a knight on horseback; English, 1250. These charming objects were very popular on the Continent as well as in England. *London, British Museum.*

Window seats were nearly always provided by the builders in living quarters and many poems describe the ladies sitting in them and watching their lovers coming or going from the castle. Shelves were hardly known until later in the Middle Ages. The most usual place to keep clothes or the charters of grants, rights, and records of payments, was in a chest – a most untidy arrangement for the latter. Clothes were sometimes stored in the lavatories where the stench kept the moths away – hence, it is said, the euphemism *garderobe* from which our word 'wardrobe' comes. Benches and trestle tables were the normal furnishings of the hall and the baron's dependants would be accustomed to standing in his presence (probably

not the strain after spending a day in the saddle that it would be to us) until he retired to his chamber. We can rarely gather an impression today, and generally only through documents, of the variety of the wall-paintings and hangings which decorated the state rooms of important castles. Just as the outside walls were frequently lime washed and otherwise decorated, so, especially from the thirteenth century, the hall, chapel, and private apartments were alive with colourful stories, moral tales, and episodes from the Bible and the lives of the saints, though it is exceptional for wall-paintings of this date, such as those at Chillon (plate 10), to survive. Elaborate furniture was not general, either because social conventions limited its use to a few cases or because life was, in contrast to our sedentary existence, extremely active. Most of the amusements of the knight, apart from chess and listening to songs or recited stories, were intensely energetic – all the forms of hunting, hawking, tournaments, and dancing.

As conditions became more peaceful, so the castle acquired more comforts and luxuries in its residential quarters. Because they were less likely to be burned in their beds, so men learned to look with love upon the scenes of their upbringing. The Sieur de Joinville could not bear to look back on his castle as he left it to go on Crusade, and the churchman Giraldus Cambrensis has left a famous description of his family's castle of Manorbier in Pembrokeshire, speaking with the warmest affection of its towers and walls, its fishpond, garden, lake, and its fine position by the sea. Playing on the beach below its walls, his brothers used to build castles and palaces in the sand but Giraldus showed his future vocation by always making churches and abbeys.[19]

The ladies of the castle
This softening of the rigours of life in the castle must to a large extent have been due to the influence of the women of the time. Between the eleventh and the thirteenth centuries a remarkable change came over the attitude to women. Although they had no rights to speak of and were never allowed to marry for love if they were heiresses, the fact that so many great estates descended into female hands, and that so many women showed themselves eminently capable of running not only large estates but also kingdoms in the absence of their husbands or because of widowhood, helped to give greater authority to their position. Characters as masterful as the Conqueror's daughter, Adela of Blois, who sent her weak-willed husband on the first Crusade because she thought it would be good for him, had in any case been known in earlier days. There is a story told of a siege of the Husterknupp when the attackers sent a message to the lady of the castle that she could take her leave before the final assault, together with anything she could carry. So she issued from the castle gate with her husband on her back. The extreme toughness of the life made some of them very formidable creatures. One *chanson* of the cycle concerning William of Orange shows his wife, Guibourc, cheering up the hero after a frightful disaster with the spirit of a Greek heroine. What is new is that women came to be appreciated for being themselves and could make their power felt through essentially feminine ways, like the simple Petronilla, wife of Arnold of Ardres, who used to scandalize the elderly and the clerics by swimming in the castle fishpond on hot days clad only in her shift and beneath the eyes of her ladies and knights.[20] In particular, those ladies who were attached to courts, such as the one at Troyes, would

have great influence in furthering the careers of young knights who would endeavour to please them. Part of the young William Marshal's success came from the charm of his manner and his singing.

The status of women varied, of course, from locality to locality. In Languedoc, if one trusts the troubadours, they were almost supreme and at the least were treated as equals in points of intelligence and manners, but further north their condition could be much harder. The Church's influence in regulating marriage was devoted largely to seeing that monogamy was observed and that no one married within an extensive list of prohibited degrees. It had little influence on the sexual morality of the men who generally treated the marriage vows lightly where they applied to themselves.

115 A thirteenth-century chest in the castle of Coburg.

William the Conqueror was considered exceptional for his fidelity to his wife. The system of marriage to extend possessions, which often involved childhood marriages between the parties, had as haphazard results as marrying for love. Divorce was not unknown and, although the husband could behave as he wished, if he suspected his wife of unfaithfulness he could murder her with impunity – providing he was more powerful than her relations.

The Church influenced the position of women in another way. Society in the early Middle Ages was deeply devoted to the Virgin Mary. This extended from the monasteries and the great cathedrals built in her honour, but also affected the knightly code whose followers were permeated with a new sense of the worth of womankind. The other great influence in raising the status of women owed practically nothing to the Church and was frequently in conflict with it. This was the effect of the literature of *l'amour courtois*.

The castle as a cradle of secular literature
The role of the castle in acting as a focus for the development of early technological and scientific skills has already been mentioned. The other great contribution of the society of the castle to the civilization of Europe was that it acted as a cradle of secular literature, in northern and southern France, in

Germany and Austria, in southern Italy, and in Spain. It was in the castle, just as much as in the other residences of the upper classes, that forms of lyric, narrative, and epic poetry were evolved that are still read with pleasure today and which still exercise a commanding influence on what is now written. Every art needs an audience and the halls of the castles brought together men and women thirsting to hear the transformations of the old Celtic, Frankish and Teutonic myths, of Troy, of Alexander, of Arthur, of Charlemagne, and of the heroes of the *Nibelungenlied*. They also heard new lyric songs in praise of the Virgin or of some famous beauty, satirical and political squibs or the elaborate and mystical *trobar clus* of some of the southern poets.

The earliest examples of this castle literature are the *chansons de geste* of which over eighty, written between the late eleventh and the early fourteenth centuries, survive. These *chansons* are divided into several groups: among them are those dealing with Charlemagne and his peers, those that cover the cycle of William of Orange, and later ones that rehearse the trials of the first Crusade. The most famous is the *Song of Roland* which tells of how Roland's rashness in refusing to call the aid of Charlemagne by sounding his horn when ambushed at Roncesvalles brings disaster and death to him and his followers. A version of this was sung to the Norman knights at Hastings and it reveals not only the depth of attachment that the feudal bond could inspire but also a new working of the Christian spirit in the turbulence of warfare which is seen in the final reconciliation between Roland and Oliver and when, waiting death,

'The Count Rollanz, beneath a pine he sits;
Turning towards Spain he begins
Remembering so many divers things:
The many lands where he went conquering,
And France the Douce, the heroes of his kin,
And Charlemagne, his lord, who nourished him.
Nor can he help but weep and sigh at this.
But his own self, he's not forgotten him,
He owns his faults, and God's forgiveness bids.'[21]

At about the same time as the *chansons de geste*, but inspired by totally different influences, there arose in Poitou and Aquitaine the school of poets known as the troubadours. The first known troubadour was William, seventh count of Poitou and ninth duke of Aquitaine. It was his father who took Barbastro from the Moors and the influence of Hispano-Arabic poetry was probably very deep on his son and his fellow poets (see page 70). The long-hidden influence of the neoplatonists revived again and the beloved became once more an ideal to aspire to and to inspire. Feudal ideas of devotion and service were adopted and transferred to the lady (*domna* or *mi'dons*) of the poet's choice and both his own *valor* or worth and his reputation were enhanced by the intensity of his love. These poets came from all classes of society: many of them travelled far, especially after Eleanor of Aquitaine married first the king of France and then, divorced by him, Henry II of England, thus diffusing a taste for the troubadour poems and songs through many lands. Many stories are told of their deeds and their loves, such as the following, which were to have a profound effect on manners and behaviour.

'Jaufre Rudel of Blaye was a gentleman of great nobility and Prince of Blaye; and he fell in love with the Countess of Tripoli without ever

116 Charlemagne finding the body of Roland, his sword Durendal, and his horn beside him at Roncesvalles; a fifteenth-century French representation from the *Grandes Chroniques de France. Paris, Bibliothèque Nationale,* Ms. fr. 6465, fo 113v.

having seen her simply because of the good he heard pilgrims coming from Antioch tell of her; and he made many poems about her with fine music and poor words. From the desire to see her he took the cross and went to sea. In the ship he fell ill and was taken to an inn at Tripoli as though dead. The Countess was told of him and she came to him, to his bed and took him in her arms. And he knew it was the Countess and immediately he recovered sight, hearing, and sense of smell; and he thanked God for having allowed him life until he had seen her. Thus he died in her arms; and she had him buried with great honour in the House of the Temple. And then that same day she took the veil for the misery she had of his death.'[22]

Where the tunes still survive, the poems are at their best when sung. They have a totally individual vigour and freshness. The first and most difficult form was the *canso* but there were many other forms permitting the poet to express not only his love but his passion for fighting, his lament for a dead patron or mistress, his disgust at paltry behaviour on the part of some noble, or his delight in the spring. The society that produced the troubadours also produced the main heresy of the Middle Ages and when that society was swept away in the Albigensian Crusade the ideals of the poets appear again in southern Italy, Tuscany, and northern France.

Northern France had its counterpart to the troubadours in the *trouvères* who were deeply influenced by the southern poets. However the most original contribution of that area was made by the rediscovery of the *Matter of Britain*, the old Celtic stories of Arthur and his knights, of Tristan and Yseult, and, above all, of the legend of the Grail. In the hands of the master, Chrétien de Troyes, these old stories were adapted to express the tensions and demands of feudal society, as in his Lancelot whose courtly love for Guinevere is at odds with his sense of the knightly code.[23] His greatest work, the *Conte du Graal* or *Perceval,* though unfinished, brought the memory of the Grail back into the consciousness of Europe. This he wrote for Philip of Alsace, the builder of the great castle at Ghent (plate 106). The theme of *Perceval,* the foolish boy who fails to ask the question, even when presented with a vision of the

Grail, that will restore the Waste Land to fertility, and his subsequent purification, remained the highest attempt to express the ideals of knighthood. In the best of these stories the didactic purpose is masked almost completely by the Celtic magic and love of symbols and subtle behaviour: in the moment, for example, when Yseult swears she has never been in the arms of other men apart from her husband King Mark, except for the beggar who has just carried her across a ford (the beggar is, of course, Tristan disguised). Or when Tristan, parted from his own Yseult and married to another woman of the same name, sings

Isot, ma dru, Isot ma mie,
En vous ma mort, en vous ma vie,
(Yseult, my love, Yseult, my dear,
In you my death, in you my life)[24]

so his wife can imagine he is singing of her while he can assuage his grief by uttering his true love's name. Or, to take an example from a later telling of the Grail legend,[25] this is the way in which King Arthur learns of the damage done by Perceval's neglect of asking the question of the Grail: 'The sun shone through the windows everywhere amidst the hall that was strewn of flowers and rushes and sweet herbs and gave out smell like as had it been sprinkled with balm'. Suddenly there appear three ladies, the first riding on a white mule and holding the head of a king sealed in silver and crowned with gold. She has been bald since Perceval failed to ask the question and she tells of the other sorrows and deaths that have arisen from this lack. The second lady carries the head of a queen sealed in lead and crowned with copper. Outside, she says, there is a cart containing the heads of a hundred and fifty knights, some sealed in gold, some in silver, and some in lead. In this way, arousing their listeners' interest immediately with hints of magic and foul deeds, the poets embark on a story that would take many nights to complete. The stories are full of battles and individual fights, often, as in Chrétien de Troyes, still very

exciting in the telling and they are also full of descriptions of manners or of the rules governing, for example, the hunt. 'The poet, of course, knew that half his audience would be listening to see if he had got it right and the other half to memorize it all for future reference.'[26] One way of making the stories come alive was to inform the audience that the events, say, in an Arthurian legend, took place locally, in that very castle or just beyond the hill. The names of the heroes would be associated with neighbouring landmarks and in this way, for example, Arthur came to be buried under Mount Etna, entombed at Glastonbury, reborn as a chough in Cornwall, or dispatched to the island of Avalon. This process probably explains why the same legends and stories recur again and again, ascribed to different castles.[27]

The inspiration of the Arthurian legends spread far beyond France and Flanders. The greatest telling of the Grail legend is the *Parzifal* of Wolfram von Eschenbach[28], who was a welcome guest in the early thirteenth century at the poetry-loving court maintained by the Landgrave Hermann at the Wartburg (plate 185). His great rival was Gottfried von Strassburg who left unfinished a long epic on the Tristan theme.[29] Epics with classical heroes also appeared in Germany, generally based on French originals, but, in the case of Henrik van Veldeke's *Eneide,* coming via the Low Countries. This survives only in a manuscript (plate 118) specially connected with the Wartburg in a translation from the Limburg into the Thuringian dialect. French and troubadour influences were also absorbed into the native German lyric tradition thus producing the school of poets known as the Minnesingers, many of whom are depicted in the pages of several later manuscripts (plate 117). They flourished particularly in the castles and courts of the Babenberg dukes of Austria and at Vienna. From that region, too, probably came the great masterpiece of Teutonic myth, the *Nibelungenlied.* Many of these poets were of the *ministerialis* class and some achieved great influence through their songs and political comments. Chief among them was Walter von der Vogelweide who was granted a fief, probably in the see of Würzburg, by Emperor Frederick II in about 1220 as a reward for his support.

Frederick's interest in poetry was by no means purely political. Although only a few poems are doubtfully attributed to him, the courts he and his son Manfred maintained in their castles of Apulia saw the development of Italian lyric poetry and of the forms that were to be used by Dante and Cavalcanti. His contemporary, St Francis of Assisi, was inspired by the ideal woman of the troubadours to create and follow the commands of his own lady, Poverty. In Spain the great epic already mentioned of the *Cantar del Mio Cid*[30], the only Spanish *chanson de geste* to survive almost complete, with its numerous accounts of attacks on castles and strongholds, appeared in the twelfth century and was followed later by the intense literary, musical, and scientific activity of the court of Alfonso the Wise (1221-84) of Castile. Also in the thirteenth century there was the remarkable Majorcan soldier, mystic, poet, and deviser of a system of universal knowledge, Ramon Lull, whose work on chivalry and whose romances on chivalric themes were to have a deep and abiding effect. This account of the

117 The poet Hartmann von Aue (fl. 1190–1210), the author of two Arthurian epics based on Chrétien de Troyes and of *Der arme Heinrich.* He was a *ministerialis* in Swabia and took part in the Emperor Henry VI's Crusade of 1197. From the fourteenth-century *Weingärtner Liederbuch. Stuttgart, Landesbildstelle Württemberg,* f. 33, no 9.

literature produced and disseminated by the society of the castle, has left out the *chansons de toile,* the sewing songs from which the English ballad probably derived, the Crusader songs with their great laments, and many other forms of writing and entertainment – the gossip of Walter Map, the *lais* of Marie de France, the first known French poetess, or the extraordinary tale from thirteenth-century Germany of *Meier Helmbrecht* by Werner der Gärtner which tells the story of a peasant lad who goes off to be a knight and of his miserable end after falling in with robber barons.[31] It is useful, though, to remember how much the society that produced this literature depended on the castle, how much was actually written and performed in the castle, and to reflect that, without the temporary tranquillity provided by its walls, we would be much the poorer today. For although in writing of castles the military aspect, especially in the early years, is bound to predominate one must not, in telling how it protected in the twelfth and thirteenth centuries, forget to ask 'what did it protect?' One answer is the slow growth of secular civilization and of the idea that a man or woman did not have to go as a celibate into a monastery or nunnery to learn to cultivate their finer tastes and aspirations, but that they could be responsive to beauty and the deeper emotions, courteous and understanding of others, while living the lives of normal human beings.

118 *Above left* A drawing from the *Eneide* of Henrik van Veldeke (*c* 1145–*c* 1200), a Limburg poet and *ministerialis* of the counts of Loon, showing Camilla and Turnus besieging Montalbanus. *Berlin, Deutsche Staatsbibliothek*, Ms. Germ. 20282, fo 46v.

119 *Above* Another drawing from the same manuscript showing (top) Mars and Venus caught in the net by Vulcan and (below) Vulcan forging armour for Aeneas at the behest of Venus. *Berlin, Deutsche Staatsbibliothek*, Ms. Germ. 20282, fo 39v.

120 *Right* A thirteenth-century French ivory mirror case. *London, Victoria and Albert Museum.* (See also opposite title page)

CAPETIANS AND ANGEVINS-CRUSADER, FRENCH, ENGLISH, AND IBERIAN CASTLES IN THE 12TH AND 13TH CENTURIES

4

The French and Norman castle builders created the great school of medieval fortification, the influence of which was to extend all over Europe. Their many conquests and their success in holding on to their gains meant that they possessed a mastery of skills that central Europe and Italy were always to copy and rarely to anticipate. It was in France and England that the development of flanking and, later, of concentric defence was understood first and best of all, and it was in France that the Gothic style first arose, bringing with it attendant benefits for the castle in improved techniques. It is this mastery of skills which dictates the order in which the castles of various countries are dealt with in the following chapters and it is the pre-eminence of the French in the first Crusades that makes it necessary to start with the castles of the Holy Land.

Castles in the Holy Land

It was generally assumed, up to the beginning of this century, that every important innovation in military architecture came from Moslem and Byzantine examples in the Holy Land. Then T. E. Lawrence[1] challenged this assumption entirely by claiming that the Crusaders learned nothing of importance from the East and had in fact introduced the form of the castle already developed in Europe to the Holy Land, pointing to the number of square keeps resembling the Norman type which were built after the first Crusade. Further light has been thrown on this question by a recent study of the Crusader castle in relation to the military needs of Frankish society. This has shown that the design of the castles built in the Holy Land during the Crusades owes far less to the influence of sophisticated theories of defence, whether these were brought from Europe or found in Asia Minor, than to the typical terrain on which the castles were sited. Nature had already provided strong sites, many of which had been fortified for thousands of years, and the design was dictated first by the need to reinforce this natural strength. Thus each of the greatest Crusader castles, those at Sahyun, Crac and Crac des Chevaliers, Markab (plate 122), and Beaufort as well as many lesser ones, was built on a similar site–a spur protected on all sides but one by steep or precipitous cliffs. The unprotected side was provided with a ditch and a wall. At Sahyun the Crusaders, or possibly their Byzantine predecessors, cut a ditch from the living rock 90ft (27m) deep, leaving one pinnacle to carry a postern bridge to the gate across the divide (plate 121). This attention to the choice of site certainly finds many echoes in Europe, the most notable

example of a similar choice being Richard Coeur-de-Lion's at Les Andelys for his Château Gaillard (plate 51). The castle of Sahyun (plate 75), where Frankish and Byzantine work stand side by side, shows the clearest evidence of Byzantine influence, which lay not in scientific principles (these as we have already shown were studied from Vegetius and Vitruvius in the West) but in details of fortification and construction.[2]

The first settlement of the Latin Kingdom was made by bold individuals seizing fortified places and converting them into strong castles with the aim of dominating newly-acquired property. This settlement was largely a haphazard business not directed by a central authority: the prime reason for maintaining an already fortified place or building a new castle was the economic one of gaining revenue. As the kingdom of Jerusalem grew, so a military system evolved, based on the relation between the Latin field army and the castles and walled towns. The castles acted as essential bases providing water and supplies for the field army. It was while moving from the castle of Saffuryia to relieve the beleaguered

121 Sahyun, Syria. The 90-ft (27-m) man-made gorge cut from the rock to isolate the castle from an easterly attack. The pinnacle was left to carry a postern-bridge. (See also plate 75)

castle of Tiberias, for example, that Guy of Lusignan's army was caught and destroyed at the Horns of Hattin, in 1187, by Saladin, the disaster that lost Jerusalem to the Moslems and caused the third Crusade.

The castles of the Holy Land, therefore, formed part of a military network across the kingdom and were frequently linked by a signalling system. They did not constitute a coherent frontier defence partly because no frontiers were well enough defined. They had a strong administrative purpose, especially because the Frankish lords were dependent on taxes and other revenues, and they were also meant to dominate the heterogeneous local populations whom the Franks could rarely trust for long periods. As we have already seen, many of the castles were built not for defence but for determined and sustained attack. Warfare may have seemed part of life at home in Europe; here it was constant and unremitting. A new professionalism, which affected the design of castles and impressed all visitors from Europe, arose in response to this challenge.

This professionalism was especially seen in the knightly orders of the Hospitallers, the Templars, and later of the Teutonic Knights. The high death-rate among the Frankish settlers and the paucity of able-bodied knights meant that from an early period the defence of the Latin Kingdom came to depend on these strange orders of fighting monks to whom the art of war was a form of worship. Being organized into permanent religious orders with great funds available from estates in many parts of Europe, they were much better placed to carry on a continuous war with the Moslem, than the knight who had come to the Holy Land to settle down and who was much more inclined to reach a compromise with his enemies. The most famous of their castles is Crac des Chevaliers (plate 123). This avoided capture by Saladin when nearly every other castle of importance had surrendered from fear or had been taken by siege. From its original occupation by Tancred of Antioch in 1109 till the eventual surrender by its few remaining Hospitaller Knights to Sultan Baibars in 1271, it remained untaken although enduring many sieges and two

earthquakes. It is a most powerful example of concentric fortification, each defence covering the one beneath it, its great chambers capable of storing grain to feed a garrison for years. Even a windmill stood on its battlements, the ultimate adaptation of the latest technical device to make the fortress self-sufficient and proof against starvation.

The Templars grew particularly rich and acted as one of the chief bankers of the time until their suppression in the early fourteenth century. They possessed many important castles outside the Holy Land, notably in Cyprus and Spain. The influence of the orders dictated, in many ways, the form the castle took in Portugal and the Teutonic Knights, on establishing themselves in eastern Europe, were to build some of the most original of all medieval castles. As a result of the Crusades

122 *Left* Markab, Syria. A view of the south side of this Crusader castle on the coast near the small harbour of Baniyas. It was visited by Richard Coeur-de-Lion during the third Crusade.

123 *Opposite Below* Crac des Chevaliers, Syria. A view from the south-west of this most powerful of Crusader castles which was built in the twelfth century and transformed into a concentric castle in the course of the next. Note the extreme scarping of the inner curtain walls.

Fig. 8 *Right* A ground-plan of Crac des Chevaliers. Twelfth-century portions in black; thirteenth-century additions cross-hatched; additions later than the middle of the thirteenth century hatched; post-1271 alterations unshaded. 1. North gate. 2. North tower. 3. Castle chapel. 4. Great hall and cloister. 5. Magazine. 6. Substructure of the three south towers. 7. Lower main gate. 8. Barrier in passage-way. 9. Upper main gate. 10. Inner gate. 11. Stables and magazine. 12. Tower of Sultan Qala'ûn. (After Müller-Wiener)

124 *Below right* Monemvasia, Greece. A castle built on a cliff at the tip of the Peloponnese, captured by William Villehardouin in 1249. It had earlier been an outpost of the Comnenos Emperors against the west and returned to Byzantium in 1262 as part of Villehardouin's ransom. It was the last Byzantine fortress to defy Mehmet II.

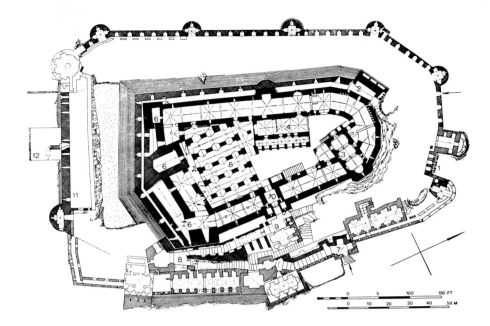

castles appeared in many regions where they had scarcely been known before. After the capture of Byzantium in 1204 by troops diverted from the fourth Crusade and the establishment of a Latin empire, western adventurers carved out feudal princedoms for themselves in parts of the Balkans, and in Greece, especially in the Peloponnese where their additions to many great citadels already existing, such as Monemvasia (plate 124) and Acrocorinth, remain to remind the traveller of these successful conquerors who, later in the thirteenth century, were regarded as the noblest knighthood in the world.

Mention of the Crusades calls to mind almost inevitably the names of Coeur-de-Lion and Philip Augustus of France and the history of their quarrels has a long background of events which in their time deeply affected the development of the castle in both France and England.

France and England

The ruling society of England was French-speaking and constantly travelling to France. Ireland and Scotland in the twelfth century were to be brought into this international community by Franco-Norman adventurers who introduced the castle into those countries. The most important factor in the building of castles was supplied, however, by the rivalry between the Capetian kings and the kings of England. The cautious Capetian monarchs, biding their time, careful of effort, form a marked contrast to the flamboyant sons of the Conqueror and to the Angevins. To hold on to and gradually extend their small domain of the Île de France was their sole ambition. The possession of one tower, that of Montlhéry (plate 125), was as much to Philip I as the realm of England had been to his contemporary, William the Conqueror, and he died, according to Suger, saying, 'Make sure, my son, that you never lose the Tower of Montlhéry. It has caused me untold trouble. Frankly that tower has made me old before my time.'[3] His son, Louis the Fat, considerably extended his power and was constantly engaged in siege warfare, including the three sieges of Le Puiset already mentioned. Even so, his energy can hardly be compared with that of Henry I who built or reconstructed a line of castles as a strategic defence for Normandy. About twenty-six castles of stone, including parts of Arques, Falaise (plate 127) and Gisors (plate 87), are attributed to him in Normandy alone and these castles were to play a vital role in the border quarrels up to Philip Augustus's conquest of

Normandy in 1204. He also built widely in England. A notable master of siege warfare, his success probably depended on the use of wooden siege-towers (otherwise known as the *malvoisin* or *beffroi*), like those we have already seen in use at Jerusalem. The energy Henry put into his campaigns and sieges is shown by a description of him at the siege of Pontaudemer in 1133 when, after setting fire to the town and preparing for the assault on the castle, he ran about like a young soldier, encouraging his men, instructing his carpenters in how to build the siege-towers, and taking the most active part in the work. Most of his sieges took place in Normandy, notably during his crushing of the great house of Montgomery-Bellême. If the Capetian kings were less spectacularly successful, however, they never suffered the appalling reactions that came upon the English crown. The reign of Henry I was followed by the Anarchy.

Stephen and the Anarchy

The first three Norman kings in England had firmly kept the building of castles under royal control. From 1135 to 1152, the period of divided succession under Stephen and Matilda, the number of private or adulterine castles multiplied. If there

125 *Below* An eighteenth-century print of the remains of the castle of
Montlhéry which was so important to the Capetians in their struggles of the
eleventh century since it controlled the road from Paris to Orléans.

127 *Above* Falaise, France. The great square keep rebuilt by Henry I in 1123,
replacing that put up by William the Conqueror to guard his birthplace,
together with the round Talbot Tower constructed by Philip Augustus after
his conquest of Normandy to guard the approach. The tower is named after
the famous English fifteenth-century soldier; from a lithograph by
Vilain, *c* 1830.

128 *Below* Castle Rising, England. The Romanesque staircase of this great
Norfolk keep, built in the mid-twelfth century for the Albini earls of Sussex.

126 *Above* Loches, France. A fortified site since the sixth century and later
belonging to Fulk Nerra, this castle received numerous additions throughout
the Middle Ages. The great keep, shown here in a French nineteenth-
century lithograph, is generally dated to the late eleventh century, though
parts of it are earlier. In the late Middle Ages the castle was used as a
prison and Ludovico il Moro died incarcerated there.

129 *Opposite* Castle Hedingham, England. One of the most elegant of the
English square keeps, built *c* 1140 for the de Vere earls of Oxford. It was
during his visit here at the end of the fifteenth century that, according to
Bacon, Henry VII fined his host 5000 marks for his defiance of the laws
against livery and maintenance. Note the finely cut ashlar, especially at the
corner, backed by a rubble core. The entrance was formerly through a
forebuilding now in ruins.

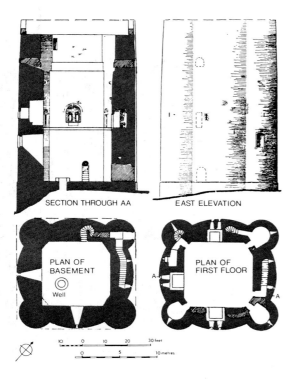

SECTION THROUGH AA   EAST ELEVATION

PLAN OF BASEMENT

Well

PLAN OF FIRST FLOOR

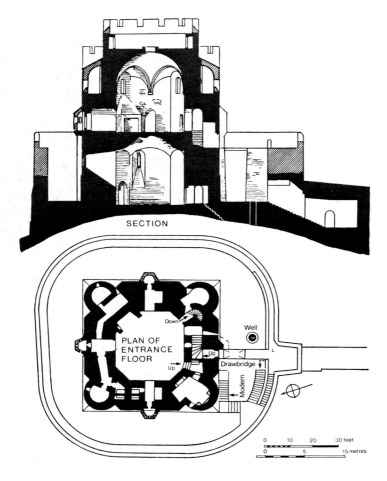

SECTION

PLAN OF ENTRANCE FLOOR

Down

Up

Up

Well

Drawbridge

Modern

were few developments in the design of English fortifications in this period, castles can never have been used so much previously. It seems likely that most of these adulterine castles were of the motte-and-bailey type and they largely consisted of refurbished castles built in the days of the Conquest. Some were very makeshift – the castle of Bampton was a construction on top of the church tower.[4] Many royal castles fell into private hands, including the Tower of London which was seized by Geoffrey de Mandeville. Castles were used as pawns in the political game; they were as important in the exchange of prisoners and in treaties as for their intrinsic military worth.

Stephen provoked the start of civil war by seizing the castles belonging to Roger, bishop of Salisbury, and his family. Stephen besieged his castle of Devizes which was surrendered by the bishop's mistress, Matilda of Ramsbury, after three days. The king's action provoked the anger of the Church. The Empress Matilda landed in England and for many years a ding-dong war of besieging castles, of taking castles, of relieving castles and exchanging castles for important prisoners distorted the government of the country and enabled barons in those parts not directly affected by the royal wars to engage in private feuds and plunder. The most famous siege was that of Oxford castle in 1141 from which, after a three months' investment, Matilda escaped on a winter's night over the ice on the Thames, dressed in a white sheet so that she could not be seen in the snow. One siege in particular brings out both the cruelty and the petty scale on which these wars were fought.[5] William Marshal, later to be called the greatest knight of his age, companion of the Angevin kings, and finally regent of England, was the fourth son of John Marshal, a supporter of Matilda. Stephen had besieged the castle of Newbury, whose castellan owed duty to John Marshal. The castellan asked for a truce to send to the Marshal for advice and the Marshal gained an extension by handing over William as a hostage and a guarantee that he would not reinforce Newbury. The Marshal then broke the truce by revictualling Newbury and by strengthening its defences. Now according to the practice of the time Stephen was free to kill the Marshal's son. When told of this, the father replied, 'What does that matter? I possess the anvil and the hammer to make many more.' William, then about five or six, was led off to the gallows not comprehending where he was being taken. Stephen heard him say to one of his knights, 'O sir, what a pretty javelin! May I have it?' and was so pierced by his charm and innocence that he refused to hang the boy. He also refused a later request by his harder-hearted followers that they should catapult the boy into the castle. But Stephen was exceptionally merciful for his time. Henry I had allowed the blinding and disfiguring of two of his grand-daughters to avenge a wrong committed by his son-in-law.

130 *Right* Saul smiting the Ammonites (top) and the annointing of David (below) from the thirteenth-century French Old Testament named after Cardinal Bernard Maciejowski who presented it to Shah Abbas of Persia in 1608. This and the illumination opposite the contents page and in plate 109 are among the numerous illustrations to this work which is not only celebrated as one of the masterpieces of the artists of the period but is invaluable for the information to be found there about the military and other aspects of the time. *New York, Pierpont Morgan Library,* M. 638, fo 23v.

131 *Overleaf* Eltz, W. Germany. The small fifteenth-century oratory in the Rübenacher Haus, one of the several dwellings into which the castle is divided. The oratory can be shut off by the doors painted to resemble wall hangings.

Fig. 9 *Top* Sections and plans of Houdan, France, one of the earliest transitional keeps designed to improve the flanking. (After Toy, 1955)

Fig. 10 *Above* Provins, France. Section and plan of the keep known as the Tour de César, *c* 1150. (After Toy, 1955)

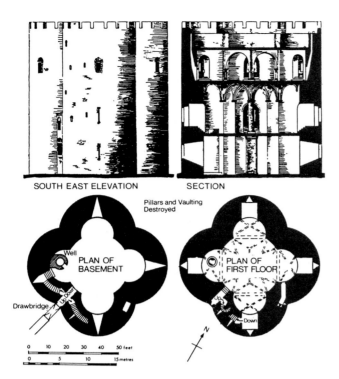

SOUTH EAST ELEVATION   SECTION

Fig. 11 *Above* Etampes, France. Elevation, section and plans of the keep of this royal castle, showing the use of stone vaulting in the hall on the first floor, *c* 1140. The means of entrance was particularly complicated.
An attacker who did not know the keep would rush straight on into a blind alley and he could be taken from the stairs on either side leading to the ground floor and the hall respectively. (After Toy, 1955)

Square and transitional keeps

Certain important castles in England do, however, date from this period. Castle Hedingham in Essex (plate 129) was built for the de Vere earls of Oxford, and Castle Rising in Norfolk (plate 128), famous for its particularly beautiful staircase, for the Albini earls of Sussex. Both are fine examples of the rectangular keep, but they are old-fashioned when compared to some of the new keeps of the transitional type already constructed in France. There the fashion for the older keeps such as Loches (plate 126) or Falaise (plate 127) waned as the disadvantages of the form became apparent. The purpose of these transitional keeps, which employed round or polygonal forms, was to avoid giving the attacker any screen from arrow fire or other projectiles such as was provided by the square corners of the rectangular keep. Rounded or polygonal edges also offered greater resistance to battering or picking engines. As early as 1130, Amaury III de Montfort built his castle of Houdan (Seine-et-Oise) as a round keep with projecting circular turrets at its imagined corners (see fig. 9). The curve of the walls between the turrets, however, prevented the full use of flanking fire. The octagonal design of Provins (Seine-et-Marne), the castle of the counts of Champagne (fig. 10) of about 1150 suffers from the same disadvantage. At the royal keep of Etampes (Seine-et-Oise) of about 1140 (fig. 11) the four-leaf plan, consisting of intersecting round towers, overcomes the problem better, and another introduction at Etampes was the use of ribbed vaulting, supported by a central pillar, for the ceiling of the hall on the first storey.[6] This innovation shows not so much the influence of the Holy Land, where the lack of wood had forced the crusaders to vault with stone, but the adaptation of a Gothic technique to fortifications. One cannot see such original forms as some of these transitional keeps solely as responses to tactical problems. Their fascinating use of cylindrical volumes or of sudden and unexpectedly sharp edges points to a desire on the part of both architect and patron to produce something different, something totally individual—in short, high fashion. In the same way old fashions return with slight or more up-to-date changes, as for example in the castle of Niort (about 1160) which has two square keeps, both with rounded corner towers, joined together by the curtain walls of the intervening courtyard. These castles reflect the growing awareness of the use of great stone constructions as a means of furthering dynastic ambitions, an aim followed by great feudatories as well as the Capetian kings. Bishops, too, built castles—the first castle at Chauvigny was built by a bishop of Poitiers some time in the twelfth century on a hilltop site near the River Vienne, so naturally strong and yet so close to an important trading route that it attracted the building of four castles by other owners.[7] In the south of France the different social conditions produced many fruitful developments.

132 *Previous page* Middleham, England. An interior of the ruined rectangular keep, begun about 1170 for Robert FitzRalph, which was later enclosed within a quadrangular enceinte. In the fifteenth century Middleham belonged to Warwick the Kingmaker.

133 *Left* Etampes, France. Etampes in the late fourteenth-century: 'August' from the *Très Riches Heures* of the duc de Berry by Pol de Limbourg. *Chantilly, Musée Condé.*

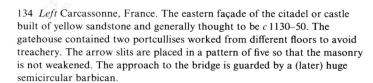

134 *Left* Carcassonne, France. The eastern façade of the citadel or castle built of yellow sandstone and generally thought to be *c* 1130–50. The gatehouse contained two portcullises worked from different floors to avoid treachery. The arrow slits are placed in a pattern of five so that the masonry is not weakened. The approach to the bridge is guarded by a (later) huge semicircular barbican.

135 *Left* Conisborough, England. An aerial view of the great round keep supported by six massive buttresses, one of which contains an oratory. It was built in the late twelfth-century for a half-brother of Henry II.

136 *Above* Arles, France. The Roman amphitheatre in 1807 before it was cleared of the accretions of medieval and later fortified and domestic buildings. From A–L Millin, *Atlas pour servir au voyage dans les Départements du Midi.*

Castles of the Midi

In the south of France the building of fortifications followed more closely the Italian pattern; society was more urban and because castles played a dominant part in the organization of these towns their lords could derive a considerable revenue from the burgesses. Also there were many more Roman remains to adapt. The arenas at Nîmes and at Arles (plate 136) were converted into circles of fortified town houses. Carcassonne (plate 158) was on the site of a Visigothic citadel and even the triumphal arch at Orange was adapted into a fortress. The mountainous nature of much of the south provided many naturally strong positions for castles, amongst them the four castles of Lastours, near Carcassonne, and one of the most superbly sited of all castles, Les Baux, set in a white lunar

landscape looking down on the plains of Provence. There, too, in the south flourished the society that produced the literature of the troubadours, and also the most dangerous heresy to challenge the Church of the Middle Ages, that of the Cathars or Albigensians, amongst whose centres was Carcassonne. Here the Trencavel family built their very original citadel in about 1130.[8] The absence of a donjon, the rectangular plan round an open courtyard, the provision of a watchtower, the placing of arrow slits in a quincuncial disposition to avoid weakening the masonry and to increase the field of fire, all these features make the citadel of Carcassonne one of the most advanced of its period and one which was to have a great influence on future building. Another subtle innovation was to provide two successive portcullises, each raised by separate machinery, placed on different floors without communication between them so that a traitor could get at one but still not be able to open the castle to attackers. (See also plates 89 and 160.)

Wide regions of the south, in Aquitaine and Poitou, were brought under the rule of Henry II of England when in 1152 he married the fascinating patroness of the troubadours, Eleanor of Aquitaine, a queen so famous that even a contemporary German poet sang of her that, were the whole world his from the ocean to the Rhine, he would give it up if he had her lying in his arms. This marriage greatly extended the Angevin empire and added many new reasons to the long-standing quarrels between the French and English kings.

Henry II

Constantly on the move, whether for the administration of justice, the pursuit of war, or to evade embarrassing suitors or

Fig. 12 *Right* A map of the Angevin Empire. (After Poole)

137 *Below* Orford, England. One of Henry II's earliest castles in England. The polygonal keep is one of the most developed forms of the transitional type. It was built between 1165 and 1173. From Grose's *Antiquities*, 1773.

138 *Below right* Framlingham, England. The great curtain walls and square flanking towers built *c* 1200 for the Bigod earls of Norfolk. It possesses no keep, trusting completely to its wall of enceinte. It was a centre of the 1216 rebellion against King John and from here in the sixteenth century Queen Mary set out to claim her throne from Lady Jane Grey. From Grose's *Antiquities*, 1773.

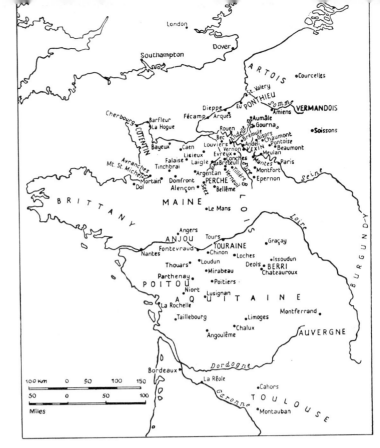

relatives, Henry needed many castles. As a descendant of Fulk Nerra, the passion for building was in his Angevin blood and hardly a year of his long reign passed without the erection of a new castle or improvements on an old one. As well as building castles or heavily reconstructing them on the main frontiers of the Welsh Marches, the Scottish border, and the south-east coast, he devoted even more attention to the castles of the interior of England. Although these would also be used as administrative centres, as treasuries, or as prisons, the attention paid to them, in spite of the fact that they formed no part of a frontier system, helps to make clear the military basis of

Angevin government.[9] One of Henry's frontier castles in England, Orford in Suffolk (plate 137) is also one of the most original keeps of the transitional kind. It is still in a fine state of preservation, standing on a hillock, commanding views over the estuary of the Alde and the flat Suffolk coast. The castle was built between 1165 and 1173 partly as a check against the activities of the Bigod earls of Norfolk who had a strong castle not far away at Framlingham (its later form is seen in plate 138) and partly against Flemish mercenaries who landed on the coast. Other transitional keeps of this time include Conisborough in Yorkshire (plate 135), built for Henry's half brother, Hamo de Warenne, earl of Surrey, and Chilham, also built for Henry. The chief impetus to his castle building in his later years was given by the rebellion of 1174-5 when Henry's wife and sons joined with all his most powerful enemies. After this tragic contest Henry imprisoned Eleanor in the castle of Old Sarum for the rest of his life and then he suffered the death of his eldest son, Henry the Young King, beloved of all wild young knights and troubadours for his largesse and his passion for tournaments.

As a result of the rebellion Henry concentrated on other castles in England. Newcastle (plate 141), a particularly fine

rectangular keep, was built by 1175-8 as an extra defence against the Scots. The architect was probably a certain Maurice the Engineer who was also associated with the building of Henry's last and finest castle at Dover (plates 140 and 53) in 1179-81. As Dover, called the 'key of England' by Matthew Paris, was one of the links between the two main divisions of the Angevin empire, the troubles of Henry II's last years made it all the more important that Dover should be held. Although its keep follows in general the traditional form, a great innovation was to encircle it completely with the inner curtain walls and this was followed by the building of an outer curtain wall (probably finished under John)–which makes this castle the earliest known example of concentric fortification in western Europe.[10] The twelfth-century outer curtain wall has largely disappeared. The inner curtain wall survives to this day, but with its rectangular towers cropped for gun emplacements in the eighteenth century to the level of the wall ramparts.

139 *Right* Newcastle, England. Heavy zigzag patterns in the window and door frames of the castle chapel. Compare this with the more elegant chapel of Dover (plate 53) built only a little later.

140 *Above* Dover, England. A panoramic view of Henry II's most powerful castle in England, built on a site occupied by a Roman light-house and possibly fortified by Harold for William the Conqueror before the Conquest as a condition of his release from captivity. In front of the great rectangular keep can be seen the late twelfth-century curtain walls with square flanking towers which, with an outer line of walls of the same period now largely vanished, formed the earliest example of concentric fortification in a castle in western Europe. Hubert de Burgh, with a garrison of 140 knights and many more men-at-arms, successfully held the castle during the invasion of 1216 against a French army whose failure to capture it significantly reduced their chances of success.

141 *Left* Newcastle, England. An exterior view of Henry II's square keep, the upper portions of which have been heavily restored. It is doubtful whether the crenellations should project as they do here.

Fig. 13 *Below* A plan of Château Gaillard, France. *A* indicates where the French began sapping operations; *B* marks the building through which they gained entry to the middle bailey. Note the pattern formed by the chemise to the inner bailey, and the pointed base of the donjon or keep. (After Toy, 1955)

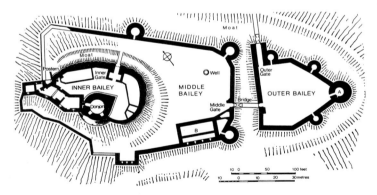

The keep itself is the largest of the twelfth-century square keeps. It rests on a splayed base or talus, the purpose of which was to bounce on to the enemy projectiles dropped from the tower. The walls are extremely thick, from 17 ft to 21 ft (5 m to 6 m), the thickness being used to provide a considerable number of rooms fitted into the walls. Water, hauled up to the top of the keep from the well, was supplied to different parts of the keep by lead pipes (a similar system has been employed at Newcastle), and the keep was provided with garderobes or lavatories. There are two chapels; the upper chapel (plate 53), with its ribbed vault and arcading, is a fine example of transitional architecture. Another feature of note is the forebuilding to the keep, which protected the entrance by a system of three drawbolted doors.

Such an undertaking as the building of Dover castle cost a great amount of money. Henry and his son Richard spent about £4000 on the keep and probably another £3000 on the outbuildings. This sum was spread over the years 1179-91 when the average yearly income of the Angevin kings was about £10,000. And they were, of course, spending sums of almost the same order on other castles at the same time. The construction of castles certainly absorbed the major part of the royal revenue and this must have been justified by the essential part they played in Angevin administration.

142 *Right* Chinon, France. The twelfth-century Tour du Moulin which guards the westernmost point of the Château du Coudray. Parts of the curtain wall on either side may be tenth-century. The tower rises from a square base to an octagon and then to a circular form.

Perhaps the most extraordinary of Henry's castles is that at Chinon[11] (plate 32). It consists of an entrenched camp on a spur overlooking the River Vienne which had been fortified by the Romans. The camp is divided into three distinct castles separated by deep moats—on the east the Fort St Georges; in the centre the Château du Milieu; and on the west the Château du Coudray. Henry had lavished much care on works here and it was in the Fort St Georges in 1188 that he died in pain and misery at the rebellion of his sons, deserted by nearly all his followers, after his servants had pillaged the room for the few belongings that remained to him. (See also plates 147 and 282.)

Coeur-de-Lion and Philip Augustus

The long quarrel between the Angevin and Capetian kings which reached its climax in the struggles between Richard and John on the one side, and Philip Augustus, on the other, ended one of its phases in a great victory for the latter. Many great castles were built during the struggle and its ending meant that both sides were free to deal with other problems: the Capetians to gain control of yet more of France and the English kings to engage in the great constitutional struggles of the thirteenth century and then to embark on the conquest of Wales and Scotland.

The rivalry was brought to a head by the building of Château Gaillard (plates 143 and 144) by Coeur-de-Lion to compensate for the loss of Gisors (plate 87), ceded to Philip Augustus by the Treaty of Issoudun in 1195. His new castle was sited on a spur overlooking the Seine near Les Andelys to cover the approach to Rouen, the capital of Normandy. The land chosen belonged to the archbishop of Rouen who was so enraged by Richard's requisition of his manors that he laid an interdict on Normandy until he was recompensed with rich lands elsewhere. Richard, it must be remembered, was the greatest general of his age, accustomed to command to build since being made count of Poitou when still an adolescent. He was a master of military skills and even carried with him on the way to the Holy Land his own transportable wooden castle with which he terrified the Sicilians during his long halt on their island. He had captured Cyprus, thus adding many years of survival to the Latin Kingdom by giving the Crusaders a secure base for reinforcements and command of the sea. At the siege of Acre he performed one of the rarest feats of medieval warfare, the defeat of an army come to relieve a beleaguered garrison. Normally under such a threat the besiegers retired. Richard, however, won a great victory against Saladin and then went on to capture Acre. His years

143 *Above left* Château Gaillard, France. The round keep from its strongest side in nature on the edge of the chalk cliff. The machicolation and keel or pointed base were on the other side, facing the inner wall of the chemise. No attack was expected from the direction of the cliff.

144 *Left* Château Gaillard, France. The wall of the chemise (right), the last protection of the keep. When he had breached this wall, Philip Augustus had won the castle. The design of closely set, bellying towers was one of the most subtle features of the castle and was meant to provide the fullest possible flanking at this point.

145 *Right* Eltz, W. Germany. The dressing-room, one of a series of small, but highly decorated rooms. The lady receiving a ring from the knight, the angel displaying a coat of arms on the chimney breast, and the vigorous decoration of vegetation and flowers, each of which had a definite meaning, add a liveliness and gaiety to what might otherwise be a poky little room.

of imprisonment in the Empire, when captured in the lands of Leopold of Austria on his return from the Crusade, did not break his spirit even though during his captivity in Dürnstein his only amusements were writing poems and wrestling with his warders. His experience of warfare was unrivalled and, as Sir Maurice Powicke says:

'We must regard Richard's wars in Normandy as a continuation of his fights as a Crusader . . . during the four years of his reign the unity of the soldier's life was never broken, and . . . his best talk was in the company of Mercadier the Brabançon or Master Ivo the Balistarius. He brought back with him from the East men who had been trained in Syria. Franks born in Syria, one of them from Nazareth, were among his artillerymen; indeed there is good evidence that he had brought back a band of Saracens to fight for him . . . We may think then, that as he supervised the workmen at Andeli, Richard's thoughts often went back five or six years to the siege of Acre or to his visit to the great Syrian fortress of Margat.'[12]

Much thought has been devoted to the question of whether or not Château Gaillard marks a new era in the history of castle building. Although it is extremely skilfully designed, it has been claimed, however, that it marks the end of the Norman fortress[13] and that most of its characteristic features had already appeared in earlier French castles–notably the basic plan which had been employed at La Roche-Guyon about twenty miles upstream from Les Andelys. Certainly its scheme of defence, in which the keep stands at the extreme end of the promontory so that it could only be reached when a whole series of defence works had been captured, looks back to past practice both in Europe and the Holy Land rather than to the recently conceived concentric design in which the castle can be actively defended from all sides of equal strength and which had already appeared at Dover.

Although many details about its building are to be found in the Normandy exchequer rolls for 1197-8, no architect is mentioned and it is generally agreed that Richard himself supervised the works. Even if he did not boast that it was built in one year, as a later chronicler claimed, the work certainly went forward with great speed. When Philip Augustus was reported to have said that he would take it though its walls were made of iron, Richard retorted that he would hold it though its walls were made of butter. A lodging on the island below the castle became his favourite residence for the last two years of his life.

Built on a spur and therefore protected on all sides but one, the castle had as its first defence a wide ditch cut across the spur (see fig. 13). Then came the outer bailey with widely projecting round towers. A further ditch separated that in turn from the middle bailey which itself was cut off by a moat from the chemise wall protecting the keep. The chemise is one of the most original and visually exciting parts of the castle. It consists of a series of round towers projecting at such short intervals that only about 3 ft (914 cm) divide one from the next and it gives the impression from a distance of a gigantic jelly

146 Eltz, W. Germany. A view of the inner courtyard which contains elements of every period, from its foundation in the twelfth century to the sixteenth century. Situated on a tributary of the Mosel (see jacket front), it came to be an example of the *Ganerbenburg* or castle under multiple ownership; four separate dwellings open on to this courtyard. This helps to explain the resemblance to later medieval town building, with every device used to gain more light and space by projections from the upper storeys, including even the oratory (painted red).

147 Chinon, France. The ruins of the great hall in the Château du Milieu. Here, in 1429, Joan of Arc met the Dauphin, Charles VII, picking him out, according to the story, when he had tried to make himself indistinguishable among his courtiers. Here she gave him the courage to go to Rheims to be crowned and to carry on the fight against the English. The level of the floor can be seen from the joist holes and the position of the fireplace.

mould. The keep is a round tower with walls 12 ft (4 m) thick and a prow-shaped projection facing the inner wall of the chemise. Around the top of the keep were machicolations of the key-arch type supported on buttresses embedded in a stone plinth reinforcing the base of the walls. The machicolation and the plinth were used by the defenders in conjunction because the point of the plinth was not so much to prevent sapping but to act as a platform off which projectiles could be bounced. The upper part is concave and the lower part oblique, thus deflecting projectiles in a fan-shaped trajectory. Most of these subtleties were intended to avoid the provision of any dead ground which would enable an attacker to mine or sap undisturbed. The remains reveal, out of all the complexity of the building, only one part, the bridge to the chemise or wall of the inner court, that provided such protection and it was here that Philip Augustus's miners were able to work in safety.[14]

Richard was not content with merely defending the promontory; the castle was linked to a series of defences extending across the river and including a barrage of stakes in it, the construction of which was a task probably as difficult to achieve as any part of the castle itself.

Richard did not have long to enjoy it. In 1199 he was mortally wounded by a crossbow shot at a minor siege of the castle of Chalus whose owner refused to surrender some figures of gold, probably Gallo-Roman, which had been discovered near the castle. John, though capable of violent bursts of energy and gifted with fitful military capacity, was no match for Philip Augustus who, in 1203, moved with a great army to seize Château Gaillard as the first stage in his conquest of Normandy. There followed one of the most famous sieges of the Middle Ages–the seemingly impregnable fortress fell after only six years of existence. In describing this siege much has been made of small points, such as the dead angle under the bridge to the chemise already mentioned, as though these were deficiencies in Richard's design. They would have been of no account had Richard been able to plan against one totally new factor–the new cohesion and organization of the Capetian army. Whenever in the twelfth century the Capetian kings had gone to war, whether against Henry I, Henry II, or Richard I, they had been defeated unless they had break-away support from the opposing side. For one thing, they were not as rich as the Angevins and, for another, they could not rival the organization of the Anglo-Norman chanceries and other royal offices. Philip Augustus, through a long and continuous preparation, had built up his army to the point where at last he was a fitting match for his old enemy. Considering this background, the unusual strength of the besieging army and the length of time that Philip Augustus was able to devote to its siege (it lasted throughout the winter) were far more important factors in the capture of the castle than any small flaws in the design of its defences.

The siege was described by a chaplain to Philip Augustus, William Le Breton,[15] in the course of a very long epic. The French king arrived with his army in August 1203 and gained an almost immediate success in destroying Richard's elaborate system of defences across the Seine. The palisade across the river was broken up by strong swimmers and the fort on the island taken. The only offensive by John's forces, a night attack under the earl of Pembroke, failed miserably. It remained for Philip Augustus to take the castle. In September he built double lines of circumvallation and sat down to wait. The garrison of the castle under a brave commander, Roger de Laci, consisted largely of Englishmen, forty knights, two hundred foot sergeants, and about sixty engineers and crossbowmen. Hundreds of refugees had fled to the shelter of the castle on the French approach. To save his supplies, de Laci expelled many who were allowed to pass through the French lines. A second wave of about four hundred were not, however, allowed to pass through by the French, who hoped de Laci would take them back. De Laci refused to do so and these unfortunate wretches had to spend the winter on the sides of the promontory, in danger of missiles from either side, living in whatever shelter they could find, and reduced to cannibalism. When Philip Augustus finally relented and let them through, it

149 Angers, France. Five of the seventeen striped drum towers of the castle begun in 1232 on the site of that of Fulk Nerra by Blanche of Castile when regent to the young St Louis. Angers had become an advance post of the French monarchy against Brittany, following the capture of the Angevin lands by Philip Augustus. The drum towers formerly rose high above the curtain walls and were capped with conical towers.

was too late for most of them and they died of the effects of starvation and exposure.

By February 1204 the French towers and siege-engines were ready and the assault began. The miners, who worked under mantlets for protection, picked holes in the foundation of the curtain wall of the outer bailey, set fire to the wooden props, and the wall collapsed. The next obstacle was the ditch, 30 ft (9 m) deep to the inner bailey whose walls rose flush from the ditch and gave no purchase for the miners who even tried sticking daggers into the chalk to make ladders for themselves. Then a French soldier noticed that the drain of a privy opened on the west side just below an unbarred window of the chapel. He managed to crawl up the drain of the privy, entered the chapel, and reached the window through which he pulled up other soldiers. There they raised an uproar to make the defenders believe a great many of them had gained entrance.[16] The defenders failed in an attempt to smoke them out, panicked, and fled to the safety of the chemise. The design of the chemise made it particularly difficult for the miners to attack it–except in one place under the stone bridge which afforded them protection. Philip Augustus brought in a great catapult named Cabalus to reinforce their efforts. The defenders made a brave attempt at counter-mining but their efforts only weakened the wall further without driving off the attackers. There was a huge fall of masonry and the defenders, not even bothering to retreat to the keep, tried to flee by a postern gate where they were met and forced to surrender.

French castles of the thirteenth century

The seizure of Normandy rapidly followed the fall of Château

150 Dourdan, France. Built by Philip Augustus in about 1220 to cover the south-east sector of the royal lands, this is an excellent example of the rectangular form favoured for his castle by this monarch. The great round keep can be seen in the background. A late fourteenth-century view from the *Très Riches Heures. Chantilly, Musée Condé.*

Gaillard and the next few years saw a remarkable expansion of Capetian control in France. Philip Augustus not only gained most of the Angevin empire but also, by the battle of Bouvines in 1215, established his power over Flanders. His son, Louis VIII, although he failed in his conquest of England (see page 135), reaped the benefit of the Albigensian crusade by bringing large parts of the south under royal control. His widow, Blanche of Castile, struggled to preserve the royal power and then handed over to her son, St Louis, a country that had never been so united even in the time of Charlemagne. This period saw the building of the most impressive and ambitious of French fortifications, the immense striped towers of Angers (plate 149), the walled city of Carcassonne (plates 158, 159 and 161), and the port of Aigues-Mortes in the marshes of the Rhône delta (plates 90, 155 and 156), which were not to be rivalled by their extent in that country until the

constructions of Vauban in the seventeenth century.

Philip Augustus, in the opinion of many a better engineer than the Lion-Heart, made great improvements to the numerous Angevin castles, adding powerful towers to their most open lines of approach. Examples of this work can be seen in the round Talbot tower at Falaise (plate 127), standing beside the Anglo-Norman keep, and in the Château du Coudray (plate 32) at Chinon.

In his own original castles, such as the Louvre and at Rouen, although he did not neglect to build keeps, he adopted a simple quadrilateral plan, perhaps owing much to the Trencavel citadel at Carcassonne, much simpler than the elaborations beloved by the Angevins but extremely effective because of the care that went into the placing of round towers, the design of the arrow slits, the use of hoarding (or wooden machicolations), and the employment of portcullises.[17] The quadrilateral plan had ancient roots in Roman practice, in the

Fig. 14 *Below* Coucy, France. A cross-sectional reconstruction of the round keep by Viollet-le-Duc, long before its destruction in the First World War. The great strength of the tower derived from the application of buttresses rising to arches which distribute the weight of the building. The stone parapet rising above the roof level supported the tiled roof of the hoarding which was built out from 48 corbels extended from the upper circumference. From *Military Architecture,* 1879.

151 *Right* Beaucaire, France. The thirteenth-century triangular keep pointing towards the Rhône, marking the old boundaries between Languedoc and the Empire. One of the most important fairs in Europe was held in the town here and it was at Beaucaire in 1216 that Simon de Montfort received his first check in the Albigensian crusade. The castle is also associated with the story of the loves of Aucassin and Nicolette, a Picard *chante-fable* of *c* 1206.

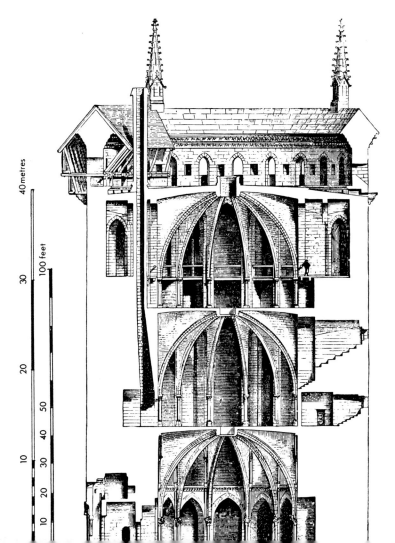

disposition of Carolingian palaces and especially in the layout of monasteries since the building of St Gall in the ninth century. Its adoption for the castle, however, reflects a new professionalism in warfare. The system of piecemeal defence had, above all, a psychological weakness, something Machiavelli was later to comment upon: the garrisons would always be tempted to retire behind the next line of defence before they had done their utmost to repel the enemy from the outer walls. The castle based on the quadrilateral plan, like the concentric castle to which we come later, presented fronts of equal strength on all sides, except, of course, for the entrances which were particularly strongly fortified. This signifies a new confidence in the castle builder and in his sense of his ability to drive off his attackers. One of Philip Augustus's best surviving castles is that of Dourdan (plate 150, shown here as the illustration to April in the Chantilly *Book of Hours*). Another given to him is Yévre-le-Chatel which has an interesting lozenge-shaped ground-plan. His work on his castles settled the general design of fortifications in France for the next hundred years, and in Germany, Holland, England, and the Iberian peninsula we will find many examples of castles laid out on the quadrilateral plan.

Under the regency of Blanche of Castile, when the royal power was perforce relaxed, private castle building continued to flourish. The most notable of these castles was that at Coucy (fig. 14) built by Enguerrand III de Coucy who had designs on the French throne. The keep, rising to a height of 180 ft (55 m) and with a diameter of 102 ft (31 m), which had defied the efforts of Richelieu's engineers to blow it up and was only destroyed in the first World War by the Germans, was considered to be the strongest and greatest ever built.

So impressive was this tower that it has even been suggested[18] that it was built not at the same time as the castle, but two hundred years later as one of the first French experiments against cannon–an opinion which is not generally held. The masons were able to raise it to such a height by providing holes for projecting beams placed at spirally rising intervals, so that a helical path could be made for carrying up materials to whatever point the circumference had risen. The castle itself was joined to the town by a continuous line of wall strongly defended with round towers. No direct approach could be made to the castle except through the town which meant negotiating a barbican, a great ditch and two sets of town gates before the castle itself was even reached. The keep was protected from the rest of the castle by a moat and the foundations of the castle were provided with a network of subterranean passages sometimes guarded by grilles to facilitate escape. According to Viollet-le-Duc, it would have been necessary to employ 800 men for the construction of Coucy over a period of five summers–an effort that must have placed a severe strain on local food resources and on the coffers even of the lord of Coucy.

Earlier we remarked on the continuance of the Romanesque *appearance* of castles throughout the Middle Ages, but here at Coucy is an example of Gothic influence which is not immediately apparent. In this donjon, and in the Tour du Tréseau at Carcassonne, in the Tour de Constance (Aigues-Mortes), and in the Wakefield Tower of the Tower of London, the interior face of the circumference is applied perpendicularly with buttresses, thus providing niches each covered by an arch from buttress to buttress. On the next floor the buttresses rise on the keystones of the arches beneath. The advantages of this method include great solidity, and distribution of the weight, at the same time making it more difficult to sap and mine because even if sappers break through to a niche, the arch sustains the rest of the building. The basic idea had been known before in, for example, the way the interior of the wall of the ring-fort at Leyden (*c* 1150) was strengthened with arches, but not with such subtlety. In general the Romanesque cathedral and castle take their strength from sheer mass; the Gothic cathedral and castle from arches and the opposition of forces.

The threat presented by such private castles impelled Blanche of Castile to build on a similar scale. At Angers between 1232 and 1238 she built a huge castle on the site of Fulk Nerra's home and seat of power. The seventeen round towers, formerly rising higher than the intervening curtain walls, were crowned with tiled conical roofs. The alternate bonding of dark shale with courses of limestone makes a fierce and almost Saracen impression on the onlooker (plate 149), and, like the later Caernarvon, probably derives its inspiration from the walls of Byzantium (plate 12). There was no keep at Angers, probably because the walls were themselves considered sufficient defence; therefore the layout permitted

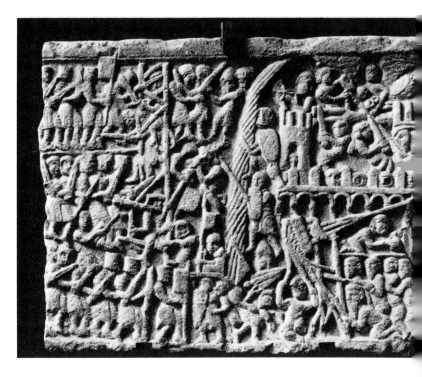

152 An early thirteenth-century bas-relief preserved in St Nazaire, Carcassonne, which is thought to have come from the tomb of Simon de Montfort, and to represent the scene of his death at the siege of Toulouse in 1218. On the right can be seen the trebuchet which is pulled down by a group of men and women. They must have released it simultaneously at a signal; otherwise it would have been very dangerous for anyone still hanging on to his rope. A stone is being inserted into the sling.

a freer disposition of the chapel and residential quarters, giving the impression of a palace within a castle such as Philip Augustus had already achieved in the Louvre, except that the Louvre was finished with a great round keep like that of Coucy.

Blanche was also deeply involved in retaining the authority in the south, newly won by the crown under the cover of the Albigensian crusade.

the crusaders were nearly everywhere triumphant, seizing town after town and castle after castle, burning the heretics pitilessly, plundering and appropriating lands at the same time. They were, in fact, destroying far more than the centres of heresy, and were deliberately ruining the liberal and gracious civilization of the south. The count of Toulouse, the leader of the south, formed a league with Peter II of Aragon and with a huge army they moved to trap Simon de Montfort at the castle of Muret, Garonne, in 1213. Simon had only 900 knights as against the 2000 of his opponents and yet he did not hide behind the walls of the castle but attacked so furiously that the southern knights were completely routed and Peter of Aragon was killed. The French knights then turned on the enemy footsoldiers who had been trying to take Muret and slaughtered thousands of them.

The first major reverse Simon met was at the siege of Beaucaire in 1216. He was forced to withdraw and although he achieved other successes the city of Toulouse, which he had taken from the counts, revolted against his barbarous treatment of the inhabitants. He began to besiege the city in 1217. Although the walls of the city had been destroyed, the inhabitants worked with such vigour at the construction of palisades

153 *Above* Montségur, France. An aerial view of the last important stronghold of the Albigensian heretics, 300 of whom held out here for nine months against a royal army until forced to surrender in 1244. Two hundred of them were burnt alive rather than abjure their faith. The exceptional thickness of the curtain walls can be seen here very well.

154 *Right* Najac, France. A view from the east showing (left) the round donjon built by Alphonse of Poitiers, younger brother of St Louis, in about 1253. This round tower, built in red sandstone on the model of the donjon of Coucy, took the place, as keep, of the earlier square donjon which was transformed into residential quarters. The earlier castle built about 1100 and later enlarged, had been involved in the quarrels of Richard Coeur-de-Lion and Philip Augustus, dominating as it does important routes leading from Guienne inland. The River Aveyron curls round three sides of the hill on which it is built.

155 *Overleaf* Aigues-Mortes, France. The Tower of Constance, built 1241–50.

156 *Overleaf, right* Aigues-Mortes, France. The lower hall (*c* 1250) of the Tower of Constance showing the great stone hood of the fireplace, the oven, and the doorway to the postern leading to the open country. A staircase goes to a gallery in the thickness of the wall, from which archers could shoot at an enemy who penetrated the hall through eleven windows set between the spandrels. All the needs of the building have been brought together in a pure and satisfying design—to note one example, the way in which the corbel above the fireplace sinks into the top of the hood.

The Albigensian crusade

The Albigensians had won either support or tolerance from the rulers of the south in the area stretching from Toulouse to Beaucaire (plate 151) on the Rhône. The cupidity of northern barons and the fear and bigotry of the Church found common cause in promoting a crusade against this dangerous heresy. The crusaders soon found a leader of genius in Simon de Montfort l'Amaury, a soldier of great integrity and passionately devoted to the Church. The crusaders set the style of the war from the beginning by sacking and burning Béziers in 1209, massacring the inhabitants indiscriminately. 'The grass of the fields was as red as a rose, for no prisoners were taken', said the poet of the *Chanson de la Croisade*. Shortly afterwards Carcassonne was forced to surrender. In the following years

and barbicans and were possessed with such enthusiasm that they repelled all the assaults of the crusaders for eight months. Then in June 1218 some women working a trebuchet mounted on a church flung a stone that struck Simon on the head and smashed his brains. The besiegers withdrew and took Simon's body for burial to Carcassonne, an event which inspired the writer of the *Chanson* to one of the most terrible judgements ever penned on fanaticism.

'Straight to Carcassonne, they carried him for burial and for the service in the Abbey of Saint Nazaire. And those who can read will see in his epitaph, that he is a saint, a martyr, that he will rise again, that he will inherit the blessing without equal, wear the crown and inherit the kingdom. I have heard say that he must be all these things for if, by

killing men and spilling blood, by damning souls, by consenting to murders, by believing in false counsel, by lighting fires, by destroying barons, by dishonouring chivalry, by taking land by force, by making pride triumph, by advancing evil and extinguishing good, by killing women, and by massacring children, one can in this world win Jesus Christ, then he must indeed wear the crown and shine forth in heaven.'[19]

Toulouse remained in the hands of its counts but the crusade revived under the direct royal control of the future Louis VIII, the husband of Blanche of Castile, who had returned from his nearly successful attempt to conquer England. One result of his wars before his death in 1226 was to establish Carcassonne as a centre of royal power in the still intensely hostile south. The Trencavels, though long dispossessed, had not given up hope of regaining their city and they attacked it in 1240.

157 Albi, France. The fortified cathedral seen from the watchtower of the Abbey of St Salvi.

The report (see note 20 to this chapter) on the siege sent to Blanche of Castile by her constables after they had successfully routed the attackers, shows the high degree of skill in siegecraft employed by both sides. The number of mining operations is almost incredible. Although these attempts failed and although the Inquisition had established a terrible power in the south, smelling out the heretics and burning them if they would not repent, the Albigensians still held out, especially in the Pyrenees in the mountain castle of Montségur (plate 153) which had been the centre of their faith since 1231. Although nothing of what is known of the Catharist religion supports this, it has been suggested that Montségur may have acted as a kind of temple for the ceremonies of the heretics.[21] There are certain unmilitary features in its construction: two great unfortified gates, far wider than was common in comparable castles, and the provision of windows instead of arrow slits. The castle acted as the last seminary for instruction in the Catharist faith and must have witnessed scenes of the most intense devotion. Acting on the orders of Louis IX in May 1243 an army laid siege to the 300 people in the castle. At first they hoped to starve out the heretics but by November, when the warlike bishop of Albi arrived to organize the siege-engines, they had determined on making an assault. Although the defenders constructed machines in answer and drove off many assaults, by March 1244, after nine months, they were forced to surrender and the victors celebrated by burning 200 of the heretics alive at the foot of the mountain.

The mountain fortress of Quéribus held out even longer, until 1255, and the opposition to the Church gradually died down. But hatred was still strong enough in 1285 for the bishops of Albi to build their cathedral as a completely fortified building (plate 157) with arrow slits, machicolation, and a single entrance. Languedoc finally came to the French throne in 1271 on the death of Alphonse of Poitiers, younger brother of St Louis who had married the daughter of the last count of Toulouse. Alphonse had been responsible for improvements to the great castle of Najac (plate 154) which had already played a part in the quarrels between Coeur-de-Lion and Philip Augustus and in the Albigensian crusade. Its most notable feature is the great round keep, constructed in the same manner as that of Coucy, and considerable attention was paid to the provision of arrow slits and murder holes.

St Louis in the south

St Louis redirected the efforts of Crusaders to the original aim of fighting Islam instead of their fellow Christians. Instead of making use of Italian ports, he decided to construct his own base and harbour on the Mediterranean coast. It is strange that, in spite of the recent Capetian successes in the south, none of the existing ports had fallen into royal hands. Therefore, he had to buy land from the Abbey of Psalmodi in a most unsuitable part, the marshes of the Rhône delta. Aigues-Mortes was Louis's greatest work of fortification and from here in 1248 he set out with 30,000 followers for his disastrous campaign in Egypt and in 1270 for Tunis where he died of the plague. Louis was responsible for the building of the huge round keep, the Tower of Constance, between 1246 and 1250 (except for the lighthouse tower of c 1300), the construction of the harbour, and for the laying out of the town on the quadrilateral pattern. The Tower of Constance (plate 155), which acquired a dismal reputation as a prison for Protestants in the eighteenth century, is a redoubtable construction owing much to the keep

158 Carcassonne, France. A view from the south-west of the most
powerful example of concentric fortifications of the medieval West. The
castle is on the far left, the cathedral is in the centre, and the huge round
Tour de la Vade (far right), the strongest in the outer walls, marks the point
at which they turn up towards the Narbonne Gate. The town contains
fortifications of the Visigothic period, and of the twelfth and thirteenth
centuries. Its name is said to be derived from a lady called Carcasse, the
widow of a Saracen governor, who, when the town was besieged by
Charlemagne and was on the point of starvation, ordered the last remaining
pig to be stuffed with the last bag of grain. The pig was then slung over by
a siege-weapon to the Frankish lines. It burst scattering grain as it did so
and the Franks, saying to one another that if the inhabitants could still
afford to feed their pigs on grain there was no chance of their ever starving
the citizens out, abandoned the siege. At that point a trumpet sounded for
parley and Carcasse married the first of the Trencavel dynasty. Needless to
say, the story is very old and is ascribed to many castles.

of Coucy. Its two entrances, one to the town, the other to the
open country, were each provided with two doors and a
portcullis and a murder hole. A corridor running round the
upper part of the ground-floor chamber has eleven bays
opening into the chamber so that should an enemy penetrate
that far he could be shot down immediately. Not surprisingly
there are no reports of the tower being taken. After Louis's
death the construction of the walls with their five gates was
continued by his son, Philip III, under the direction of Louis's
favourite military architect, Eudes de Montreuil. The work
probably continued into the reign of Philip the Fair and was
not finished until about 1295. The walls, it is interesting to note,
are constructed in the masonry with roughened exteriors
known as *appareil-à-bossage,* mentioned in Chapter 3.
Formerly they stood higher but now the moat has been filled in.
Some way outside the town the highway was blocked by a
square tower, the Tour Carbonnière, again provided with two
portcullises, to hold up any enemy and gain time for a
warning to reach the town. Money for the building of the walls
was arranged by the Genoese doge, William Boccanegra,
whose townsmen had grown rich on ferrying Crusaders and
pilgrims across the Mediterranean, and he was paid by a share
in the ownership of the town and the taxes. After his death in
1274 another Genoese took over the finances.[22]

One fascinating aspect of Aigues-Mortes, apart from its
present melancholy air of desolation amongst the dead waters
of its name, is that, unlike Carcassonne, it was a totally new
creation, dependent on no earlier fortifications but representing
a completely thirteenth-century design. It can be compared to
Edward I's creation of new towns within military complexes
in Wales at Conway and Caernarvon, but the military purpose
was not the same. The Welsh towns were centres of coloniza-

tion. At Aigues-Mortes there was a great arsenal for overseas
operations; a more apt comparison would be with the new
town of Winchelsea on the south coast, which Edward laid
out and fortified as a new Cinque Port later in the century,
whose harbour, like that of Aigues-Mortes, also silted up so
soon that it was made useless in a hundred years.

Among St Louis's other great military works was his adding
to the fortification of Carcassonne. This work, continued by
his son after his death, consisted of encircling the town with a
double line of walls and towers, thus creating the greatest
complex of concentric fortifications in western Europe. Seen
today, they largely bear the mark of the great restorer, Viollet-
le-Duc, who began his task as long ago as 1844, and although
many features of his work have provoked criticism the general
impression is excellent. An extraordinary round barbican
(plate 158) and a winding road protected the entrance to the
castle. The two gates of the town are like castles in themselves,
especially the famous Narbonne gate (plate 159) with the
extremely subtle ogival points attached to its twin drum
towers. These, of course, were yet another device to eliminate
dead ground. Should an enemy manage to break through the
first line of walls, he would find himself completely exposed in
the lists to fire from the second line. Should he somehow break
through the second line he would then, given a sufficient spirit
in the garrison, have to take each of the twenty-five towers
one by one because each was designed for independent
defence.

Ghent and Chillon
These great works of St Louis signalled the extension of
Capetian power in France. Much of the country still remained
in other, and frequently, hostile hands, such as Guienne
where Edward I of England was to build a series of small
fortresses. Again, neighbouring countries, though deeply
influenced in many ways by French civilization, were slow to
pick up the sophistications of French military architecture
either because they had firm traditions of their own or
because, in terms of the scale of attack expected, the elaborate

159 *Overleaf* Carcassonne, France. The statue of the Virgin above the
doorway of the Narbonne Gate. After its surrender to Simon de Montfort
in 1209 Carcassonne became a base for the establishment of Capetian power
in the south and a bulwark of the Church in its persecution of the heretic
Albigensians.

160 *Overleaf, right* Carcassonne, France. A view looking down the narrow
lists of the western walls of the town.

161 *Left* Carcassonne, France. The Tour Carrée de l'Evêque, and a sector of the walls near the cathedral; the bishop had the use of this and a nearby tower in time of peace.

162 *Above* Winchester, England. The twelfth-century great hall of the castle which was completely remodelled by Henry III and is one of the finest rooms of its type now remaining; an eighteenth-century engraving.

devices used at Carcassonne were too expensive for their usefulness. One example is the famous Gravensteen at Ghent (plate 106), built in 1180 for Philip of Alsace, count of Flanders on his return from the Holy Land.[23] Constructed on the site probably occupied by a ring wall, having been a comital fortress since 1000, its exterior wall shows little regard for flanking. The bartizans or projecting towers are probably a fourteenth-century addition. The most notable feature of the castle is the great keep, making use of the earlier stone castle in its cellars and containing the hall of the counts who seemed to have used it as a setting for displays of pomp and authority rather than as a permanent residence. The placing of a palace (plate 99) within the enceinte and separate from the keep resembles Corfe as redesigned by John but also looks to contemporary German practice. Another famous castle, Chillon [24] (plates 9 and 33) in Switzerland, again well within the sphere of French influence, also looks more to German practice than to France, with its comparative lack of flanking, its reliance on a naturally strong position on Lake Geneva, and its *Bergfried*-like central tower. Although its site was occupied

from prehistory, as it now appears it is largely of the thirteenth century when it was redesigned by Pierre Mainier for Peter II of Savoy. Its fine series of wall-paintings of this and later date reflect the light from the water of the lake and the harshness of its history melts in the evanescence of the atmosphere.

The country still most open to French influence was, of course, England.

Castles in thirteenth-century England
After the breakdown of negotiations over Magna Carta in 1215, England came close to becoming another province of France. The future Louis VIII, son of Philip Augustus, landed with a great army in 1216 and it was only the energy and skill shown by John and then by William Marshal, as regent to the minor Henry III, that saved the country. The warfare was conducted largely by sieges of towns and castles. These sieges, which are well-documented, provide some of the best evidence we have of the techniques at the command of the armies of the period. In many cases the beleaguered castles had been standing for many years, for example Rochester (plates 47 and 48) or Dover (plate 140). During the struggle for Rochester in 1215 a square corner tower fell an easy prey to miners. After they had dug their hole and supported it with props, they filled the mine with the carcasses of forty fat pigs and set fire to them. The heat was so intense that the masonry cracked and the corner came crashing down, resulting in the eventual capture of the castle. As was mentioned in Chapter 2,

later that century the corner was repaired with a round tower (plate 48). When a few years after this, Henry III attacked the castle occupied by Fawkes de Bréauté at Bedford in 1224, he used siege-engines on the outer walls, built wooden towers from which to harry the garrison, and successfully mined the inner walls and the great tower.

Baronial building in the later part of the twelfth century and throughout most of the thirteenth kept pace with the royal castles. To around 1200 can be ascribed the great curtain walls of Framlingham with their square projecting towers (plate 138) and William Marshal's domed round keep at Pembroke (plate 163). Caerphilly, which is, like the earlier Kenilworth, notable as a castle making use of great expanses of water in its defence, dates from the middle of the century, and in many of its features foreshadows Edward I's Welsh castles. Kenilworth was one of Simon de Montfort's seats of power in the great constitutional struggles with Henry III.

Henry III shared to the full his family's passion for building and, although during his reign there began, probably under the direction of his son, the future Edward I, the conversion of the Tower of London into one of the most powerful concentric castles in Europe (plate 49), it accords with his mild but extravagant nature that where castles are concerned we should think of him as a great innovator of comforts and beauty. Rendered devious and unstable in government by his powerful Savoyard relations and by the barons who surrounded him, in matters of interior decoration he knew exactly what he wanted. Great numbers of his directions to his masters of works survive and these examples show him paying the same attention to detail in decorating rooms as when he superin-

include the following orders: the queen's chamber was to be panelled and entirely whitewashed inside and newly painted with roses. (This was only two years after it had been painted before.) A partition wall of panelling was to be made between that chamber and the garderobe which had to be tiled outside. His great chamber had to be whitewashed and repainted and all its shutters remade with new wood, new catches, and hinges, to be painted with his arms and newly barred with iron. The glass windows in the chapel of St John the Baptist needed repairing, as did the windows in the great chamber towards the Thames. The eastern corner of this great chamber was to receive the addition of a great round tower, the lowest chamber of which was to go down into the Thames.[25]

Again, in 1256, we find him instructing William the Painter,

monk of Westminster, to execute a painting at Westminster in the chamber where the king washes his head, the painting to show the tale of the king who was saved by his dogs from the plots of his seditious subjects.[26] How he must have longed to have owned such dogs!

At Winchester all that remains of his additions to the castle is the twelfth-century great hall which he remodelled (plate 162), one of the finest rooms of its type to survive, and on one wall

tended the sculptors during the rebuilding of Westminster Abbey. Tiling for floors, wall-paintings especially including the colour green which was his favourite, plasterwork, carpets on the floor for his Spanish daughter-in-law, Eleanor of Castile, in 1255 to make her feel at home, glazed windows – all these tastes he either encouraged or introduced.

His directions in 1240 for improving the Tower of London

163 *Left* Pembroke, Wales. An eighteenth-century print of a painting by Richard Wilson. The round keep built by William Marshal in about 1200 is notable for its domed roof.

164 *Above* Kenilworth, England. This great Warwickshire castle, once defended by large expanses of water, contains elements of every period from the twelfth to the sixteenth centuries, and among its most famous owners were Simon de Montfort, John of Gaunt, and the earl of Leicester, favourite of Elizabeth I; an eighteenth-century engraving.

165 *Above right* Lucera, Italy. A view of one of the two corner round towers, known as the 'Lion' and the 'Lioness' which were added at two particularly important positions in the wall of enceinte after 1270 by Charles of Anjou, the conqueror of the son and grandsons of the former owner of the fortress, the Emperor Frederick II, who planted a colony of Moslems nearby. The scarped platform made it almost impossible for attackers to approach the base of the tower itself.

166 *Below right* Castel del Monte, Italy. Built on an octagonal plan with eight octagonal corner towers, this most famous and beautiful castle was constructed in about 1240 for the Emperor Frederick II chiefly as a hunting lodge. It is unlike any other castle and had no stylistic successors. The entrance shown here reveals the combination of classical and Gothic influences that are so harmoniously joined in other parts of the building. Its shape may represent the form of the imperial crown.

still hangs the painting of King Arthur's Round Table which was ancient in the reign of Henry VIII. This taste for greater comforts, appreciation of beauty, and luxury spread naturally from the court to his richer subjects. His own brother, Richard of Cornwall, who possessed lofty aspirations to become Emperor, also lived in a style of great ostentation and wealth. The connection between Church and castle building was still very important and this is shown by one of Henry's most interesting buildings, the very original Clifford's Tower (see plate 168) at York, begun in 1245 on a quatrefoil plan using the motte of William the Conqueror's original castle as its base. It was designed by Henry III's master-mason, Henry de Reyns, the architect of the Westminster chapterhouse.

entirely to its sea defences and he never forgot the importance of controlling lines of sea traffic. It is interesting, therefore, to see the influence of his years in the East on the siting and building of the great castles he built or reconstructed for the subjection of north Wales. Nearly all of them have access to the sea, thus enabling Edward to ring his enemies about and deprive them of outside aid or supplies. There is one notable difference between what Edward saw in the Holy Land and what he did in Wales. There, the dying Latin community was forced to use the sea as its last defence. Here, he used his castles as bases in a strategy of attack, linking land and sea forces to crush the resistance of the Welsh.

'I did not think there had been such buildings. It surpassed my ideas,' murmured Dr Johnson in amazement after seeing

Edward I in Wales

Under his son, Edward I, there was, however, a return to the object of making the castle an even more impregnable military unit. Edward was in the Holy Land on Crusade when he learned of his father's death. He had already gained considerable experience of warfare by his opposition to, and final defeat of, Simon de Montfort. He was the last great medieval monarch to visit the Holy Land at a time when it was reduced

167 *Left* Almourol, Portugal. A castle built on an island in the River Tagus. Owned by the Templars from the twelfth century until 1312 when King Dinis I handed it over to the Order of Christ, it has a central tower with ten towers in its wall of enceinte.

168 *Above* A view of York, England, in the fifteenth century seen here in a reconstruction. The quatrefoil-shaped Clifford's Tower (centre) was begun for Henry III in 1245. It is unusual both in its shape and in being sited on an artificial motte. Earlier, stone buildings were rarely placed on man-made earthworks because of the risk of subsidence. This motte and the one on the opposite bank of the river were the work of William the Conqueror.

Caernarvon Castle in 1774, and modern visitors still feel the same surprise. Edward's Welsh castles were built to subjugate and to pacify and did their work so well that scarcely any of them, apart from Harlech, have provided any very dramatic historical interest after the story of their actual building. They include Rhuddlan (1277-82), Flint (1277-*c* 1285), Harlech (1283-90), Caernarvon (1283-1327), Beaumaris (1295-*c* 1330) and Conway (1283-89)[27], all highly individual in design, which was determined by their different sites, and, in some cases, by the existence of earlier fortifications that could be adapted and made use of. Each castle is treated as though it were a separate problem and this is due to the skill of Edward's chief military architect and engineer, Master James of St George, who was to Edward what Eudes de Montreuil had been to St Louis.

James of St George had been architect to Edward's cousin, Count Philip of Savoy, and it was from the count's castle of Saint-Georges-d'Espéranche near Lyons which he himself had built that he took his name. After sixteen years of working

169 *Left* Conway, Wales. Two drum towers, with the smaller round watch-towers projecting from their ramparts which characterize the towers of the inner ward: (left to right) the Chapel Tower and the Stockhouse Tower. Part of the Kitchen Tower defending the outer ward can be seen (right).

170 *Below left* Flint, Wales. A view in 1742 by the brothers Buck of one of the first of Edward I's great series of Welsh castles (1277–c 1285), Flint includes much earlier work and, with its great round keep (right) detached from the castle and the town walls and having separate connection with the sea, resembles the Tower of Constance at Aigues-Mortes. It was here that Richard II surrendered to Henry Bolingbroke, soon to be Henry IV, in 1399.

presented a series of obstacles to the enemy. On the other hand, the separate connection of the keep with the sea–resembling in this the Tower of Constance at Aigues-Mortes–shows a strong awareness of contemporary practice. All the others are closer to the principle of aggressive defence. At Harlech (plates 171 and 172) for instance, the gatehouse, formerly considered the weakest part of the defence, is made the strongest. Caernarvon and Conway resemble one another in many ways: both were seats of government overlooking newly created towns and forming part of the complex of walls defending the towns.

for the count building castles and other edifices in all parts of the wide Savoyard lands, in about 1277 he was transferred to Edward I's service. As master of the king's works in Wales he was in a position of enormous authority and supervised numerous experts in masonry and the various forms of labour required. He was so valuable to the king that in 1284 he was awarded a pension for life of 3s a day and a further grant promised to his wife, Ambrosia, of 1s 6d a day if she were to survive him. His powers of organization must have been prodigious to deal with the variety and numbers of workmen on a site, which might reach as many as 1500, as at Conway in the season of 1285. The experts under him came from various parts of Europe; for example, Master Manasser from Vaucouleurs in Champagne was in charge of the diggers at Caernarvon. Other types of workmen included quarriers, stonecutters, masons, workers in lead for the roofing, carpenters, smiths, and many others; these seem to have been drawn for the most part from England and there was hardly a county that did not contribute to the labour force.

Although these castles are remarkable for their individual designs they have many similarities in common. Flint (plate 170), with its round keep cut off from the bailey beside it, in some ways looks back to the older style of castle which

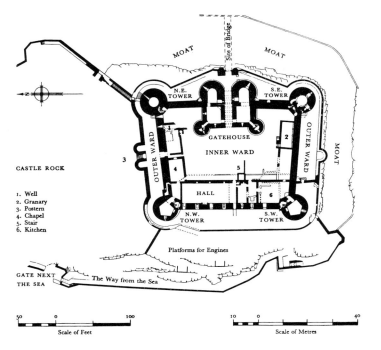

Fig. 15 *Above* A plan of Harlech, Wales. The gatehouse protecting the only side of approach was made the strongest part of the castle. The buildings, such as the hall built in the inner ward, have now disappeared. (After Colvin, H. M. et al. *History of the King's Works*)

171 *Right* Harlech, Wales. The south outer and inner curtain walls. The inner curtain wall rises 80 ft (24 m) and the cliff drops another 200 ft (60 m) Harlech saw the longest siege of the Wars of the Roses when Daffydd ap Jeuan held the castle for the House of Lancaster for two years until surrendering in 1468.

172 *Overleaf* Harlech, Wales. The steps leading up to apartments in the gatehouse; a view from the north curtain wall into the inner ward (built 1283–90). In Owen Glendower's heyday he held court here. His family was forced to surrender the castle when besieged by Henry IV's soldiers in 1408–9.

173 *Overleaf, right* Conway, Wales. Looking up inside one of the drum towers. These towers were formerly capped with tiled pepperpot roofs.

174 *Below* Caernarvon, Wales. The front on the River Seiont, showing (left to right) the Eagle Tower, the Queen's Tower, the Chamberlain Tower, the Black Tower, and part of the Queen's Gate. Note the banding of the masonry thought to be influenced by the land walls of Byzantium.

Fig. 17 *Right* A plan of the castle and town of Caernarvon, Wales, in the early fourteenth century. Note the position, protected on three sides by the waters of the River Seiont, the River Cadnant, and the Menai Strait. (After Colvin, H. M. et al *History of the King's Works*)

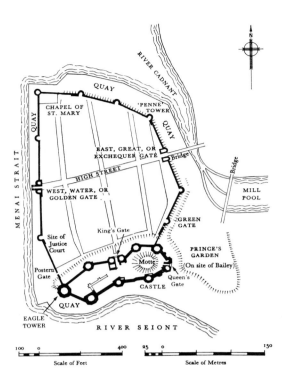

Both depend on a single wall line of defence of such strength that little was to be feared from mining or other means of penetration. They differ most in the design of the towers, those at Caernarvon being multiangular and those at Conway being round and, therefore, formerly capped with tiled conical towers. Because of their different styles of towers they present totally contrasting views to the onlooker (plates 169, 173, 174 and 175). The sharpness of the angles of Caernarvon is terrifying, expressing the harsh legalism of the man who was to be known as the hammer of the Scots and who made his subjects tremble by the thoroughness of his inquisitions into their rights and possessions. The Eagle Tower takes its name from the sculptures of eagles that formerly stood on its battlements, showing that Edward drew on Roman symbolism to express his *imperium* over the Welsh. The castle stood on the site of the Roman Segontium and the banded masonry used at

Caernarvon, in conjunction with polygonal towers, seems to have been directly inspired by the walls of Theodosius at Byzantium (plate 12). During the building of the castle a body, supposed to be that of the Emperor Maximus, was found and reverently re-buried. This is the emperor who appears in the *Mabinogion* as Macsen Wledig, who dreams at Rome of a beautiful girl seated in a gold chair with eagles on it in a castle beyond the seas and mountains, and who finds her at last at Caernarvon and marries her. All these associations, or similar ones, would appear to have been present in the minds of Edward and his advisers in the planning and design of this castle.

Conway has a milder look, the product of gently encroaching shadows on its drum towers. Here again the differences between the two fade when compared with the concentric designs of Rhuddlan and of Beaumaris. Rhuddlan, built in the valley of the Clwyd, is of a comparatively simple design but it is Beaumaris (plate 176 and fig. 18) that always arouses admiration for being the most perfect surviving expression of the concentric castle. The complete freedom of the defenders to make their way round the ramparts and to concentrate their fire from any point, the way in which the archers on the inner walls can fire over the heads of their fellows on the outer walls, the complexity of the turns in the entrance from the sea, the strength of the two gatehouses, all these advantages have been provided with the greatest skill and in the most elegant design. It almost seems a pity to record that Beaumaris never saw any siege of any importance and that fifty years after its partial completion nearly all its timbers had perished. But it is to

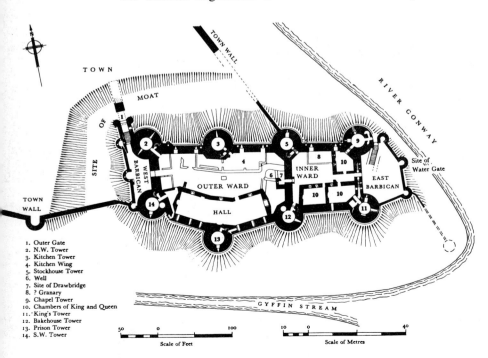

1. Outer Gate
2. N.W. Tower
3. Kitchen Tower
4. Kitchen Wing
5. Stockhouse Tower
6. Well
7. Site of Drawbridge
8. ? Granary
9. Chapel Tower
10. Chambers of King and Queen
11. 'King's Tower
12. Bakehouse Tower
13. Prison Tower
14. S.W. Tower

Fig. 16 *Left* A plan of Conway, Wales. Note the curious kinked great hall, made to follow the lines of the outer wall. The outer gate to the town was particularly strongly defended and so was the division between the outer and inner wards. The royal apartments were in the inner ward.

175 *Right* Caernarvon, Wales. The Eagle Tower, named after the statues of Roman eagles which were among the many sculptures once embellishing the battlements. The tower was the residence of the first constable of the castle, Sir Otto de Grandson who, like James of St George, the architect of the castle, was a Savoyard.

Fig. 18 *Right* Plan of Beaumaris, Wales, showing the perfectly regular layout of this concentric castle. (After HMSO guide)

176 *Below* Beaumaris, Wales. The moat, the south-west corner tower of the outer curtain wall, and the gate next the sea; the mill and the fortifications of the dock giving into the Menai Strait are beyond the tree.

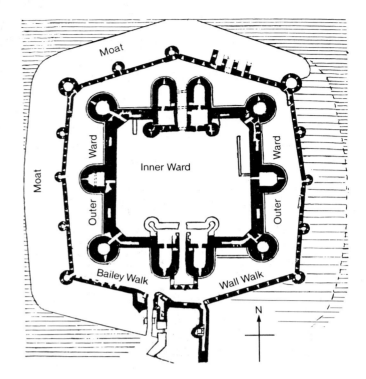

forget one of the chief purposes of a castle to anticipate a history of sieges; the first object was to make rebellion seem vain before it arose and to deter attack by obvious impregnability.

Edward turned from his successful conquest of Wales to attempt a similar victory over the Scots. There, he was to be less happy in the outcome and the huge sums he had spent on the Welsh castles seriously embarrassed the finances of the later part of his reign, especially in the financial crisis of 1296 which was followed in the next year by a constitutional crisis.[28] Castles were constantly in his thoughts and he even had a toy wooden castle made to give to his son who had been born to him in Caernarvon Castle and whom he is said to have presented to his newly conquered subjects as a prince who was born a Welshman and who could speak not a word of English. This toy castle was made at a cost of 44s for the future Edward II in 1290 when he was six by a member of his household.[29]

Castles in Scotland and Ireland

When Edward I turned from Wales to attempt the conquest of Scotland, he found a country where the presence and importance of the castle had already been recognized. Under the influence of Norman-French adventurers, and with the

active help of the Canmore monarchs, feudal institutions came to lowland Scotland in the twelfth century. The castles they built were entirely, it seems, of the motte-and-bailey type although, as we have seen, these were being superseded in England by the stone keep and bailey. Numerous examples of these motte-and-bailey castles remain and several have been excavated. Further north, however, the periphery of Scotland was controlled by Norse jarls, one of whom possibly built the stone keep known as Cubbie Roo's Castle on the island of Wyre in the Orkneys in about 1150. The earliest existing stone castle in Scotland itself is Castle Sween in Argyllshire, probably built in the late eleventh or early twelfth century,[30] consisting of 40 ft (12.2 m) high walls now forming a quadrangular enclosure on a rock in the sea-loch of Sween. These walls were probably in fact a keep. Little is known of its early history, and one has to wait for the thirteenth century, when lowland castles were being built of stone, for Scotland to come well to the forefront of contemporary developments in castle building. The singular round form of Rothesay (plate 380), the triangular ground-plan of Caerlaverock (fig. 19) and Kildrummy, with its great gatehouse and round keep, showing affinities on the one hand with Coucy and on the other with Edward I's castles in Wales, are a few examples that demonstrate this late but notable arrival on the European scene. During the Anglo-Scottish wars, sieges and recaptures of castles, notably Edinburgh (plate 180), and Stirling, played a far more prominent part than they had in Wales and it was in this hard school that the English armies received much of the experience they were to use in France in the Hundred Years War.

During the conquest of Ireland in the twelfth century the

177 *Right* Bodiam, England. One of the most celebrated of English moated castles, Bodiam was built in the years following 1385 by Sir Edward Dalyngrigge, a veteran of the French Wars. It is also typical of the quadrangular castles being built in the fourteenth century. The main entrance is on the other side while a lesser gateway, protected by heavy machicolation, is shown on the left. The main living quarters for its owner were on either flank of the nearest drum tower.

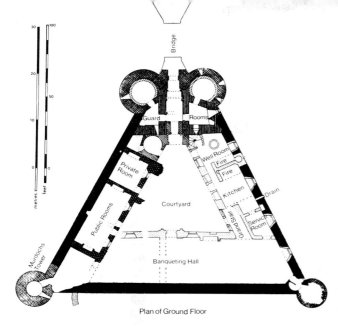

Bridge

Guard Rooms

Private Room

Well Room
Fire
Fire
Kitchen

Public Rooms

Courtyard

Drain

Gate Stair

Service Room

Murdoch's Tower

Banqueting Hall

Plan of Ground Floor

Fig. 19 *Left* Plan of Caerlaverock, Scotland, showing the triangular ground-plan. (After Macgibbon, D. and Ross, T. *The Castellated and Domestic Architecture of Scotland*, 1887)

180 Edinburgh, Scotland. An eighteenth-century view of this most famous of Scottish castles. During the 1745 rebellion it was still of military importance, holding for the Hanoverians against the Young Pretender throughout.

Anglo-Norman adventurers again demonstrated the continuing usefulness of the motte-and-bailey castle. About 150 of these can still be traced, mostly around the perimeter of the central plain.[31] In certain cases the motte was added to existing Irish earthworks, or *raths,* as at Killaloe. As the success of the conquest became assured, so in the thirteenth century the new aristocracy began to build in stone, in a few cases achieving the sophistication of the contemporary European castles as at Trim (plate 181) or Carrickfergus (plate 179).

This chapter began with the Crusader castles in the Holy Land and it must end with the older struggle of Christendom against Islam which still continued bitterly in Spain and Portugal.

178 *Left* Bunratty, Eire. The great hall of this fifteenth-century towerhouse.

179 *Above* Carrickfergus, Northern Ireland. Built on the shores of Belfast Lough *c* 1180–1205, unlike Trim, its keep is joined to the curtain walls.

181 Trim, Eire. The largest Anglo-Norman castle in Ireland, with its square keep and projecting wings, was built *c* 1190–1200. The curtain walls, enclosing an area of more than three acres (300 sq. m) were later, *c* 1220.

Spain and Portugal in the twelfth and thirteenth centuries
One of the most important events to affect the Iberian peninsula
in the twelfth century was the seizure of Lisbon from the Moors
in 1147. A heterogeneous party of adventurers including
Germans, Flemings, and East Anglians had set off for the
second Crusade from Dartmouth in a large number of ships.
They were deflected in their journey by an invitation from the
first king of Portugal, Afonso Henriques (1111-85), to join him
in taking the Moorish citadel and town of Lisbon whose
inhabitants had already repulsed several earlier attempts to
take it. An East Anglian priest wrote an account of the events[32]
in the form of a letter home, addressed to Osbert of Bawdsey.
Afonso could offer the Crusaders no money, only a share in
the spoils if there were any. The Crusaders, who had no overall
commander, and who, according to the account, disputed
vigorously among themselves, nevertheless came to an agree-
ment with him, chiefly under the influence of powerful sermons.
The Moorish city stood on an arm of the Tagus protected on
one side by a tributary, now built over, and the summit of its
defences was a citadel whose place is now occupied by the
later castle of Lisbon (plate 183). For all the expedition's
diversity and lack of notable feudal commanders, it obviously
included many skilled engineers and others versed in the latest
techniques, among them a Pisan engineer killed in the later
assaults, because they made there one of the first recorded uses
of the trebuchet which was worked by relays of a hundred men
at a time (see plate opposite Contents page).

Although the Crusaders easily took the suburbs, they
were brought to a halt by the walls of the city, from which
the Moors taunted them with insults about the infidelity of
their wives at home and with blasphemies against the Christian
religion. The Flemings and Germans were constantly foiled in
their attempts to mine by sorties and missiles and the siege-
tower of the English became stuck in the sand. After six weeks,
however, the Crusaders captured letters which showed not
only that the Moors were facing starvation but that a local
ruler on whom they were depending for relief refused his help
and advised them to buy their way out. This, and a successful
engagement with the Moors at Almada by the Anglo-Normans,
after which they were able to display eighty impaled enemy
heads before the walls of Lisbon, gave heart to the besiegers.
The Germans and Flemings constructed a mine under the
walls of the city with five entrances and completed it in a month.
They then set fire with inflammable material to the supports of
the mine and a large portion of the walls crumbled to the
ground. However, the terrain still suited the defenders who
rapidly constructed a barrier of wood in the breach from which
the attackers were always repulsed. Now it was the turn of the
Anglo-Normans again, who had built a great siege-tower
83 ft (25 m) high aimed to attack a tower on the south-western
corner of the city wall. The incoming tide cut off the men in
the siege-tower from their fellows; the following passage
shows the violence and difficulties of the assault:

'When the Moors observed that the rising tide had cut us off, they
issued in two companies through the gate and attacked our machine
[the siege-tower]. And the others upon the wall, an incredible multitude,

182 *Above right* Guimarães, Portugal. The later medieval castle
replacing the one where the first Portuguese king, Afonso I, was born.

183 *Right* Lisbon, Portugal. A wall-walk in the fifteenth-century castle that
took the place of the earlier Moorish citadel.

brought up articles of wood, together with pitch and flax and oil and every kind of inflammable matter, and hurled them at our engine. And still others discharged an intolerable hail of stones upon us. But there was beneath the wings of our engine, between it and the wall, a penthouse of plaited osiers, which is commonly called a Welsh cat, in which were seven youths from the district of Ipswich who kept it constantly in position . . . And under this some of our men, with the assistance of those who were inside the engine, beat out the burning matter piece by piece as best they could. And others dug trenches underneath the engine and, lying in them, drew away the balls of fire. Still others in the upper storeys poured water through holes upon the hides which were suspended from above, so that the tails hanging in order on the outside irrigated the whole engine. And still others, drawn up in fighting formation, manfully resisted those who had come out from the gate. So the engine was defended through that night by a prodigious effort, very few of our men being wounded, thanks to the protection of God, but the greater part of the Moors being cut to pieces in hand-to-hand or distant combat.'[33]

The knights and soldiers defended their tower for two days and nights before being relieved. When the siege-tower was pushed to a distance of only 4ft (1.2 m) from the wall in a position enabling the Crusaders to lower the drawbridge, the Moors capitulated after a siege of seventeen weeks. Afonso was thus established on a basis of firm territorial power: Portugal begins her separate existence from the time of this siege.

In the same year Alfonso VII of Castile took Cordoba, sacked Granada and Seville, and for a time held Almería (plates 13 and 14). Most successes on both sides were short-lived; there was a wide area in the centre of Spain so fought over that no one held it long enough to build castles there, thus giving rise in twelfth-century France to the expression 'castles in Spain' for a much longed-for but impossible dream.[34] The situation had changed by the end of the century. Just as the great Christian successes of the previous century had provoked the terrifying reaction of the Almoravides, so retribution came again in the shape of the Almohades who dealt a terrible blow to the Castilians at the battle of Alarcos in 1195. The king who lost then was Alfonso VIII and seventeen years later, in 1212, under the banner of a Crusade he gathered an army of 60,000 knights at Toledo and marched south to meet the Almohade caliph, Mohammed-al-Nazir, at Las Navas de Tolosa. There the Spanish footmen armed with spears managed to hold off the mounted Moslems with the help of the Knights of Santiago after the Knights of Calatrava had been virtually destroyed. This great Christian victory finally assured the success of the Reconquest and, although Granada was not to fall for another 280 years, the Moslems never again threatened to rule the peninsula.

The knightly orders deservedly played a notable part in the final victory and it is their castles that form the most interesting examples of military architecture in the Spain of this period.[35] The Knights of Calatrava took their name from a castle (now called Calatrava la Vieja, lying between Toldeo and Cordoba) which even the Templars had refused to defend. Though themselves driven from it by the Almohades the numbers of their other conventual castles grew. After the victory of Las Navas de Tolosa they transferred their head-quarters to Calatrava la Nueva in about 1216. There they built a great church with a superb rose window, a keep with double curtain walls, and monastic quarters. An earlier and somewhat similar castle belonging to the Templars is Loarre in Huescà

(plate 95), a fascinating complex of religious and military buildings.

It was the concentration of power and wealth in the hands of the kings and the orders that gave them such superiority in the possession of castles. The great, privately owned castles in the rest of Europe, such as Coucy, Caerphilly, or some of those on the Rhine, were unknown in the peninsula while the finest examples of castle building in Spain will be discussed in Chapter 7.

184 Calatrava la Nueva, Spain. The chapel, with its rose window, of this castle which from about 1216 onwards was the headquarters of the Order of the Knights of Calatrava.

HOHENSTAUFENS AND COMMUNES-GERMAN, AUSTRIAN, SWISS, AND ITALIAN CASTLES OF THE 12TH AND 13TH CENTURIES

185 The Wartburg, E. Germany. A romantic etching by Preller of this famous castle at Eisenach, one of the great centres of secular literature and learning in the Germany of the early thirteenth century.

Castles under the Hohenstaufens

In 1152 the princes of Germany chose as their king Frederick I, Barbarossa, partly in the hope that he would be strong enough to put an end to the quarrels that had lasted since the investiture contest. The lands and powers of the Emperor had been severely curtailed in the disturbances following the investiture contest and the social changes that took place at the same time, and Barbarossa, himself a member of the new nobility which had arisen at the expense of the imperial lands, was firmly committed to the new feudal society. He came of a family noted for its castle building, and for the founding of towns. Of his grandfather, Frederick of Swabia, the historian, Otto of Freising, says, 'Duke Frederick always drags a fortress with him at the tail of his horse'.[1] Barbarossa's own lands were largely concentrated in Swabia, then including part of modern Switzerland. His high awareness of the political role of the Emperor in Christendom led him to reassert the imperial rights in Italy, at the same time furthering his dynastic ambitions by making Swabia the centre of a greatly enlarged empire instead of an outpost. His more energetic predecessors had derived most of their basic power from the extent of their demesnes, and Barbarossa devoted great attention to the increase of his lands, building an estimated 350 palaces and castles and setting them under the command of *ministeriales* for their administration. These *ministeriales* gradually achieved more and more freedom, either as they received more power from the Emperor, or when in periods of disturbance they were able to use the castles they were entrusted with as bases for personal advancement. One *ministerialis*, Markward of Anweiler, rose to great power as Henry VI's lieutenant in Italy. Another, Werner of Bolland, under Barbarossa, possessed seventeen castles and had over 1000 knights in his service.[2] This class also produced many of the great poets of the age and played a significant part in the civilization of the Hohenstaufen period.

Imperial palaces and castles

Deeply influenced by the classical revival of his era, Barbarossa saw himself as the heir not only of Charlemagne but also of the whole ancient Roman Empire. He introduced a new ostentation into the buildings of his reign, a policy to be followed in Germany by his son and successor, Henry VI, and in Italy by his grandson, Frederick II. Efforts were made to emulate the open disposition of the Carolingian palaces, such as Aachen, and, according to Rahewin who continued Otto of Freising's history, he restored those at Ingelheim and Nijmegen. Rahewin described Barbarossa's own palace at Kaiserslautern

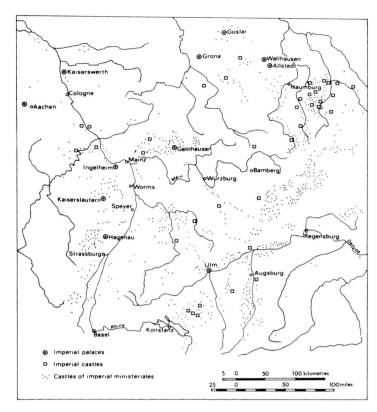

Fig. 20 Map of imperial palaces, imperial castles, and castles of imperial *ministeriales* in the Hohenstaufen period. (After Bäuml)

as built of red sandstone and surrounded on one side by a wall and on the other by a fishpond like a lake. Thus the preference of the imperial court for life in *Pfalzen* or palaces was to have a profound effect on the development of the German castle. There were many imperial castles or *Kaiserburgen,* such as Nuremberg, but these were administrative centres placed for the protection of trade routes, and not sufficiently luxurious for the Emperor. The palaces for the most part were imperial; the Wartburg at Eisenach[3] (plate 185) is one of the few princely examples, and that was built by the Landgraves of Thuringia, members of a new rank attached to the imperial cause and intended to offset the power of the great territorial magnates. The German preference for a plan based on the open court is evidence of the pacifying and civilizing effect of the Emperors at their strongest, and many of the castles occupied by imperial *ministeriales* include smaller versions of their masters' residences, though contained within strong walls. But, to a palace such as Goslar, fortifications were added only as an afterthought; the comforts and amenities of life were not cramped or deprived of light simply because of military needs and precautions. The effect on the design of castles was, however, to delay the adoption of French improvements in flanking, to continue to trust in the choice of an impregnable site, and to stick to the more haphazard arrangement already mentioned as common to Germany. Goslar is the most famous of the imperial *Pfalzen,* now almost entirely a nineteenth-century reconstruction (plate 186) of what it presumably looked like in about 1200. Many previous Emperors had held court there, notably Henry III. Its most outstanding feature is the *Kaisersaal* on the first floor with its arcaded Romanesque windows opening on to the courtyard so that crowds could watch the ceremonies taking place within. Another very

beautiful palace, now in ruins, lies at Gelnhausen, Hesse (plate 187), which was built by Barbarossa who made the town an imperial city in 1170 and which was also a favourite residence of his son, Henry VI. At Gelnhausen, however, the palace was completely surrounded by a strong military enceinte and guarded by a *Bergfried.*[4] In contrast to these palaces are the imperial castles such as Nuremberg, restored since the war, Eger, Bavaria, and Trifels (plate 93), which were all sites previously belonging to other families, taken over by the Emperors. They lay on or near important trading routes, and at this time there was a remarkable commercial growth in German-speaking lands. The castle at Nuremberg controlled the route from the important city of Ratisbon (Regensburg) to the upper Main. Eger was no less important for trade from

186 *Top* Goslar, W. Germany. A view of the imperial palace set in the Harz mountains. It was reconstructed in the last century to its probable form in the early thirteenth century. Note the extent of windows and the general lack of defensive characteristics.

187 *Bottom* Gelnhausen, W. Germany. A nineteenth-century engraving of this important Hohenstaufen fortified palace, showing some of the rich Romanesque carvings that still remain.

Bohemia to the Main valley and thence to the rest of Germany. Trifels, which is near Annweiler, lies near the great route from Speyer to the Saar, thus connecting the middle Rhine area with France. Barbarossa enlarged Trifels in 1153 and he is credited with the residential buildings at Eger in 1175.[5] Nuremberg, Eger and Hagenau, in Alsace, are embellished with double chapels on two levels intended to separate the imperial suite from the lesser court followers at their devotions.

The castle and the growth of trade

The trade which Barbarossa tried to nurse became a new and fruitful source of revenue to the nobility across whose lands the merchants had to pass. The cities themselves burst out of their old limits and had to build new fortifications. The richer burghers built themselves tower houses of stone, of which one example survives at Trier. The towns were convenient sources of wealth and the bishops and dukes built castles in or near towns for purposes of administration and taxes. In some cases too, they may have been urged by the same reasons that made Philip of Alsace build his great castle in Ghent – to control the proud burghers who had constructed so many fortified towers in the city. The effect of trade on castles is particularly clear in the Rhine valley; under Barbarossa there were nineteen castles acting as toll stations levying fees on the merchants; after his death the number rose to sixty-two[6], far too many either to attain their object or to be endurable for long, and in the thirteenth century the cities formed leagues to fight their oppressors. Many of the most famous castles of the Rhine were built mainly as toll stations. The archbishops of Mainz, Cologne, and Trier ringed their lands with castles, one of the most famous being that on the Drachenfels (plate 188), constructed by Archbishop Arnold of Cologne in 1147 on an old site, and previously fortified against Henry V in 1117. Bad Godesberg (plate 193) was begun by Archbishop Theoderich I, also of Cologne, in 1210.[7] The best preserved of the Rhine castles, the Marksburg near Braubach (plates 190, 191 and 192), first mentioned in 1231, continuously added to, and restored by the last Kaiser's favourite architect, Bodo Ebhardt, to its

appearance in the late Middle Ages, was not, however, an episcopal castle. Its grouping of the *Bergfried,* with the residential quarters superbly placed on the summit of an impregnable hill (it was the only Rhine castle to escape capture in the Thirty Years War) provides one of the most characteristic examples of the West German castle.

Further south, the increase in trade across the Alps en-

188 *Left* Drachenfels, W. Germany. An episcopal castle built 1050 ft (315 m) above the Rhine by an archbishop of Cologne in 1147, it was celebrated in *Childe Harold* by Byron. Siegfried is said to have killed, in a cave in the mountainside, the dragon guarding the hoard of the Nibelungs and then bathed in its blood; from Tombleson's *Views of the Rhine,* 1832.

189 *Above* The Emperor Frederick I Barbarossa depicted here as a Crusader *c* 1188. It was during his journey to the Holy Land to join the Third Crusade that he was drowned while crossing the Anti-Taurus mountains. *The Vatican,* Vat. Lat. 2001.

190 *Right* The Marksburg, Braubach, W. Germany. As a prospective attacker might have seen it, a view of the only Rhineland fortress to resist capture in the Thirty Years War, now restored to its probable appearance in the late fifteenth century. Its building was probably begun in the early thirteenth century by the counts of Eppstein with the square central tower or *Bergfried*; round this were grouped the palace (on the other side), the building known as the Rheinbau (centre), and the Kaiser Heinrich Tower (far right), named after the Emperor Henry IV but much later, which contains the chapel of St Mark dedicated in 1437, from which the castle derives its name. As with numbers of other Rhine castles, its purpose was the regulation of trade and to guard its owner's right to tolls on passing merchants and their goods. In 1282 Rudolf of Habsburg granted the nearby toll of Boppard to the Katzenelnbogen family who controlled the castle. They had also to defend their rights to the toll of Braubach from the claims of the archbishop of Mainz.

couraged the building of yet more castles in valleys followed by important routes and in the passes. These castles never reached the size or grandeur of many on the Rhine and generally consisted of a single tower with minor outworks, as at Kirnstein in the Inntal, though this does not apply to Churburg on the Swiss borders of Austria, later the seat of the lords of Matsch. Many belonged to bishops or great families who naturally preferred more comfortable areas to dwell in and therefore put *ministeriales* in charge of them to further their interests. Barbarossa had a strong political interest in the Alpine castles because he wanted to keep open the passes to Italy. The low passes to the Adige were too vulnerable to pressure from Verona and after 1157 he had to depend on the western passes to Lake Como, either the Septimer Pass or the Splügen Pass by way of Chur, both leading to Chiavenna. He was most careful, for example, not to offend the bishop of Chur, even though the latter would not support him against the Pope, and despite the fact that Barbarossa already had an ally in the Vogt of Chur.[8]

The castles of the knights

In general the castle in German-speaking lands followed the plan already settled by the end of the eleventh century and

194 Wildenberg, W. Germany. A reconstruction of a thirteenth-century castle built on a spur. Note the care that has gone into protecting the chief line of approach. The residential quarters are provided with many windows.

191 *Previous pages, left* The Marksburg, Braubach, W. Germany. The gatehouse to the upper castle, one of the series of gatehouses guarding the constantly turning and rising approach, a characteristic of German hill or mountain castles built on sites so naturally strong that all defences were concentrated on the entrances.

192 *Previous page* The Marksburg, Braubach, W. Germany. A window seat in the residential quarters. The general lack of chairs made the provision of window seats a necessity. Note the thickness of the wall.

193 *Above* Bad Godesberg, W. Germany. The ruins of another episcopal castle on the Rhine; from a steel engraving *c* 1840.

195 *Right* Dankwarderode, Brunswick, W. Germany. A woodcut of *c* 1880 showing Henry the Lion's palace before its reconstruction. The palace and the cathedral of St Blasius were completely enclosed by a large defensive enceinte. Outside stands a lion, the largest known example of Romanesque bronze casting, erected by Henry the Lion.

described in Chapter 2. The palaces of the Emperors had an effect in influencing their subjects' desire for more spacious living quarters within their fortifications. If these were not always on the scale of the Wartburg (plate 185) or Henry the Lion's Dankwarderode at Brunswick (plate 195), nevertheless many castles reveal their builders' developing taste for greater comfort and ease. Stone was used more frequently for the perimeter walls which could then be provided with tile-covered wall-walks. By the beginning of the thirteenth century, many castles, such as Münzenberg, Wetterau[9] (plate 197), and Wildenberg im Odenwald[10] (plate 194), were provided with two *Bergfrieden,* to cover different areas of approach. The residential quarters with their halls, their rooms, their up-to-date sanitary arrangements, bear out the high standard of living of the knightly classes which is otherwise confirmed by the evidence of manuscript illuminations and the descriptions of interiors and manners left by the poets. Many of the most attractive castles of this period are in Austria where, under the Babenberg dukes, the minnesingers were particularly en-

couraged. Among them are two castles, both subsequently much altered, Heidenreichstein (plate 198) built by the Burggraf von Gars in 1190 and generally considered one of the most important Austrian *Wasserburgen*, and Rappottenstein (plates 201 and 348) begun in 1157 by Rapoto von Kuenringer.[11]

One of the chief reasons for the highly individual nature of the German castle and for its late surrender to French influence is a geographical one: the large numbers of mountainous and hilly sites which provide naturally strong positions close to much-frequented routes such as the Rhine. It was the form of the site that causes the great varieties of ground-plan, whether roughly triangular as at Trifels (plate 93), or elliptical as at Münzenberg or just irregular as at Wimpfen. Many of these positions could be approached only by one possible route and so all the main defences are concentrated on the gate and its approaches. Here there was no possibility of a policy of concentric defence and so the castle would be divided, like Wildenberg, into sectors cut off from one another by deep ditches and passable only by drawbridges. In some areas, especially in the Neckar valley, in the Palatinate, and on the Rhine, use was made of the *Schildmauer*, an exceptionally strong wall provided with galleries and arrowslits, as at Neuscharfeneck (plate 199). In many cases the chapel was included in the gate tower as if to bring heavenly power to bear on the place where it was most needed.

Behind these strongly defended approaches stood the residential quarters which in certain castles could be very scattered. These were the castles known as *Ganerbenburgen*, that is castles under joint ownership by inheritance. This arrangement was also known in the Midi where brothers or different families would take different parts of a castle and make separate homes. One of the most notable German examples is the castle of Salzburg in Franconia[12] which was owned by the bishops of Würzburg and divided into six sectors. Burg Eltz, on a tributary of the Mosel (see jacket front, plates 145 and 146), first mentioned in 1157, became a *Ganerbenburg*, and so did the mainly fourteenth-century Rhine castle, Schönburg at Oberwesel (plates 102 and 200). As time went on the number of heirs increased so that Münzenberg, for example, the major part of whose construction began in the early thirteenth century under the Hohenstaufen *ministerialis*, Kuno von Hagen, came to acquire as many as forty-eight!

The conquest of the east

Barbarossa and his son, Henry VI, brought a firm and settled government to the German parts of their Empire. This settlement largely survived their deaths because, although Frederick II (1212-50), Barbarossa's grandson, preferred southern Italy as his place of residence, the Hohenstaufen chancery and network of *ministeriales* remained to protect his German interests. But the fascination that Italy exercised on these Emperors left them little time for one of the most important movements of their period. This was the intensification of the conquest of the east from the Slavs, and other heathen tribes, which led to the development of the castles of the Teutonic Knights. Although Barbarossa settled the Pleissenland and the Erzgebirge under the direction of his *ministeriales*, the great leader of the eastern conquests during Barbarossa's reign was Henry the Lion, head of the Welf family, son-in-law of Henry II Plantagenet, and until his fall in 1181 virtually an independent monarch in the north. A great builder, notable at Lübeck and at Brunswick, where he was responsible for the castle of Dank-

Chur.

196 *Top* Chur, Switzerland. This town played a vital role in controlling one of Barbarossa's main routes into Italy; from Merian the elder, *Topographia Helvetiae*, 1644.

197 *Above* Münzenberg, W. Germany. The two round *Bergfrieden* of this early thirteenth-century castle act as watchtowers covering the main lines of approach. The elliptical ground plan of the castle follows the lines of the hill.

warderode, erecting opposite it in about 1160 the bronze lion which symbolized his ambitions, his conquests in the east were to make new lands suffer the power of the castle as an instrument of domination. His fall from power was to arouse the sleeping quarrels of Germany into the Guelf-Ghibelline wars in which Italy as well was to be fully involved as a result of Barbarossa's fatal fascination for control of the south.

Although leaders such as Henry the Lion and Albert of Brandenburg played an important part in the conquest of the east a steadier and stronger impetus was given by the merchants of the cities on the Baltic coast which formed the Hanseatic League whose beginnings can be dated partly from the treaty concluded between Hamburg and Lübeck in 1241. German merchants made their power felt in Scandinavia and they were responsible for the remarkable fortifications of Visby (plate 202) in Gotland in the thirteenth and fourteenth century.

The winning of the east from the heathen Prussians and other Slav tribes has been called the greatest achievement of the German people in the Middle Ages; as with the Norman expansion over Europe, the castle was to play a notable role in the settlement. As early as 1108 the Germans in the west were incited to move by inflammatory proclamations such as the following:

'[the Slavs] are an abominable people but their land is very rich in flesh, honey, grain, birds, and abounding in all products of the fertility of the earth, so that none can be compared unto it. Wherefore, O Saxons, Franks, Lotharingians, men of Flanders most famous—here you can both save your souls, and, if it please you, acquire the best of land to live in.'[13]

Later in 1147 the bishops of Magdeburg, Brandenburg, and Halberstadt preached a crusade against the heathen and great numbers of peasants were encouraged to go east, attracted by the promise of lands, special exemptions and freedoms. As many as two million, it has been estimated,

199 *Above* Neuscharfeneck, W. Germany. A reconstruction of this thirteenth-century castle showing the immense *Schildmauer*.

200 *Right* Schönburg, W. Germany. A rectangular *Bergfried*, one of two at this Rhine castle. The other, a round tower, can be seen in plate 102.

settled on Slav land. In many parts the freedoms offered meant that the nobility never acquired the dominance and superior position over the peasantry they had acquired in the west. The princes kept the rights of castle building strictly in their own hands and only in some areas, as on the borders of Brandenburg, allowed the erection of private castles as a protection against border raids from the Poles.

The final success of the conquest of the east was assured by the involvement of the order of the Teutonic Knights who were to found, in areas now belonging to Poland, Russia and East Germany, one of the most modern of medieval states—a state which by the celibate nature of the order did not depend for continuity on hereditary succession but on devotion to a religious ideal and a powerful administrative service based on a network of castles and fortified towns which grew up round the castles.

The Teutonic Order was founded in the Holy Land first of all as an order devoted to the sick in the late twelfth century. Too late to achieve there the authority of the Templars and the Hospitallers, the Teutonic Knights only possessed one notable fortress, Montfort or Starkenberg, now in Israel, which Frederick II secured for them in 1221. The rule was strict. Members lived in common, slept on hard beds, and were required to attend daily services. The knights took monastic vows, adding a further one that they would devote themselves to the cure of the sick and to fighting the heathen. It was the heathen religion of the Slavs that gave them the great opportunity to conquer which was denied them by the decline of Frankish power in the Latin Kingdom. Gradually they were to withdraw from the Holy Land as the chances of success in Prussia grew. Even though their territorial ambitions had been made plain in Hungary, from which they had already been

198 Heidenreichstein, Austria. The most important Austrian *Wasserburg*, this castle was founded in the twelfth century. The square *Bergfried* (centre, distance) is thirteenth-century. Later numerous additions include the great round tower whose hoarding is included in the conical tiling. The castle underwent sieges by Hussites and by rebellious peasants.

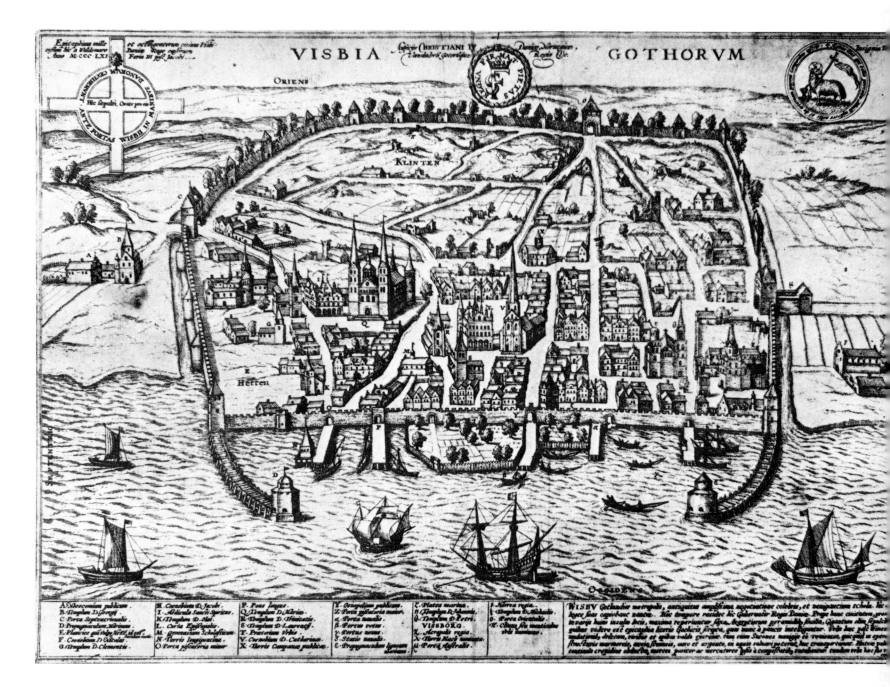

201 *Left* Rappottenstein, Austria. The defended approach to the castle built
on massive rocks. Founded in the twelfth century by Rapoto von
Kuenringer, the castle received many later additions including a particularly
fine arcaded courtyard in the sixteenth century. The curtain walls support
Italianate merlons.

202 *Above* Visby, Gotland, Sweden. A view *c* 1580 of the thirteenth-century
town walls of this once immensely important mercantile centre.

expelled, in 1226 the Polish duke of Masovia invited the Order
to subdue the Prussians. By 1233 the Order had built the
fortified town of Marienwerder, now Kwidzyn (plate 321). At
first their castles were wooden structures but later in the century
they began to build in brick. Part of their success depended on
their understanding of sea power, perhaps, as with Edward I,
a legacy of service in the Holy Land, and on the close connections they kept with the Hanseatic League. They met
reverses, as when an army of the Order was defeated on the
ice of Lake Peipus in 1242 by Alexander Nevsky defending
Novgorod. They had to put down an uprising of the Slavs
that lasted for twenty years but by 1283, by which time

Marienburg, now Malbork (plate 318), was built, they were
masters of the country and were able to produce in the
fourteenth century the most sophisticated and original forms
of the German castle. Just as the French and Norman castle
builders had needed the pressures of conquest to develop their
fortifications to their fullest extent, so at last the German
builders received and reacted to the challenge of maintaining
a permanent hold on the new lands they had seized.

The interregnum and the first Habsburg
These influences did not react on the castle in the older settled
regions of Germany until the fourteenth century. For the first
half of the century Frederick II ruled by proxy, giving more
and more power to the great princes so that he did not need
to be distracted from his ambitions in Italy. After his death the
strife between the cities and the nobility which led to the
formation of the leagues continued during the miserable period
of the interregnum 1250-73. This was the time of the robber
barons when, from impregnable castles such as Rheinfels
(plate 203) or those along the Danube, they could plunder with

203 Rheinfels, St Goar, W. Germany. Built in 1245 by Count Dieter von Katzenelnbogen as a toll station, it was later converted into one of the strongest castles on the Rhine and provided with a great Renaissance palace by the Landgrave Philip II of Hesse-Cassel. It was captured by the French and blown up in 1794; from Tombleson's *Views of the Rhine*, 1832.

were not in the countryside, which had been the Hohenstaufen practice, but were placed in or near cities, or in certain cases cities were founded near imperial castles. Special groups of knights were formed for the defence of the city castles in case of war. The commander of these groups, the *Burggraf*, was often also entrusted with the administration of the surrounding imperial estates.[15]

Castles in Bohemia and Hungary

One of the chief reasons for the success of the Germans in colonizing the east was their genius for creating permanent urban settlements. This meant that they were welcomed as colonizers where they did not come to conquer, as in Bohemia and Hungary. Strong native rulers saw the advantages of increased wealth from their trade. The numbers of towns and castles in close combination grew; for example, Prague dominated by the Hradschin, or Bratislava, then in Hungary. The Přemyslid rulers of Bohemia encouraged German knights and *ministeriales* to settle as counterweight to the unruly native Slav nobility. In the thirteenth century the chief royal seat was the castle of Zvíkov (Klingenberg) which, although following the characteristics of a German castle, was adorned with a richly ornamented chapel designed by a French architect. French designers also worked in Hungary, notably the famous Villard de Honnecourt (see plate 112). The kings of Hungary had, under the impact of the Mongol invasion of 1241, been forced to relax their strict control over the building of private fortifications. Already in the twelfth century the royal castles included those of Sárospatak and Esztergom and these were later rivalled by many castles built by the nobles.[16] German settlers were especially prominent in Transylvania where the largely peasant population were later to protect themselves by castle-like fortifications round their churches and villages.

The castle in Scandinavia

German influence also spread into Scandinavia which, in the twelfth century, began to see castles being built in many parts. Although Denmark had already known a variety of fortifications ranging from the late tenth-century Trelleborg to examples of the motte-and-bailey, it was in this period that the first stone castles were built. The Danevirke still acted as the line of the March to the south, and in the reign of Waldemar I (1157-82) it was further strengthened in parts with stone or brick walls. The bishops had come, in the late christianization of the country, to play an extraordinarily powerful part, not always, however, making their flocks as up-to-date as their position might have warranted. At the battle of Fotevik in 1134 five Danish bishops died in the defeat of Danish infantry by German cavalry, one of the battles which, like Hastings and Homburg on the Unstrut, demonstrated the general superiority of the trained mounted soldier in the warfare of the time. Other great ecclesiastics were foremost in the building of castles, including Archbishop Eskil who constructed a stone castle at Søborg in Zeeland in about 1150 on a site previously occupied by an octagonal wooden

ease in the knowledge that there was no central authority capable of dealing with them, when the value of money had risen and that of land had gone down, and when the old values of knighthood were in decay and were satirized. This last development is seen particularly clearly in the depiction of the foolish hero of *Meier Helmbrecht*, although in his case the authorities manage to catch up with him after his career as squire to a local knight, robbing, raping, and murdering comes to an end, and, when after being blinded and mutilated, he is hanged by his fellow peasants – a fate his father warns him of at the outset by relating a terrifying series of dreams. By the time that Rudolph of Habsburg was made king, in 1273, most of the imperial possessions had fallen into the hands of private individuals. One example of how this happened is shown by the imperial castle of Landskron which Frederick II gave in charge to the *ministerialis*, Gerhard of Sinzig. Even before Frederick's death he was calling himself *dominus de Landscrone* and after 1250 he gave up using his family name altogether and became a noble with an independent lordship.[14] Rudolph of Habsburg, whose family was named after the castle shown in plate 61, and whose chief family lands were in Alsace, began a systematic policy of regaining imperial lands. By defeating and killing Ottakar of Bohemia in battle in 1278 he gained possession of the territories of the defunct Babenberg dukes of Austria, a victory which established the basis for the later successes of his dynasty. Rudolph's ambitions were infinitely smaller in scope than those of the Hohenstaufens but his concentration on setting his lands in order was to have lasting effects. He provided military security for the imperial estates by renewing the network of imperial castles, such as Nuremberg, which had fallen into abeyance. The castles Rudolph built himself, however,

204 An illumination from the *Grandes Chroniques de France* by Jean Fouquet. Charles V of France is giving a banquet in honour of the Emperor Charles IV. Among the guests are Wenceslas, king of the Romans and son of Charles IV, the archbishop of Rheims and bishops of other towns. Below is a representation of the embarkation for Crusade, and the taking of Jerusalem. Note the crenellations on the ship and on the gold 'boats' on the table. *Paris, Bibliothèque Nationale*, Ms. fr. 2813, fo 473.

ꝛenmierement fiſt laꝛceneſſ
de Reims ⸱ Apꝛes ſeoıt
lempereur⸱ Apꝛes ſeoıt
le ꝛoy ⸱ A dioıne on mılıeu
du front de la ſale⸱ Apꝛes
le Roy de france ſeoıt le ꝛoy

des ꝛomaıns⸱ Et auoıt autant de dıſtance
du ⸱ Roy au Roy des ꝛomaıns come du
Roy a lempereur⸱ Et auoıent lempereur
le Roy et le Roy des ꝛomaıns chaſcun ſe
pairement vn cıel de dꝛap doꝛ boꝛde de velu
au aus armes de france⸱ et par deſſus ceulx

tower. In its layout his new castle probably owed much to Goslar for its inspiration. In 1211 Archbishop Absalom built the fortress (now almost completely disappeared) which formed the nucleus of Copenhagen. Many of these castles have, as in the case of Nyborg, been incorporated in later buildings or they have since disappeared because of the successful growth of the towns they nurtured. As the Danish monarchy grew strong in the early thirteenth century, so the number of castles brought directly under the royal power, such as Hammershus with its great keep on the island of Bornholm, increased.

Norway scarcely knew feudal institutions and the number of castles, again either ecclesiastical or royal, was few. Sweden, on the other hand, had to be protected from the inroads of pirates on its east coast at the end of the twelfth century by a series of castles. Flanking was introduced there in the later thirteenth century in the walls of Visby, nearly two miles long, whose German inspiration is shown by their resemblance to the walls of Cologne. Kalmar, a Swedish royal castle of late in the same century, introduced the French fashion for round corner towers, but it remained exceptional in that country for some time.

The castles of Holland

The lack of good building stone in many parts of the Netherlands meant that it was not until the thirteenth century, when techniques of brickbuilding were more advanced, that permanent castles became general in Holland. A few examples of stone ring-walls remain from the twelfth century and earlier at Utrecht, Leyden and Horn, showing the characteristics of the perimeter plan that was retained at Ghent. In the thirteenth century Floris IV, count of Holland, gave a great impetus to the building of castles with Muiden (plate 205), which shows strong French influence in its drum towers and rectangular layout, and with his great hall, the *Ridderzaal*, in his palace, Het Binnenhof, now the seat of the Dutch government at the Hague. The low-lying nature of the land lent itself to the development of the *Wasserburg* or water castle and numerous examples exist of castles, both of regular and irregular ground-plan, making use of natural and artificial waterways in their defences.

Barbarossa in Italy

Although the German cities were flourishing in the second half of the twelfth century, they were widely scattered and thinly populated compared with the cities of northern Italy. Rich from the Crusades and the expansion of trade, enjoying a high standard of literacy compared with other parts of Europe, the communes of Milan and the other great cities had evolved a political system that was very difficult for outsiders to comprehend or countenance. Otto of Freising says that of the feudal rulers of the north, by 1160, only the bishop of Asti and the marquis of Montferrat had escaped the dominion of one of the cities.[17] He also notes with some horror that the communes made knights of men of inferior station, 'workers of the low mechanical crafts', in their efforts to have at their

206 San Gimignano. Italy. The famous towers of this small Tuscan town which still give a good idea of the density of fortifications which once was a feature of great numbers of Italian cities; from a lithograph by E. Ciceri, 1863.

command a large enough body of mounted soldiers owing the city cavalry service.

Something must be said on the origins of the different political system of northern Italy. After the break-up of the Carolingian empire the bishops had become the natural leaders of each town, exercising either comital or *de facto* authority. Imperial authority had been reasserted by numerous expeditions in the eleventh century but, in the need to gain allies, rights would be granted to compliant cities. For example, in 1081 Henry IV had agreed with Lucca to build no palace in the city and no castles within a distance of six miles.[18] By the middle of the twelfth century the main matters of government, the provision of defence, administration, and the law, had in most cities become the responsibility of the commune, the body of local landowners, nobles, merchants, and notaries (any one of whom might come under all these categories) who had taken over the power of the bishops or the lord. The interdependence of city and countryside meant that nobles came to live in the cities to be close to the centres of power and that merchants bought land outside. There was great social mobility while at the same time much respect was paid to the ideals of chivalry. The nobles who came to live in the cities and towns brought with them from the countryside the design of the tall, generally rectangular watchtowers and these they added to their town houses. These towers are mentioned as early as about 1100 in Pisa when the consuls tried to regulate the height to which they could be built. The violence of city life and the never-ceasing vendettas between rival family groups made it essential to possess a castle in the city which could stand up to siegecraft. Families that were not powerful enough individually would form *consorzerie,* or formal alliances for mutual defence and for constructing a tower and house in common. In a contract of 1177 made in Bologna, the purpose of the tower is given as defence and for harming the enemy or enemies of the *consorzeria*.[19] In spite of the close concentration with which they were built, there are accounts of siege engines being used

205 The Muiderslot, Muiden, Holland. One of the most notable Dutch brick castles, this was begun by Count Floris IV of Holland in the thirteenth century and was added to later in the fifteenth and seventeenth centuries. Machicolation is confined to the sunken entrance but a covered wall-walk runs the length of the curtain walls.

against them, and Benjamin of Tudela, a Jewish traveller in the 1160s, describes how in Genoa they fought one another from the tops of towers. Although most of these towers have now disappeared, a number remain. Many old prints of Florence give us an impression of how the city bristled with lean, rectangular towers, to which families fled from attack in

207 *Below* Bologna, Italy. A seventeenth-century view by Matthaeus Merian in his *Topographia Italiae,* showing the extent of the fortifications and some of the family towers.

208 *Right* Castel Ursino, Catania, Sicily. The powerful drum towers which characterize this castle built for Frederick II *c* 1239. The interior disposition of the corner towers is based on the octagon. Note, on the right, the lava from the eruption of 1669.

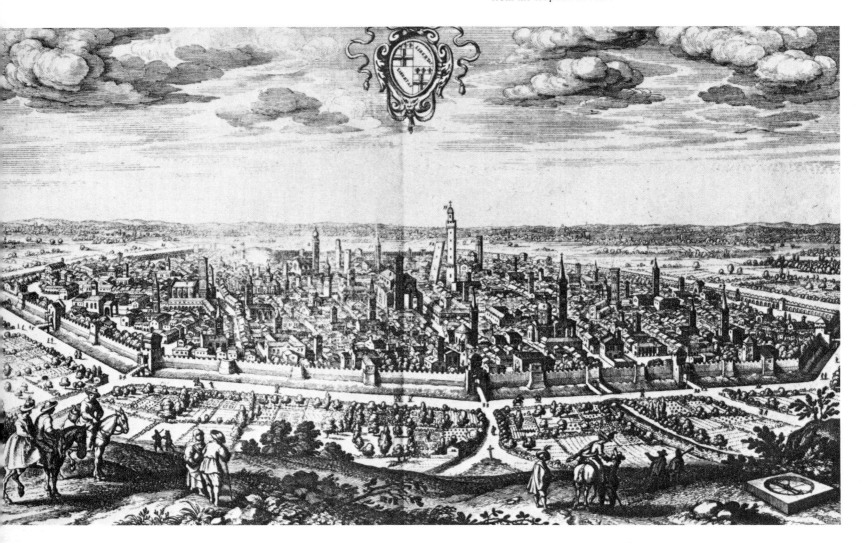

quarrels that lasted for generations. San Gimignano has thirteen remaining out of forty-eight (or, traditionally, seventy-six); in Bologna (plate 207) only two famous towers are left out of about 180. In Rome the Frangipani family made a series of fortresses within the confines of the Colosseum from the safety of which they terrified the Popes. This violence was reflected on a wider scale in the wars the cities of the north fought to secure the mastery of trading routes.

Barbarossa was drawn into Italian politics partly because on his way to be crowned Emperor at Rome and to curb the king of Sicily, he wished to be accepted as peacemaker by the northern cities, a role in which he had enjoyed some success in Germany. His peace-making involved him in some of the bloodiest wars of the twelfth century and these campaigns of his are thought to have introduced to the Germans the most up-to-date techniques of siege warfare. Otto of Freising, for example, describes the use of mining at the siege of the castle of Tortona in 1155 during Barbarossa's first invasion of Italy as 'a quite unusual device' when it had been known for years in other parts of Europe – though the preponderance of mountain

castles and *Wasserburgen* in Germany, neither of which type could usually be mined, would be enough to explain this. In 1158 Barbarossa besieged Milan for a month and forced it to surrender. He installed a magistrate or *podestà* who took over the tolls, exacted new taxes, and used forced labour in the building of imperial castles.

The difficulties Barbarossa had to overcome in taking cities and the barbarisms to which both sides resorted are shown by his siege of the small city of Crema[20] in 1160 which, although defended by double walls and a ditch, could be invested from all sides. At one point, Frederick ordered prisoners, earlier sent to him from Milan and Crema, to be bound to the front of a tower which was then pushed up to the walls and lit with candles at night. His hopes that the Cremese would spare their relations and not attack the tower were proved wrong, and the tower was repulsed. Both sides slaughtered their prisoners in the sight of their friends. Hunger and disease finally forced Crema to surrender after six months. Milan rebelled and again Barbarossa besieged it continuously from 1160 until 1162 when it surrendered, a victory he compelled by building a

series of castles which could prevent all supplies of food from reaching the city; this time he razed Milan to the ground. But he had entirely underestimated the power of the Lombard cities and the importance of the site of Milan. One result of the strong opposition to him was the founding of the fortress town of Alessándria on the Tanaro in northern Italy, named after the Pope he was fighting against. In 1167 the other cities of the Lombard League started to rebuild and it was not until 1174 that Barbarossa was free enough to invade Italy in order to punish the rebels. In 1176 the Lombard cities won a decisive victory over the Emperor at the battle of Legnano, a turning point from which many events followed. Henry the Lion, Barbarossa's chief vassal, had refused to come to his aid in the campaign that led to Legnano when Barbarossa had balked at handing over Goslar as payment for his aid. Barbarossa pursued him seeking vengeance for other reasons, drove him into exile at the Angevin court, and thus gave a new impetus to the Guelf-Ghibelline struggle which was to convulse Italy and the rest of the Empire in the next century. Another result was that the power of the cities continued to grow, those of Tuscany following the same pattern as their northern counterparts. Barbarossa came to terms with the papacy and with Italy and married his son to Constance, the heiress of the Norman kingdom of Sicily. The offspring of this union was the Emperor Frederick II. Henry VI and his son Frederick were to construct between them 196 castles in Italy and Sicily, and those built by Frederick include some of the most original secular buildings of the Middle Ages.

Frederick II

Frederick II yielded further to the fascination which Italy exercised over his predecessors in the Empire by making Apulia his preferred country of residence and devoting most of his energies to Italian politics. Salimbene makes him say that: 'the God of the Jews had not seen his land, the Terra di Lavoro, Calabria, Sicily, and Apulia; otherwise He would not so often have commended the land which He promised and gave to the Jews.' Germany, on the other hand, he could scarcely bear, complaining of long winters, sombre forests, muddy towns, and rugged castles. Apart from these tastes and the fact that he had a Sicilian mother (he was brought up in the south and part of his youth was spent in the castle of Rocca Maggiore at Assisi), there was a strong political factor to confirm him in his choice; this was the highly developed Norman-Sicilian administration which he re-organized and improved and extended to the parts of northern Italy under his influence. These methods, it is thought, he intended to introduce into

Austria and the old Hohenstaufen lands in Swabia, thus controlling the Empire from the south. He had been made Emperor in 1212 by the great Innocent III in the hope that he would prove docile to papal claims and injunctions. No monarch in the Middle Ages defied the papacy so consistently or with less fear of its spiritual power. The papal lands in the centre and the papal influence in the north were the chief barriers to the uninterrupted rule throughout Italy he desired. No Pope could endure being totally surrounded by another powerful ruler, and so up to his death in 1250 Frederick was in an almost continuous state of excommunication, constantly at war and constantly building fortifications. Although he was at frequent periods in the north, building, for example, his castle at Prato (plate 210) and forming alliances where possible with cities or with tyrants such as Ezzelino of Romagna, here we are concerned with his castles in the south and, as these in their turn reflect his political aims and personal tastes, something must be said of these sides of him.

A poet in whose court the great Italian tradition of lyric verse began, a sceptic who inclined rather perhaps to Islam than to Christianity, a devotee of the chase who wrote a book on falconry, a natural scientist given to revolting experiments on men and children, a philosopher with a reputation for tastes in magic and astrology, a patron of the plastic arts of the highest connoisseurship, and an Emperor who drew upon classical precedent to claim obedience and suzerainty beyond all his predecessor's dreams, he aroused the terror and forced the admiration of his contemporaries. Matthew Paris, the English chronicler, calls him *stupor mundi*, the wonder of the world. A widely travelled man, he had fought for his rights in Germany, he had been crowned both at Aachen and at Jerusalem, he had seen many of the fortresses and studied the military organization of the Holy Land and, therefore, he attracted a cosmopolitan court where many influences met and were synthesized. At the beginning of his rule he made use of the already existing Norman fortresses such as Adranò in Sicily (plate 57) for establishing his power. Soon, however, he began to build on his own account and, taking the absolute

209 *Left* Gioia del Colle, Italy. An exterior view of this much-restored Hohenstaufen castle. The original castle was built in 1090 by a son of Count Drogo of Hauteville, one of the Norman conquerors of southern Italy, and it was greatly altered by Frederick II.

210 *Right* Prato, Italy. The castle built by Frederick II in 1237 in one of his centres of support in Tuscany. The gateway of this castle, which has a rectangular ground-plan, bears some resemblance to that of Castel del Monte (plate 166).

211 *Overleaf* Lucera, Italy. A view inside the base of Frederick II's palace. The corbels formerly supported a gallery from which archers could use the nine embrasures on each side fitted with arrow slits.

212 *Overleaf, right* Lucera, Italy. A detail showing the corner vaulting of the sloping roof of the base of Frederick II's palace.

regularity of layout that his Norman predecessors with Moslem help achieved in their palaces of La Zisa (plate 58) and La Cuba (plate 21), he and his architects added to that regularity a diversity of shapes and further influences from the Moslem world, from Burgundian Gothic, and from classical examples. His castles can be divided into the following types: those, such as Lagopesole (Lucania), Gioia del Colle (plate 209), Castel Ursino (plate 208), and Lucera (plates 165 and 211), which were fortresses containing residential quarters, barracks, and prisons; those, of which only Gravina (Apulia) survives, which were summer hunting-lodges; and other buildings, such as his triumphal arch and fortified bridge at Capua, the palace at Foggia, and Castel del Monte, the best preserved and most remarkable construction of all (plates 166, 216, 217 and 235).[21]

Gioia del Colle was badly restored at the beginning of this century (indeed so badly restored that much of the restoration has fallen down again). Originally, however, it was constructed with a symmetrical layout and four towers. Stronger Islamic influences, especially from the plan of the caravanserai, are to be seen in Frederick's later castles in Sicily, such as Syracuse and Castel Ursino, Catania (plate 208) which, according to a letter from Frederick to Richard of Lentini, his *praepositus aedificiorum* in Sicily, were under construction in 1239. Castel Ursino was formerly on the sea but a flow of lava in 1669 from Etna destroyed ramparts and trenches and extended the land out to sea. Its exterior is protected by four massive round towers whose internal arrangements are based on the octagon. The walls contain smaller intermediate round towers. Everything points to its having been built at great speed, as though the builder feared attack during the construction.

At Lucera, where Frederick imported and settled a Moslem army, allowing them their own mosques and customs, there stood formerly one of his greatest constructions, a square tower with a top storey whose internal arrangements were based on the octagon. The tower, which Frederick is said to have filled with antique statues and splendid furnishings, is known, however, only from the paintings and drawings of J. L. Desprez executed in 1778, twelve years before the ruins were blown up (plate 213). The great base of the tower, measuring 50 m by 50 m

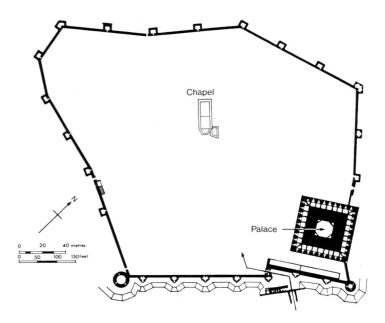

Fig. 21 A plan of Lucera showing Frederick II's palace in relation to the later Angevin enceinte. (After Hahn)

(165 ft square), had continuous galleries for archers in its walls and still preserves its sloping upper part. The other remains at Lucera are the later work of Charles of Anjou and date from between 1270 and 1283.

Frederick's use of the octagon is to be seen at its most complete in Castel del Monte. It is one of the supreme achievements of medieval secular building; every writer dwelling on its splendours echoes the tones of Gregorovius when he described it as 'the crown of Apulia' and 'the diadem of the Hohenstaufen empire'.[22] It lies isolated on a hill in central Apulia so that it can be seen from afar. The ground-plan of the whole is octagonal; so is the enclosed courtyard; all the corner towers are octagonal, and also almost all the rooms in the towers (with the exception of the round staircases). This exceptional complexity of design has provoked an enormous amount of literature, comparing it with the chapel of Charlemagne at Aachen, with Barbarossa's Hagenau, with San Vitale at Ravenna, and with the Dome of the Rock in Jerusalem. These comparisons show that the octagon was used widely as the design of many important buildings, both sacred and secular. Frederick had been crowned at Aachen and knew all the buildings referred to, including the Dome of the Rock.

All sorts of symbolism have been read into its shape. Its design may owe something to Frederick's other buildings: the octagonal vaulting in the round towers of Castel Ursino, the Capua bridge (plate 396) with its octagonal bases to the drum towers on either side of the triumphal arch, and the final stage of the great tower of Lucera. The windows and niches of Lucera and Castel del Monte would seem to have resembled

213 Lucera, Italy. A drawing made in 1778 by the French artist J. L. Desprez showing how the tower of Frederick II's palace rose from its splayed base. The internal arrangements of the top storey were based on the octagon. In 1790 the tower was blown up to provide building materials for a local courthouse.

214 *Right* Karlštejn, Czechoslovakia. Begun in 1348 by Charles IV, the 'priests' Emperor' to house the crown jewels and his vast collection of relics and as a centre of his power in Bohemia, this castle was extensively restored in the last century. Although it can be compared to the contemporary Valois castles in its height and its internal splendour, the disposition of its defences with their trust in the naturally strong site and the emphasis on disputing the main line of approach by a series of successively more powerful obstacles, owes more to traditional German practice. The huge keep houses the Hall of the Empire and the Chapel of the Holy Rood. Other chapels and the residential quarters are in the lower buildings. The strength of the castle is shown by the fact that it stood out for the Emperor Sigismund all through the Hussite Wars when nearly every other imperial or Catholic stronghold fell.

each other and a comparison of the cross-sections reveals some other striking similarities. Both owed much still to the inspiration of Norman-French keep design.

It is impossible to tell how much the idea of an octagon was Frederick's own, but he must certainly have taken the closest interest in the plan as well as the decorations. These include the use of expensive marbles in the portals, windows, pillars, pilasters and wall decoration, in motifs combining classical and oriental features. There were luxurious sanitary arrangements, water conduits, and bathrooms. On the top of one of the towers may have been a mews for hawks; Frederick was the author of the notable work on falconry, *De arte venandi cum avibus*, a work with a didactic purpose because he believed the art could be of the greatest value in training young noblemen in self-control and patience. Some of his hawks were brought all the way from Iceland by way of Lübeck and the Alps.

Earlier buildings in Italy, notably the eleventh-century baptistery at Florence, had already anticipated the Renaissance in the spirit and the style in which classical details or craftsmanship were used. Such a spirit was largely absent from Frederick's earlier castles and this points to new influences and new architects in the mid-1230s, the period during which the Capua bridge was being built. One particularly Roman feature at Castel del Monte is the pattern on the wall made by the method known as *opus reticulatum* – the incorporation of regular diagonal courses. Other classical individual features are the main entrance (plate 166), the chamfered pilasters, the so-called 'egg-and-dart' pattern and the mouldings on the consoles. A Roman relief was built into one of the walls. The torso of a rider, definitely classical in spirit, remains above the main door from the inner court to the private apartments, and other similar fragments are preserved in Bari Museum. The main entrance was protected by a very medieval portcullis.

The overall octagonal form dictated that the rooms in between the towers should be trapezoidal in shape and the idea of vaulting over the trapezoidal rooms as a single unit was Gothic: this had already been done in the choir surrounds of French cathedrals having the same ground-plan. In the same vaulting at Castel del Monte one finds the stylistically advanced early Gothic capitals of cup-shaped leaf buds, which, together with the realistic supporting figures on the vaulting consoles and bosses, display the 'modern' influences of France and northern Italy, especially the influence of Cistercian architecture.

Castel del Monte can be seen as an architectural expression of the synthesis of various cultures that Frederick was trying to achieve in other spheres; whether in politics, to make the Empire a truly international revival of the power of his Roman predecessors; whether in religion, as shown by his interest in other creeds apart from western Christianity; or whether in literature, where perhaps his court achieved the most fruitful success in making a synthesis. This building has always posed the question, 'What did Frederick use it for?' Although basically a defensible hunting-lodge, it seems too grand, too original for so simple a purpose. Attempts have been made to

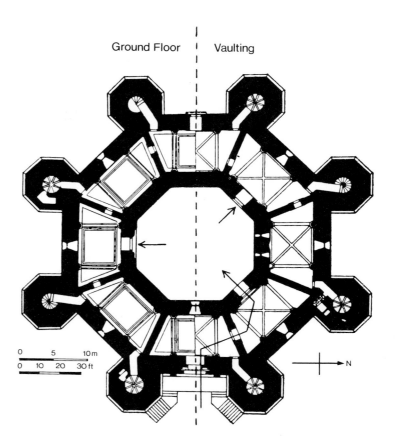

Ground Floor | Vaulting

0   5   10m
0   10   20   30ft

N

Fig. 22 *Above* A plan of the ground floor dispositions of Castel del Monte, the right-hand side showing the vaulting. Notice the turned route into the inner court. (After Hahn)

216 *Overleaf* Castel del Monte, Italy. The inner side of the first doorway into the court on the ground floor.

217 *Overleaf, right* Castel del Monte, Italy. One of the many superb capitals in the rooms on the first floor.

show that it was much more of a fortress than might at first appear, but these are not all convincing. Nevertheless, on a comparatively small scale, it brings together the functions of a castle, a palace, and a hunting-lodge. And in addition, all the previous experience of imperial castle building in Italy, the characteristics and the shapes, were combined within it. It is not so much of a fortification as Bari or Castel Ursino, it is not as light and intimate as Gravina once was, yet one forgets the mass of the building in its crystal-clear outline and the fineness of its detail.

Castel del Monte is unique in western Europe and if it can be compared with buildings of another epoch it is with the work of Akbar the Great at, for example, Fatehpur Sikri in India. There is a curious resemblance between Frederick II and Akbar, in their determination to synthesize various religions and philosophies, their aspirations to international government, their passions for warfare, hunting, poetry and the arts, and in both cases their architecture depended upon the combination of the most disparate and apparently conflicting influences harmonized into new and satisfying styles.

Angevins and other tyrants

After the Emperor Frederick's death at his castle of Castel Fiorentino in Apulia in 1250, his lands in the south fell to his bastard son Manfred. Charles of Anjou, a younger brother of St Louis, made himself the weapon of the papacy, whose one desire was to extirpate the hated Hohenstaufens, and at the same time fulfilled his ambition of having a kingdom to himself.

215 Karlštejn, Czechoslovakia. A doorway and wall decoration from the Chapel of St Catherine, one of the series of chapels served by a college of priests. This chapel was the private oratory of the Emperor Charles IV, who is shown in the painting above the door with one of his wives, Anna von Schweidnitz.

At Benevento in 1266 he defeated and killed Manfred and at Tagliacozzo in 1268 he won a great victory over the last Hohenstaufen at large, the sixteen-year-old Conradin, whom he had publicly executed at Naples. Charles brought the latest French influences to the design of castles in Italy. At Lucera (plate 165) he added the great series of towers and curtain walls which form its perimeter and in Naples he began the Castel Nuovo (plate 218) and rebuilt the Castel del Uovo. Castel del Monte he made a prison for the remaining members of the Hohenstaufen family.

His Sicilian subjects rebelled against him in 1282, in the episode known as the Sicilian vespers, and invited the king of Aragon to become their ruler. The wars between the Angevin and Aragonese royal families over the possession of the south

in the history of the castle comes to an end, except that their memory and example remained, not least in the legend of the Kyffhäuser mountain in Thuringia. There, beneath a castle built at the end of the eleventh century and occupied by imperial *ministeriales* to about 1350, it was said Frederick II slept until he should wake to vanquish the priests. The legend seems originally to have been applied to Wotan and later to Barbarossa, but it remained so powerful that in the fifteenth century the Church organized pilgrimages there to exorcize the imperial spirit and, in 1525 during the Peasants' Revolt, the unhappy rebels of central Germany, drawn by a dream of vanished justice that was sure to come again, met at the foot of the mountain before their defeat at the battle of Frankenhausen.[23]

were to continue for many years. Aragon had already shown its strength, especially in naval power, by the capture of the Balearic islands from the Moslems in the course of the thirteenth century, and the other kingdoms of the Iberian peninsula were now playing an important part on the European scene. How these events and the new situation in Italy were to affect the castle will be considered in Chapters 7 and 8. With the extinction of the Hohenstaufen line, a particular force

218 Castel Nuovo, Naples, Italy. An eighteenth-century engraving of this castle (left), planned for Charles of Anjou after 1265 by Pierre d'Angicourt, who also worked on the walls of Lucera. Extensively altered at later dates, it included the triumphal arch of Alfonso of Aragon (1401–58).

WARFARE, COURTS, AND CASTLES IN THE 14TH AND 15TH CENTURIES

The castle in a changing world

By the end of the thirteenth century many of the tendencies that were to lead to the supersession of the castle, both as a military weapon and as one of the chief types of residence of the ruling classes, had already appeared. The autonomous feudalism of an earlier age had long departed. The era of the paid soldier had arrived and with it a new professionalism that brought many changes to the art and practice of war. The bigger and richer towns which had grown up since the twelfth century were now even more politically powerful, offering both more effective obstacles to attacking armies and richer plunder if captured. Gunpowder was known although it had not been used in warfare. The strong rule of Edward I in England and of St Louis and his immediate successors in France provided examples of kingdoms, comprising wide areas of peaceful settlement, that needed defence only at their limits. All these tendencies for the most part met many set-backs. Gunpowder and firearms proved more useful at first to the defenders than to the attackers of a castle and it is only in the fifteenth century that provisions began to be made specifically against the effect of cannon. And then the peace attained in England and France was wrecked by the Hundred Years War whose damaging effect spread through Spain, Italy, the realms of the Empire, and Flanders.

The castle was still therefore militarily, politically, and socially a necessity. So far we have seen the castle arising as a response to invasion and to private warfare, as a means of conquest and of consolidating gains, as a centre of government and administration, as the provider of defence in depth or as part of a strategic network, as the court of rulers and great nobles, and as the seat of country landowners. Castles continued to exercise all these functions in one way or another. The threat of the Turks, for example, enforced from the fifteenth century onwards the building or reconstruction of castles in the Balkans, Hungary, Bavaria, and Austria. Private warfare in numerous parts of Germany made it vital to keep castles in repair. In Ireland and Scotland the same cause made the building of castles a necessity continuing into the seventeenth century. For the castle as a means of consolidating gains one can point to the Ordensland where the Teutonic Knights had to protect the 1000 new villages and 93 towns that had been settled in their lands; or, for an example of consolidation over a smaller area, the use Henry V made of castles in keeping his grip on Normandy after the siege of Rouen. An instance of the use of the castle as part of a strategic network or for providing defence in depth is the group of castles built or reconstructed by Sicard de Lordat, for Count Gaston-Phébus of Foix between 1365 and 1380.[1] A little later, between 1392 and 1407, Louis d'Orléans added Pierrefonds and La Ferté Milon to the network of older castles, including Coucy, that he already controlled over the wide region to the east and north-east of Paris so enabling him to threaten the capital when necessary and break up the forces of his rival Burgundian relations should they attack.[2] Monarchs and rulers, whether Valois kings or tyrants of Italian cities, still found it essential either to build castles close to their palaces or actually to keep their courts in castles. In Spain, the success of the Reconquest and periods of weakness in the Castilian monarchy permitted for the first time the construction of huge private castles by bishops and rich nobles.

These examples show the continuity of the reasons for building and using castles, but in design and in function they continued to evolve and to change in response to new military, technological, social, architectural, and artistic pressures. The thirteenth century had been in general a period of expanding trade and economic health. By contrast the fourteenth century is an unhappy age, with famine over wide areas in its earlier years and the pandemic of the Black Death in the mid-century causing depopulation and economic depression. To these miseries can be added the longer-lasting and more devastating warfare now practised.

Later medieval warfare and the castle

In the earlier Middle Ages elaborate theories of war remained unpractised in the field because tradition and physical conditions played a greater part than ideas in moulding military methods. Most of the ideas had in fact gone into the design of castles and fortifications. Now, with the decay of the feudal levy as the basis of the royal army and the increase in the hiring of indentured troops, a new professionalism marks the warfare of the fourteenth and fifteenth centuries. Although by modern standards the armies were still small (the total number of troops engaged at Crécy was 18,000, at Poitiers 10,000, and at Agincourt 11,000[3]), they were now much larger than previously and the kings of this period could put into the field armies of a size which could only have been raised for a Crusade in earlier centuries.

Against such armies there were few castles that could hold out for long, and, even though many French castles gave Henry V a lot of trouble, in the end he won all he besieged. Again the castle garrisons could do little to halt the smaller *chevauchées* or raiding cavalry parties the English sent through

France; they could only keep themselves shut up and hope to re-establish the rights of the Valois after the raiders had done their damage. Battles in the open field had been comparatively rare in the earlier period; they now became more frequent and a victory such as Philip Augustus's conquest of Normandy won by a siege is revenged by Edward III on the field of Crécy, followed up by the successful siege of the town of Calais.

The causes of employment of indentured troops varied in different parts of Europe. Edward I, for example, to enforce his will on Wales and Scotland, needed troops who would serve for a long period, especially through the winters.[4] They had to be organized according to a proper chain of command, and be accustomed to respond to discipline. From the Welsh wars the English learned their special superiority in the use of the longbow to which they owed so many triumphs in the Hundred Years War. The feudal levy had shrunk in numbers as it became more convenient to make payment in lieu of service, and thus the English armies after 1327 consisted entirely of paid soldiers. Troops were hired by professional soldiers, such as Sir John Chandos, who would contract with the monarch to provide so many men for a certain length of time. In Italy, the towns had to employ mercenaries because, although citizen armies had been raised over a long period, the mercenaries were rather more efficient. Here the contracts were with professional war leaders or *condottieri* who raised bands of heavily-armoured horsemen.

The feudal army had depended on the mounted knight as its main arm and, although there had been important battles such as Tinchebrai in 1106, in which the issue had been decided on foot, the tendency was to despise the footsoldier and to neglect his provision, especially in France and Germany. It is a sign of the rigidity of thinking in the upper classes that the French could not bring themselves to understand the English success in mixing their arms at Crécy. At Poitiers they dismounted and still lost, and, in spite of the intervening victories of du Guesclin using other tactics, reverted to relying on their heavily-armoured knights at Agincourt. Earlier, the French knights had been slaughtered at Courtrai in 1312 by Flemish footsoldiers. In Switzerland, the halberdiers of the Swiss infantry cut to pieces the cavalry of Leopold of Austria at the

battle of Morgarten in 1315. They won another resounding victory at Sempach in 1386 (plate 219). Here the Swiss had achieved a new professionalism and discipline, with their device of the infantry phalanx armed with the pike or halberd. This formation was designed to resist the impact of a cavalry charge, and to allow those in the hinder ranks to fill in the gaps of the fallen. This same formation won them great victories against Burgundy, first at Laupen in 1339, and over a hundred years later against Charles the Bold. The Hussites, too, were to demonstrate how powerful determined and well-trained infantry could be against cavalry. The outcome of battles depended, of course, on who was in command; at Roosbeke in 1382 the French cavalry routed the Flemish foot, but the general tendency of success was in favour of the infantry.

One result of this new professionalism was the emergence of great captains, such as Bertrand du Guesclin, often of comparatively humble origins. Several English professional commanders, such as Dalyngrigge who built Bodiam (plate 177), Delamare who built Nunney (plate 222), and Fastolf who built Caister (plate 223), were able to make large fortunes out of the warfare in France, and build themselves grandiose

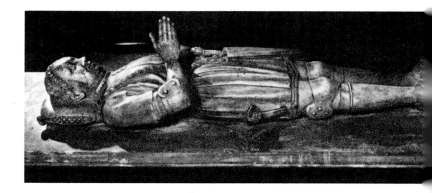

220 *Above* The effigy in St Denis of Bertrand du Guesclin (*c* 1320–80), constable of France and chief aide to Charles V in driving the English from French royal territory in the latter part of the fourteenth century.

221 *Right* The brass in Fletching church, Sussex, of the builder of Bodiam castle, Sir Edward Dalyngrigge and of his wife.

219 A scene from the *Weltchronik* of Rudolf von Ems probably depicting the battle of Sempach in 1386, in which Swiss infantry defeated a force of the Habsburgs. *Kassel, Murhardsche Bibliothek der Stadt*, Handschrift 2°, Ms. theol. 4, fo 46v.

castles to announce their arrival in the upper ranks of society. Another result of the need to pay troops was (in France) the raising of special taxation or *aides permanentes* and an increased dependence on the banker. Although Edward III of England had helped to ruin several great Florentine banking houses, by his refusal to repay the money he had borrowed for the diplomatic alliances that preceded his assault on France, there are many examples of more successful relationships. Dick Whittington financed Henry V's campaigns. Jacques Coeur of Bourges, whose house is shown in plate 250, provided much of the money used to drive the English out of France. Thus the more sophisticated means of finance available offset to a certain extent the lack of supplies caused by the general economic regression.

Castle garrisons still remained small. That this was accepted in general is shown by the tendency to reduce the perimeter to be defended, making use of greater heights, and a disregard for the truly concentric formation (except at Queenborough, fig. 26) which had obviously been too expensive for frequent adoption in any case. Pierrefonds would have required less than 200 defenders, and in 1449 Surienne had to await an attack on the town and castle of Fougères by the Duke of Brittany's forces with only 600, of which 150 went to the castle, 250 to the town, and the rest were kept in reserve.[5] Apart from the effect of cannon (see Chapter 9) there appear to be no major introductions in the form of siege weapons and methods. Mining, the casting of flaming projectiles or carcasses of animals to spread disease, escalation, and induced starvation, all continue to find a mention. The defences of many castles were improved by the widescale adoption of stone machicolation, obviously much safer than wooden hoarding, and, especially in French castles, the provision of continuous wall-walks and wide platforms to allow the defenders to rush to any threatened area. The sieges produced many terrifying and dramatic incidents; for example, at the siege of Caen in 1417 Sir Edward Springhouse fell off a scaling ladder into a ditch and the French dropped burning straw on him, roasting him in his armour.[6] On occasions women still led or helped in the defence: Black Agnes, countess of March, shrieked in

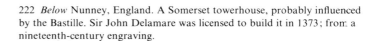

222 *Below* Nunney, England. A Somerset towerhouse, probably influenced by the Bastille. Sir John Delamare was licensed to build it in 1373; from a nineteenth-century engraving.

triumph, 'The English sow has farrowed!' when her men managed to crush a penthouse or 'sow' guarding a ram about to batter her walls[7]; and the countess of Montfort, wife of the claimant to the dukedom of Brittany, backed by Edward III, when besieged in 1342 in the castle of Hennebont led sallies against the French dressed in armour. After the castle had taken a terrible battering by siege weapons, her advisers begged her to surrender but she insisted on waiting for English

223 *Right* Caister, England. This Norfolk castle of brick and limestone dressings, bearing a close resemblance to certain lower Rhineland castles, was built for Sir John Fastolf (c 1378–1459) who at one period in his career commanded the Bastille. During the Wars of the Roses the castle was held by the Paston family for the Yorkists and it fell to the cannonfire of the duke of Norfolk who besieged it in 1469.

225 *Right* A tourney; one of John Rous's drawings in the *Life and acts of Richard Beauchamp, Earl of Warwick*, *c* 1485. *London, British Museum, Cotton Ms Julius E. IV Art VI, fo 11v.*

224 *Above* An illumination from the *Grandes Chroniques de France* depicting King John of France with members of his Order of the Star. The members wore scarlet cloaks with huge blue and gold star-shaped badges. The order lapsed shortly after it was founded. *Paris, Bibliothèque Nationale, Ms. fr. 2813, fo 394.*

226 *Below* The helm of George Castriota, called Scanderbeg, Prince of Albania (1412–68). *Vienna, Kunsthistorisches Museum.*

228 *Right* The surcoat embroidered with his arms, his shield with the arms modelled in gesso, and his gauntlets, all *c* 1376; from the Black Prince's funeral achievements in Canterbury Cathedral.

help. 'Then the countess looked down along the sea, out of a window in the castle, and began to smile for great joy . . . Then she cried out aloud and said twice, "I see the succours of England coming!" Then they of the town ran to the walls and saw a great number of ships, great and small, freshly decked, coming toward Hennebont.'[8]

An important development, stemming from old feudal customs and also from the law of nations, was the observance of a law of arms regulating the behaviour of soldiers to one another, and to their enemies. It was applied in military courts, and did much to ensure, at least for prisoners, some degree of humane treatment.[9] These rules applied to the surrender of a castle or town garrisons as well as to field engagements. One of the most characteristic features of this period was the founding of knightly orders such as Edward III's Order of the Garter in 1348 and Philip the Good's Order of the Golden Fleece in 1429. King John of France, captured at Poitiers in 1356, was less fortunate in his Order of the Star (1352), the 300 members of which took an oath never to flee in battle (see plate 224). Within a year, nearly a third of the knights had died in one engagement, and the order fell into abeyance. There are many stories of knights deliberately handicapping themselves to gain more glory, of deliberately spurning professional advice because it was unchivalrous, as in the

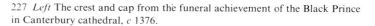

227 *Left* The crest and cap from the funeral achievement of the Black Prince in Canterbury cathedral, *c* 1376.

229 *Below* Helm with visor and mail from the harness of Philip the Fair, presented to Chartres Cathedral after his victory at Mons-en-Pevèle in 1304. *Chartres, Cathedral Museum.*

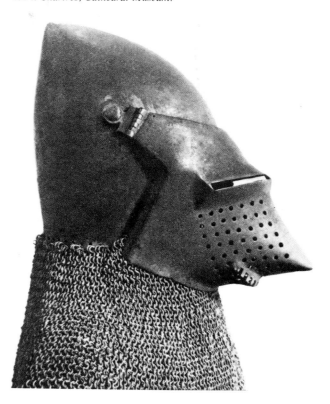

disastrous charge of the western knights in the battle of Nicopolis against the Turks in 1396, when the survivors had to cut off the long points of their fashionable shoes so they could run faster. Froissart tells of a number of young Englishmen who went to fight, each with one eye bandaged until they performed some deed of note.

Not all soldiers were so foolhardy, as is shown by the developments in armour in this period.

Arms and armour

As warfare became more professional, so the richer fighting man was forced to spend more on protecting his body. The mounted knight had to contend against much the same dangers as in earlier centuries when fighting members of his own class – the cavalry charge was still followed by hand-to-hand fighting – but the infantryman, armed according to his nation, with the halberd, the crossbow, or the longbow, became increasingly a foe to guard against. Much as he disliked it, the knight often had to dismount from his horse, because it was so vulnerable to arrows, and fight on foot. Otherwise, he had to shield his horse, as well as himself, with armour.

The surviving armour and funeral effigies of the fourteenth century show an increasing use of plate armour, articulated so as to allow movement (see plates 220 and 228). Gradually the whole body came to be encased like the exoskeleton of an insect. The shield became of less importance as protection, and the shape of the helmet altered, becoming rounded so that it presented a glancing surface to blows, instead of the earlier flat-topped helm. During the fourteenth century it was provided with a visor, thus completely protecting the eyes and nose. For purposes of recognition the crest became much more necessary. Only a few examples survive, notably the horns preserved in the family armoury of the Lords of Matsch in their castle of Churburg (see also plate 226), and among the magnificent funeral achievements of the Black Prince in Canterbury Cathedral (plate 227). Helmets acquired many shapes according to the rank, function, or country of the wearer, including that of the *chapeau de Montauban* (plate 238) specially designed for scaling operations. Footsoldiers wore much lighter armour, a brigandine and a light helmet, but they could be protected in the field or during siege operations by large body shields called pavises or targes, by stakes, or even by trenches.

The chief centres of armour production were Milan and in

230 *Above* A German helm *c* 1400–10 from a harness of plate armour, now in the museum of Coburg, W. Germany. The visor is of a particularly frightening design.

231 *Above right* A sallet, the technical name for this type of helm; south German 1470–80. *Glasgow, Art Gallery and Museum.*

Germany, Nuremberg and Augsburg, and their products were in demand all over Europe. Superbly applied with designs in gilt-brass, ornamented with flutings and ripplings in the metal, some of these late-medieval harnesses are remarkable works of art, quite transcending in their accomplishment, and in the skill with which they follow the lines of the human body, their often grisly purpose. Sometimes the armour was inscribed; for example, the breastplate of the earliest complete harness surviving at Churburg of about 1390 bears the often repeated words, 'Jesus autem transiens per medium illorum ibat' ('But he, passing through the midst of them, went his way'–Luke IV, 30), as a charm.[10]

Of all the weapons, the lance remained the most important of a knight's equipment. Although his sword retained a special place of honour, the dagger was often much more useful as a means of forcing a fallen enemy, completely encased in armour, to surrender or to agree to a ransom. It acquired many forms and many apt names, including the ballock dagger and the ear dagger. Another weapon which became more popular, especially as the shield became obsolete, was the two-handed poleaxe. The earlier and dangerous tournaments were replaced by the individual encounters of the joust, a rather more skilful sport, and this meant the development of a separate class of armour and weapons, often particularly richly decorated and adorned. The joust frequently accompanied banquets,

marriages and diplomatic celebrations, occasions which also provided opportunities for the most lavish displays of fashion and wealth.

The towns and technology

The skills, wealth, and political power of great cities and towns in this period all have a bearing on warfare, technology, and, therefore, on the castle. The Valois kings, from Charles V onwards, were only able to pay for their armies and garrisons

232 *Below* The seal of Guy of Flanders attached to a deed of 1345, now in the Gravensteen, Ghent.

233 *Bottom* A saddle coated in bone chased with scroll decoration *c* 1480–90; probably Hungarian. *Glasgow, Art Gallery and Museum.*

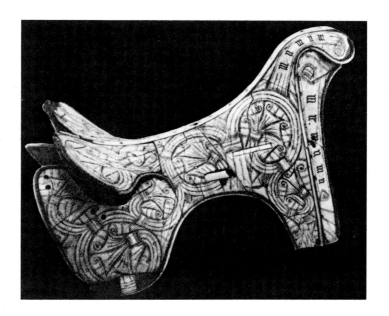

234 *Right* Rappottenstein, Austria. Interior of the chapel.

Ren: 1942.

by raising extraordinary taxation, the *aides permanentes,* and the burden of this fell on the townsmen. Bankers, too, were men of the towns, eventually providing one dynasty in the Medici, and employed in many countries in great affairs. Although it was the towns which received the severest challenges from starvation, and from the plague (if grain failed in eastern Europe then Flanders suffered, and the same was true for Venice and Genoa, dependent as they were on sea-borne food), nevertheless, they survived and became formidable military obstacles. In Germany and Italy, especially in periods of weak rulers, they became independent and autonomous states, conquering and controlling castles for their own ends. By 1370, at the Peace of Stralsund, the Hansa had won the fortifications of the Sound from the Danish monarchy and a

houses with walls, varying in strength and efficiency according to the needs and the resources of the place. Rouen, to take one example, was able to hold out against Henry V in 1418 for six months, despite the fact that he possessed artillery. Temporary forts were still built outside besieged cities and during the long siege of Calais (1346-7) Edward III constructed a siege camp like a town, complete with shops and markets.

Continuous warfare ensured that in spite of general economic regression and the effects of depopulation, great advances in technology continued to be made, especially in metallurgy because the demand grew for iron to fashion plate armour and later for casting cannon. Mills were increasingly used for hammering and for furnace bellows, while the introduction of a new smelting technique meant that iron could now

little later the tough mayor of Rothenburg ob der Taube, Heinrich Toppler, was acquiring fortified houses for his territorial ambitions.[11] The city of Siena gave Simone Martini a special payment for a journey in 1328 to study the castles of Montemasso and Sassoforte, whose sieges had been raised by their general Guidoriccio da Fogliano, before he started his fresco in the Palazzo Pubblico (plate 236 above), to make sure he painted them correctly. Thus it is interesting to observe the city fathers including in their civic buildings many of the characteristics of the castle, as at Bruges, or at Toruń (Poland), or at Florence or Siena in Italy, amongst them being belfries, watchtowers, crenellations, shutters, and iron grilles. In this they shared the opinion of the noted Italian military architect, Francesco di Giorgio Martini, that 'a *palazzo pubblico* should be constructed like a fortress, in anticipation of popular risings, and of the inconstancy of events'.[12] From their beginnings most medieval towns provided themselves with stone walls or palisades: here again the experience of the castle builder was used in extending old fortifications or making new ones, devoting especial attention to gates, and to the defences of bridges, as at Cahors over the Lot (plate 241), and ringing the

235 *Left* Castel del Monte, Italy. Two of the octagonal corner towers.

236 *Above* The fresco by Simone Martini in the Palazzo Pubblico, Siena, showing the General Guidoriccio da Fogliano in 1328. The general had just defeated the Ghibelline leader Castruccio Castracane and raised the sieges of Montemasso and Sassoforte, both of which are shown in the background.

be cast like bronze.[13] These new skills resulted in a greater concentration of effort in industrial centres, and this is reflected in the fact that it was the great urban complexes of Florence and of Flanders that first grasped the significance of firearms. Diffusion of the products was, however, made easier by the invention of the mobile fore-carriage which increased the efficiency of haulage waggons.

Just as the warrior became more professional, so the military engineer became increasingly specialized. This applied especially to artillerymen (see Chapter 9) but also to other trades. Increased literacy meant that new ideas could be spread further by the diffusion of manuscripts, such as those of the German Konrad Kyeser, whose *Bellifortis* was dedicated to the Emperor Rupert of the Palatinate in 1405, and which contained an astonishing range of recipes and techniques (plate 240). The drawings of the Hussite manuscript (plate 334) recorded the new artillery methods of Jan Žižka, and his followers. In Italy, the main technological advances were made, not so much in the city states, but at the courts of the great tyrants such as Urbino, Ferrara, and Milan. For, although specialization had increased in the towns, it was still possible for a man skilled as a military engineer to share this ability with many other activities. The great example, of course, is Leonardo da Vinci, who in writing to offer his services to Ludovico il Moro of Milan in about 1483 recites first his skill in making bridges, draining trenches, methods of bombardment, armoured cars capable of withstanding artillery and covering the advance of infantry, and a host of other sug-

237 *Below* An artillery-carrying chariot from the *Bellifortis* of Konrad Kyeser. It was this very device that the Hussites were to use with such devastating effect. *Göttingen, Niedersächsische Staats- und Universitätsbibliothek*, Cod. phil 63.

240 *Right* An escalading machine and ram from the *Bellifortis* of Konrad Kyeser. *Göttingen, Niedersächsische Staats- und Universitätsbibliothek*, Cod. phil 63.

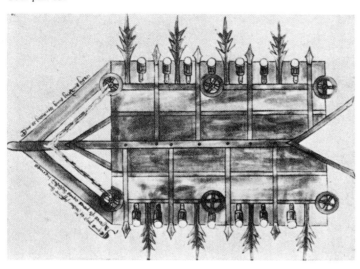

gestions. Only afterwards does he mention architecture, sculpture, and painting.[14] Many of the great Renaissance architects, artists, and engineers were just as deeply involved in the business of war and in their writings on architecture, to varying degrees, Alberti, Filarete, Francesco di Giorgio Martini, and Taccola all dealt with problems of siegecraft and of fortification. This fascination with military matters was also shared by Dürer, whose last book, on fortifications, *Unterricht zur Befestigung der Städte, Schlösser und Flecken*, was published in 1527. Even if he had not written this book, his interest in castles would still be plain from such water-colours as the Hinterburg at Innsbruck, or the Trento (plate 244), or the innumerable towers in the landscapes of

his paintings and engravings.

Improvements in the design of shipping from the beginning of the thirteenth century, notably with the introduction of the stem rudder and more efficient rigging and sails, had already had a pronounced effect, as we have seen, both on trade and the scope of warfare. These tendencies were to increase in importance throughout the fourteenth and fifteenth centuries and the ships illustrated, for example, in manuscripts of Froissart depicting sea battles, like that of Sluys in 1340 (plate 242), show a strong influence from the castle, with their crenellated superstructures and crow's nests, an influence still remembered in the terms foc'sle (or forecastle) and aftercastle.

The courts and the castle

One of the reasons for the continuing use of the castles in Europe is that they still acted in conjunction with only partly defended or unfortified residences as the courts of kings or territorial rulers and magnates. In the area now covered by France, in about 1370 there would have been not only the royal court of Charles V but also courts maintained by his brothers, Jean de Berry and the duke of Burgundy, the court of the Popes at Avignon, and the numerous courts of great magnates such as Enguerrand VII at Coucy or of Gaston-Phébus of Foix at Orthez. The princes and bishops of Germany and the tyrants of Italy in the next century kept state in a sometimes similar splendour. Allowing for the accidents of war, kings were growing richer and the nobility felt the need

238 *Far left* Armour designed for scaling operations: a huge wide helm, known as the *chapeau de Montauban*, and extra protection for the shoulders. The drawing, based on one dated *c* 1420 in the Bibliothèque Nationale, Paris, comes from Viollet-le-Duc, *Dictionnaire Raisonné du Mobilier Français* 1874.

239 *Left* A dagger, fifteenth-century. *Paris, Musée de l'armée.*

241 *Right* Cahors, France. A tower on the Pont Valentré built in 1355. The 'Breton' machicolations are built on consoles which sharpen to a point to give the defenders as wide a field of fire as possible.

for more money. (The accidents of war could have a very severe effect: the examples of the ransom demanded by Edward III for John of France, or of the Emperor Sigismund, deprived of his Bohemian revenues by the Hussite Wars, forced to pawn the Garter insignia he had been given in England to be able to continue on his journey home in 1416, are enough to show this. But once the reason for the loss vanished, the money started coming in again.) Although the movement, general in the west though not in the east, towards the commutation of labour services for cash payments might have helped the landowning nobility to grow rich, it was offset by the effect of depopulation, caused by famine and plague, making prices rise and rents fall. To become really rich, therefore, the great noble had to keep in constant contact with the court, the one certain source of heiresses, grants of land and appanages, of new and more grandiose titles, and of

There was another result of the commutation of labour services for money which is perhaps related to the supersession of the feudal levy by indentured troops. The great lord now had to pay for his servants and, if he were exceptionally rich, he housed these by the hundred. The design of castles and other residences had to be more generous to allow for the

money itself. This dependence on the court was welcomed by the rulers who would employ their power in bestowing wealth and honour to bind the nobility ever closer to them, using rivalry with other courts and their own orders of chivalry as devices to ensure loyalty. The successful noble would maintain his own minor court in his own territory and thus the fashions originating in Paris or Burgundy would spread down through local society, arousing a greater demand for comforts and luxuries. The concentration in the towns of skilled artisans made these comforts possible, so that a castle like Saumur on the Loire could shine with gold leaf on elaborate metalwork, sparkle with windows of clear and stained glass, have its chambers panelled, hung with tapestries, or painted with strange and beautiful devices, and be a boast in stone of its master's power and superiority. This was the period of International Gothic, in which Italian artists would paint in Avignon and Bohemia and Frenchmen in England.

242 *Left* The battle of Sluys in 1340, an illustration to Froissart's 'Chronicles'. *Paris, Bibliothèque Nationale*, Ms. fr. 2043, fo 72.

243 *Above* Saumur, France. This castle, shown here in the miniature depicting September in the *Très Riches Heures*, has a history going back to the time of Fulk Nerra. At the time of this painting it had been transformed into one of the most luxurious castles of France. *Chantilly, Musée Condé.*

244 *Right* Trento, Italy. A water-colour by Albrecht Dürer (1471–1528). This has many interesting features, notably the shutters protecting the crenels, the open balcony like those of Venetian palaces, and a number of projections. *London, British Museum.*

245 *Left* Poitiers, France. Detail of 'July' in the *Très Riches Heures*. This castle (no longer existing) shared with Caerlaverock (Fig. 19) in Scotland and Sarzanello in Italy a triangular plan. *Chantilly, Musée Condé.*

246 *Below* Castles appear again and again in Dürer's work as in this engraving of the 'Sea Monster' of 1500.

accommodation of households that in many cases must have been much larger than those of earlier times. The hotel of Jean de Berry in 1398 had to provide room for 200 servants, and that figure does not allow for the courtiers attending on him. The maintenance of such large numbers, whether by a monarch, or by a great lord, had many implications. Monarchs or great territorial princes still led a peripatetic life, whether for reasons of warfare, administration, or amusements such as hunting, and, therefore, they had to keep several castles or palaces in commission, each well provided with stores for the travelling entourages and with permanent servants who would keep the place in readiness and arrange for the cleaning out of rooms and garderobe pits after they had gone.

Another change was brought about by the fact that the castle was defended by hired soldiers. Their professionalism meant that the owner of the castle and his courtiers could live more openly and could pay less attention, in many ways, to the needs of defence. But, also, he had to ensure greater privacy. He could not trust the soldiers too close to his person, and he had to provide barracks within the castle. His own lodgings, frequently furnished with great splendour although by our standards with meagre comforts, would be placed close to the donjon for easy refuge, or, not infrequently, the donjon itself was constructed as a new well-lit and comfortable stone or brick building, as in the tower-houses of England. One suggestion of a factor that would have impelled everyone in this period to look to his comforts, is that in general the weather grew much worse in the fourteenth and fifteenth centuries, with short wet summers and long, freezing winters. Whether or not this was the case has been hotly contested.

Many of these introductions, whether military or decorative in purpose, had the effect of intensifying the Gothic appearance of the castle. Roofs were pitched higher, not only to deflect projectiles but because they were thought more attractive in that style. Machicolation in stone lent itself to decoration. Flanking towers, as at Pierrefonds, France (plate 270), either had their sturdy massiveness relieved with sculptures or elaborately carved finials, or else became much thinner, as at Aigle in Switzerland (plate 251), or at Valencia de Don Juan in Spain (plate 384). Aigle, with its narrow pointed towers and its elegant tiling, is a superb example of the late-Gothic castle.

The later styles of the Gothic not only show more pro-

nounced national tastes and influences, whether flamboyant, or perpendicular, or *isabelino,* the Spanish version of the flamboyant style; they also provided a greater freedom for decoration and love of ornament, which can be seen in the embellishment of every kind of artefact, from the windows of great halls to the jewellery of reliquaries, and for a short period

247 *Overleaf* Aigle, Switzerland. A guardroom serving the wall-walk in the curtain wall projects over the entrance. It is built out on consoles which also provide machicolation. Note the chimney for the guardroom fire.

248 *Overleaf, right* Aigle, Switzerland. A view of the keep of this particularly fine late-medieval castle, showing also the square turret seen in plate 251, and one of the round corner towers.

or the castles of the Teutonic Knights, and above all, the love of a many-spired and pinnacled outline. Eltz (jacket front) is a fine example of this, dating from the fifteenth century and later. The complex of buildings rises like a clump of plants bunched together and having to thrust higher to gain their share of light. The use of the bartizan, or projecting turret, originally devised, as in the perimeter wall of Ghent (plate 106), to increase the flanking power of the castle, became more and more a decorative motif—so that, for example, at Eltz the altar end of an oratory bulges out, suspended in the air. The use of such projections, whether for throwing missiles, for privies, or for providing elegant window seats, reached particularly elaborate forms in many later German castles.

One of the effects of the more obviously Gothic appearance of the castle was to add to its air of enjoyment, of adventure, and of lightheartedness. To understand more of this, we must turn to the people living in the castles at this time.

Conspicuous chivalry

There are two changes in the life of the later medieval nobleman that contrast him with his ancestor of two or three centuries earlier. One is that life has become much more formal: there are many more rules of behaviour to observe, whether in heraldry, hunting, fighting, or court life. The other is that fashion is much more important; styles of clothes change more rapidly, youth is a time to prolong as far as possible, and a sense of melancholy at the passing of time pervades the lyrics of poets as different in their upbringing as Guillaume de Machault, Charles d'Orléans, and François Villon. Numbers of surviving tapestries, such as the great Unicorn series (plate 254), or illuminations such as the *Très Riches Heures* (plates 150, 245 and 268), or wall-paintings and frescoes testify, however, to a delight in nature, in flowers and gardens and in lovemaking.

Both the increase in formality and the new responsiveness to fashion were due to the influence of the great courts and the new capacity of towns to provide for these luxurious tastes. Enormous sums of money would be spent on banquets, tournaments, and display, especially at royal weddings or other great diplomatic occasions. The rich court of Burgundy would take almost any excuse to hold a banquet. In 1454 Philip the Good gave one at Lille to express his grief at the fall of Constantinople after he, in common with all the other

249 *Above left* Aigle, Switzerland. Inside the covered wall-walk which runs round the curtain walls.

250 *Left* A fireplace in the House of Jacques Coeur, Bourges, *c* 1443–51, which illustrates admirably how the features of the castle entered the decorative language of the time. The upper frieze consists of a stone wall-walk with projecting tourelles themselves provided with machicolation, a style very similar to Pierrefonds (plate 270). Jacques Coeur was banker to Charles VII and immensely powerful until his fall in 1451.

251 *Right* Aigle, Switzerland. A delightful example of the late-Gothic castle with its attenuated conical tiled roofs to its drum towers. Of thirteenth-century origin, it acquired its present form after its capture by the Bernese in 1475. The central buildings stand almost free of the surrounding rectangular curtain walls with the three round towers and one great tower (in the distance) guarding the corners.

252 *Overleaf* Karlštejn, Czechoslovakia. The Chapel of the Holy Rood, intended by Charles IV to house his relic of the cross on which Christ died. The lower walls are embedded with semi-precious stones while the upper panels contain the portraits of saints by the otherwise unknown master, Theodric (see plate 253). Note especially the superb metal arch of the roodscreen.

in the fifteenth century, fashionable ladies could even be crowned with conical hats resembling the spiral towers of the castles in which they lived. The luxury of the courts demanded more light and more space, and so we find that in the fourteenth century halls were added to the earlier fortifications, as at Coucy, or John of Gaunt's great hall at Kenilworth or Jean de Berry's hall in the Palace of the Counts at Poitiers. The chimney-pieces were often elaborately carved, as at Tattershall, and the one shown in plate 250, from the house of Jacques Coeur, is especially interesting because its mock machicolation and crenels show how the characteristics of the castle had become part of the decorative language of the time.

Other Gothic influences continuing in the castle include the increased use of ribbed vaulting, as in the Hradschin at Prague

western leaders, had done nothing to help the unfortunate Byzantines in their last despair. (The Burgundians may have felt that, having had to ransom John the Fearless after Nicopolis fifty years earlier, they had done enough.) Olivier de la Marche describes the elaborate set pieces[15], including the castle of Lusignan with Melusine in the shape of a serpent on the top, and with orange water flowing from two of the towers into the moat, while facing the high table was the carving of a naked woman guarded by a live lion chained to a pillar. Hippocras wine flowed from her right breast and she was adorned with a cloth with Greek writing on it. The guests were moved by all this to take an oath to go on Crusade, but nothing came of it.

Yet one should not think that all this symbolism was the result of an empty vanity. Symbolism and imagery provided another language of expression, frequently very subtle and economical, and, in the works of great Flemish painters and tapestry makers, acquired a height of intensity that was only equalled in contemporary Italy. Every flower, every colour, every gesture was endowed with a particular meaning in a language to which, particularly when expressed by Van Eyck, we respond immediately. But the noblemen of the time were trained to respond to this language in numbers of other ways, in heraldry, in courtship, and in war. One extreme example was the use of the colour yellow to express hostility and, when Henry of Würtemberg paraded with all his retinue dressed in yellow past Philip the Good, it was to let Philip know of his enmity.[16] Much of this symbolism was related to the abiding strength of the chivalric code and the secularization of rituals, with meanings taken over from the Church. The ceremonies connected with a knighting, the vigil and fast, the mass and the accolade, all share this love of semi-ecclesiastical ritual. The ideals of chivalry were still very strong and were set out and discussed in numbers of treatises.

Thus one of the features of the later medieval period that emerges is the way in which artefacts of all kinds and sizes, whole castles, suits of armour, or jewellery, became conscious works of art. The artist accepted his obligations to a warlike society, and the warrior wished to appear with greater panache and splendour. This artistry was applied to the clothing of the upper classes, which at the same time permitted freer movement and was much better cut. The miniatures of Jean Fouquet and other painters and the evidence of tomb effigies reveal infinitely greater elegance and style. The hennins or spire head-dresses of the women of the fifteenth century, the drawn-in waists, the low-cut bosoms are echoed by the scalloped edges of the houpelandes of the men, their floppy hats, their ridiculously long, pointed shoes, and their brazenly cut tights stressing their masculinity, and they show an enjoyment of dressing-up that we are only slowly beginning to recapture.

The furnishings they surrounded themselves with reflected the same love of display. They would, of course, vary in different parts of Europe; Eltz still contains its vigorously painted but comparatively humble rooms of the fifteenth

century (plate 145) but it is amazing to think that, in the same century, Mantegna was executing his great frescoes of the Gonzaga family in the castle at Mantua (plate 255). Italy was, of course, far in advance of the rest of Europe, both in its architecture and its furnishings. Further north, the later-Gothic style was applied to the decoration of wooden furniture, producing the most elegant roundels and panel-carving on

253 *Left* Karlštejn, Czechoslovakia. Two royal saints from the series of paintings by Theodric in the Chapel of the Holy Rood (plate 252). The one on the left is St Louis.

254 *Above right* 'Taste', a tapestry from *La Dame au Licorne* series made in a Loire studio in the early sixteenth century. *Paris, Musée Cluny*.

255 *Right* Part of the frescoes depicting the Gonzaga family painted by Mantegna in the Castello Ducale at Mantua.

256 *Right* A late-medieval Gothic cupboard in the castle of Heidenreichstein, Austria.

257 *Below* A chest ornamented with roundels and hatchings in the castle of Coburg, W. Germany.

of the rich and the production of illuminated books in town workshops, whether devotional works such as the duke of Bedford's *Book of Hours,* or books of the poems of Eustache Deschamps, or chronicles such as those of Froissart, added by the beauty of their paintings to the desire to know their contents.

The great Italian courts also encouraged poets and writers, as they did painters and sculptors, especially as will be seen in dealing with Urbino (Chapter 8). And it was the old themes, of Alexander, Troy, Charlemagne, and Arthur, that continued to exercise their fascination. Thus Arthur reappears in his own country in English in the fourteenth century *Sir Gawaine and the Grene Knight.* The old love of descriptions of battles, whether real or imaginary, remained. Of more rigorous works, Vegetius stayed a favourite. Christine de Pisan, an Italian woman but writing in French, translated and adapted him in the fourteenth century, and a little later an English writer produced a verse translation of him which is one of the ugliest works of the period.

The chief connection between the castle and the literature of this period was an enforced one, where the writers were actually imprisoned in castles. King James I of Scotland is said to have written his *King's Quhair* while a prisoner in Windsor Castle in the early fifteenth century and Charles d'Orléans, captured at Agincourt in 1415, then spent many years as a prisoner, chiefly in the Tower of London, where he wrote great numbers of lyrics and conducted at least two love affairs. Then again the Arthurian tales received their latest and one of their most magnificent tellings in *Le Morte d'Arthur* of Sir Thomas Mallory. Thanks to the recent work of an American scholar[17], we can now think of this Thomas Mallory, not as the rowdy Knight of Newbold Revel who seems to have given too much attention to a life of crime ever to have put pen to paper, but as another man of the same name from a Yorkshire family living near Fountains Abbey. This man was probably taken prisoner towards the end of the Hundred Years War and was immured in one of the castles belonging to Jacques d'Armagnac, duke of Nemours, who happened to possess one of the very few libraries of Arthurian manuscripts extensive enough to provide Mallory with all the sources he is known to have used. Cycles come full cycle, and the very castle in which he was imprisoned provided him with the means of spiritual escape his genius and his feelings could have most desired.

chests, sideboards, and standing cupboards (plates 256 and 257). The sideboard was the most important introduction, again used more for display than for comfort, because all the plates and vessels of gold that were a necessary concomitant of rank could be exhibited on it. The Valois kings and dukes were probably the greatest patrons of the goldsmith in this period and a few examples of Parisian goldsmiths' work survive to show the exquisite shapes and enamelling achieved.

It must be stressed again in mentioning these aspects of life that the castle was only one of the types of building in which the upper classes now lived, and then, often in peaceful areas, only out of habit, inertia, or because they were useful country headquarters. Rules of behaviour still owed much to the warlike beginnings of the castle and the ideals of chivalry continued to receive added lustre and respect in the literature of the period.

The castle and later medieval literature

Poets and chroniclers were attracted to the royal and princely courts for rewards and for their audience. To draw a writer of Froissart's reputation to your court and to get him to record your deeds was an extremely successful exercise in public relations. In many countries the upper classes had become literate to some extent by the thirteenth century and the tendency was to spread considerably in this later period. Charles V of France, with his libraries at St Germain-en-Laye and Vincennes, shared his tastes with considerable numbers

258 The building of a river fort outside a town; a detail from the fifteenth-century *Histoire du Grand Alexandre. Paris, Petit Palais,* Ms. 78607, fo 48v.

FRENCH, ENGLISH, SPANISH, AND PORTUGUESE CASTLES OF THE 14TH AND 15TH CENTURIES

7

The fortified building that best shows the difference between the later and earlier Middle Ages is the Palace of the Popes at Avignon[1] which Froissart called the 'finest and strongest building in the world'. The collapse of papal authority that followed Philip the Fair's victory over Boniface VIII at his family's castle of Anagni, south-east of Rome, in 1305 forced Boniface's six immediate successors to maintain their authority not at Rome but at Avignon, a town that owed its importance to the possession of a bridge over the Rhône. Here, the Cistercian Benedict XII built the old palace and this was added to considerably by Clement VI who built the new palace, the two parts forming one immensely strong military complex. The severity of the outside of the Palace belies its reputation, described by Petrarch, as,

'an abode of sorrows, the shame of mankind, a sink of vice . . . a sewer where all the filth of the universe is gathered. There God is held in contempt, money is worshipped, and the laws of God and man are trampled underfoot. Everything there breathes a lie; the air, the earth, the houses, and above all the bedrooms.'

The interior of the new palace contains some of the most splendid medieval chambers, most of them the result of the special requirements of the papal court for halls of audience and consistories. The ground area of the vast echoing Clementine chapel is equal to that of the nave of Amiens cathedral. One dominating feature of the severe exterior is provided by the use of pointed-arch machicolations which are held on buttresses sunk down to the foundations. Machicolations of this type had two advantages: one was that very large projectiles, such as treetrunks, could be cast down them on to rams or sappers, and the other was that, should the sappers get through the wall, the buttresses and the arch would not collapse, and the damage would be localized. Two of the towers, the Tours Trouillas and Campane (1339-46) also are embellished with examples of some of the earliest known stone machicolation on consoles to be found in France.[2]

The general reason why the Avignon Popes felt it necessary to provide so gigantic a fortress for their protection can only be seen in relation to events in France, Italy and the Empire.

The Hundred Years War
The castles of France, although they witnessed few of the most dramatic events of this long war, played an important and abiding part in its events.[3] The English, despite their frequent triumphs in the field, found it impossible to capitalize on their successes partly because of the difficulties of supply and

259. The Palace of the Popes, Avignon. On the left is the Tour de la Campane with its machicolation on consoles of c 1340 contrasting with the old-fashioned machicolation on buttresses of the façade (centre).

partly because there were so many castles that remained faithful to the Valois cause and so acted as bases for re-establishing the royal power. Constant fear of attack meant that castles all over France continued to be built, or to be improved, and many new developments were introduced. Again, after the French recovery in the later fourteenth century, they found it impossible to expel the English utterly because of the line of fortresses the English controlled all the way down the coast, from Calais to Bordeaux and Bayonne, which were linked to improved coastal defences across the channel.[4]

The Hundred Years War had been under way a long time

before the parties actually engaged in battle. Edward III's claim to succeed to the French throne by right of his mother had been rejected in favour of that of Philip of Valois. Clashing interests and indecisive campaigns in Flanders and in Gascony brought the struggle nearer, but it was the disputed succession of Brittany in 1341 that gave the English the chance to gain a foothold across the channel, where they won the battle of Morlaix. A little later Edward himself crossed for the campaign of 1346 that ended in the astounding victory of Crécy and the long siege of Calais, the capture of which resulted in the establishment of a permanent English base in France. Ten years later the Black Prince turned seemingly certain disaster into victory at Poitiers, where the French king John was captured. The first part of the war was concluded by the Treaty of Brétigny in 1360, whereby Edward III gained great advantages of territory and power, but failed in his objective of the French crown. Thereafter the able French king, Charles V, swung the tide against the English by a policy of piecemeal recapture of castles and possessions and by never giving battle. The French progress in this was halted by the madness of his successor, Charles VI, and by the desperate civil war that broke out between the Armagnacs and the Burgundians in their struggle for control of the regency. England had her own problems at home, and the dramas of the reigns of Richard II and of Henry IV allowed no time or money for adventures abroad.

Henry V restored his great-grandfather's power in France by the victory of Agincourt where the French nobility, spurning all tactical advice and the help of archers, died in the mud of a ploughed field under a hail of arrows. Much of northern France, including Paris, was his by the time Henry died in 1421, together with the promise of the succession to the throne. The French recovery under the Dauphin, who was to be the future Charles VII, was slow and again wrecked by civil disputes—until Joan of Arc came to meet him in the great hall of the Château du Milieu at Chinon (plate 147) and gave heart to his dispirited followers. The expulsion of the English was gradual at first and then finally very rapid as the artillery trains of the brothers Bureau blasted them off the fields of battle, the levying of extraordinary taxation and the coffers of Jacques Coeur of Bourges supplied the money for the campaigns, and the first standing army since Roman times

to be formed of a combination of all arms, made certain that the fortunes of France would never again depend on the tactics adopted at Agincourt. It was now the turn of the French to watch and benefit from the troubles of their neighbours as England plunged into the Wars of the Roses which were to see the destruction of numbers of her great families and were to end in the establishment of the Tudor monarchy. Froissart saw the events of the Hundred Years War, which he chronicled, as results of the turns of Fortune's wheel, raising monarchs up to victory and casting them as abruptly to despair, defeat or death. It is against this background that we must trace the developments in the building of castles in these years.

In France in the first half of the fourteenth century there was no major change in the design of castles. Introductions included the new stone machicolations built on consoles and these assumed various types. The most efficient, known as Breton machicolation, was supported on a console cut like a reversed pyramid to give a wider field of fire to the defender. An example of this can be seen in plate 241 which shows the Pont Valentré at Cahors on the River Lot built in 1355. Another tendency in France, already realized at Harlech in Wales, was the concentration of attention upon the gatehouse. This was to lead to such creations as the entry to the Fort St André, probably built between 1362 and 1368, at Villeneuve-lès-Avignon, a royal frontier town up to the annexation of Provence in 1480 (plate 261), with its thick encrusting of machicolation on the twin towers on either side of the gate.[5] No part of the ground below on the wall-walk is left safe from these gaps.

It was the effect of Poitiers in 1356 that led to great changes in

260 *Left* Villeneuve-lès-Avignon, France. The tower of Philip the Fair, built up to the first storey from 1293–1307. Later in the fourteenth century the higher portions were added, together with the machicolation. Villeneuve-lès-Avignon was a vital outpost of royal power in the south and it attracted much defensive building, notably the great gatehouse towers shown in plate 261.

261 *Right* Villeneuve-lès-Avignon, France. The gatehouse of the Fort St André *c* 1360 with its immensely impressive stone machicolations on consoles covering every part of the ground near the walls.

262 *Overleaf* Vincennes, France. Charles V's great donjon of six storeys which rises to a height of over 170 ft (51 m) and formerly was even higher. The only entrance was originally by a drawbridge and postern to the chemise (plate 265) which itself was cut off by a moat from the rest of the castle.

263 *Overleaf, right* Vincennes, France. The superb octagonal central pillar supporting the vaulting of the great chamber on the second floor of the donjon. The original oak vaulting remains–probably devised to prevent heat loss by the chilling of warm air on bare stone.

the design of castles. King John was a prisoner in the Tower of London, and the peasantry rose against their lords. Marauding bands patrolled the countryside. In an uprising in Paris, Etienne Marcel murdered the followers of the future King Charles V before his eyes. It was this last experience that probably made Charles V take the castle of Vincennes and

turn it into not only one of his favourite, but also the safest of his residences. The open plan generally favoured since Philip Augustus is rejected, and the ruler once more retires into the keep to dwell–a keep which is strongly defended against treachery within the bounds of the castle, as the outer walls are against rebellion in the kingdom. It is interesting to compare Charles V's experience at the hands of Etienne Marcel, and his subsequent use of Vincennes as a residence, with the young Louis XIV's early brush with the Frondeurs, and his later determination to avoid the indignities of Paris by living at Versailles.

Vincennes[6] had long been a favourite hunting box for the Capetian kings. There, St Louis loved to dispense justice seated under an oak tree, as Joinville describes. The fourteenth-century rebuilding began under Philip VI, and was continued and completed by John and Charles V. A huge rectangle, 1096ft x 604ft (334m x 174m) described the perimeter of the castle – large enough to hold a considerable army. Formerly nine towers, rising to a height of 138ft (42m), marked the corners and the intervals of the curtain walls. Their original appearance can be seen in the miniature in plate 268. All except one have gone, some in the time of Napoleon who used the castle for his political prisoners, and who had the duc d'Enghien shot there. The remaining tower, the Tour du Village, was provided with two drawbridges, one for carts and one for pedestrians. Each tower, by reason of its height, was built with large windows looking into vaulted chambers. The stone platforms at the top of each tower were made especially strong to stand up to the force of projectiles, while their walls were elaborately buttressed. There were no flanking towers in the curtain wall on the side containing the donjon; this was to avoid the possibility of an enemy, if he gained the wall, using a tower to mount an attack on the donjon. Here the curtain wall breaks to allow room for the square moat from which the great donjon and its splayed chemise rise. This complete separation of the donjon from the bailey of the castle, designed to guard against treachery from within, nevertheless considerably weakened the outer defences of the castle, for it was by this gap that in 1432 Jacques de Chabanne entered and recaptured it from the English. The donjon is 170ft (51m) in height and is constructed on six storeys, each finely vaulted and magnificently appointed (plate 262). Not only was access to the chemise guarded by a drawbridge across the moat but passage from the wall-walk of the chemise into the donjon was only possible by another drawbridge on the second floor level. The top of the donjon was defended by two tiers of battlements at the summit. Each corner is protected by round turrets and a fifth projecting turret isolated the privies. A very deep well provided the inhabitants with water. Wooden panelling on the walls, and even, most unusually, in the vaulting, rich furs, tapestries, goldwork displayed on open shelves alleviated the chill of this stony eyrie for Charles V, and in the gatehouse to the donjon he kept the library of books which he loved to study in the intervals of directing du Guesclin and his other commanders in the task of freeing France from the English.

Charles V was also responsible for completely transforming the Louvre, built by Philip Augustus, and withdrawing it from the outer defences of Paris. It became a luxurious palace, though still within a complete defensive enceinte and retaining its round thirteenth-century donjon. To St Germain-en-Laye Charles added a massive donjon. The most important fortification in Paris now became the Bastille, built between

1370 and 1382 (plate 266) to guard the Porte St Antoine. Though as much an innovation in its own way as Vincennes, it was entirely different. The castle was strengthened by eight round towers of equal size and, a most unusual feature, the curtain walls were raised to the same height as the towers so that an active defence could be conducted by rushing troops to any threatened point without their being delayed by negotiating entrances and towers· blocking the way. The Bastille was entirely a military fortress but one finds its basic spirit adapted later to residential castles. The furthest flung imitation of the Bastille is said to be Nunney in Somerset (plate 222). More important developments of its style are to be found in Pierrefonds[7] (plate 270) and Tarascon[8] (plate 271). Pierrefonds was built by Louis d'Orléans between 1392 and the time of his murder by the orders of his cousin, John the Fearless, duke of Burgundy, in 1407, and was transformed in the last century into a medieval fantasy by Viollet-le-Duc for Napoleon III. It was defended by a continuous, covered wall-walk projecting from both curtain walls and towers forming the most impressive stone machicolations of the Middle Ages, and further protected by higher open wall-walks for firing over the roofs of the lower one. Like Tarascon, it also inherits

264 *Above left* Vincennes, France. A view from the north-west of the donjon within its defences. The chapel of the castle can be seen on the right. Jutting out from the donjon on the left is the wing containing an oratory and the drainage systems.

265 *Left* Vincennes, France. The Tour du Village containing the main entrance to the castle reached by a bridge and drawbridge across the moat. This is the only tower in the perimeter wall left at its original height. The bases of two others can be seen far left and near right.

266 *Above* The Bastille, Paris, in an eighteenth-century view engraved by J. Rigaud. The curtain wall is raised to the same height as the flanking drum towers.

268 *Right* Vincennes, France. This detail of 'December' from the *Très Riches Heures* shows all the towers in the curtain wall standing as they did up to the time of Napoleon and shortly after. *Chantilly, Musée Condé.*

267 *Left* Bertrandon de la Brocquière offers to Philip the Good of Burgundy a translation of the Koran at the Abbey of Pothière during a siege of Mussy-l'Evêque; from *Avis Directif pour faire le passage d'Outremer*, 1456–9. *Paris, Bibliothèque Nationale*, Ms. fr. 9087, fo 152v.

from Vincennes the separation of the residential quarters from the rest of the castle but neither of these patterns weakens the outer defences as at Vincennes. Tarascon, built from 1400 onwards for Louis II of Anjou, king of Naples, and later the castle of the good King René, continues the Bastille style and improves on it by having a wider roof platform thereby giving the defenders even greater mobility.

Castles such as Vincennes were the work either of monarchs or else of royal holders of great appanages, such as Jean de Berry. One must not forget that, especially during the troubles of the Hundred Years War, the practically independent lords still maintained great courts – such as, for example, Gaston-Phébus, count of Foix who patronized Froissart and owned the castle of Foix in the south. To his castle of Orthez Froissart travelled and gathered there some of his best material, describing the machinations of the evil king of Navarre, who so poisoned the count's mind against his own son that he murdered him, and the narration of the Bascot of Mauléon, the old soldier who told what it was like to live as a *routier*, depending on war as the only means of survival, and who could boast of the twenty-seven towns and castles that in palmier and earlier days had been his. Other castles were the work of military commanders grown rich in the service of the state. Such a one is the beautiful castle of Josselin[9] (plates 1 and 279) purchased in 1370 by the Constable de Clisson who rebuilt it

and made it into one of the strongest supports of the French monarchy in Brittany. An idea of the riches he gained can be gathered from the inventory, made on his death in 1407, which listed: '109,053 *francs*, 11,857 *écus*, 9539 *moutons*, 993 *guyennois*, 966 *florins*, 611 *nobles*, 4 *réaux*, and 17 *pavillions*'.[10] Josselin is also interesting because it shows the gradual transformation, in the late fifteenth century, of the *château-fort* to the *château* or country house. The façade to be seen in plate 1 is largely the work of the constable but in 1488 the castle was dismantled by order of the duke of Brittany, and then at the turn of the century it was transformed into a magnificent country palace by Jean, duc de Rohan, in the flamboyant style (plate 279). He added the dormer windows, the elaborate finials and other carving, and Breton machicolations, more because they fitted in with the style rather than for pressing needs of defence. The great donjon at Josselin was blown up on Richelieu's orders in 1629, and the most impressive surviving tower keep in France is probably that of Largoët-en-Elven (plate 100), another Breton castle, built in the late fourteenth century and now a lonely ruin in the forests of the Morbihan.[11] Another castle which continued to be improved throughout this time was Fougères[12] on the north side of Brittany. It had a long history – Henry II razed it to the ground in 1166 and it had been rebuilt in 1173 by Raoul II, baron of Fougères. Frequently added to since that rebuilding, a remarkable use was made of water in its defences; it was isolated from the town by a series of pools which could be kept flooded by sluices from the River Nançon. In the first moat still stands the seigneurial water-mill. Here in the fourteenth century the existing towers and some of the curtain walls were

270 Pierrefonds, France. A reconstruction drawing by Viollet-le-Duc who, in the last century, rebuilt the ruins of Louis d'Orléans's castle for Napoleon III. It had two lines of wall-walks, one with a covered roof.

269 *Left* Tarascon, France. One of the castles influenced by the style of the Bastille in which curtain walls and flanking towers are of the same height thus permitting the rapid movement of troops to the defence of any threatened sector. This example is largely the work of Louis d'Anjou, king of Naples, who began it in 1400 and the famous good King René (1408–80). The kingdom of Provence was separate from France at this time and across the Rhône on the left can be seen the outline of the keep of Beaucaire, an outpost of the French kings until the annexation of Provence in 1480. The crenellations are restored.

Fig 23 *Below* France during the Hundred Years War. From left to right: France in 1328; France in 1360 (Treaty of Brétigny); France in 1420 (Treaty of Troyes). (After Fowler)

heightened and provided with stone machicolations. In the next century, the arrow slits were adapted to firearms and, most significant of all, towards 1480 were built the Surienne and Raoul towers which are among the first French experiments in designing fortifications specifically against cannon fire. These towers, constructed in horseshoe shapes, are ahead of their time when compared with many of their contemporary fortifications – for example the royal castle of Langeais, built by Louis XI not far from Fulk Nerra's keep in about 1465, whose designers, apart from providing loops for firearms, acted as though the trebuchet were still the most dangerous weapon in use. Rambures,[13] a brick-built castle in Picardy of an exceptionally satisfying design based on interlacing circles, begun in 1421 but not finished for another forty years, shows by its numerous embrasures and by being partially

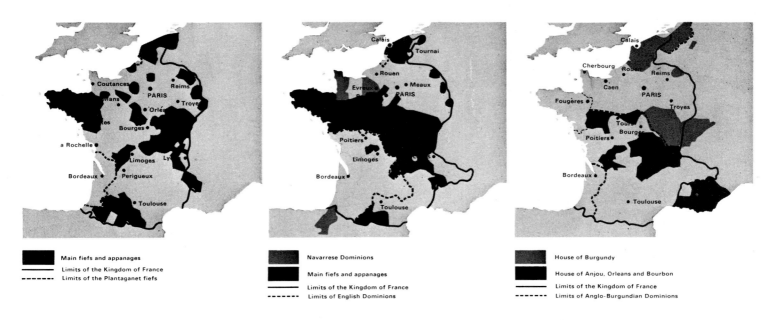

| Main fiefs and appanages |
| Limits of the Kingdom of France |
| Limits of the Plantaganet fiefs |

| Navarrese Dominions |
| Main fiefs and appanages |
| Limits of the Kingdom of France |
| Limits of English Dominions |

| House of Burgundy |
| House of Anjou, Orleans and Bourbon |
| Limits of the Kingdom of France |
| Limits of Anglo-Burgundian Dominions |

hidden in a dry moat some understanding of the measures to be taken against the new weapons. But, for a close example of how to design fortifications as a whole against gunpowder, the French had to wait till after 1497, when the Spanish engineer Ramirez began to build the fortress of Salses[14] to defend the rights of his countrymen to Roussillon; in a great siege in 1503 the French artillery managed to wreck all the highest parts of the castle and were on the point of capturing it when Spanish reinforcements arrived. The Spanish now took advantage of a truce to repair Salses and thus produced the revolutionary construction shown in plate 395 which totally reverses the dominating character of the medieval castle built to demonstrate its power over the surrounding countryside, and instead uses the lie of the land to conceal itself as much as possible from its attackers.

These were the exceptional castles of the period in France. Many others remain, but the lesser nobility could not compete financially to equip themselves with anything more than strong houses, capable of standing up to the minor dangers of war but yielding instantly to harder threats. One must not forget, on the other hand, the continued usefulness of earlier fortifications. The Black Prince, for example, in his *chevauchée* of 1355, burnt the bourg of Carcassonne but did not even dream of attacking the *cité*, so impregnable did it seem. Another use for the older castles was found by the captains of the mercenary

bands, who would use them as bases for their raids. The trouble caused by these immensely skilful brigands could be immense. Mérigot Marchès, for example, had made, according to Froissart, 100,000 francs (probably a wild exaggeration) by pillaging and laying tribute to his part of the Auvergne in the borderland between English and French territory, in the ten years up to 1391. In that year, regretting the sale of one castle, he remembered that, 'to pill and to rob (all things considered) was a good life, and so repented him of his good doing'.

271 *Left* Tarascon, France. A view of the castle from across the River Rhône which reveals its particularly clean-cut and subtle design.
A postern gives access to the boats and the only frontage containing windows looks out on the river from the royal apartments.

272 *Below* Tarascon, France. The altar end of the chapel.

273 *Right* A staghunt from the *Livre de la Chasse* of Gaston-Phébus, count of Foix, a great lord of the south in the later fourteenth century, builder and owner of many castles and patron of Froissart. *Paris, Bibliothèque Nationale*, Ms. fr. 616, fo 87.

274 *Below right* Graffiti on the interior wall of one of the chambers at Tarascon used as a prison.

Froissart makes him say to his comrades:

'Sirs, there is no sport nor glory in this world among men of war, but to use such life as we have done in time past; what joy it was to us when we rode forth at adventure, and sometime found by the way a rich prior or merchant, or a rout of muleteers of Montpellier, of Narbonne, of Limoges, of Fougans, of Béziers, of Toulouse, or of Carcassonne, laden with cloth of Brussels, or leatherware, coming from the fairs, or laden with spices from Bruges, from Damascus, or from Alexandria; whatsoever we met, all was ours, or else ransomed at our pleasures; daily we got new money, and the villeins of Auvergne and Limousin daily provided and brought to our castle wheatmeal, bread ready baken, oats for our horses and litter, good wines, beefs and fat muttons, pullens, and wild fowl; we were ever furnished as though we had been kings. When we rode forth, all the country trembled for fear, all was ours, going or coming. How we took Carlaste, I and the Bourge of Compayne? And I and Perrot of Bernois took Chaluset? How did we scale with little aid the strong castle of Marquell, pertaining to the Earl of Dolphin? I kept it not past five days, but I received for it on a fair table five thousand francs, and forgave one thousand for the love of the Earl Dolphin's children. By my faith this was a fair and a good life . . .'[15]

The memory and the temptations were too much for him. He and his followers seized an empty castle called La Roche

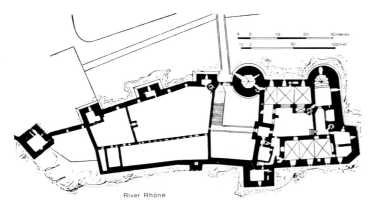

Fig. 24 *Above* Plan of Tarascon, France. (After Finó)

275 *Left* Fougères, France. The immensely strong Tour Raoul which, together with the Tour Surienne, was added *c* 1480 to protect a long stretch of enceinte formerly reinforced by smaller rectangular towers. The Tours Raoul and Surienne, with their horseshoe-shaped groundplans represent some of the earliest French experiments to construct fortifications capable of withstanding artillery.

276 *Below* An illumination from René of Anjou's *Le Livre des Tournois*, 1460–5, written about the tournaments held in 1446. The duke of Brittany is handing over to the king-at-arms the sword intended for the duke of Bourbon. *Paris, Bibliothèque Nationale*, Ms. fr. 2695, fo 3v.

277 *Top* Fougères, France. Three towers (from left to right), Guémadeuc, Mélusine and Gobelins, in the perimeter wall of this castle which dates originally from the eleventh century and contains elements of all later periods.

278 *Above* Detail from the door of a dressoir at Bunratty, Eire.

Vendeux and returned to that fair and good life pillaging and terrifying the neighbourhood. Though he was besieged by the Vicomte Meaux, he used his connections with the English court to try to get the siege raised through negotiations with Jean de Berry. When that failed, he left the castle secretly to

look for more companions, and it was given up by his uncle who had remained behind. Mérigot was eventually betrayed by a cousin, to whom he had gone for help, and he was executed in Paris. 'Thus fortune payeth the people when she hath set them on the highest part of her wheel, for suddenly she reverseth them to the lowest part', says Froissart on his end.

English castles

The development of the English castle in this period, especially in the south, shows a much greater tendency towards domesticity than in France; the strongly fortified castle changes into a palace, to express the power of the monarch or lord, and then is transformed into the country house, still perhaps retaining the symbols of nobility—the moat and the crenellations—but reflecting in its peaceful atmosphere the unwarlike aspirations of its owner. It is interesting to note the much smaller part sieges play in the warfare of the time—especially in the Wars of the Roses, with their terrifying list of engagements on the battlefield. The castle was no longer fulfilling its purpose of delaying an advancing army and, except in the north and in Wales, the possession of the towns was of all-dominating importance. Castles certainly underwent sieges but they nearly always fell; these sieges were merely part of the mopping-up operations following a battle which had been the turning-point in the fortunes of the parties.

Although England had to contend with no prolonged or successful invasions in this period—only raids by the French on the south coast and forays by the Scots in the north—civil

Fig. 25 *Below* A plan of Raby Castle, England. (After Allen Brown)

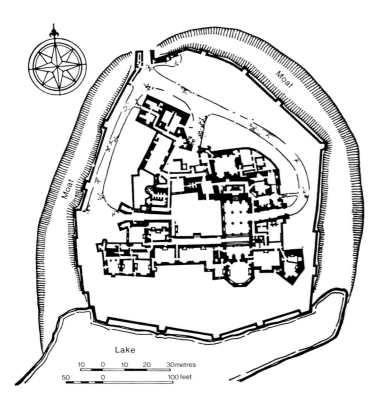

279 *Left* Josselin, France. Exuberant Breton carving on the landward side of the complex of buildings in plate 1 showing the work in the *flamboyant* style ordered by Jean, duc de Rohan, in about 1500. The castle had been dismantled by the duke of Brittany in 1488 and its adaptation into a particularly splendid country house soon followed.

280 Goodrich, England. A drum tower strengthened at the base with spurred taluses. This contained a state chamber in its top storey and other rooms for important guests and connected with the great hall of the castle on the right. Goodrich was one of the most powerful Marcher castles. It has a rectangular twelfth-century keep and many later towers and walls dating from its ownership by the de Valence earls of Pembroke who remodelled it between 1300 and 1350.

war was frequent. In times of weak or child monarchs, great lords, backed by the resources of great estates from which they drew their followers, frequently rebelled under the excuses of a threat to the rights of their order, or of removing the evil counsellors surrounding the king. Four kings, Edward II, Richard II, Henry VI and the boy Edward V were murdered in their castle prisons; Richard III died on the battlefield and Prince Edward, the son of Henry VI, was murdered after his capture at the battle of Tewkesbury. The fates of kings were frequently those of their adherents, and their enemies.

To have large possessions was still to invite the threat of attack. The change from dependence on feudal levies to the use of paid and indentured troops has already been mentioned. In England this gave rise to what historians have called bastard feudalism, the system whereby a lord entrenched himself in his district by extensive payments and patronage, a system in many ways bestowing remarkable stability, but liable to many upsets depending on the fortunes of the lord. This system tended to perpetuate the administrative and social functions of the castle. Just as in France, room had to be found for the hundreds of servants, and other dependants, halls for audiences, galleries for suitors to wait in, barracks for the professional soldiers, and private apartments for the lord and his family. In time of civil disturbance, the castle becomes a base for the gathering of troops, but when the lord is defeated it is only by chance, and not by choice, that he himself retreats to his castle to withstand a siege. That is what he pays his soldiers to do for him. He himself prefers to escape to the Continent, and to await more favourable times at the French or Burgundian courts. Such

281 Bellver, Majorca. One of the few completely circular castles, this view shows the exterior round tower connected to the castle by a bridge on the other side. The entrance is on the right. The Majorcan branch of the Aragon dynasty enjoyed a brilliant reputation for its style of living and chivalrous attainments. This castle probably inspired the design of Edward III's Queenborough (Fig. 26).

was the choice made, for example, by Warwick the Kingmaker. The plan of his great castle of Raby, Durham (fig. 25) shows a haphazard arrangement, grown up over many years and which was suited more to residential than to defensive purposes.[16]

English castles of this period can be divided into those still intended for a major military role, those that were adapted from earlier works, and those that were built to new designs, and were primarily royal or baronial courts or simply fortified manor houses. An example of the first is Queenborough Castle, built by Edward III between 1361 and 1377 in Kent, on the Isle of Sheppey, as a barrier to French invasions.[17] It was built by John Box under the supervision of William of Wykeham. Edward III was particularly proud of it and often lived there in his later years. Probably owing something to the earlier round castle of Bellver (plate 281), Queenborough was unfortunately destroyed by order of Parliament in 1650, but the plan (fig. 26) shows a remarkable development of the concentric castle. The only entrance to the round keep was at the opposite end to the main gateway, and the bailey itself was cut in two by corridors leading from the gates to the keep. The design combined the merits of the Norman plan of defending the castle sector by sector with the full benefits of active defence which was allowed by a concentric plan.

Where older castles are adapted in the fourteenth century, it is generally to add to the domestic comforts and to extend the residential areas of the original buildings—as, for example, John of Gaunt's great red sandstone hall at Kenilworth, with its wide and traceried windows. Thus it was at Windsor (plate 56), which Edward III turned into one of the great palaces of Europe to be a worthy setting for his new Order of the Garter, and which was embellished by later monarchs

with the Chapel of St George. On the other hand, there are castles such as Goodrich (plate 280), belonging to the de Valence family, where a successful attempt had been made by the early fourteenth century to bring the higgledy-piggledy accretion of earlier buildings into a rational scheme of defence with the provision of a barbican to defend the main entrance. Again at Warwick (plate 283), the building of Guy's Tower (1394) and Caesar's Tower (c 1400) by Thomas Beauchamp, earl of Warwick, to flank the gatehouse and barbican in the fourteenth century, show that it was still thought necessary to redress the imbalance caused by too great an insistence on domestic needs—though these towers, too, were provided with lodgings for the earl's officials.[18]

The new castles of the fourteenth and fifteenth centuries generally fall into two classes: the quadrilateral castle and the tower house. In many cases in the south, because not so much attention was paid to the choice of site from the point of view of immediate defensive needs, castles were no longer built to follow the contours of the hill or country in which they were placed. This meant that the quadrilateral plan, with its open court or series of courts like the contemporary (and fortified) colleges at Oxford and Cambridge, could be followed. The most famous example of a castle built on the quadrilateral plan is Bodiam (plate 177 and fig. 27), originally pronounced 'Boojum'. This castle was built by Sir Edward Dalyngrigge in the reign of Richard II.[19] Dalyngrigge had made his money in the French wars serving under the grim Sir Robert Knollys, whose men used to speak of his 'mitres' in Normandy and Brittany, comparing the burnt gable ends of houses to the episcopal crown. This was at the period of French recovery, when Rye on the south coast had been sacked and burnt in 1372 and when, in 1386, Olivier de Clisson, the owner of Josselin, had a prefabricated castle or encampment of wood made at Boulogne as part of his preparations for an invasion of England.[20] The castle at Bodiam was to prevent the French penetrating up the River Rother, and the licence of 21 October 1385 to crenellate empowered Dalyngrigge 'to strengthen and crenellate his manor house of Bodyham near the sea in the

282 *Right* Chinon, France. The Tour de l'Horloge from which entry is gained to the Château de Milieu from the Fort St Georges. This tower, built in the later fourteenth century, is extraordinarily narrow when seen from the side.

Fig. 26 *Below* A plan of the now destroyed Queenborough, England. (After Allen Brown)

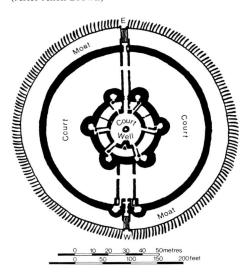

283 *Above* Warwick, England. A water-colour by Peter de Wint (1784–1849) showing the two great later fourteenth-century towers flanking the gatehouse: (right) Guy's Tower with a polygonal shape and (left) Caesar's Tower built on a trilobed ground-plan.

284 Herstmonceux, England. The gatehouse as seen *c* 1830 in an engraving by W. Tombleson of this splendid brick castle licensed for Sir Roger Fiennes, a veteran of the French wars, in 1441. It is now the official residence of the Astronomer Royal. Many features of its design reflect the influence of the not far distant Bodiam built sixty years earlier.

Fig. 27 *Below left* A plan of Bodiam, England. *A*. Later causeway. *B*. Octagon. *C*. Bridge foundations. *D*. Barbican. *E*. Chapel. *F*. Hall. *G*. Kitchen. *H*. Well. *I*. Dungeon. *K*. Stables (?) (After National Trust *Guide*)

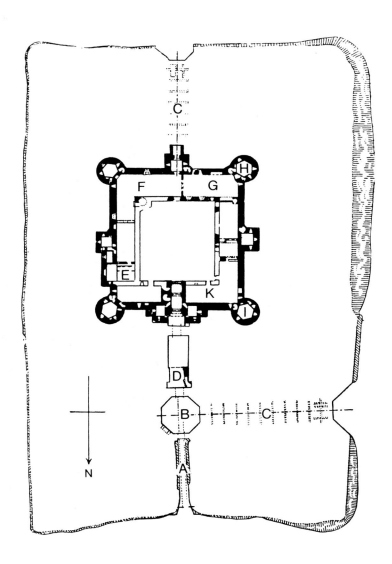

county of Sussex with a wall of stone and lime, and to construct and make thereof a castle in defence of the adjacent country-side, and for resistance against our enemies'. In fact, the castle, like so many, never withstood a siege; the nearest it came to this was in 1483, when Sir Thomas Lewknor who then held it was attainted by Richard III. This has led several writers to call it 'an old soldier's castle' and to belittle the resistance it could have put up to attack by a powerful fourteenth-century army, even though at the time it was built England, for the first time since the battle of Sluys over forty years earlier, had no control over the shipping lanes of the channel. It was one of the first castles in Europe to be equipped with gun-loops.

The castle consists of a rectangular area with round towers at each corner, square flanking towers, and two opposed machicolated gatehouses. To reach the castle, the visitor or the attacker had to cross the moat by a wooden bridge at right-angles to the main gate, thus exposing his undefended sword-side to the enemy. The turn to the gate was defended by an outwork which led by a drawbridge to a barbican and then by another drawbridge to the gatehouse. The gatehouse was fitted with three portcullises and three sets of folding doors, and the bosses of the vaulting contain murder holes. The arrangements within the quadrangle show a sharper demarcation between the rooms for the lord and his family, and those for his retainers. The south-east tower probably contained Dalyng-

285 *Right* Beersel, Belgium. Two of the three horseshoe-shaped towers added to the perimeter of this thirteenth-century brick castle in 1491. Additions were made to the towers in the early seventeenth century.

rigge's private apartments, and he also had a great chamber for audiences and a hall whose small dimensions show that he was accustomed to eating in private. There are even two kitchens, one for the lord and one for his retainers.

Bodiam was one of many quadrilateral castles. The great northern castle, Bolton in Yorkshire, a seat of the powerful

Scrope family, had preceded it in 1379. Here, a strong tower was provided with a rectangular courtyard and it was obviously still thought necessary to pay attention to the choice of site from the point of view of defence. Yet another famous commander in the French wars, Sir John Fastolf, from whom Shakespeare derived his fat knight, built the rectangular Caister Castle in Norfolk (plate 223), again incorporating a tower, this time a tall, slender one nearly 90 ft (27 m) high, containing his private suite. Fastolf paid for the castle with the ransom he obtained for the duc d'Alençon captured at the battle of Verneuil in 1424,[21] and the castle was famous in its day for the luxury of its appointments, since its builder, who at one time under Henry V was commander of the Bastille, clothed its rooms with tapestries and decorated its walls with

gargoyles and machicolations. Like several other castles of its time, it is constructed of brick with limestone dressings, and comparisons have been drawn between it and castles of the lower Rhineland. Forty years after its construction, when it was in the possession of the Paston family, it underwent a siege by the duke of Norfolk, and fell to his artillery. Other quadrilateral castles include Kirby Muxloe (plate 287), built for Lord Hastings by the noted architect John Couper who had worked at Eton and Winchester, and the great palace known as Herstmonceux Castle, Sussex (plate 284). These quadrilateral castles are important not only in themselves, but because from them developed the great Tudor houses which, whether in ruin like Cowdray, the last English house for which a royal licence to crenellate was granted, or in preservation like the first quadrangles of Hampton Court, impress by the sheer quality of their architecture – the finest expressions of domestic tranquillity, order, and responsibility that England has achieved.

The tower houses reflect the contemporary French interest in the keep, as at Vincennes, and the isolation of the lord from his professional soldiers. This renewal of interest in the keep has been interpreted as an archaizing movement, a harking back to the days when the baron was at peace in his good, strong keep. It is better seen, however, as something that happened in many parts of Europe, and can be explained as a fashion, released by changing methods of warfare and systems of defence, that did not require the exigencies of the concentric layout. The tower house also derives from a thirteenth-century custom of placing a solar tower containing the great chamber next to the hall in an unfortified manor house.[22] The keep in any case never went entirely out of fashion; now it was to be made more comfortable. The tower houses of the fourteenth and early fifteenth centuries appear in diverse shapes: at Wardour, licensed for Lord Lovell in 1393, the tower is hexagonal with a central court; the Yellow Tower of Gwent (1430-45) at Raglan (plate 383) is also hexagonal but has no inner court and is isolated from the main body of the castle. Guy's Tower at Warwick has twelve sides and rises to

286 *Left* Hohensalzburg, Austria. The Golden Room built for Archbishop Leonhard von Keutschach (1495–1519) showing the famous stove, a supreme example of late-medieval ceramic work, richly decorated with saints and religious scenes in the upper series of panels and with fantastic devices in the lower. The splendour of the stove is echoed in the gildings and elaborate carvings of the apartments. These interiors give a fine example of the outward display surrounding the courts of the princely magnates, both ecclesiastical and secular, in the Empire of the fifteenth century. Externally, however, at the same time, Hohensalzburg's defences were being increased against the threat of Turkish invasions.

287 *Above* Kirby Muxloe, England. An aerial view of the remains of this quadrilateral brick castle (1480–4) in Leicestershire built for the Yorkist magnate William, Lord Hastings, by John Couper. The full plan was never completed because of the execution of Lord Hastings at Richard III's orders in 1483. The accounts surviving are so full they allow one to follow its progress week by week, and they include a payment to five men in May 1481 to sit up all one night to watch in case the moat overflowed and flooded the site.

288 *Right* Tattershall, England. The towerhouse built for Ralph, Lord Cromwell, the Lancastrian Lord High Treasurer, by Baldwin Docheman between 1434 and 1446 as an addition to the thirteenth-century castle. Parallels have been drawn between this towerhouse and, on the one hand, the donjon built by Jean de Berry at Poitiers and, on the other, the Grand Master's lodgings at Marienburg, Poland.

289 *Left* Warkworth, England. The unusual towerhouse or keep built on the ground-plan of a Greek cross *c* 1380 as dated by the stone heraldic devices on the exterior. It was a stronghold of the Percy family and was besieged by Henry IV and taken in 1405. A central well supplied light to the inner rooms of the keep; from Hearne's *Antiquities of Great Britain*, 1789.

290 *Below left* Borthwick, Scotland. The Scottish form of the towerhouse seen in this border castle built *c* 1440 by Sir William Borthwick. This almost blind exterior forms a marked contrast with, for example, the contemporary towerhouse at Tattershall (plate 288).

291 *Bottom left* Bunratty, Eire. An oratory furnished with ornaments of various dates.

292 *Right* Borthwick, Scotland. A closer view showing the deeply incut passage covering the entrance to the castle.

128 ft (39 m); its fellow, Caesar's Tower, is even higher (133 ft, 41 m) and has a trilobed plan. The design of the tower at Warkworth in Northumberland (plate 289) is singular, not so much in its height as in its ground-plan based on a Greek cross. An addition to a much older site, in the sophistication of its building it is a far cry from some of the severely practical designs of the eleventh and twelfth centuries. From the evidence of heraldic carvings on the tower it was built in about 1380.[23] Just as Nunney, one form of the tower house, has been ascribed to the influence of the Bastille, and Caister compared to the lower Rhineland castles, so Tattershall (plate 288), the great brick tower built for the Lancastrian Lord Cromwell in the 1430s, was the work of Baldwin Docheman, who may have been a Hanseatic German and, therefore, influenced by the great brick castles of the Teutonic knights.[24] The tower castle has many points in its favour as a residence, especially at this period, since it could be well lit with large windows and provided with fine fireplaces and stairways. It is also much the most impressive form of castle; the lord is seen to be a lord simply by the Babel-like heights to which he can build. And this applies to Karlštejn in Czechoslovakia, to Pierrefonds in France, and to Fuensaldaña in Spain, just as much as it does to Tattershall. One of the most remarkable tower castles in Scotland is Borthwick, *c* 1440,[25] which, as can be seen in the illustration (plate 292), makes use of its severe angles and deep incut entrance to create the most chilling impression of fear and domination. Here, as in common with most Scottish castles of the period, the needs of defence permitted no large window openings, and the keep contains the most intricate pattern of staircases to confuse an intruder and put him at the mercy of the defender. A similar castle, this time in Ireland, also showing little allowance for the comforts of life, except in its splendid great hall, is Bunratty (plates 178, 291 and 293).

The border between England and Scotland, at a time when country gentlemen much further south often sought licences to crenellate as a sign of their social position, now saw the building of the small castles commonly known as pele towers.[26] Sometimes these were built with walled enclosures known as barmkins, into which the cattle, the object of raiding parties, were driven. These pele towers were built as a response to the dangerous and continuous wars of the Border. They were almost entirely defensive in character although some, such as Chipchase (*c* 1340) and Belsay (*c* 1340) have machicolations and turrets. In their small and uncomfortable interiors, the young and the old sought refuge until the raid was over or had passed by, and by their puny scale they illustrate the smallness of the numbers involved in the raids, and the poverty of

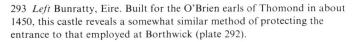

293 *Left* Bunratty, Eire. Built for the O'Brien earls of Thomond in about 1450, this castle reveals a somewhat similar method of protecting the entrance to that employed at Borthwick (plate 292).

294 *Above* Pontefract, England. An important royal castle, now much decayed compared with its appearance in this painting by Joos de Mompers (1564–1635). Richard II was murdered here in 1400.

295 *Above right* Craigievar, Scotland. An Aberdeenshire castle finished in 1626, it is a late example of the Scottish towerhouse but it also shows that the form was still capable of development.

296 *Right* Blarney, Eire. This famous Irish castle was built *c* 1446 by Cormac MacCarthy. The origin of the practice of kissing the Blarney-stone, which is just below the battlements, is unknown. Note the fine machicolation.

resources of the society that produced the great and savage poetry of the Border ballads. In Scotland itself the nobility continued to build castles long after the English lords had turned to the country house. This was partly because of the continually unsettled state of society, and partly because they could not afford to build on the scale, or in the style, of Longleat or Castle Ashby. Thus we find a perfect example of the tower house castle as late as 1626 in Craigievar, Aberdeenshire (plate 295), and the curious combination of Palladian styles with turrets and drum towers that feature in other seventeenth-century Scottish buildings. Some French influences affected the Scottish castle and among these were the iron grilles, such as one sees in the illustration of Saumur (plate 243), which enabled larger windows to be inserted in the towers.

Castles in England in this period acquired another, more sinister function as prisons and as places for execution. Edward II was kept at Berkeley in a dungeon through which the castle sewer ran, and was murdered by a method of which various tales are told, all unspeakable. His wife, Isobel of France, after her lover Mortimer was killed, was kept in Castle Rising for twenty-one years, while her son prosecuted his claim to the throne of France which he derived solely from her. One can extend the list to include Pontefract (plate 294), scene of the murder of Richard II, and the imprisonments and executions in the Tower of London, and later to Mary Queen of Scots beheaded at Fotheringhay after nineteen years of imprisonment. Disgust, with the weight of unpleasant associations, superstitious stories, and fears–all these could become too much for the heir who had been bequeathed too much horror. Richard II ordered a retreat in the grounds of his palace at Shene (now Richmond) to be destroyed in his grief at the death of Anne of Bohemia, so that he should not be disturbed by the memory of past happiness.

This sense of disgust was, of course, offset by the new skills in making life more comfortable and luxurious. The tastes that Henry III had worked so hard to nourish now burgeoned, and Chaucer's *Boke of the Duchess,* written to commemorate the death of John of Gaunt's first wife, gives in its opening an idea of how delightful it must have been to be surrounded by original carvings and glass. 'In the dawenynge' in May as he lies naked on his bed he is woken by the birds and he looks about the room:

And sooth to seyn my chambre was
Ful wel depeynted, and with glas
Were al the windowes wel yglased
Ful clere, and not an hole y-crased,
That to beholde hit was gret joye;
For hoolly al the storie of Troye
Was in the glasyng y-wroght thus,
Of Ector, and of kyng Priamus:
Of Achilles, and of Lamedon,
And eke of Medea and of Jasoun;
Of Paris, Eleyne, and of Lavyne;
And al the walles with colours fyne

Were peynted, bothe text and glose,
And all the Romaunce of the Rose.'[27]

One such painted chamber survives in Longthorpe Tower, dating from about 1330 (plate 298). This was probably made for an anchorite of the Thorpe family, but the astonishing range of subjects crammed on the walls gives an idea of the contents of the residential parts and chapels of many castles.[28] England, it must be remembered, unlike France, did not suffer from a cessation of work on churches and cathedrals and the same masons and the same painters were, as we have seen, frequently employed on secular as well as ecclesiastical buildings. Another peculiarly English development affected the design and adornment of castles. It was soon realized that the perpendicular style was exceptionally well suited for domestic purposes. It was very economical: stone could be cut in an almost mass-produced manner so that ornamentation frequently became very stylized. It is fascinating to see the exchange of stylistic ideas between features predominantly characteristic of castles and those of the perpendicular style. The adaptation of this style gave to the castle more open and glazed windows, elegance to the form of its courtyards, vaultings and doorways, and broke down its defensive and light-hating characteristics in such a way as to turn the castle into the country house. But on the other hand, the style found in the castle some of its richest inspirations for design. If one looks at many of the surviving roodscreens of the fifteenth century, for example, one finds very often that the upper lines of decoration consist of crenellation, complete even to the roll-top on the merlon designed originally to stop stray arrows from glancing over on to the wall-walk. Crenellations are to be found on the exteriors of numbers of fourteenth and fifteenth-century churches, such as Launceston, but transformed from their vulgar military use into part of the integral design intended to uplift the onlooker into praise of God and delight in his works. Even church towers, which sometimes in the past had defensive purposes, now sprout angels and

297 *Below* Crenellation used as decoration on a church: Stanton-in-Vale, Berkshire, England.

298 *Above* 'The Wheel of Senses': one of a series of wall-paintings *c* 1330 in Longthorpe Tower, near Peterborough, England.

299 *Right* Embid, Guadalajara, Spain. The corner of the keep said to have been undermined in a siege. The open inner face of the corner tower (centre) prevented an attacker from making use of it as cover should he penetrate that far.

apostles on their battlements as at Gresford.

This was a very natural development. Castles, however grim many of them look now, deprived of their white walls, their blue roofs and their gilded finials, were considered objects of beauty and worthy of admiration. Perhaps it was this realization of the beauty in castles that shows better than anything that their period of greatness was coming to a close. They were no longer capable of inspiring quite such fear if their features could be taken up and transformed into decorative motifs. This is paralleled by the decay in the fifteenth century in the old skills of horsemanship which once characterized the knight, something noted by Caxton in his version of Ramon Lull's *The Book of the Order of Chivalry,* and lamented by Mallory also.

For some of the most splendid later-medieval castles where stern military necessity was still kept in balance with the desire to produce a beautiful building, those of Spain are certainly among the finest.

300 *Overleaf* Alter do Chão, Portugal. The gatehouse to this fourteenth-century royal castle built by Pedro I from 1321 onwards. The capping of the round corner tower is a feature common to many Portuguese castles.

301 *Overleaf, top right* A Spanish thirteenth-century illumination showing an assault with a siege-tower. The incident depicts a siege of the citadel of Belinas, now in Syria, during the early Crusades. Note the barrel helms of the knights on the left and the Moorish horseshoe arch of the gate. *Madrid, Biblioteca Nacional, Conquista de Ultramar,* fo 2v.

302 *Overleaf, bottom right* King David of Scotland before Newcastle in 1346. An incident depicted in a fifteenth-century manuscript of Froissart's great chronicle of the Hundred Years War. The armour shown is contemporary with the manuscript, not with the war depicted. *Paris, Bibliothèque Nationale,* Ms. fr. 2643, fo 97v.

303 *Left* Doornenburg, Holland. A total but faithful reconstruction of the fifteenth-century keep destroyed in 1945. The keep is divided from the bailey (right) by a moat of running water and entrance is gained only by a narrow bridge and drawbridge.

304 *Right* Embid, Guadalajara, Spain. Typical of the more regular ground-plan favoured in Spain from the fourteenth century onwards, this small castle was first built after 1331 by Diego Ordoñez by permission of Alfonso XI of Castile as a border fortress against Aragon. Border wars between the two kingdoms in the next century caused its reconstruction. In 1710 it was severely damaged in the War of the Spanish Succession.

305 *Below* Coca, Spain. A view of this massive fifteenth-century episcopal fortress. The gun ports low down in the scarped plinth would indicate that the moat was never flooded.

306 *Overleaf* Fuensaldaña, Spain. Machicolation and round corner towers of the massive fifteenth-century keep.

307 *Overleaf, right* Peñafiel, Spain. Looking up at the keep from below the curtain wall, a view that impresses with the quality of the masonry. The turrets project on rounded rings of stone. The arms are those of the Girón family, owners of Peñafiel during its last stages of building, and they quarter the royal arms of Castile and León.

Spain and Portugal in the fourteenth and fifteenth centuries

One of the effects of the containment of the Moors in a small area round Granada was to enable the rulers of the three main kingdoms to play a larger part in European affairs. Thus, in the thirteenth century, Alfonso the Wise of Castile attempted to become Emperor and Aragonese power was successfully established in Majorca and Sicily. This tendency continued in the fourteenth and fifteenth centuries, especially as Castile was drawn into the Hundred Years War and as trade and wealth grew. French influences, therefore, are increasingly found in the Spanish castles of the later period and greater attention is paid to laying out regular, geometrical ground-

plans. One example of this is the small pentagonal castle of Embid in Guadalajara (plates 299 and 304) which was built by Diego Ordoñez after 1331 on the borders of Aragon by permission of Alfonso XI.[29] It was reconstructed in the fifteenth century because of border warfare between Castile and Aragon and was taken in 1452 by partisans of the king of Navarre. The truly concentric castle never gained favour in the mainland of Spain, nor did the round castle, although on Majorca the castle of Bellver (plate 281),[30] built by Pedro Salvat for King James II in the first years of the fourteenth century, probably influenced the later Queenborough (fig. 26) in its perfect circular form. Its almost blind exterior, with its entrance guarded by a detached round tower, is in complete contrast to the elegant, arcaded courtyard of the interior. A particularly fine example of the trapezoidal ground-plan is Montealegre (Valladolid)[31], of the early fifteenth century, with its great square corner defences superbly set off by the slender round towers rising in the centre of each wall (plate 330). It was exceptionally strong; Pedro the Cruel tried to take it and failed against a defence organized by the wife of one of his enemies.

The preference for a regular and generally rectangular form was equally strong in Portugal where the knightly orders remained influential. A fourteenth-century example is the castle of Amieira[32] (Alto Alentejo) built by Don Alvaro Pereira, prior of the Hospitallers, with its square corner towers, one built to a much larger scale to act both as keep and gatehouse. A less regular form appears in Alter do Chão which Pedro I ordered to be rebuilt in 1321 (plate 300).[33]

The really great castles of Spain belong to the period when the nobles and prelates of Castile took advantage of the weak Trastamara monarchy, especially under Henry II (the Impotent), to seize power and wealth; they expressed their new-found dominion in castle-palaces which, though owing something to the influence of the French royal castles such as Vincennes or Mehun-sur-Yèvre, nevertheless were expressed in a thoroughly Spanish form. The Spanish had always clung to the tower form, the *torre del homenaje*, and new fashion and new building skills impelled them to construct castles centred on immensely tall keeps rising high above elaborate lengths of curtain walls, now provided with gun loops and built to withstand the artillery of the period. Such a castle is Peñafiel[34] (plate 331), interesting in any case as an example of the fortress type known as *gran buque,* or 'great ship'—for so it appears, riding on a great rounded hill on the southern banks of the River Duero between Valladolid and Aranda de Duero. The site had been fortified for centuries when Don Pedro Girón, master of the Order of Calatrava, decided to rebuild it in the middle of the fifteenth century. Its defences consist of two lines of curtain walls, the inner thickly studded with round

towers and containing an almost continuous wall-walk; these lines circumscribe the crest of the hill and in the middle stands the keep, 112ft (34m) high, with elegantly severe turrets projecting from its corners and the centre of its sides. For all its height and dominating position it has few windows and this omission, together with the height of the entrance above ground level and the dog's-leg entrance to the hall, confirms its strongly military character.

At Fuensaldaña there stands a keep similar in many ways to that of Peñafiel. Here, however, the corner towers rise from the ground and the outworks are built in a rectangular form more suited to the plains. This castle, which was never finished or occupied[35], was the work of Don Alfonso Perez de Vivero, John II's treasurer who was murdered by order of the king's favourite, Don Alvaro de Luna, in Burgos in 1453.

Coca (plates 305, 310 and 368), one of the famous Castilian palace-fortresses, forms a complete contrast to these two castles.[36] Unlike Peñafiel and Fuensaldaña it was built largely of brick and it is generally claimed as the finest example of *Mudéjar* military work in Spain. The *Mudéjars* were Moslems, living and working in the reconquered areas, and their particular style

309 The arms of León-Castile from León Cathedral, Spain.

308 *Left* Almodóvar del Rio, Spain. The great *torre del homenaje* or keep is connected to the rest of the castle by a high stone bridge. It bears the traces of a more recent war.

310 *Overleaf* Coca, Spain. A close view of the amazing brickwork of the crenellations, showing the cross-and-orb gun loops and a small embrasure for a cannon. Note the decoration of the base of the projecting turret.

311 *Overleaf, right* La Mota, Medina del Campo, Spain. The oldest parts of the castle are the square towers of the inner curtain wall built partly of *mamposteria* (like the Moorish *tapia,* a mixture of pebbles and mortar). Before them rises the fifteenth-century outer curtain wall which shows, by the scarping nearly to its full height and its gunloops, the attention that had to be paid to guarding against cannon.

of craftsmanship forms an important part of the highly individual, decorative nature and profile of the Spanish castle, as at Segovia or farther south at Almodóvar del Rio (plate 314). Coca was built by the archbishop of Seville, Alfonso de Fonseca, perhaps in the middle of the fifteenth century and it played an important part in the struggles of Isabella of Castile in her efforts to establish her rights to the throne. Quite apart from its huge and dominating size, the architectural quality of Coca is exceptional, depending mostly on the tension set up between the rigour of its extremely regular layout and the fantasy and richness of its decorations, a tension harmonized by the variety of geometrical forms employed, squares, hexagons, circles and hemicircles. The main design consists of a square within a square and the keep is an enlarged corner tower of the inner part guarding its single entrance. This could only be reached by turning a corner from the entrance from the bridge over the moat. The brickwork is astonishing, especially the crenellations which are ornamented with rounded furrows and, as if to emphasize their downfall to the Moslem workmen who built it, the walls are interrupted by square gun loops of the cross-and-orb type. There are even embrasures provided for heavy cannon. One of the most interesting features of the corner towers in the external wall is the provision of hexagonal bartizans (a device known as an *escaraguaita*) from each hexagonal face which seems to serve no special purpose here for flanking but adds considerably to the fantastic air of the castle. Of the famous ceramics and other *Mudéjar* decorations inside the castle unfortunately nothing remains.

A more severe example of the brick built castle is La Mota[37] (plates 311, 312 and 313), with its dominating and terrifying keep. Probably a thirteenth-century castle built to guard the important trading centre of Medina del Campo, La Mota was transformed in the fifteenth century into a fortress equipped for using and withstanding gunfire. The new buildings were begun in about 1440 by Fernando de Carreño for John II and were completed in about 1479 by Alfonso Nieto. They probably included the outer curtain wall, which was provided with two galleries in its thickness, and the keep itself supporting four pairs of twin turrets with the corner angles protruding between them and its machicolations on stone consoles. The castle has an unpleasant reputation as a prison; among its unwilling guests were Joanna the Mad, the daughter of Isabella the Catholic, and Cesare Borgia who nevertheless managed to escape. The castle chaplain gave him a file to break through the grille on his window and a rope with which to slide down to the dry moat.

The powerful ruins of Valencia de Don Juan (León) (plate 384), remarkable for its clusters of very tall, very thin round towers in its keep and curtain walls offer an example of castle building in the north. And further south there are two that show a strong Moorish influence: San Servando at Toledo (plate 70), built by the archbishop of Toledo, Pedro Tenorio, with its pointed merlons typical of *Mudéjar* style; and the much-restored but still very striking Almodóvar del Rio (plate 308) in the province of Cordoba. But the castle which shows best the new style of splendid living, common to the higher nobility of the great countries of Europe at this time, is Manzanares el Real.[38] The earlier castle built nearby in the Guadarrama hills belonged to the Marquis of Santillana, the writer of enchanting lyrics, to whom it was granted by John II. His son, who became duke of the Infantado in 1475, reconstructed the castle, building a palace defended by strong,

low curtain walls. The machicolation of the main building is, however, false and all the energies of the *Mudéjar* craftsman went into the decorative possibilities of the form. Perhaps the decorations were intended to deceive their Catholic Majesties, who had already expressed their dislike of any new castle building in their territories, so that their agents might be distracted by the charm and invention of the building from noticing its still powerful military strength. From each of the round corner towers of the western façade there springs another round tower of lesser diameter studded with round bosses like the stone cannon-balls then in use. A similarly decorated tower, this time octagonal, rises from the roof of the keep. In about 1480 the second duke of the Infantado added the famous gallery (plate 315), the finest example of the *isabelino* or Spanish flamboyant style in Spain. The architect was Juan de Guas who had designed the church of San Juan de los Reyes in Toledo.

With the fall of Granada in 1492 and the opportunities provided for all the adventurous and unruly spirits of the peninsula by the discovery of America in the same year, the power of the joint monarchies of Spain was established and the great period of Spanish castle building came to an end. When Philip II in 1574 ordered an inventory to be taken of the castles of Spain, the returns showed a picture of consistent decline and decay among these great and proud buildings that a new age had no use for.

312 *On previous pages, left* La Mota, Medina del Campo, Spain. Machicolation and bartizans crowning the keep, now the haunt of jackdaws.

313 *Previous page* La Mota, Medina del Campo, Spain. The stupendous brick built *torre del homenaje* or keep of this important Castilian royal castle. Although a castle stood here protecting the important trading centre of Medina del Campo at least as early as the twelfth century, this keep is part of the vast programme of new building and reconstruction carried out between 1440 and 1480. It is attributed to Fernando de Carreño who worked for John II.

314 *Right* Almodóvar del Rio, Spain. A Moorish castle, rebuilt in the fourteenth century by Pedro the Cruel and heavily restored in the last century, on the banks of the Guadalquivir.

315 *Overleaf* Manzanares el Real, Spain. Part of the famous gallery in the *isabelino* style designed for the second duke of the Infantado by Juan de Guas. The octagonal tower is bossed with rounded boulders, a pattern followed on the two towers rising above the wall-walk of the western façade.

316 *Overleaf, right* Manzanares el Real, Spain. The gateway in the outer walls of this most richly decorated of all fifteenth-century Spanish castles, built near Madrid in the Guadarrama hills by the first duke of the Infantado. The machicolations are blind, i.e. only there for their decorative function, and the main defence is horizontal, not vertical, from the gun-loops which have an interesting double-cross pattern.

CASTLES OF EASTERN, CENTRAL, AND MEDITERRANEAN EUROPE IN THE 14TH AND 15TH CENTURIES

The castles of the Teutonic Knights

The great fortifications of the Teutonic Knights, now scattered in various parts of Poland and Russia, formed the nuclei of one of the most original political foundations of the Middle Ages. The final defeat of the Latin Kingdom had caused the removal of the headquarters of the Order first, after the fall of Acre in 1291, to Venice, and then, under the Grand Master Siegfried von Feuchtwangen, to Marienburg (plate 318) in 1309. The great period of castle building therefore lasts roughly from this time, throughout the fourteenth century, and until the battle of Tannenberg in 1410 which marks the decline of the Order. The splendour and comforts of these castles reflect the extraordinary authority that the knights secured in the east. Working with the Hanseatic League, they grew rich on the trade of the Baltic, controlling Visby (plate 202) and the coasts of that sea. Kings, among them John of Bohemia and the future Henry IV of England, were proud to visit them and take part in a crusade against the heathen—and so the greater castles grew to resemble palaces worthy of their visitors.

There are three features that mark the originality of these castles, especially when compared with earlier German castles. The first, of course, is that they were military convents and, therefore, strongly influenced by monastic designs and needs in their construction. The second is their regularity of layout, generally rectangular, which has been claimed as a direct influence of the Crusades but which may be seen as a revival of the practice going back to Carolingian times.[1] They were generally built on low ground by rivers and provided with moats and, therefore, their form was not dictated by hills or mountains. And third, the most important castles were built

317 Marienburg, Poland. The exterior of the Grand Master's lodgings, in an early nineteenth-century engraving. Its particularly original features include the manner of breaking the buttresses with slender pillars to allow more light into the state apartments, and the ornate consoles of the corner towers.

318 *Below* Marienburg, Poland. The river frontage.

of brick, thus adding an extra impetus to the movement along the north of Germany, Holland, and East Anglia where the lack of good ashlar had delayed the spread of the great Gothic buildings more common further south. A brickworks, one must mention, stood in the outworks of the castle of Marienburg. Because of this use of brick the great castles of the Teutonic Knights share many characteristics with both the churches and cathedrals of the Hansa towns and of Poland and with the town halls of those regions as well. These characteristics include the use of stepped gables and of great expanses of bare brick walls which could be relieved of monotony either by blind, sunken panels or by patterns of different coloured bricks. By the acceptance of this style,[2] and by adapting it to their own military, conventual, and administrative needs the Teutonic Knights brought a new dignity and beauty to the architecture of the castle.

Marienburg, now Malbork, heavily restored in the last century and badly damaged in parts in World War II, used to be known as 'the queen of all the castles of the Order in the East'. By 1280 it consisted of two main parts, the *Hochschloss* which contained a chapel and a chapterhouse from which the great possessions of the Order were ruled, and the *Mittelschloss* which contained barracks and necessary offices (see fig. 28). A remarkable feature of the *Hochschloss* was the *Wehrgang* or covered gallery with machicolations that ran all round the building and which could be reached from the chapel, the chapterhouse, and the dormitories of the knights by staircases in the walls. From their dormitories the knights could also reach the *Danske*, or sewage-tower, which contained their lavatories and which was built out over the River Nogat. A similar arrangement existed at Marienwerder. The transfer from Venice, however, led to great changes at Marienburg. Between 1335 and 1341 the Grand Master Dietrich von Altenburg added a tower and a bridge over the Nogat, trans-

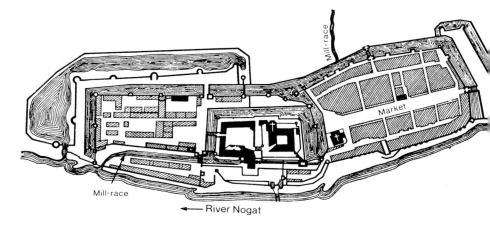

Fig. 28 *Above* A plan of Marienburg, Poland. (After Hotz)

319 *Below* Marienburg, Poland. The interior of the summer refectory in the Grand Master's lodgings, designed by Nikolaus Fellenstein, and probably influenced by the chapter houses of some English cathedrals.

320 *Above* Marienburg, Poland. The exterior of the chapel showing the great statue of the Virgin with (left) the *Hochschloss*, the older part of the castle, and (right) part of the *Mittelschloss*. This engraving shows the condition of the castle at the time when it was an inspiration to the poet Eichendorff and to the Neo-classical architect Schinkel before the mid-nineteenth-century restoration.

321 *Left* Marienwerder, Poland. A view of the great complex of ecclesiastical and military buildings comprising (left to right) the *Danske* or sewage tower connected by a bridge to the castle of the Teutonic Knights, and the cathedral with its bell tower.

322 *Below left* Marienwerder, Poland. Part of the bridge to the *Danske* and the castle.

lodging of the grand master which is a wing of the *Mittelschloss*. This building was constructed in the late fourteenth century by the Rhenish architect Nikolaus Fellenstein[4] and was intended to express the power and majesty of the Order and to entertain the grand master's royal and princely guests. Its luxuries included the provision of underfloor heating in the winter refectory. The most beautiful room was the summer refectory, with its windows looking onto the river by which communication was made to many of the other towns and castles of the Order. Here the vaulting is supported by a single granite pillar, reminiscent of the English chapterhouses, and the whole forms a room of exceptional power and originality. The romantic poet Eichendorff sighed 'Here one truly understands what in the exuberance of youth Schlegel meant when he called architecture "frozen music" '[5] (plate 319).

For all its splendour and despite the extent to which it had been allowed to grow (it has a river frontage of 550 yards or 503 m), Marienburg was still a thoroughly defensible castle. When, in 1410, the Grand Master Ulrich von Jungingen went off to fight the Poles he took with him the cannon of the castle. He died, together with thousands of his followers, at Tannenberg and his cannon were captured, to be brought back to Marienburg by the victors and turned on its walls. Heinrich von Plauen, a young member of the Order, rushed to the defence of Marienburg, set fire to the town so as to prevent the Poles using it as a base, mustered a large garrison, and managed to hold off the armies of King Vladislas for two months. Several storming attempts failed and dysentery broke out among the besiegers so that they were forced to retire. The great days of Marienburg were soon to be over. Von Plauen was disgraced in an intrigue for power and no grand master of his capabilities succeeded him. In 1457 the grand master was so short of cash that he had to pledge twenty castles and towns, including Marienburg, to his own mercenary soldiers, largely Hussite Bohemians. These mercenaries finally revolted and drove the grand master and his magnates from the castle with whips and insults. A brave attempt by other knights to regain the castle from the Poles, to whom the mercenaries sold it, failed and, after the siege of 1466, it was formally ceded to Poland.

Marienburg draws most attention but something must be said of the other castles which the Order built over their wide lands. Chief among these is Marienwerder[6], now Kwidzyn (plate 321), also severely war damaged, which consists of a castle of the Order attached to a cathedral, built together in a powerful architectural group on a steep bank of a river valley. Its most unusual feature was the great *Danske* or sewage-tower which was detached from the main body of the castle and could only be reached by a gallery 176 ft (54 m) long supported on five great arches resting on four freestanding brick pillars (plate 322). Quite elaborate examples of lavatories and provisions for the disposal of waste are to be found in much earlier castles (Henry II's castles and the Wartburg, to take two instances), but never had so much effort, expense, and superb architectural skill been devoted to a

formed the *Mittelschloss* into residential quarters, and added a third element to the defence, the *Unterschloss* which contained, among other things, the brickworks and a foundry. The most splendid innovations were those of his later successor as grand master, Winrich von Kniprode – appropriately so for, under his long rule from 1352 to 1383, the Order achieved its zenith. He enlarged the chapel in the *Hochschloss* and added to its eastern exterior a gigantic statue of the Virgin holding the Christ child[3] set in a window niche and studded with gold mosaic (plate 320). She stood there as a reminder that the knights were members of a religious state devoted to crushing the heathen and that her faithful were guarded in the folds of her cloak. Beneath her statue lay the graves of the knights. The most admired of all the buildings was the new sewage-tower in a secular fortress. Perhaps we must look to the conventional nature of the Order's building for an explanation; in many monasteries the horror of bodily functions was taken to such a length that each monk was provided with a separate privy.

The most easterly castle of the Teutonic Knights was Hermannsburg at Narva, not far distant from the future site of St Petersburg. On the opposite bank Ivan the Great built his fortress of Ivangorod in 1492 and the two castles still glare at one another across the Narva (plate 326).[7] One of the most beautiful Teutonic castles must have been Rehden (1290-1300) (plate 324), where the square shape of the main block was relieved with elegant patterns in the brickwork, with hatchments of different coloured bricks picked out on the main mass of the walls. Other examples include Gollub (c 1300) and Nidzica, both in Poland.

The chief reason for the existence of the Order in the east was the war against the heathen. This reason suddenly disappeared in 1386 when the Jagellon duke of Lithuania accepted baptism and married the heiress of the Polish crown. From this time the Order was under attack from an increasingly strong Poland. Many of its members became affected by

Hussite doctrines and its military reputation was severely damaged, as we have seen, by the battle of Tannenberg and by later Bohemian invasions. It finally disappeared as an outpost of the Catholic Church when the last grand master of the east, a Hohenzollern, accepted the teachings of Luther and secularized the lands under his control.

The Emperor Charles IV and Karlštejn

With the Emperor Charles IV and, later, the Hussites in Bohemia we come to new roles for the castle, first as a shrine and then as a bulwark of Christian communism. Charles IV was a remarkable ruler who combined great personal holiness with the most civilized of tastes.[8] The son of the blind King John of Bohemia who died at Crécy, he was deeply affected by his upbringing at the French court. He saw Bohemia as the best basis for building up the territorial power necessary to a strong emperor and so continued the shift of gravity of power in central Europe to the east which had already begun in the thirteenth century. To him the Czechs owe the introduction of the vine, the building of the Charles bridge and the reconstruction of St Vitus's cathedral in Prague, the founding of Prague University, and the establishment of peace by

323 Niedzica, Poland. A corner tower of a hill-top castle near Cracow, built about 1325 and reconstructed in 1601.

324 *Above* Rehden, Poland. Enough remains of this once exceptionally elegant castle, built 1290–1300, to show the quality of the brickwork, a feature common also to the ecclesiastical and civic buildings of the area in the same period.

clearing the roads of brigands. To dominate the road from Germany to Prague and to act as his treasure house and as a shrine for his vast collection of relics, he built his great castle of Karlštejn[9] (plates 214, 215, 252 and 253) between 1348 and 1357.

Charles's close connections with the French court have led some writers to speak of Karlštejn as a French *château* set down in Bohemia. In scale and splendour of decoration it is comparable to the great Valois castles but its ground-plan and the omission of flanking towers in the curtain walls, except at the entrances, show it to be more typical of the castles of central Germany. And its wall-paintings and interior decoration owe more to Italy, where Charles had acted as regent for his father, than to France. The use of wooden hoarding (now completely restored, as in our illustrations) was superseded in the western European castles of similar importance by stone machicolation. Karlštejn is defended piecemeal by five

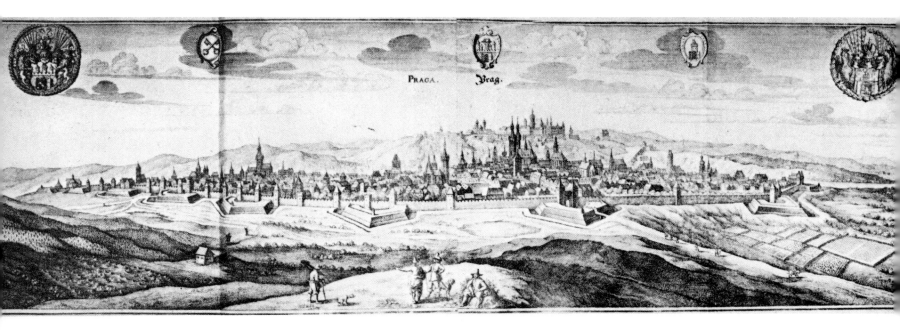

325 *Above* Prague, Czechoslovakia. A panoramic view by Matthaeus Merian the elder in 1650. from *Topographia Bohemiae, Moraviae et Silesiae*. The Hradschin and St Vitus Cathedral overlook the whole city. Note the addition of sharp-angled bastions to the medieval walls.

326 *Below* Narva, Russia. In this depiction of the battle of Narva in 1704 between Peter the Great and Charles XII of Sweden can be seen (centre left) Hermannsburg, the most easterly castle of the Teutonic Knights. From an eighteenth-century engraving.

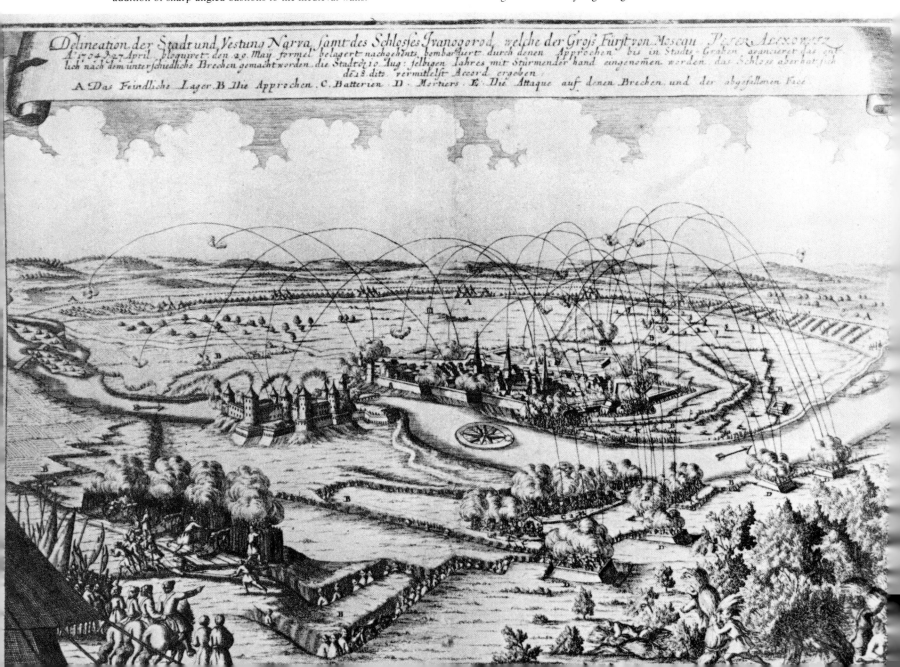

buildings: first by the well tower which was furnished with supplies by underground passages from the River Morina; second, by the lodgings of the *Burggraf*, the commander of the castle; third, by the imperial palace containing the chapels of St Nicholas and St Wenceslas; fourth, by the tower of the Virgin containing the collegiate church of Our Lady, and a subsidiary chapel of St Catherine (plate 215); and fifth and last, by the great keep, 121 ft (37 m) high. This holds the Hall of the Empire and above it the chapel of the Holy Rood (plate 252) where Charles kept the crown jewels of the Empire and of Bohemia and his vast collection of relics, including the piece of the True Cross which gave the chapel its name. Thus the castle is built according to a progression of degrees of holiness and the external might of each tower is related to the value of what it is intended to preserve and defend.

The first stone of the castle was laid on 10 June 1348 by the archbishop of Prague, Ernest of Pardubiça. The architect is thought to have been a Czech or a German who had worked at Prague under the master-mason Matthew of Arras, who had come to Prague from Avignon in 1342. The interiors of the castle contain some of the most complete series of medieval wall-paintings surviving. The chapel of the Virgin is painted with scenes celebrating Charles's collection of relics, including a depiction of him receiving the relic of the True Cross from Pierre de Lusignan, king of Cyprus. There is also a series of *trompe l'oeil* architectural panels showing a marked Italian influence. The most remarkable paintings were the works of a painter, known only as Theodric, in the chapel of the Holy Rood. Nothing is known of his origins and nothing similar to his powerful, lumpy figures (plate 253) links his style with any contemporary fashion.[10] The paintings are on the upper parts of the walls, while beneath runs a high frieze of gilded plaster embedded with about 3000 chunky semi-precious stones. The paintings, together with the golden vaulting, the superbly elegant roodscreen, the altarpiece by Tomaso di Modena, give the chapel an overpowering impression of richness and mystical splendour.

To Charles the castle was as much a place of retreat as a weapon of his power. He liked to spend Holy Week in the small chapel (plate 215) off the chapel of the Virgin and his meals and papers requiring his urgent attention would be pushed to him through a hatch. His devotion to the Church did not, however, mean that his other duties suffered. His contemporaries noted the care with which he listened to a report,

327 *Above* Tabor, Czechoslovakia. The fortress-town of the Hussites as it appeared in Merian's *Topographia Bohemiae, Moraviae et Silesiae*, 1650. The engraving shows well the defensive possibilities of the natural features of the site. The Hussites were told to go up into 'the high places' to await the coming of the Lord and this site and that of Oreb were renamed after biblical mountains.

whittling away all the time at a piece of wood, and offered an instant decision. He was deeply concerned with the advancement of his family (another of the Karlštejn series of paintings, this time in the great hall, depicted important figures from his genealogy), and was married four times. Villani tells a story of one of his wives who was so frightened that he might be attracted by one of the court beauties that she gave him a

love potion to draw him to her. Unfortunately it poisoned him and he nearly died. To protect herself, she accused some gentlemen of his chamber of a plot to kill him and they were about to be put to death when the truth came out. So flattered was he that he forgave her the lies and the poison, restored the wrongly accused men to his favour, and, 'considering the frail nature of women, with his usual meekness he received her honourably to his love'. His fourth wife, Elizabeth, had the strange endowment of hands that could grip like steel and Charles used to make her show his court how she could rip wood and parchment to pieces. She was the mother of Richard II's beloved Anne of Bohemia and she herself was so devoted to Charles that when he was dangerously ill in 1371 she walked barefoot from Karlštejn to the shrine of St Sigismund to make an offering of gold for his recovery.

Charles's great reforms in Bohemia, his fostering of the Czech language, his endowment of the University, and his own deep concern for the purity of the Church were to have an effect totally opposite to his intentions. These traits in his policy awoke, however, the reforming zeal of the Czechs, first under Jan Hus and then under two great military leaders, Jan Žižka and Prokop the Bald.

The Hussite wars
The burning of the great Czech reformer, Jan Hus, at Constance in 1415, a direct contravention of the safe-conduct given him by Sigismund, the king of the Germans, was the chief event that led to the Hussite wars; in these wars time and again the Bohemians were to defeat great crusading armies gathered from all over Europe and their final collapse only came about through internal dissensions. Hus had stirred popular feeling against the Church's vast possessions (at the beginning of the century half Bohemia was in ecclesiastical ownership) and his demands for reform of abuses, for communion in both kinds, and for poverty of the clergy united the lesser nobility and the

328 *Above left* A page from a German 'Firework Book' *c* 1440 showing an attack on a castle. The barrel of the large mounted cannon consists of long segments bound together with hoops. The crossbowmen are shooting incendiaries at the castle and the defenders have special hooks for pulling them off the roofs. Note the barrels of the handguns on the right. *Tower of London.*

329 *Left* A reconstruction of a Hussite camp, showing the artillery-laden wagons acting as the first line of defence. The wagons carrying the cannonballs form the second.

330 *Above right* Montealegre, Spain. The grandeur and subtlety achieved by the use of simple geometrical shapes are shown at their best in this striking Spanish castle built on a trapezoidal ground-plan. Shadows play an important part in the impression made by the various parts of the castle: here the sharp black patterns of the corner towers seem to express dominion and defiance, while the smaller intervening towers with their softer shadows evoke the shelter and security to be found within the walls.

331 *Right* Peñafiel, Spain. This powerful castle whose name means 'the faithful rock', received its present form in the fifteenth century when it was rebuilt by the Grand Master of the Order of Calatrava, Don Pedro Girón. This type of castle running along the crest of a hill is known as *gran buque* or great ship. A series of turned entrances leads to the tall keep or *torre del homenaje*, characteristic of Spanish castles of all periods.

332 *Overleaf* Hunting remained one of the chief amusements of the upper classes throughout the Middle Ages. This savage bear hunt comes from the *Devonshire Hunting Tapestries* executed in Tournai *c* 1425–50. The tapestries may be connected with the marriage of Henry VI of England to Margaret of Anjou in 1445.

common people against both the great landowners and the Church. The death of King Wenceslas in 1419 meant the succession as king of Bohemia of the hated Sigismund, who was determined to stamp out this heresy. In 1420 he besieged Prague (plate 325) and his armies suffered disaster in an engagement with the Hussites under their great general,

Jan Žižka of Tronor. Žižka was a member of the lesser nobility who had already seen service abroad, fighting at the battle of Tannenberg against the Teutonic Knights and conducting a successful defence of their castle of Radzyn which the Poles had taken. Deeply imbued with the Hussite doctrines, he was one of the many who had flocked to Mount Tabor (plate 327) near Bechyne to form a new Christian community, where for a time all was owned in common, set up in 1420 by pilgrims on a hill. The priests of the movement told their followers, 'The end of the world is approaching, resplendent castles shall fall into ruins, proud cities shall perish, magnificent monasteries crumble into dust, and all existing society is to be destroyed.'[11] But for all their hatred of castles as the symbol of the old feudal and ecclesiastical order, the Taborites were forced to make their new home one of the most powerful fortresses of the land. Even the widely travelled Aeneas Sylvius, the future Pope Pius II and builder of the Rocca Pia at Tivoli (plate 376), was impressed with its strength. Žižka was as good a builder of fortifications as he was a general. He reinforced Tabor with a great double wall completely encircling its natural position, a steep hill on a peninsula formed by the joining of the Luznice river and the smaller Tismenice river. The only approach by land was guarded by a moat and then by three walls. The ground-plan was roughly hexagonal and at each projecting corner a great tower was built.[12] It was difficult to shake off old habits in other ways. Žižka wished to change his name to Jan of the Chalice, that being the symbol of the Hussite demand for communion in both kinds. As men were known by the names of the castles they owned, he took a castle, called it Kalich (or Chalice castle) and named himself after it.

333 *Left* Fuensaldaña, Spain. One of several great castles built by the Spanish nobility in the unruly period of the fifteenth century, this was built for Don Alfonso Perez de Vivero, treasurer to John II who was murdered in 1453. The castle seems never to have been finished or occupied. The light slanting through the machicolation shows how well provided for defence it would have been.

334 *Above* A drawing from the Hussite ms, showing a cannon with a device for raising and lowering the barrel. *Munich, Staatsbibliothek,* cod. Lat. 197, fo 28v.

335 *Right* Pernštejn, Czechoslovakia. A passageway in the thickness of the castle walls.

From the fortress of Tabor and, later, from the similar foundation of Oreb (named after a biblical mountain, as Tabor was), Žižka led forth his armies, first to defend Prague and then to a series of resounding victories against the invading crusaders. Although notable as a builder of fortifications and extremely skilled in siegecraft, his main contribution to military tactics was his use of artillery mounted in great wooden wagons which on the field were formed into squares (plate 329). At first these wagon formations were used as defensive positions but during the night-battle of Kutna Hora in 1421, when he was surrounded by Sigismund's troops, Žižka ordered the wagons to move on the enemy and, stopping only to fire, cover the advance of his own troops. Žižka had invented a mobile castle, the ancestor of the modern tank, thus opening new possibilities for artillery which had previously been used only in static warfare. His other introductions included a degree of discipline quite exceptional in a medieval army, a speed of movement which enabled him to surprise his enemies again and again, and an ability to follow up a victory relentlessly. This discipline was backed by the strength of the Hussite religious convictions; they would enter battle singing their great hymn 'Ye Warriors of God' and beating drums, producing an effect of such terror in their enemies that it was put about after Žižka's death that his flayed skin had been stretched over a drum. Well before Žižka the Bohemians had an exceptional reputation for their military skills, their ingenuity, and their courage. This extended to their women followers who are said in one early battle of the wars to have laid their veils on the ground to entangle the spurs of the enemy knights advancing on foot. It has been said of Žižka that he 'revolutionized warfare'.[13] The eclipse of the knightly cavalry of the Middle Ages was due quite as much to Hussite forms of military organization, Hussite methods of fighting, and the development of the recently invented fire weapons under Žižka, as to the Swiss mercenary infantry. This legacy is still seen in the names of weapons today–howitzer from the Czech word *houfrice,* and pistol from the Czech word *pistàla.*

Even after Žižka's death in 1424 the Hussite armies, especially

under Prokop the Bald, continued to hold off Sigismund's troops. They were only defeated by their own countrymen using their own tactics against them at the battle of Lipany in 1434. Sigismund died a matter of months after his return to the country that had rejected him for so long, the main effect of the revolution being to confirm the Bohemians in an independence they preserved to varying degrees until 1620. Another effect was the seizure and redistribution of the Church lands amongst the nobility, who naturally began to reconstruct the old fortresses and make them more comfortable and more splendid. A notable example of one of these castles is Pernštejn (plate 338).[14] William and John of Pernštejn began to reconstruct it in 1457 after a fire. Improvements continued to be made for another hundred years, generally in the late Gothic style, a fine example being the cellular vaulting in the entrance hall (plate 336 and see also plates 335, 337 and 342).

The Turks and castles in the east

Under the rule of two monarchs of the Neapolitan Angevin house (1304-82), Hungary absorbed many of the influences of French chivalry: a feudal army, the establishment of military orders, and the attraction of the nobility to the court. This naturally had an effect on the design of castles and the standard of living enjoyed there. The most original fortifications were, however, built in response to the increasing danger of Turkish invasions which, although repelled in the fifteenth century by the two great leaders John Hunyadi and his son Mathias Corvinus, finally ended in the disaster of Mohacs in 1526 and the Turkish conquest. One response to this threat was that of the German settlers in Transylvania, who constructed fortresses surrounding their churches with a perimeter wall with covered wall-walks, as at Tartlau, now Prejmer, or at Kelling, which contains two *Bergfrieden* and a moat.[15] The grandest fifteenth-century castle is that of Vadyahunyad or Hunedoara (plate 340), now in Rumania, the palace of John Hunyadi whose great hall, with its gallery of oriel windows, seems to owe much to the influence of the Teutonic castles further north. Under Mathias Corvinus strong Italian influences came to Hungary, one of the most important in the next century being the introduction of the bastion.

The threat of the Turks to Europe had been made more apparent at the battle of Nicopolis in 1396 when the defeat of a large army of Crusaders, including the future Emperor Sigismund and members of the French and Burgundian royal houses, showed how out-dated the old chivalric cavalry charge had become. The siege and capture of Byzantium in 1453 shocked the consciousness of Europe with the new power of gunpowder. This was followed in 1480 by the siege of Rhodes in which the Knights of St John barely beat off repeated Turkish attacks. All the countries in danger of invasion were forced to look to their defences and it was to the Italians, with their mastery of fortification, that they turned for advice

336 *Left* Pernštejn, Czechoslovakia. Cellular vaulting of about 1520 creates an apparently simple but extremely satisfying pattern above this staircase in the entrance hall.

337 *Above right* Pernštejn, Czechoslovakia. A late Gothic doorway.

338 *Right* Pernštejn, Czechoslovakia. The way to the main entrance of the castle is defended by a particularly strong polygonal tower connected by a bridge to the main block and encircled by a series of machicolated turrets (left).

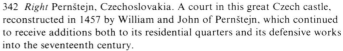

342 *Right* Pernštejn, Czechoslovakia. A court in this great Czech castle, reconstructed in 1457 by William and John of Pernštejn, which continued to receive additions both to its residential quarters and its defensive works into the seventeenth century.

340 *Above* Hunedoara, Rumania. A view of this much-restored fifteenth-century Transylvanian castle, the seat of Jan Hunyadi.

339 *Above left* Schönburg, W. Germany. The great fourteenth-century *Schildmauer* protecting the most accessible part of the site. The round *Bergfried* on the right also appears in colour plate 102.

341 *Above* Schönburg, W. Germany. A view from Oberwesel with the Frauenkirche in the centre.

Later German, Austrian, and Swiss castles of the fourteenth and fifteenth centuries

Only one Emperor in this period attempted with any success to re-establish the authority of his office in the style of his predecessors, Ludwig of Bavaria (1314-47), and his attempt was wrecked by quarrels over the papacy at Avignon and the ambitions of the Valois kings to interfere in German politics. Even an Emperor as strong in many ways as Charles IV preferred to buy peace by the privileges he granted to the electors in the Golden Bull of 1356 and to build up his own territorial power outside Germany proper, in Bohemia. This resulted in the fragmentation of Germany into almost autonomous electorates and states whose princes eventually were to gain almost complete sovereignty. These princes, having won a large measure of independence, now found it necessary to crush the resistance of the towns and of the lesser nobility who still dared to defy them from their castles. One feature of their rule was the increasing power they gained over Church lands and appointments, a movement that helps to explain the success of the Reformation in those regions where the princes supported Luther. This was, however, no easy task: the leagues both of towns and nobles had arisen in many cases as a reaction against the anarchy caused by the withdrawal of imperial power and frequently they possessed cohesivenesss and strength. The castle still played a notable part in these struggles. One of the most important new arrivals to the princely ranks in the fifteenth century was that of the Hohen-zollern, who took their name from a castle south of Tübingen and who had risen from obscurity to become hereditary *Burggrafen* of the imperial castle of Nuremberg and then electors of Brandenburg. Before Frederick I became the first

and help. Even Russia, where the Tsars of Moscow now regarded themselves as the heirs to the Byzantine imperium, showed a belated interest in the art of fortification and the Italian architect Fioravanti was employed on the walls of the Kremlin as early as 1475. But it was not only the eastern European countries that had to fear the Turk; Germany and Austria still show many traces of the threat that did not cease until long after our period in 1683 when Jan Sobieski came from Poland to help save the city of Vienna from its Turkish besiegers.

Hohenzollern elector in 1415, every princely castle in Brandenburg, apart from Spandau, had been appropriated to private ownership. After violent struggles with a league known as the Stellmeiser he managed to defeat them in 1414 and to issue laws condemning private feuds as criminal offences.[16] These leagues of knights were known elsewhere in Germany, especially amongst the unruly nobility in the old imperial lands of Swabia and Franconia, notably the League of the Growling Lion founded in 1379 and so called because of the arms borne by its knights. Wide areas were given over to anarchy and the peasantry suffered terribly in these feuds. It was only as the princes established their power, gained control of taxation, and began to expend their hard-won wealth on gunpowder and artillery, which the nobility could not afford to a significant extent, that the private castle declined in importance.

In common with France and England, fewer castles were built in Germany in this period. Where the new castles were associated with princes or great ecclesiastics, they took on the appearance of palaces. The vast numbers of servants and courtiers required at these courts meant that castles such as Coburg (plate 346) or Hohensalzburg (plate 63) had to spread in extent and provide enough living space. In their general disposition both these examples show the old German trust in a strong natural site and an irregular layout. In other castles, however, one noticeable development is the adoption of a regular ground-plan and due attention paid to flanking. An exceptional example, with its hexagonal plan, is the enchanting Pfalzgrafenstein bei Kaub[17] (plate 344) begun in 1327 by Ludwig of Bavaria on an island in the Rhine to act as a toll station and seeming itself like a ship about to sail. Another adoption was the form of the tower-house as at Eltville, on the Rhine[18], one of a series of fortresses constructed by Archbishop Baldwin of Trier (1307-54) and memorable for its connection with Gutenburg who had a printing press installed there. Two later Rhineland castles of the fifteenth century, Heyden near Aachen and Hülchrath, also reveal adaptations of the tower-house idea.[19] So many castles had, however, been constructed in earlier centuries that it was more usual to add to an already existing complex, which is visually sometimes very exciting, as at Eltz (jacket front and plates 131, 145 and 146). In some cases, as at Harburg in Swabia, the device of double walls with lists in between (as at Carcassonne) now played the part of the *Schildmauer* on the only side of approach.[20]

The areas liable to attack from the Turks, notably Austria and Bavaria, were especially well fortified, the most notable and impressive example being Burghausen in Upper Bavaria, which consists of six castles strung along the 1,000 yards (914m) of a mountain top, built largely between 1479 and 1503. In the same period Hohensalzburg (plate 63) was

343 *Above right* Wildenstein, W. Germany. A seventeenth-century view by Merian from *Topographia Sueviae* of this extraordinary castle on the Swabian reaches of the Danube. Four drawbridges had to be crossed before reaching the main castle. Its form, as seen here, was the work of Count Werner von Zimmern in the first half of the sixteenth century.

344 *Right* Pfalzgrafenstein and Gutenfels, Kaub, W. Germany. Ludwig of Bavaria's toll station in the Rhine built from 1327 onwards and given a baroque roof to its central tower in the seventeenth century is overlooked by the earlier thirteenth-century castle of Gutenfels.

345 *Right* Hohensalzburg, Austria. Twisted columns of red marble in the Golden Hall, the centre of which carries the devices of the builder, Archbishop Leonhard von Keutschach, and the date 1501. These columns help to support an elaborately panelled ceiling embossed with gilded studs.

346 *Overleaf* Coburg, W. Germany. The main entrance and part of the curtain walls of this late but famous castle, seat of the Saxe-Coburg family and refuge of Martin Luther in 1530 during the diet of Augsburg. First mentioned as a castle in the thirteenth century, though occupied as a site from prehistory, most of its earlier buildings were destroyed in a great fire in 1499, though the Hohes Haus (centre left) with its steep pitched roof is as it was rebuilt in 1450. Much of the rebuilding was the work of the first duke of Saxe-Coburg Johann Casimir (1564–1635). Wallenstein besieged Coburg in 1632 for seven days and had to withdraw. Three years later it fell to the imperial armies after a siege lasting five months. The handsome baroque gateway (1671) is crowned with cannon, powder kegs and balls.

347 *Overleaf, right* Coburg, W. Germany. Another view of the Hohes Haus and below it one of the towers of the perimeter wall.

provided with four round towers, new bulwarks, and a granary in the later fifteenth century as a protection against the Turks.[21] The most striking parts of Hohensalzburg are the state apartments built by the Archbishop Leonhard von Keutschach (1495-1519), the great hall (plate 345), and the Golden Room with its stove (plate 286), one of the most astonishing achievements of the late-medieval potter.

However much the nobility despised and hated the townsmen, they were not slow to adopt the tastes and luxuries the towns developed and provided. One example is given by the numbers of small rooms now built, the result being more like a town house than a country mansion. This love of lavish decoration is to be found not only in great princely castles but also in castles of the nobility, such as Eltz[22] (plates 131, 145 and

146), with the delightfully painted walls of its chambers and its rich oratory. Frequently the exterior of the castle was modified, regardless of consideration of defence, simply to provide greater comfort inside – for example the great chimney stacks of Heidenreichstein (plate 351),[23] although this particular castle was besieged in the fifteenth century by both Hussites and rebellious peasants.

As a final example of the German castle one cannot choose better than Coburg[24] (plate 346) where the disposition of its defences exactly conforms to the great dolomite rock on which it is built. Although it was a thirteenth-century foundation, nearly all that remains now dates from after a great fire in 1499. Many of its residential portions, therefore, show a marked Renaissance influence, a feature Coburg shares with numbers of other German and Austrian castles that continued to be occupied in the sixteenth and seventeenth centuries, Rheinfels, Heidelberg and Rapottenstein being among them. Coburg's defences, reinforced in 1614 and later, were so strong that Wallenstein besieged it for seven days without success in 1632 and three years later it held out for five months against another imperial army, only falling this time through a trick. Although fascinating as the place where Luther sheltered during the diet of Augsburg and as the home of the Saxe-Coburg family,

348 *Left* Rappottenstein, Austria. A view looking up to the castle perched on a high outcrop of rocks. The corbels probably supported wooden hoarding.

349 *Below left* Rappottenstein, Austria. The kitchen.

350 *Below* Hohensalzburg, Austria. The gateway to the inner castle built by Archbishop Leonhard von Keutschach (1495–1519) whose emblem of a turnip appears in the armorial devices and who is recorded in the inscriptions. He had to take up residence here because of the opposition of the citizens of Salzburg and of peasant risings. During his successor's reign the castle underwent its only siege during the Peasants' Revolt of 1525.

351 *Right* Heidenreichstein, Austria. Chimney stacks, one with a stork's nest, and projecting privies, of various dates, show residential needs overcoming those of defence.

closely connected with the British royal family, it also shared in the astonishing but short-lived resurgence in the military importance of the castle that took place in seventeenth-century Europe, whether in the Thirty Years War, Richelieu's struggles against the French nobility, or the English Civil War.

Castles of the Netherlands

The landscapes of the seventeenth-century Dutch landscape painters, notably of the Ruysdaels, frequently concentrate upon the ruins of a brick castle slowly tumbling down into its reed-thick moat as the focus of sunlight before the storm breaks. Today Holland has about 300 castles remaining out of the 2000-odd it once possessed[25] and, as in the Baltic areas, these castles were largely built of brick. The proximity of the Flemish cities, however, with their great wealth and luxurious tastes, strongly influenced the later Dutch castle. To this period we owe the great Dutch brick castles, among them the additions to Muiden (plate 205), built by Albert of Bavaria between 1370 and 1386, and Doornenburg (plate 303) of the early fifteenth century. The keep of Doornenburg, which was separated from a large bailey by a moat and could only be approached by a wooden postern, was totally destroyed in 1945; it has now been completely restored. Another brick castle of the fifteenth century, Beersel (plate 285) in Belgium, shows signs of French influence in its use of the tower with a horseshoe ground-plan designed to withstand gunfire and adopted earlier at Fougères (plate 275). The three great towers of Beersel were added in 1491 to an existing roughly circular perimeter wall which keeps the general appearance of the castle well within the characteristic style of the region. A desire for comfort and luxury did not yet mean that all considerations of defence were neglected, so one finds such curious hybrids as Walzin (plate 352) with its elegant palace-like façade gazing out above a sheer and rugged cliff of extraordinary height.

From the Netherlands we must turn to a country with which they had many links of trade and commerce and which resembled them in the intensity of its urban development – Italy.

Italian castles of the fourteenth and fifteenth centuries

The death of Frederick II in 1250 had brought to an end one age of castle building in Italy. Although, in the second half of the thirteenth century, the Guelf party had triumphed in Tuscany, the quarrels that broke out amongst the Guelfs themselves provoked further disorders especially in Florence and the lands it controlled. One of the chief victims of these disorders was Dante Alighieri who, from 1301 until his death in Ravenna in 1321, was an exile, punishable with an unspeakable death should he be taken, living in hiding in Apennine castles, taking shelter with Ghibelline nobles or at the court of some new, powerful family of the north, such as the Scaligeri at Verona, enjoying a few ecstatic months when it seemed likely that the Emperor Henry of Luxembourg would restore peace to Italy, but certain at the end of every journey of nothing but disappointment. One legend tells of him receiving warning of a Florentine emissary coming to seize him at the castle where he was staying. Dante left but met the emissary on the road going up to the castle. The Florentine asked him whether Dante Alighieri was in the castle and received the truthful reply, 'He was there when I was'. They parted and Dante escaped.

In earlier times the most original castles in Italy were the creations of foreign invaders and their descendants; now, in the

352 Walzin, Belgium. This fine castle near Dinant was founded in the thirteenth century and rebuilt c 1581 for the de la Marck family, incorporating many Renaissance features. It was enlarged 1880–3.

fourteenth and fifteenth centuries, with the rise of indigenous rulers establishing their power over comparatively small but very rich areas, a new Italian style develops, strongly helped both by the brilliant line of architects who preceded and brought in the Renaissance and by the intense technological development encouraged in the cities and, more especially, at the courts of military leaders.[26] The fourteenth century sees the widespread adoption of machicolation on consoles, together with merlons with rounded incuttings and the gradual use of more regular ground-plans; and the next century, an increasing awareness of the dangers of firearms and a host of experiments from which emerged the sharp-angled bastion described in Chapter 9. One can divide the Italian fortifications of this period into those built by the cities, by the papacy or its representatives, and, most interesting of all, by the tyrants. All of them employed mercenaries, more especially the tyrants who could not trust their unwilling subjects. The numbers of mercenary troops in Italy greatly increased after the Treaty of Brétigny in 1360 and for a few years the infantry tactics so successfully practised in France and Scotland by the English became common south of the Alps. In the fifteenth century, however, as native mercenaries assumed the ascendancy, there was a reversion almost entirely to the use of cavalry in battle and to protracted sieges of castles and cities. Cities such as Florence and Siena continued to fortify their public buildings and their walls.

One of the most famous examples is the Palazzo Vecchio (plate 355) at Florence, built at the beginning of the fourteenth century. According to the historian Villani, it had to be given a trapezoidal ground-plan instead of a regular form simply to avoid building on a site once occupied by the dwellings of the Ghibellines then in exile.[27] Between 1310 and 1328 Villani himself was in charge of the building of a third series of city walls with fifteen gates and seventy-two towers, an extent made necessary by the fact that Florence had probably the highest population of any city in Europe at the time. These walls were made necessary from fear of attack, first, by Henry of Luxembourg and, later, by Castruccio Castracane, the tyrant of Lucca, who built in 1324 the great triangular fortress of Sarzanello which later fell into Florentine hands. Another way in which the castle was adapted to urban needs can be seen in

the great complex of palaces at Gubbio.[28]

The papacy had earlier led the way in the development of the castle into the palace, notably at Viterbo (plate 353) and Anagni, the seat of the Gaetani family, where Boniface VIII was imprisoned by Nogaret and Sciarra Colonna, an event which so scandalized Dante that his hatred for his old enemy

353 *Above* Viterbo, Italy. The loggia of the papal palace, built *c* 1267.

354 *Below* Benevento, Italy. The tower built by a papal rector in about 1320 to guard the interests in the area of the absent Pope at Avignon.

355 *Right* Palazzo Vecchio, Florence. Built in the late thirteenth and early fourteenth centuries, it is the most famous of the municipal palaces common to many Italian cities; detail from an engraving by Zocchi.

was changed into indignation at the shame brought upon the Vicar of Christ. Although after 1305 the papacy was absent at Avignon its representatives were not always idle. For example, the papal rector in the south built the great keep of Benevento (plate 354) in about 1320, not far from the plain where Manfred had died fighting the French invaders in 1266. Later the great Cardinal Albornoz prepared for the return of the papacy by a series of campaigns and by rebuilding or constructing castles. Among these were the Rocca Maggiore at Assisi (plate 97) which he rebuilt in 1367 and the great fortress of Spoleto (plate 356) which Matteo Gattopone constructed for him between 1362 and 1370.[29] At Spoleto the castle was fed with water by a great aqueduct, the *ponte delle torri,* 750 ft (229 m) long, but even more amazing is the height of 260 ft (79 m) it attains above the gorge it spans. After the return to Rome in 1377 and the long squabbles of the Conciliar movement, at last, by the middle of the fifteenth century, the popes were rich enough to start building again in the most up-to-date styles. One such example is the Rocca Pia built on the site of a Roman amphitheatre by the much travelled Pius II in 1452 to keep a firm hold on his subjects at Tivoli. With its great round towers it forms part of a series of similar castles, such as the Castel Nuovo[30] at Naples (plate 218), built or reconstructed at this time as one of the experiments to withstand artillery.

The papacy was constantly involved in the wars conducted by the tyrants who had arisen in many cities in the north – the Visconti and, after 1450, the Sforza in Milan, the Gonzagas at Mantua, and the Estensi at Ferrara and, in the Romagna, the Malatesta at Rimini and the Montefeltri at Urbino. These families, all famous in the history of civilization for their courts and their encouragement of the arts, were also great builders of fortifications. One of the most notable families in the fourteenth century was the Scaligeri who had gained control of the city and territory of Verona. The Cangrande della Scala whose statue rides so proudly at the Castelvecchio (plate 358) was the patron of Dante. Among the Scaligeri castles is Sirmione (plate 361) on Lake Garda on the peninsula

celebrated by Catullus. Constructed between the late thirteenth and early fourteenth centuries it was intended far more for military purposes than for residence and incorporated a fortified harbour in its defences. The main keep with its slender form resembles the family towers of the great cities and its wide, projecting machicolations and striking crenellations add to the elegant architectural effect gained by the grouping of the towers.[31] For their chief residence the Scaligeri built the great Castelvecchio in Verona with its famous bridge, destroyed in the Second World War and now totally reconstructed (plates 362 and 364).[32] The bridge linking the Castelvecchio with the far side of the Adige is castellated and is protected by two draw-bridges. This bridge, together with most of the castle, was built for Cangrande II della Scala between 1354 and 1356 and it was completed probably by Francesco Bevilacqua in about 1375. The castle itself is divided in two by the road leading to the bridge which also separates the palace on the south-west from the barracks for the mercenaries on the north-east—a division, as we have seen, that was also common in France. Its lack of symmetrical planning or of flanking, however, is uncommon in contemporary French castles.

The most impressive fortification of this family, a ten-mile

356 *Left* Spoleto, Italy. The castle built for Cardinal Albornoz by Matteo Gattopone 1362–70, from an engraving of 1793 by B. T. Pouncy. The great aqueduct cannot be seen here.

357 *Above* Gubbio, Italy. The Palazzo Municipale in a late nineteenth-century woodcut, built *c* 1332–46 by the consuls who governed this small Umbrian town.

358 Castelvecchio, Verona. The equestrian statue of Cangrande della Scala, carved 1335 by an unknown artist. Similar statues commemorate other members of his family outside S. Maria Antica in Verona. The horse is wearing a cloth trapper skilfully suggested in stone and Cangrande's great crested helm rests on his shoulders.

359 *Right* Sirmione, Italy. The fortified docks on Lake Garda. The chief purpose of building the castle there was to control traffic on the lake and to exact dues from shipping.

wall connecting their castles at Nogarole, Villafranca di Verona, and Valeggio has mostly vanished. After their fall to the Viscontis in the late fourteenth century, however, a further section known as the Ponte Rotto was built for Gian Galeazzo probably to act as a dam to strip Mantua of the water used in its defences.[33]

To provide such technological marvels the tyrants had to surround themselves with brilliant engineers: Sigismondo Malatesta employed Roberto Valturio, the author of a work on siegecraft (see contents page), Federigo da Montefeltro had Francesco di Giorgio Martini and, most famous of all, Ludovico il Moro had Leonardo da Vinci. War was then the temptation of the architect and the artist as it is now to the scientist.

At the same time one traces the inevitable development of the castle into the palace. The most notable fourteenth-

century example is the Castello Visconteo at Pavia, built *c* 1360-5 by Galeazzo II Visconti and completed by Gian Galeazzo. Here one finds two main influences – the town palace, both private and public, and the desire to provide a cloister. The two storeys on its inner façade of wide, twin-lighted Gothic arcades reveal how far the transformation had gone; it was defended only by mercenaries and by a deep, wide moat. Not every tyrant felt so secure. At Ferrara Nicolo II engaged Bartolino da Novara in 1385 to build the brick Castello d'Estense following a serious uprising against his rule. The same architect built the Castello di Giorgio for the Gonzaga at Mantua from 1395 onwards. Each castle consists of an isolated, symmetrical block enclosing a rectangular courtyard and with corner towers showing a far greater concern for flanking than, for example, is to be found at Verona.[34]

The castle was still essential to these tyrants. In 1452 Francesco Sforza, who had quelled a short-lived republic in Milan on the death of the last Visconti duke in 1447, wrote that the safety of the state depended on the castellans of his 130 castles. To make himself secure in his own city he had begun in 1450 the great fortress-palace known as the Castello Sforzesco[35] (plate 365) on the site of a Visconti castle destroyed by the republic. Much of its exterior is now a restoration but architects such as Bramante, Filarete, and Leonardo worked on it and on the luxurious residential quarters within its huge rectangle. Here Francesco and his descendants, notably Ludovico il Moro, held a brilliant court attracting humanists and artists, holding great displays and tournaments until the fatal involvement with the French which led to the invasions of Charles VIII and Louis XII and the death in exile in 1508 of Ludovico il Moro in the castle of Loches where he was reduced to painting the walls of his prison with geometrical designs in red and black.

Even more important as a centre of civilization and infinitely more attractive, is the Ducal Palace of Urbino.[36] It is not strictly a castle, though it fulfilled all the functions of a great castle at this date – as a seat of government, as the headquarters of a military commander, and as a court. It was an extraordinary improvement on the Valois palace-castles of the previous century. It was begun in about 1465 for the duke of Urbino, Federigo Montefeltro II, and the chief architect was a Dalmatian military architect and engineer, Luciano Laurana. Piero della Francesca may have influenced the design of the palace, with its exquisitely proportioned rooms and chambers, and the superb decorations of its door frames and windows.

360 *Left* Sirmione, Italy. The top of the central tower round which the rest of the castle is grouped. The tower is reminiscent both of the earlier family towers built in Italian cities and of the *Bergfried* of castles further north. The machicolations are particularly striking and the notched merlons indicate the Scaligeri support of the Ghibelline or imperial cause.

365 *Overleaf, right* Castello Sforzesco, Milan, Italy. The highly restored main front of Francesco Sforza's powerful fortress built from 1450 onwards to replace a Visconti castle destroyed during the period of the Ambrosian republic in Milan. The central tower of Filarete was built at the end of the last century as a copy of Filarete's original tower which had been pulled down. The massive round towers with their impressive pillow ashlar mainly survive from the original building.

361 *Top* Sirmione, Italy. The landward side of this castle built by the Scaligeri lords of Verona on the peninsula jutting into Lake Garda whose waters were employed as defences and for the fortified port in plate 359. It was built between 1290 and 1310.

362 *Centre* Castelvecchio, Verona, Italy. A view from the River Adige of the bridge leading to the castle.

363 *Bottom* Castello Visconteo, Pavia, Italy. An exterior view of the castle begun by Galeazzo II Visconti *c* 1360-5 and finished by Gian Galeazzo. It combines the characteristics of the town house with those of a castle.

364 *Overleaf* Castelvecchio, Verona, Italy. A view over the entirely restored bridge leading to the chief castle of the Scaligeri. The road from the bridge runs through the castle, dividing the residential parts from the barracks.

366 *On previous pages, left* Castello Sforzesco, Milan, Italy. The device of the Visconti family adopted by Francesco Sforza, tyrant and self-styled duke of Milan to give an appearance of legitimacy to his rule. The carving, which appears on the two corner drum towers, shows a viper swallowing a child and refers to a legend connected with a Crusader member of the Visconti family.

367 *Previous page* A stylized fifteenth-century castle from the Otter and Swan Hunt section of the *Devonshire Hunting Tapestries*, nevertheless showing well one method of raising drawbridges. *London, Victoria and Albert Museum.*

368 *Left* Coca, Spain. The great brick-built fortress of Coca was constructed by Moslem workmen for the archbishop of Seville, Alfonso de Fonseca. Built at a time when the use of artillery favoured the defender rather than the attacker, it is provided with embrasures for cannon and gunloops of the cross-and-orb type.

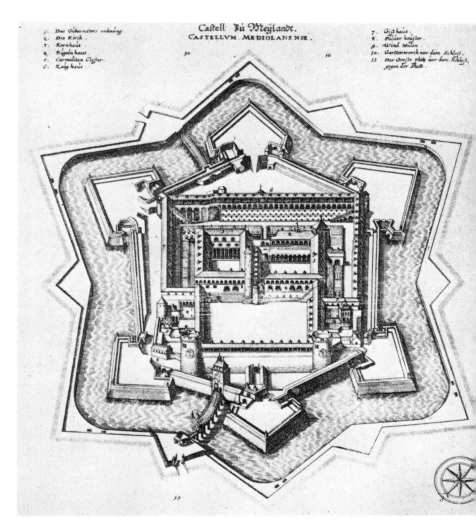

It was completed by another famous military architect of the day, Francesco di Giorgio Martini, who also provided outlying fortresses for its protection. Alberti and Mantegna were visitors to Urbino, and Bramante and Raphael were born there. Federigo made it not only a centre of humanist learning but also one of the forcing-houses of Renaissance technology. His great preoccupations are strikingly contrasted in the painting by Justus van Ghent (plate 369) which shows him in full armour, prepared for instant warfare while he sits fully absorbed in the book on the Gothic lectern before him. Beside him stands his son Guidobaldo under whom, when duke, Urbino became 'that grammar school of courtesies'. This is as fine a reason as any other for taking Urbino as our last castle, for at this court there took place the conversations which

Castiglione wrote down in his book *Il Cortegiano*. Everything that is best in the society of the previous centuries which had been nourished in castles, the courage, the chivalry, the individualism, the delight in fine action and the stress on modesty, everything that was good in the ideals of the troubadours and the minnesingers, receives a rebirth there, refreshed in the clear light of Platonic thought. This book interprets the old age to the new and, though the court at Urbino lasted only a few years before Cesare Borgia besieged and plundered the palace, its influence spread throughout Europe to Spain, to France, to Sir Philip Sidney and to Shakespeare. In its earlier days the castle had witnessed the restoration of the Arthurian legends; in its last moments Urbino provided the setting in which everything good in its past was preserved or transformed.

369 *Left* Portrait of Federigo da Montefeltro by Justus van Ghent (fl. 1460–80) now in the Palazzo Barberini, Rome, and formerly in the *studiolo* of the ducal palace at Urbino. His son Guidobaldo stands beside him.

370 *Above* Castello Sforzesco, Milan, Italy. The elder Merian's view from *Topographia Italiae* showing how the Sforza buildings had become outdated for defensive purposes against artillery and were now protected by massive sharp-angled bastions.

KINGS, CANNONS, AND GUNPOWDER

Although the use of gunpowder was widespread from well before the middle of the fourteenth century, it is evident that it was not until after about 1450 that the revolutionary effect of cannon, in completely altering the design of castles and other fortifications, became apparent. One reason for this was a gradual improvement in the technology of artillery weapons, but there were other, economic, and political reasons. Kings or sovereign rulers, through taxation and customs revenue and through the reversion to the crown of appanages and other estates, continued to grow richer. As warfare became more and more a professional matter and no longer the natural concern of every nobleman from his youth, so it became more expensive, and so it came about that only a monarch could afford to buy guns on an increasingly large scale, and to rebuild fortifications to withstand them. For example, the money spent by the French crown between 1440 and 1490 on artillery quintupled, from 10,000 to 50,000 *livres* a year.[1] In the fifteenth century many sovereigns were deeply interested in everything to do with cannon, among them being Duke Alfonso d'Este, King John II of Portugal, James II of Scotland, who was actually killed by the explosion of one of his guns at the siege of Roxburgh in 1460, and the Emperor Maximilian.

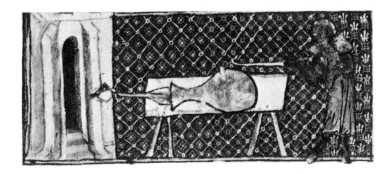

371 *Below left* A gunpowder mill from a German 'Firework Book' of *c* 1440. The need to produce a consistently reliable gunpowder led to the invention of a method of corning the grains, one example of the many ways in which the introduction of artillery made heavy demands on western technological expertise. *Tower of London.*

372 *Top* The earliest known representation of a cannon *c* 1325. The vase-shaped weapon is shown discharging a metal arrow somewhat like a crossbow bolt. From the Milemete ms, *Oxford, Christ Church*, Ms. 92, fo 70v.

373 *Bottom* A fifteenth-century cast-iron cannon preserved at Eltz, W. Germany. Owing to impurities in the metal, or to overloading, these early cannon not infrequently blew up, as in this case.

They were followed in the next century in this interest by Charles V and Henry VIII of England.

In its earlier history a castle which possessed its own smithy could be, to a certain extent, self-sufficient for the supply and maintenance of weapons for its soldiers and for its other defences. The immensely complex techniques of casting or welding cannon, of corning gunpowder, of carving and calibrating stone balls or of casting metal ones, and the new techniques of smelting, all demanded a much higher degree of industrial organization, of finance, and of professional knowledge. These in their turn depended on urban society, and it is not surprising that the earliest manuscript reference to cannon is in the *Registro delle provisione* of Florence of

1326,[2] or that the later municipal accounts of towns of northern France and Flanders include many references to the purchase and provision of artillery.[3] It was probably in this last area that the casting of iron, made possible by higher furnace temperatures and the production of an iron with a relatively high carbon content, was developed to a state in which it was useful for casting cannon.[4]

The first representation of a cannon is in the Milemete manuscript of *c* 1325 at Christ Church, Oxford (plate 372) The vase-shaped weapon is shown discharging a large arrow—like a crossbow quarrel. After this time there are ever increasing references to the use of the new weapons, on the field of battle, at sea and in sieges, and a contemporary poem describes them in use at the siege of Calais in 1346. Artillerymen acquired a patron saint in St Barbara who has only recently been removed from the calendar.

In fourteenth-century battles cannon seem to have had little but psychological value and not always that. The battle of Aljubarotta in 1385 was won by the Portuguese without artillery, against the Castilians who had sixteen bombards. It was the Hussites in the next century, and then the French armies driving the English from France, who showed how effective they could be on the battlefield. In sieges they were used for some time alongside the old stone-throwing artillery of trebuchets and mangonels, which, if not so terrifying in action, were more reliable. The Hospitallers were using a trebuchet at the siege of Rhodes as late as 1480. There were many reasons for the lack of reliability in early cannon. One was varying mixtures and strengths of gunpowder; the invention of a method of corning the grains so that they were evenly distributed throughout the mixture, which seems to have been made in about 1420, helped to put this right.[5] Another was that a wise gunner did not pack his guns with very much powder, for fear of the barrel exploding and killing him. (See also the gun in plate 373.) Or else the saltpetre content was kept deliberately low to prevent this happening, which meant a much weaker explosive effect. There was no standardization in the calibres or the charging instruments. As late as the early sixteenth century a Spanish report on the weapons in the Castello Sforzesco complains that 200 different types of charging instruments were necessary, when eleven would have been enough had the guns been standardized.[6] Each gun was an individual and was given a name, like a ship. It had to have its cannonballs cut or cast specially for it, and it required special experience in handling.

These cannon could be made of iron bars welded into a tube and strengthened with hoops, or cast from bronze or iron. Some were breech-loading and some were muzzle-loading. The muzzle-loader was generally more popular because the problems concerned with escaping gases and the danger of explosions in breech-loading cannon were not solved until the nineteenth century.[7] The cannon came in many sizes, from the semi-portable culverins which could be carried on horseback, to giants of huge weight and calibre, like the famous Mons Meg at Edinburgh Castle (plate 374), which weighs 14,560 lb (664 kgm) and has a calibre of 20 inches (50 cm). When cannon of such size were cast they were frequently made in two parts so they could be more easily transported. Then they had to be put together again: if they were made to screw together, the heat of the explosion would expand the thread and the gunners would have to wait for several hours before the breech block was cool enough to unscrew.[8] Very large cannon, therefore,

374 *Top* Mons Meg, the great bombard kept at Edinburgh Castle, made probably at Mons in about 1460. When last fired in 1682, it cracked.

375 *Above* Bronze cannon cast for Mehmet II by Munir Ali in 1464 now at the Tower of London. They were so large they had to be made in two parts and fitted together for firing.

like those made for Mehmet II besieging Byzantium, could only fire once every seven hours or so. Everything to do with these cannon was cumbersome. Imagine what it was like to be in charge of a train of oxen-pulled wagons, each piled high with huge, stone cannonballs, all liable to avalanche at a sudden jolt, on a journey from Medina del Campo to Granada, for Isabella the Catholic's great victory!

The French realized that metal cannonballs are more efficient. They do not break on impact and have a much higher projectile force. Therefore the calibre of the guns could be smaller. It was armed with light, bronze cannon, shooting metal balls, that Charles VIII demonstrated, first to the Bretons, that the day of the great castle was now over; and then he descended into Italy in 1494 to wage the campaign that shocked the Italians into becoming the chief military theorists of the next hundred years.

The bastion

As a result of the growing effectiveness of firearms between the middle and the end of the fifteenth century, Italian engineers evolved the sharp-angled bastion, an invention which has been described as the most significant of all the architectural forms of the Renaissance.[9] Up to this point in the Middle Ages a wall had been defended by hurling missiles vertically from hoarding or machicolation or from flanking towers. The introduction of the cannon meant that attackers could deliver for the first time a horizontal blow with considerable effect. One answer to this was to make the walls thicker and to scarp them for two-

thirds of their height to deflect the balls, thereby also weakening siege ladders by increasing their inclination to the wall. Scarping to this extent, however, prevents the efficient use of machicolation and, therefore, the whole burden of defending a wall directly under attack was laid on its flanking towers. A high tower presented too much front to the attackers' guns and so, as we have seen at Salses, instead of dominating the countryside, the builders were eventually to try to conceal their fortresses in the lay of the land.

There were two other reasons for lowering towers to the height of the curtain: one was to enable the commander to run troops from one side of his castle to the other without meeting obstacles, as had already been understood in the design of the Bastille and Tarascon. Another was to enable guns to be moved around the ramparts as easily as possible.

In general, during the later fourteenth century, the introduction of firearms favoured the defending forces rather than the attackers, which explains the gun-loops one finds as early as the date of Bodiam (1385). Improvements in gunnery in the next century were to put the advantage on the side of the attacker and so the defenders had to allow for heavier cannon mounted in or on their walls. Mounting a heavy cannon within a tower presents many difficulties: not too many embrasures can be made without weakening the structure; thick masonry reduces the arc of fire; recoil adds to the structural dangers; and gases would accumulate and choke the gunners without the provision of ventilation. Where the builders did make embrasures for the cannon they could, therefore, only provide a few, as at Coca (plate 368).

The advantages of gunfire in breaking up concentrations of attacking troops soon became apparent to the builders of

376 *Left* Rocca Pia, Tivoli, Italy. The massive towers of this castle built by Pope Pius II between 1458 and 1464 are among the first Italian experiments to deal with the threat of artillery.

377 *Below* Volterra, Italy. The great round tower of this Medici fortress begun in 1472. Note the combination of machicolation with scarped base producing a dramatic architectural form.

378 Studies and designs of fortifications by Leonardo da Vinci. *Milan, Biblioteca Ambrosiana,* Codex Atlanticus, fo 43v-a.

fortifications, and the problem was how to bring enough cannon effectively to bear on any approach the enemy might make. The first answer was to place the guns on platforms at the tops of towers, and eventually the bastion developed from the tower as a solid platform. This was thrust as far forward as was consistent with the flanking cover needed by its adjoining walls, and to give it as wide a field of fire as possible. We have already mentioned that scarping the wall reduced the efficiency of machicolation. The placing of heavy cannon on the battlements meant that crenellation gave way to pierced ramparts and that machicolation changed first to bracketing, without holes for dropping missiles, and finally disappeared.

The round tower at first remained the chief defence against cannon as, owing to its superior strength and suitability for flanking, it had been evolved to deal with earlier siege-engines. But although it had considerably less dead ground at its base than the rectangular tower, some dead ground remained. While machicolation was still in use this ground remained covered by vertical defence but, without machicolation, it became more and more imperative to eliminate it. In earlier fortifications this had sometimes been done by making the towers elliptical, as at Loches, or adding sharp projections, as at the Narbonne gate at Carcassonne, thus making an ogival ground-plan, or by adding a raised platform to the drum, as at Lucera (plate 165). The solution adopted in Italy was the gradual evolution of the bastion with a sharp angle pointing directly outwards. It seems to have appeared first in some obscure Italian hill towns, but its adoption was made slow by the relative smallness of the attacking forces taking part in wars and by the fashion for great round towers in palace-fortresses. These are to be found in many regions and include the Castel Nuovo at Naples (1443-58) (plate 218), the Rocca Pia at Tivoli (plate 376) built between 1458 and 1464, the fortress at Volterra (plate 22) dating from 1472, and Imola (1472-3) and Forlì (1481-3), both in the Romagna.

379 *Below* Deal, England. One of the series of forts built by Henry VIII in the later part of his reign along the south coast from Kent extending to Cornwall. These low-lying constructions make use of rounded bastions, a form that was already outdated by contemporary Italian practice.

380 *Bottom* Rothesay, Scotland. A castle of the twelfth and thirteenth centuries notable for its irregularly circular ground-plan. A massive forework was added in the later Middle Ages.

381 *Below right* Detail from 'The siege of a fortress', a woodcut of 1527 by Dürer. Note the scarped rounded bastion provided with cannon on the platform and in a double gallery with embrasures. As much as possible is concealed from attackers by building it well below ground level in a wide ditch which is given further protection by two isolated round gun turrets.

disposition of the defences. That siege was the last attempt of the Florentine republic to throw off the rule of the Medicis and, when that family returned, they employed the new form of bastion to make fortresses in many parts of Tuscany, including Siena and Florence, and to ensure they never knew exile again. Their most admired building of this style is the Fortezza da Basso at Florence, designed by Antonio da Sangallo the younger, a nephew of the two elder Sangallos, in 1534, which the widely travelled Francesco da Hollanda, the friend of Michelangelo (he executed the drawing of Salses in plate 395) called the 'finest fortress in Europe'.

Cannon had already been, for some seventy years, the greatest threat to fortifications. At one end of Europe the Wallachian gun founder, Orban, had in 1453 gone over to

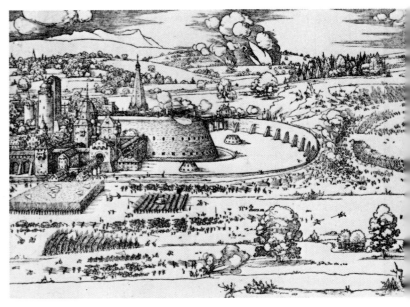

In the decade preceding the French invasion of 1494 the sharp-angled bastion is introduced more frequently and with greater understanding. Poggio Imperiale, planned in 1487 by Giuliano da Sangallo,[10] combines, for the first time, a bastioned fortress with a bastioned town wall. In 1492 Alexander VI made another architect of the same family, Antonio da Sangallo, modernize the round towers at the corners of the Castel Sant'Angelo and reinforce them with seven-sided bastions. The same architect altered Civitacastellana for the Pope's son, Cesare Borgia, in 1494, and there he abolished not only machicolation but also the bracketing which had temporarily succeeded it.

The form fascinated many architects and designers, including Michelangelo, whose designs for the fortifications of Florence in 1530 were criticized for being too subtle in the

Mehmet II, because the Byzantine Emperor could not pay his wages, and it was he who constructed the cannon which smashed a breach in the ancient walls of Byzantium. One of a series of forty-two cannon cast later for Mehmet II by Munir Ali, for a battery on the Dardanelles, can be seen today in the Tower of London (plate 375). At the other end of Europe, Bamburgh castle on the Northumberland coast fell in 1464 before a terrific bombardment. The barbicans and outworks that frightened owners erected before the new and obvious targets their beetling towers now presented, as at Bonaguil in France, or Rothesay (plate 380), were at best only palliatives In 1523 Philip of Hesse was to bombard the Rhineland castle of Landstuhl to a ruin on a single day.

In response to this challenge, the Italians were to give to the rest of Europe, and to the New World, the bastion form they had already invented. Their work can be seen as far afield as Russia, Poland, and Hungary. Henry VIII was to experiment with his round and clover-leaf shaped, low fortresses such as those at Deal (plate 379) and Camber, and Pendennis Castle, but the future lay with the Italian model, and the theory of the polygonal shapes, which provided the most complete network of lines of fire from a given fortress area, exercised many of the best minds from the time of Leonardo da Vinci and Michelangelo to that of Vauban and beyond.

CHANGES AND TRANSFORMATION-THE LATER HISTORY OF THE CASTLE

What happened to the castle? In the course of the sixteenth century in most countries, it split into its separate functions, home and fortress, which now continued to exist independently. Large numbers of castles fell into desuetude and then ruin. No longer essential in the military or political senses, they could not match in comfort the new styles of the Italian or Flemish Renaissance. Where private castles continued to be occupied, it was because of family pride or because their particular designs allowed additions, or because of poverty. Many royal castles, such as Windsor, or viceregal castles, such as the Castel Nuovo at Naples, continued to receive embellishment and additions but this was because of their past associations rather than because their double nature as fortress and residence was still needed. Once the master creation of medieval technology, the castle was hopelessly outdated by the rapid advances in other fields of Western engineering and applied science.

This does not mean that castles did not continue to be used in time of trouble, but only as refuges, not as centres for aggression and extending power. Many a German nobleman during the Peasants' Wars of 1525 must have blessed his ancestors for building walls of such strength, although the peasants did manage to seize and sack several castles. A hundred years later, during the Thirty Years War, artillery had reached a new and terrible intensity of power and the size of armies in the field had increased enormously. Consequently, although many castles were besieged, only the exceptional few, like the Marksburg (plate 190), defied their attackers either successfully or for long. In France they played a considerable part in the Wars of Religion of the later sixteenth century, notably the battle of Arques (1589) one of the turning points for Henry IV in his campaigns against the Ligue, but, during the rule of Cardinal Richelieu, many great structures from which rebellious nobles might otherwise have defied the state were blown up or dismantled. Although the *château* retained its name, it was no longer a *château-fort* but became instead a country palace or house, following the example already set by Francis I with his stupendous palaces on the Loire, such as Chambord (plate 392), where the aim was to find a refuge, not from the enemies in the physical sense but from those of the mind and spirit. In another Loire castle, Chenonceau, many of the originally military features, the drum-towers, the false machicolation, the crenellation, the concept of a fortified bridge, are retained but employed solely as intrinsically architectural forms.

In England, too, the castle's chief legacy was to the country

382 Bolsover, England. An aerial view showing the great keep *c* 1590 designed by Robert Smythson the elder, a remarkable attempt to make use of older practice to create an impression of power and domination.

house. From the moated, quadrangular castle came the moated Tudor house, built round a courtyard, and the great houses of the Elizabethan era, some of which, especially those of the Smythsons, such as Bolsover castle (plate 382), with its great keep, hark back deliberately to the castles of the past. This was part of an archaizing movement with effects on many spheres: the establishment of the Royal College of Heralds for one, and the labours of antiquaries for another. From the labours of one, Sir Edward Coke, came the rediscovery and reinterpretation of Magna Carta and it was he who said: 'the house of everyone is to him as his castle and fortress'. Other historians and writers brought into the popular consciousness the idea of the Norman yoke, the idea that the Saxons had been happy and free until the Normans came, stole their land, and took away their basic rights.[1] When the Civil War broke out, many castles were again refurbished and garrisoned in the king's name; it is not surprising that to the members of the other side the castle itself should have seemed to be the very symbol of the Norman yoke, especially after the trouble caused by such

383 *Below* Raglan, Wales. One of the large series of engravings by the brothers Samuel and Nathaniel Buck carried out in the first third of the eighteenth century which did much to evoke interest in the remains and ruins of castles. In the foreground is the Yellow Tower of Gwent built by Sir William Ap Thomas *c* 1432–45. Raglan underwent one of the most famous sieges of the Civil War; it was held for the king by the earl of Worcester who was forced to surrender after a heroic defence in 1646. Afterwards it was slighted on the orders of Parliament.

384 *Right* Valencia de Don Juan, Spain. A fifteenth-century castle in León remarkable for its cluster of narrow towers and its striving for height. It was built for the counts of Ortoñez.

the seat of government from St Petersburg but actually installed it in the Kremlin – from which orders can be dictated to communists sitting in yet another castle, the Hradschin in Prague.

For the most part, after the civil wars of the seventeenth century, castles were technological dinosaurs, useful as quarries but too big still for most stonecutters to be able to carry away altogether. Once they were in the very forefront of Western technology, and in going on to deal shortly with the aesthetics of the castle, and with how we are conditioned to look at them today, it is this aspect I want to stress first.

Historians of military architecture generally consider the design and functions of castles solely from the points of defence and attack. But, granted their relation to the technology of

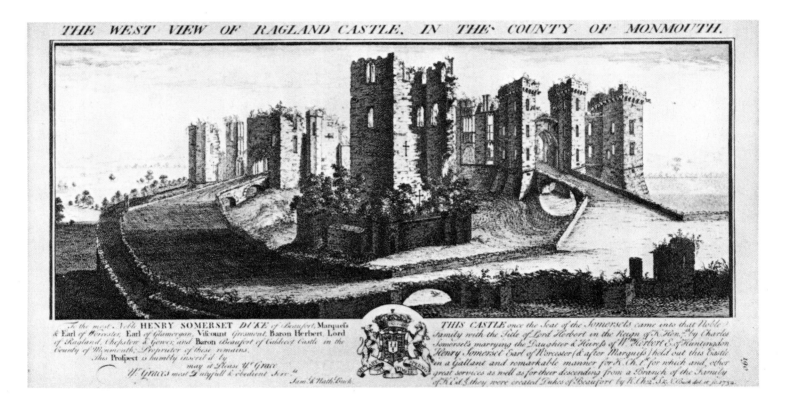

THE WEST VIEW OF RAGLAND CASTLE, IN THE COUNTY OF MONMOUTH.

sieges as those of Raglan or Scarborough.[2] After the victory of Parliament, therefore, great numbers of castles were ordered to be 'slighted' or so damaged that they could not be used again.

In the French Revolution the castle was also associated from the very beginning with the old régime and the hated feudalism that was being abolished. After all, the Revolution was sparked off by the capture and destruction of the Bastille, the castle which symbolized most of all the *Ancien Régime*. The castles of the Rhineland suffered severely in the ensuing Napoleonic wars, as did those of Spain in the Peninsular Campaigns. But if castles had to be blown up or shelled, it was rarely because they presented any major military obstacle; their towers were being used as observation posts or for the temporary shelter of parties of soldiers.

Later wars have been equally cruel to castles, as will have been realized from the numbers already mentioned as having been destroyed in the two world wars. Later revolutions have, however, been kinder; the French revolutionaries may have destroyed the Bastille but the Russian ones not only removed

the age, they resembled powerhouses storing energy and releasing it according to necessity, storing it in terms of the inertial mass the castles offered to attackers and releasing it in terms of the violent action of an army of cavalry issuing from their gates. Just as a great cathedral keeps in reserve all the ideas, symbols, and spiritual achievements of two or three hundred years of striving, so a great castle in its shorter period of effective functioning, sucked in the labour of peasant, stonecutter and mason, the fodder and produce of the surrounding fields, the obedience and acknowledgement of political power from villages and towns, and stored it until it could be used in time of crisis. The ten or twenty-foot thick walls, the great ashlar blocks, the splayed foundations were not intended to withstand one short siege but were built for a lasting and useful purpose.

This point of view may help to explain the difficulties that historians of architecture have in considering the aesthetics of the castle. Some are obviously deterred by the appalling difficulties of dating walls and piles of rubble bare of any decoration that would enable an estimate on stylistic grounds.

385 *Left* A joust from the fifteenth-century 'Ordinances of Chivalry', written and illuminated in England for Sir John Astley who was famous for his feats of arms at tournaments and jousts and who was victualer for Edward IV's castle of Alnwick in 1463. The rider on the left is Sir John, as can be seen from the crest, a crowned harpy. *New York, Pierpont Morgan Library* M. 775, fo 2v.

386 *Above* One casualty of World War II: Marienburg after seven weeks of shelling in 1945.

387 *Right* The taking of the Bastille, 14 July 1789. In the minds of the revolutionaries this castle was connected with all that was bad in the *ancien régime*.

It is not uncommon to find authorities differing by as much as five centuries and this is not surprising since naturally strong sites always attract builders in every age. Many historians shy away from castles, obviously disliking them. Frankl, for example, in his book on Gothic Architecture says: 'Castles and the whole field of military architecture have their own immanence; their artistic quality lies in the fact that their form was made to symbolize threats, arrogance, and the instillation of fear'.[3] He quotes from an earlier German art historian, Dehio: 'They seek to give the effect of a Gorgon's head'.[4] This reveals only part of the truth. Clearly it is difficult to fit a castle into the same aesthetic categories as a Greek temple, a Gothic cathedral, or a Palladian villa, but if one sees it as a feat of engineering built with a definite technical purpose, then it appears to be in the same line as the Pont du Gard or the aqueducts of the Roman campagna and the great warehouses of the industrial revolution or the nuclear power stations of our own day. The difference between the castle and the cathedral lies in their functions. The various forms of the cathedral arise from the desire to find an expression in stone of man and his relation to the divine in the universe. Only in much later forms of the castle, such as Warkworth, with its keep built in the form of a Maltese cross, Longford, an Elizabethan hunting-lodge with its three towers joined in a triangle to symbolize the Trinity, and, to take a purely literary example, the mystical castle of Alma described by Spenser in

Book II of *The Faerie Queene*,[5] does one come across attempts to express religious or metaphysical ideas through the design. Its practical function dominated the design of the castle and although, as we have seen, this did not exclude the influence of fashion and of elaborate design and decoration, it colours our appreciation of the castle today. Seen at a distance Beaumaris can seem stunningly beautiful, in the same way as does the not-so-distant Menai bridge by Telford linking Anglesey with the mainland. Approach both structures more closely and one is struck by an objective sense of practical purpose dominating everything; there is a lack of the numinous. Dehio, writing of German castles, thinks that they are appreciated not as architecture but as painting, as part of the landscape they enhance.[6] To add to this, one nearly always brings to a building or a landscape certain associations, ideas,

388 *Below* Pierrefonds, France. An early drawing by Viollet-le-Duc before it was decided to rebuild and remodel the *château* completely to make a medieval fantasy for Napoleon III and his court.

389 *Right* The castle as a symbol of domination and power: the Alsatian fortress of Fleckenstein, of various dates and shown here in a highly idealized form. It was blown to pieces in 1670. From Merian the elder, *Topographia Alsatiae*.

or prejudices about the history that formed it. So that at Harlech, for example, one is affected not only by the noble position, overlooking the sea, by the power of the walls and the gatehouse keep, and the terrible sieges it endured during the times of Owen Glendower and the Wars of the Roses, but by an even older magic dating back to the story described in the *Mabinogion,* of Bran the Blessed seated upon Harlech hill watching the thirteen ships coming from the south of Ireland that were to bring him to his fate. After deeds of great prowess in Ireland, he commanded that his own head should be struck off and that it should be buried where the Tower of London now stands to guard the country from invasion.

There is, however, another architectural quality castles certainly possess, quite apart from the expression of terror and domination; it is to be seen in their geometrical forms, their massive square keeps and cylindrical towers, and it can be called stored energy. An excellent example of this is Montealegre (plate 330). Medieval masons were frequently known as geometers and although, when using the science of geometry in building the cathedrals, they continued in the Pythagorean tradition of associating number and form with religious and philosophical ideas, when it came to designing castles, they maintained the relation only in the use of simple proportions, for example in the relation of height of towers to height of curtain walls. Perhaps, therefore, we can see in the castle one of the earliest expressions of Western philosophy and technology with its emphasis on the practical and the mechanical. This is certainly borne out by the close part

played by military engineers such as Petrus Peregrinus, the author of the first description of magnetism in the West, in the development of medieval science and technology. From this point of view at least one can think of the castle as a machine, a machine for ruling and for fighting.

But something else also happened to the castle which colours our appreciation of it today. This process had already begun in the fifteenth century with the use of special features as decorative motifs (see Chapter 7). But in the sixteenth century the castle appears fully as a symbol, above all, to Luther who had good reason to know and be thankful for the practical refuge afforded by such castles as Coburg and the Wartburg. When he wrote,

Eine feste Burg ist unser Gott,
Ein' gute Wehr und Waffen,
(A mighty castle is our God,
A strong defence and weapon),

he sent the castle on a long journey that has survived its debasement even by insurance firms and makers of toothpaste. Eleventh-century monastics used to describe their monasteries as 'Castles of God', smugly contrasting them with the secular buildings of their noble neighbours. Now the castle entered strongly into religious language. At the other end of Europe, St Teresa, who had been brought up among the mighty walls of Avila and where she read innumerable tales of chivalry as a child, took the castle as a symbol for the soul in her book *Castillo interior*. This was a treatise on prayer based on a vision of 'a most beautiful crystal globe made in the shape of a castle, and containing seven mansions, in the seventh and innermost of which was the King of Glory, in the greatest splendour, illumining and beautifying them all'.[7]

Some of the great English Palladian houses were still called castles, such as Mereworth Castle or Castle Howard, and Vanbrugh who designed the latter consciously tried to endow his buildings with the massiveness and solemnity of great medieval fortresses.[8] He loved them so much that he castellated his house at Greenwich in 1717, still called Vanbrugh Castle. The admirable engravings of the brothers Buck in the 1730s (plate 383) helped the English to realize how much of their medieval heritage remained to them. The taste for ruins in classical landscapes diffused by the original works, or engravings of them, of such artists as Claude or Gaspar Dughet, probably had a strong influence in making people turn with interest to the ruins of their own countries.

Thus a further interest in castles began to awaken partly through the literary efforts of Thomas Gray and Horace Walpole in cultivating the Gothic taste. They saw them as ruins and loved them as ruins, sensing in them 'old mortality and the ruin of forgotten times'. Where landowners had no genuine ruins in their parks they built sham ones and made their lodge keepers live in miniature castles to maintain the illusion.

A far more powerful urge to understand and admire the castle and the society that produced it was given by Sir Walter Scott in his historical novels. He awoke the imagination of Europe to their charms and horrors. He was followed in this by many of the Romantics who were inspired far more by castles than by cathedrals in their reverence for the Middle Ages. Chateaubriand was actually brought up in a castle–the ancient Breton Château de Combourg (plate 391). Eichendorff's poems are full of scenes of ruined castles and castle legends. But perhaps it was Byron's *Childe Harold*, seeing the

'. . . chiefless castles breathing stern farewells
From gray but leafy walls, where Ruin greenly dwells,'

391 Château de Combourg, France. This Breton castle was built in the eleventh century and enlarged in the fourteenth and fifteenth centuries. Among its earlier owners was the du Guesclin family and in the eighteenth-century it passed into the hands of Chateaubriand's father. It was in his *Mémoires d'Outre-Tombe* that Chateaubriand recalled his lonely years spent in the gloomy castle.

that did most, after Scott, to arouse a general fascination with the castle. It satisfied the new taste for the picturesque and tourists in their thousands came to the Rhine to repeat his lines addressed to his sister:

'The castled crag of Drachenfels
Frowns o'er the wide and winding Rhine,
Whose breast of water broadly swells
Between the banks that bear the vine,
And hills all rich with blossom'd trees,
And fields which promise corn and wine,
And scatter'd cities crowning these,
Whose far white walls along them shine
Have strew'd a scene, which I should see
With double joy wert *thou* with me . . .

And peasant girls, with deep blue eyes,
And hands which offer early flowers,
Walk smiling o'er this paradise;
Above, the frequent feudal towers
Through green leaves lift their walls of gray,
And many a rock which steeply lowers,
And noble arch in proud decay,
Look o'er this vale of vintage bowers;
But one thing want these banks of Rhine,–
Thy gentle hand to clasp in mine.'[9]

Such verses encouraged battalions of artists, Turner amongst them, to record great numbers of castles all over Europe. The newly invented techniques of lithography and steel engraving diffused their pictures even further in albums and works such as Tombleson's *Views of the Rhine* (see plates 188 and 203).

But the appeal of the castle to the Romantics was not only that it was picturesque. They sensed, as we do still, its strange and mixed nature. Like the French revolutionaries' reaction to the Bastille, they saw it as a symbol of oppression and tyranny, with every justification too if one remembers Napoleon's use of Vincennes, or the Austrian and papal castle prisons in this period, or Dumas's description of Danthès's long years in the Château d'If. Byron was inspired by the story of François Bonnivard to write his *Prisoner of Chillon* and Gotthelf, the Swiss poet and novelist, wrote his remarkable story *Die Spinne* with its ferocious feudal lord terrorizing from his castle the poor peasants in his power. Samuel Rogers caught an agonizing mood in his strange *Captivity*:

'Caged in old woods, whose reverend echoes wake
When the hern screams along the distant lake,
Her little heart oft flutters to be free,
Oft sighs to turn the unrelenting Key.
In vain! the nurse that rusted relic wears,
Nor moved by gold – nor to be mov'd by tears;
And terraced walls their black reflection throw
On the green-mantled moat that sleeps below.

Imprisonment and the desire to escape, as in Beethoven's *Fidelio* or Pushkin's *Prisoner of the Caucasus*, was one of the great romantic themes and the castle provided the perfect symbol for the predicament of the artist. More recently this theme was taken up again in a new and individual way by Kafka in his novel, *The Castle*. Yeats in his later years lived in a medieval tower frequently mentioned in his poems and it

was while walking on the battlements of the castle of Duin that Rilke was inspired with the great cry that begins his *Duineser Elegien*: 'Who, if I cried, would hear me amongst the angelic orders?'

Curiously enough many of the Romantics found an escape in a longing for the very society that had produced the castle. This is the ambivalent nature of the castle; on the one hand it expresses tyranny and the force of alien laws but on the other it means tranquillity, security, and peace – as it did to the Russian poet Lermontov who, in one of his most powerful lyrics, asks why he is not a bird, a raven of the steppes to fly far across the sea to his ancestral Scottish castle. (He was descended from a seventeenth-century Scottish soldier of fortune.) In this sense, as to Tennyson or the young William Morris, the castle is the magic centre of a lost civilization, or of a lost and innocent childhood, the castle whose towers shine with promise in a mind overcome with the misery, the human suffering, and the dirt of the industrial revolution.

'The words of Mercury are harsh after the songs of Apollo.' After the poets and the storytellers came the scholars, the imitators, and the restorers. Some were remarkable, like Viollet-le-Duc, the famous restorer who, inspired by Victor Hugo and the scholar Arcisse de Caumont with a passion for the Middle Ages, came to see in the rise of the Gothic a lay civilization forcing itself free of the clerical domination of the Church and he found in the various forms of the donjon the most original and powerful architectural invention of this new secular society. Some lovers of castles now seem unexpected, as for example Napoleon III who, when incarcerated in the great castle of Ham (destroyed in the 1914-18 war), wrote studies in the history of artillery and who, later, had trebuchets constructed and tried out at Vincennes. The re-creation of Pierrefonds for him was echoed by Ludwig of Bavaria's famous Neuschwanstein. The castle was also considered suitable for prisons, like Reading gaol, or the suburban residences of rich English businessmen, in the style

392 Château de Chambord, France. This vast and magnificent palace standing in a park as large as Paris was built for François I (1494–1547) and his son Henry II as a pleasure retreat from the international quarrels of the sixteenth century.

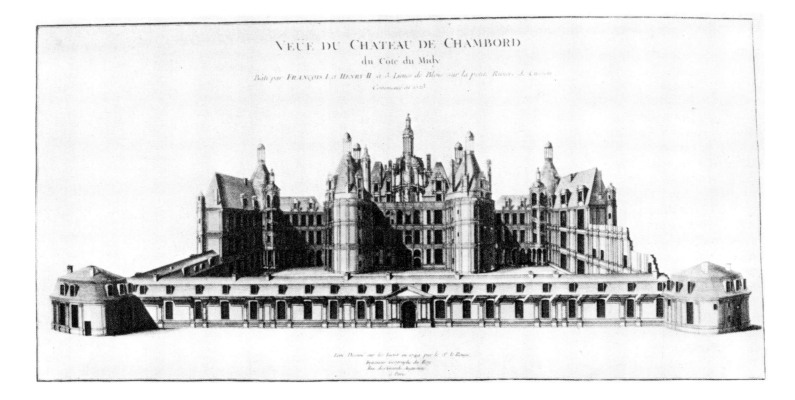

VEUE DU CHATEAU DE CHAMBORD
du Coté du Midy

known as 'Wimbledon baronial'. Some restorers, prompted
by the most vulgar nationalism, rebuilt relentlessly as at the
Wartburg and Goslar. Others, like Lord Curzon, were more
sympathetic; he returned from India, where he had saved
the Taj Mahal, to restore both Bodiam and Tattershall.
The last Kaiser also had a passion for castles, devoting much
energy to restoration work and, very suitably, he spent his
long exile and died in one. But of all modern castle-fanciers
perhaps the most extraordinary was Lawrence of Arabia
whose journey when an undergraduate to find the castles of the
Crusaders first introduced him to the countries where he was
to make his name. According to Robert Graves,[10] much that is
difficult to understand in his character and motives becomes
clearer if the influence of the troubadours and his devotion to
the ideals of chivalry is taken into account.

Castles are immensely popular still. All that remains in
some cases is a battered wall sticking out of mounds of turf
on which cows are grazing. Yet, even so, it will attract visitors
to muse on vanished races and history. For this reason there is
little point in restoring castles; most restorations, unless
extremely well done, jar on the sensibilities. There is something
unnatural about them, unlike ruins. Ruins provide the
foundations of dreams and exercises of the imagination; they
also comfort us in a curious way because they are evidence
of the dust that all will become. If nothing of the splendour
and the riches survives, then neither does anything of the
guilt, the bloodshed, and the oppression. In this we are at one
with the Sultan Mehmet II who, at the consummation of his
desires in the conquest of Byzantium, was heard to murmur
to himself as, on the day of his entry into the city, he wandered
through the half-ruined Sacred Palace of the Emperors, the
words of a Persian poet,

'The spider weaves the curtains in the palace of the Caesars;
The owl calls the watches in Afrasiab's towers.'[11]

393 *Above The Enchanted Castle* by Claude Gellée le Lorrain (1600–82).
This painting did not receive its present title until the eighteenth century
but it is not difficult to see why it received that name. It inspired John
Keats's *Epistle to John Hamilton Reynolds*. Keats noted the various styles of
building, ascribing part to 'a banished Santon of Chaldee', part to
'Cuthbert de Saint Aldebrim', and a little wing to 'a Lapland witch
turn'd maudlin Nun . . .'

394 *Richmond Castle, Yorkshire* by J. M. W. Turner (1775–1851). *London,
British Museum.*

Acknowledgements

The Publishers would like to thank all those individuals and organizations who permitted Wim Swaan to photograph the castles owned by them. He was given enormous co-operation and met nothing but courtesy during his tour of ten countries. In addition the Publishers would like to express their appreciation to all the museums, libraries, collections and individuals from whom they received information, encouragement and photographs during their search for pictures. In particular The London Library staff were always helpful. All the illustrations in this book are acknowledged to the following sources who also gave their permission for reproduction.

Wim Swaan: 1, 7, 9, 10, 12, 13, 14, 15, 16, 17, 20, 21, 22, 26, 32, 33, 36, 40, 47, 48, 51, 52, 53, 58, 59, 63, 70, 71, 72, 73, 74, 89, 90, 92, 99, 102, 103, 104, 106, 115, 128, 129, 131, 132, 134, 139, 140, 141, 142, 143, 144, 145, 146, 147, 148, 149, 151, 152, 155, 156, 157, 158, 159, 160, 161, 165, 166, 167, 169, 171, 172, 173, 174, 175, 176, 177, 178, 183, 190, 191, 192, 198, 200, 201, 205, 208, 209, 210, 211, 212, 214, 215, 216, 217, 220, 229, 230, 232, 234, 235, 236, 241, 247, 248, 249, 250, 251, 252, 253, 256, 257, 259, 260, 261, 262, 263, 264, 265, 269, 271, 272, 274, 275, 277, 278, 279, 280, 282, 285, 286, 290, 291, 292, 293, 299, 300, 303, 304, 305, 306, 307, 308, 309, 310, 311, 312, 313, 314, 315, 316, 330, 331, 332, 333, 335, 336, 337, 338, 339, 341, 342, 345, 346, 347, 348, 349, 350, 351, 354, 358, 359, 360, 361, 362, 364, 365, 366, 367, 368, 373, 376, 377, 384. Courtesy of the Trustees of the British Museum: Front end papers, 2, 3, 11, 49, 54, 55, 56, 84, 91, 101, 105, 113, 114, 162, 163, 170, 180, 196, 207, 218, 222, 225, 244, 246, 284, 289, 325, 327, 355, 370, 381, 392, 394. W. Meyer, *Die Deutsche Burg*, Verlag Weidlich, Frankfurt: 4, 8, 24, 27, 60, 62, 65, 66, 194, 199, 329. John R. Freeman, London: Opposite contents page, 5, 6, 25, 28, 88, 125, 136, 137, 138, 164, 188, 203, 238, 340, 380. National Gallery, London: 18. Stiftsbibliothek St Gall: 19. Landesbildstelle Rheinland Pfalz: 23. Institut International des Châteaux Historiques, Holland: 28. Nationalmuseet, Copenhagen: 29. Dr Herrnbrodt: 30. Yan, Toulouse: 31, 69, 94, 95, 96, 153, 182, 390. Landeskonservator von Hessen, Wiesbaden-Biebrich: 34. Kölnisches Stadtmuseum: 35. Archives Photographiques, Paris: 37, 87, 100, 154, 391. Victoria and Albert Museum, London: Opposite title page, 120, 221, 332, 367. Stenton, Sir F. M. *The Bayeux Tapestry*, Phaidon Press Ltd: 38, 39, 42, 46, 77. Country Life, London: 41, 50, 98, 135, 287. Norwegian National Tourist Office, London: 43. Hammonds and Kilpeck Church, Hereford: 44. Crown Copyright: 45, 81, 168, 294, 328, 371, 374, 375, 379, 382. By courtesy of the Italian Tourist Office, London: 57, 97, 353, 363. Swiss National Tourist Office, London: 61. Germanisches Nationalmuseum, Nuremberg: 67 (S.P. 80476; 1090), 68 (S.P. 2978a; 1125), 185 (K. 6119; 279). A. F. Kersting, London: 75, 121, 122, 123. Pierpont Morgan Library, New York: Opposite list of plates, 76, 109, 130, 385. Kunsthistorisches Museum, Vienna: 78, 226. Landesbildstelle Württemberg, Stuttgart: 79, 80, 83, 117. F. H. Crossley, Chester: 82. Bayerisches Nationalmuseum, Munich: 85. Glasgow Museums and Art Galleries: 86, 231, 233. Historisches Museum der Pfalz, Speyer: 93. Bodleian Library, Oxford: 107. Bibliothèque Nationale, Paris: 108, 110, 111, 112, 116, 126, 127, 204, 224, 242, 266, 267, 273, 276, 302, 387, back end papers. Foto Marburg: 118, 119, 197, 319, 324. National Tourist Organization of Greece, London: 124. Photographie Giraudon, Paris: 133, 150, 243, 245, 254, 268. Northern Ireland Tourist Board, Belfast: 179. Bord Fáilte, London: 181, 296. A. A. Weissmüller, Rome: 184. Deutsche Staatsbibliothek, Berlin: 118, 119, 186, 193, 321, 343, 389. Städelsches Kunstinstitut, Frankfurt: 187. Vatican Library: 189. Niedersächsisches Landesverwaltungsamt, Brunswick: 195. Antikvarisk Topografiske Arkivet, Stockholm: 202. Bertarelli Collection, Castello Storzesco, Milan: 206, 356, 357. Kungl. Akademien for de Fria Konsterna, Stockholm: 213. Murhardsche Bibliothek der Stadt Kassel und Landesbibliothek: 219. Edwin Smith, Saffron Walden: 223, 227, 228, 288, 297, 298. Niedersächsische Staats- und Universitätsbib., Göttingen: Half title, 237, 240. Musée de l'Armée, Paris: 239. Mansell Collection, London: 255, 369. Bulloz, Paris: 258. Courtauld Institute, London: 270, 388. Spanish National Tourist Office, London: 281. Christies, London: 283. Paul Popper, London: 295. Biblioteca Nacional, Madrid: 301, 395. Museum Zamkowe Pracownia Fotograficzna, Warsaw: 317, 320, 386. Teodor Hermanczyk, Warsaw: 318, 322, 323. Universitetsbiblioteket, Uppsala: 326. Bayerische Staatsbibliothek, Munich: 334. Fotoarchiv Landesamt für Denkmalpflege Rheinland Pfalz: 344. Commissariat Général au Tourisme de Belgique, Brussels: 352. Christ Church, Oxford: 372. Biblioteca Ambrosiana, Milan: 378, back end papers. Property of the author: 383. Property of the Trustees of T.C. Loyd, London: 393.

The Publishers would like to acknowledge the sources of the maps and plans and some of the reconstructions reproduced in this volume and to thank the publishers and/or the authors specifically for permission to use them. Fig 2: C. Perogalli *Castelli della pianura Lombarda*, Electa Editrice; fig 4: R. W. Southern *The making of the Middle Ages*, Hutchinson and Co. (Publishers) Ltd; fig 5: D. F. Renn *Norman Castles in Britain*, John Baker Publishers Ltd; fig 6: M. Bertolani del Rio *I castelli reggiani*, ENIT; figs 7 and 24: J. F. Finó *Forteresses de la France Médiévale*, Editions A. et J. Picard et Cie; fig 8: W. Müller-Wiener *Castles of the crusaders*, Thames and Hudson Ltd; figs 9, 10, 11 and 13: S. Toy *A history of fortification*, Heinemann Educational Books Ltd; fig 12: A. L. Poole *From Domesday Book to Magna Carta*, The Clarendon Press; figs 15, 16 and 17: R. Allen Brown, H. M. Colvin and A. J. Taylor *The history of the King's Works*, HMSO and reproduced by permission of Her Britannic Majesty's Stationery Office; fig 18: HMSO *Guide* to Beaumaris Castle; fig 20: T. H. Baüml *Medieval civilization in Germany*, Thames and Hudson Ltd; figs 21 and 22: H. Hahn, *Hohenstaufenburgen in Süditalien*, Verlag F. Bruckmann; figs 25 and 26: R. Allen Brown *English medieval castles*, B. T. Batsford Ltd, artist Mr Gilbert Howes; fig 27: National Trust *Guide* to Bodiam; fig 28 and plate 396: W. Hotz *Kleine Kunstgeschichte der deutschen Burg*, Wissenschaftliche Buchgesellschaft-Abteilung Verlag; plate 64: P. Munz *Frederick Barbarossa*, Eyre and Spottiswoode Ltd.

For extracts quoted from published books the Publishers would like to acknowledge permission to reproduce from the Publishers whose names are given in the notes, and to George Scott Moncrieff for permission to quote from C. Scott Moncrieff's translation of *The song of Roland*. The two lines from Andrew Young's poem *The Dead Crab*, from his *Collected Poems*, are reproduced by permission of Jonathan Cape Ltd.

Glossary

Arrow slit
Narrow slits in towers or curtain walls to allow archers to shoot through, carefully spaced to avoid weakening the masonry. Generally they are of two kinds: the single, upright slit and the cross slit, for the use of the crossbow.

Ashlar
Worked stone, masonry, or squared stone in regular courses.

Bailey
The outer enclosure or court of a castle and later applied to any court within the series of walls. Sometimes used synonymously with ward.

Barbican
An outer defence to the castle, often defending the approaches to a bridge and gatehouse.

Bastion
A low, solid projection, generally sharp-angled, designed to provide the maximum amount of flanking to the curtain walls and to its neighbouring bastions and at the same time providing as small a target as possible to the attackers.

Bergfried
The tall, narrow tower characteristic of many castles in German-speaking countries (see note 13 to chapter 2).

Bracket
A piece of stone or wood projecting from a wall, to support hoarding or machicolation (see also *Console*).

Chemise
Usually applied to the wall protecting a keep either by surrounding it completely or joining on to it.

Concentric castle
A term generally applied to the form of castle introduced in the late 12th century and more frequently in later centuries which consists of two or more complete circles of walls within one another, the aim being to present the enemy with sides all of equal strength, at the same time permitting a quicker response to attack on the part of the garrison.

Console
A synonym for bracket, generally applied to the supports from which machicolation was built out.

Crenel
The notch or indentation in battlements (see *Merlon*).

Curtain wall
The wall connecting two towers or bastions.

Dead ground
Any area at the base of fortifications where the attackers cannot be reached by the arrows or projectiles of the defenders (see *Flanking*).

Ditch
A wide trench designed either to stop the enemy crossing or hampering them in doing so. Here it is used to mean a dry trench.

Donjon
Another and older term for the keep, deriving originally from the Latin *dominus* ('lord'), and revealing the dominion it was meant to express. It was later corrupted into dungeon meaning a prison.

Drawbridge
A bridge, generally hinged at one end and free at the other, that could be drawn up to prevent an enemy crossing the ditch or moat in front of the gate. Its simplest form is a movable plank; others were pulled up by chains worked by pulleys. The most elaborate worked on a counterpoise system: the chains were suspended from beams which, when the bridge was drawn up, fitted into recesses provided for them above the entry. Others worked on a pivot so that the inner part of the bridge fell into a pit while the outer part completely covered the entry.

Embrasure
An opening for guns to fire through in the parapet or in the wall.

Enceinte
The main enclosure of a castle.

Flanking
The art of disposing fortifications so that, for example, the approaches to each tower are covered by neighbouring towers. Its chief purpose is to eliminate dead ground.

Ganerbenburg
A German term for a castle under the mutual ownership of several heirs.

Gatehouse
The fortifications specially designed to guard the main or other points of entry into a castle.

Gunloop
An aperture for firing hand guns through – the equivalent in artillery terms of the arrow slit. These took many forms: the essentials were a round hole for the barrel of the gun and a slit, sometimes vertical, and sometimes in the shape of a cross (making the cross and orb pattern), for sighting and to allow the gases to escape.

Hoarding
A covered wooden gallery projecting from the top of a tower or from a curtain wall to provide vertical defence.

Keep
The English term for the donjon, the strongest and generally biggest building in the castle, used often both as the last refuge and, more especially in the 12th century, as a residence. Its earliest known use is 1586.

Lists
A term for the area set aside for jousting and wrongly applied in the last century to the spaces between two lines of towers and curtain walls in concentric castles in the belief that jousts took place there. It is, however a useful term.

Machicolation
An opening or, more often, a series of openings either built out on consoles or provided by the gap between a recessed wall and the buttressed arch standing before it, from which projectiles and liquids could be thrown on to the enemy at the foot of walls or towers. The term is usually reserved for the stone constructions which in many countries superseded the use of wood for the same purpose (see *Hoarding*).

Merlon
The rising part of a parapet – in contradistinction to the crenel.

Moat
The water-filled ditch surrounding a castle, sometimes wholly artificial, sometimes partly natural in origin. Just as 'donjon' from signifying the highest part of a castle came in dungeon to denote its lowest, so moat, deriving from motte, was transferred from the motte to the ditch from which it was excavated.

Motte
A hillock either artificially created or natural, often carrying a wooden tower (see chapter 2).

Murderhole
A term sometimes used for the openings in the floors of rooms in gatehouses above the passage from the entrance or in other important places.

Oubliette
A secret dungeon or prison whose opening was a trap door from above. Almost mythical and few seem to have existed.

Portcullis
A heavy grating suspended on chains worked by winches which could be dropped quickly down vertical grooves in the gatehouse or at other important entrances.

Rampart
A mound of earth raised as a defensive wall.

Ringwork
A loose term describing any earthen defensive enclosure, regardless of period, size, or function.

Schildmauer
The especially strong wall guarding the only line of approach of a castle built on a mountain or on a spur in certain parts of Germany (see chapter 5).

Spur
An angular projection applied, for example, to the base of a drum tower to hinder mining. It had the same purpose as the *talus*.

Talus
The sloping or scarped side of a wall (also called the batter).

Tourelle
A turret projecting from a larger tower acting either as a watchtower or, if provided with machicolation, for vertical defence, or just for decoration.

Towerhouse
The term applied to residential towers of the 14th and 15th centuries.

Transitional Keep
The term applied to French and English polygonal keeps of the 12th century whose design was intended to overcome the disadvantages of the square or rectangular keep.

Turret
A slender tower or a tourelle projecting from a larger tower.

Ward
A courtyard of a castle.

Bibliography

Works consulted

Works on castles and military architecture

AGNELLO, G. (1935) *L'architettura sveva in Sicilia*. Rome

ALLEN BROWN, R. (1954) *English medieval castles*. London

ALMEIDA, J. DE (1945-8) *Roteiro dos monumentos militares portugueses*, 3 vols. Lisbon

ANDREWS, K. (1953) *Castles of the Morea*. Princeton

ARMITAGE, MRS E.S. (1912) *Early Norman castles of the British Isles*. London

BERTOLANI DEL RIO, M. (1959) *I castelli reggiani*. Reggio Emilia

BOASE, T.S.R. (1967) *Castles and churches of the crusading kingdom*. London

BRAUN, H. (1936) *The English castle*. London

CLASEN, K.H. (1924) *Der Hochmeisterpalast der Marienburg*. Königsberg

CLASEN, K.H. (1931) *Marienburg und Marienwerder*. Berlin

CRESSWELL, K.A.C. (1954) *Fortification in Islam before AD 1250*. London

CRUDEN, S. (1960) *The Scottish castle*. Edinburgh

EBHARDT, B (1908) *Deutsche Burgen*. Berlin

EBHARDT, B. (1909-27) *Die Burgen Italiens*, 6 vols. Berlin

EDWARDS, SIR J.G. (1951) *Edward I's castle building in Wales*. London

ENGEL, H.U. (1961) *Burgen und Schlösser in Böhmen*. Frankfurt

ENLART, C. (1927-32) *Manuel d'archéologie française depuis les temps mérovingiens jusqu'à la Renaissance. T.2. Architecture civile et militaire*. Paris

EYDOUX, H.P. (1969) *Châteaux fantastiques*. Paris

FEDDEN, R, and THOMPSON, J. (1957) *Crusader castles*. London

FINÓ, J.F. (1967) *Forteresses de la France médiévale: construction, attaque, défense*. Paris

GÉBELIN, F, tr. EATON HART, H. (1964) *The châteaux of France*. London

HAHN, H. (1961) *Hohenstaufenburgen in Süditalien*. Munich

HAMILTON THOMPSON, A. (1912) *Military architecture in England during the middle ages*. London

HINDLEY, G. (1968) *Castles of Europe*. Feltham

HOTZ, W. (1937) *Staufische Reichsburgen am Mittelrhein*. Berlin

HOTZ, W. (1956) *Burgen am Rhein und an der Mosel*. Deutsche Lande, Deutsche Kunst series

HOTZ, W. (1965) *Kleine Kunstgeschichte der deutschen Burg*. Darmstadt

LAWRENCE, T.E. (1936) *Crusader castles*, 2 vols. London

LEASK, H.G. (1941) *Irish castles and castellated houses*. Dundalk

VON LORCK, C. (1965) *Kastelle, Paläste, Villen in Italien*. Frankfurt

MEYER, W. (1963) *Den Freunden ein Schutz, den Feinden zum Trutz: die Deutsche Burg*. Frankfurt

MÜLLER-WIENER, W. (1966) *Castles of the Crusaders*. London

NEBBIA, U. (1955) *Castelli d'Italia*. Novara

PEROGALLI, C. (1960) *Castelli della pianura Lombarda*. Milan

PIPER, O. (1912) *Burgenkunde: Bauwesen und Geschichte der Burgen zunächst innerhalb des Deutschen Sprachgebiet*, 3rd edn. Munich

PIPER, O. (1902-10) *Oesterreichische Burgen*. 8 vols. Vienna

POUX, J. (1925) *La Cité de Carcassonne*. Toulouse

OMAN, SIR C. (1926) *Castles*. London (G.W.R.)

O'NEILL, B.H. ST. J. (1960) *Castles and cannon: a study of early artillery fortifications in England*. Oxford

ORTIZ ECHAGÜE, J. (1956) *España: Castillos y Alcazares*. Madrid

RENN, D.F. (1968) *Norman castles in Britain*. London

RITTER, R. (1953) *Châteaux, donjons, et places fortes: l'architecture militaire française*. Paris

SAINZ DE ROBLES, F. (1962) *Castillos en España*. Madrid

SARTHOU CARRERES, C. (1932) *Castillos de España*. Madrid

SCHUCHHARDT, C. (1931) *Die Burg im Wandel der Weltgeschichte*. Berlin

SIMPSON, W.D. (1949) *Castles from the air*. London

SIMPSON, W.D. (1969) *Castles in England and Wales*. London

TILLMANN, C. (1958-61) *Lexicon der deutschen Burgen und Schlössen*, 4 vols. Stuttgart

TOY, S. (1955) *A history of fortification from 3000 BC to AD 1700*. London

TOY, S. (1953) *The castles of Great Britain*. London

TUULSE, A, tr. GIRDWOOD, R.P. (1958) *Castles of the western world*. London

VON USLAR, R. (1964) *Studien zu frühgeschichtlichen Befestigungen zwischen Nordsee und Alpen*. Cologne and Graz

VIOLLET-LE-DUC, E.E, tr. MACDERMOTT, M. (1860) *An essay on the military architecture of the middle ages*. Oxford

WEINGARTNER, J. (1950) *Tiroler Burgenkunde*. Vienna

WEISSMÜLLER, A.A. (1967) *Castles from the heart of Spain*. London

Histories of art and architecture

CAIGER-SMITH, A. (1963) *English medieval mural paintings*. Oxford

CHASTEL, A, tr. MURRAY, P. and L. (1963) *Italian art*. London

CLARK, K. (1962) *The Gothic Revival*. London

CLASEN, K. H. (1939) *Die mittelalterliche Bildhauerkunst im Deutschordensland Preussen: die Bildwerk bis zur Mitte des 15 Jahrhunderts*, 2 vols. Berlin

COLVIN, H. M., ALLEN BROWN, R. and TAYLOR, A. J. (1963) *The history of the king's works*, 2 vols. and plans. London

CONANT, K.J. (1959) *Carolingian and Romanesque architecture*. Harmondsworth

DEHIO, G. (1923) *Geschichte der deutschen Kunst*, vol. 2. Berlin and Leipzig

EVANS, J. (1948) *Art in medieval France*. Oxford

EVANS, J. ed. (1966) *The flowering of the middle ages*. London

FRANKL, P, tr. PEVSNER, D. (1962) *Gothic architecture*. Harmondsworth

GIROUARD, M. (1966) *Robert Smythson and the architecture of the Elizabethan era*. London

HARVEY, J. (1950) *The Gothic World*. London

KNOOP, D. and JONES, G.P. (1933) *The medieval mason*. Manchester

LAMPÉREZ Y ROMEA, V. (1908-9) *Historia de la arquitectura cristiana española en la Edad Media, segun el estudio de los elementos y los monumentos*. Madrid

MARTINDALE, A. (1967) *Gothic art*. London

ROSENAU, H. (1959) *The ideal city in its architectural evolution*. London

SALZMANN, L.F. (1952) *Building in England down to 1540: a documentary history*. Oxford

SHEARER, C. (1935) *The renaissance of architecture in southern Italy*. Cambridge

STENTON, SIR F.M. ed. (1965) *The Bayeux Tapestry*. London

TERRASSE, H. (1932) *L'art hispano-mauresque des origines au XIIIe siècle*. Paris

VIOLLET-LE-DUC, E.E. (1858-68) *Dictionnaire raisonné de l'architecture française du XIe au XVIe siècles*. 10 vols. Paris

WEBB, G. (1956) *Architecture in Britain: the middle ages*. Harmondsworth

WHITE, J. (1966) *Art and architecture in Italy 1250 to 1400*. Harmondsworth

WHITEHILL, W.M. (1941) *Spanish romanesque architecture of the eleventh century*. Oxford

WILLEMSEN, C.A, and ODENTHAL, D, tr. WOODWARD, D. (1959) *Apulia*. London

WOOD, M. (1965) *The English medieval house*. London

General histories and biographies

ALLEN BROWN, R. (1969) *The Normans and the Norman Conquest*. London

BAETHGEN, F. (1951) *Europa im Spätmittelalter*. Berlin

BARRACLOUGH, G. (1947, reprinted 1966) *The origins of modern Germany*. Oxford

BARRACLOUGH, G. ed. and tr. (1961) *Medieval Germany, 911-1250: essays by German historians*, 2 vols. Oxford

BÄUML, F.H. (1969) *Medieval civilization in Germany 800-1273.* London

BLOCH, M, tr. MANYON, L.A. (1961) *Feudal society.* London

BROOKE, C. (1954) *Europe in the central middle ages 962-1154.* London

BULLOUGH, D. (1965) *The age of Charlemagne.* London

CALMETTE, J. (1962) *The Golden Age of Burgundy.* London

CARSTEN, F.L. (1954) *The origins of Prussia.* Oxford

CLAPHAM, J. and POWER, E, ed. (1941) *The Cambridge economic history of Europe, Vol. I. The agrarian life of the middle ages.* Cambridge

COULBORN, R, ed. (1956) *Feudalism in history.* Princeton

COULTON, G.G. (1910) *A medieval garner.* London

DAVIS, R.H.C. (1957) *A history of medieval Europe from Constantine to St Louis.* London

DAWSON, C. (1953) *Medieval essays.* London

DOUGLAS, D.C. (1964) *William the Conqueror: the Norman impact upon England.* London

FAWTIER, R, tr. BUTLER, R. and ADAM, R.J. (1960) *The Capetian kings of France.* London

FOWLER, K. (1967) *The age of Plantagenet and Valois.* London

HALE, J, HIGHFIELD, J.R. and SMALLEY, B, ed. (1965) *Europe in the late middle ages.* London

HALPHEN, L. (1906) *Le comté d'Anjou au XIe siècle.* Paris

HASKINS, C.H. (1918) *The Normans in European history.* New York

HAY, D. (1966) *Europe in the fourteenth and fifteenth centuries.* London

HEYMANN, F.G. (1955) *Jan Žižka and the Hussite revolution.* Princeton

HUIZINGA, J. (1937) *The waning of the middle ages.* London

JONES, G. (1968) *The Vikings.* London

LEWIS, A.R. (1958) *The northern seas.* Princeton

LEWIS, P.S. (1968) *Later medieval France: the polity.* London

LIVERMORE, H. (1966) *A history of Spain,* 2nd edn. London

LIVERMORE, H. (1966) *A history of Portugal.* Cambridge

MAČEK, J. (1958) *The Hussite Movement in Bohemia,* 2nd edn. Prague

MACK SMITH, D. (1968) *A history of Sicily: medieval Sicily 800-1713.* London

MASSON, G. (1957) *Frederick II of Hohenstaufen: a life.* London

MENÉNDEZ PIDAL, R., tr. SUNDERLAND, H. (1934) *The Cid and his Spain.* London

MUNZ, P. (1969) *Frederick Barbarossa: a study in medieval politics.* London

NORGATE, K. (1887) *England under the Angevin kings,* 2 vols. London

NORWICH, J. J. (1967) *The Normans in the south 1016-1130.* London

OLDENBOURG, Z. (1959) *Le Bûcher de Montségur. 16 Mars, 1244.* Paris

OXENSTIERNA, COUNT F, tr. and ed. HUTTER, C. (1966) *The Norsemen.* London

PAINTER, S. (1961) *Feudalism and liberty.* Articles and addresses, ed. CAZALET, F.A. JR. Baltimore

PAINTER, S. (1933) *William Marshal, knight-errant, baron, and regent of England.* Baltimore

PAINTER, S. (1940) *French chivalry; chivalric ideas and practices in medieval France.* Baltimore

PEERS, E.A. (1929) *Ramon Lull: a biography.* London

PERROY, E, tr. WELLS, W.B. with intro. by DOUGLAS, D.C. (1962) *The Hundred Years War.* London

POOLE, A.L. (1951) *Domesday Book to Magna Carta 1087-1216.* 2nd edn. Oxford

POSTAN, M and RICH, E.E, ed. (1952) *The Cambridge economic history of Europe, vol. II. Trade and industry in the middle ages.* Cambridge

POWICKE, SIR M. (1961) *The Loss of Normandy,* 2nd edn. Manchester

PREVITÉ-ORTON, C.W. (1912) *The early history of the house of Savoy.* Cambridge

RÖRIG, F, tr. BRYANT, D. (1967) *The medieval town.* London

RUNCIMAN, SIR S. (1965) *The fall of Constantinople, 1453.* Cambridge

RUNCIMAN, SIR S. (1951) *A history of the Crusades,* 3 vols. Cambridge

RUNCIMAN, SIR S. (1960) *The Sicilian vespers.* Harmondsworth

SOUTHERN, R.W. (1953) *The making of the middle ages.* London

THOMPSON, J.W. (1928) *Economic and social history of the middle ages.* New York

THOMPSON, J. W. (1928) *Feudal Germany.* Chicago

WALEY, D. (1964) *Later medieval Europe: from Saint Louis to Luther.* London

WALEY, D. (1969) *The Italian city-republics.* London

Warfare, weapons, and armour

BLAIR, C. (1958) *European armour* circa *1066* to circa *1700.* London

CIPOLLA, C. (1965) *Guns and sails in the early phase of European expansion 1400-1700.* London

DELBRÜCK, H. (1900-36) *Geschichte der Kriegskunst im Rahmen der politischen Geschichte,* 7 vols. Berlin

HOLLISTER, C.W. (1965) *The military organization of Norman England.* Oxford

KEENE, M. (1965) *The laws of war in the late middle ages.* London

LOT, F. (1947) *L'art militaire et les armées au Moyen Age en Europe et dans le Proche Orient.* 2 vols. Paris

MACHIAVELLI, N, tr. FARNEWORTH, E, in *The Works of Nicholas Machiavelli* (1775) *The art of war.* London

MANN, SIR J. (1960) *An outline of arms and armour in England.* London

MORRIS, J.E. (1901) *The Welsh wars of Edward I.* Oxford

OMAN, SIR C. (1924) *A history of the art of war in the middle ages,* 2nd edn, 2 vols. London

PRESTON, R.A, WISE, S.F. and WERNER, H.O. (1956) *Men in arms: a history of warfare.* London

SMAIL, R.C. (1956, reprinted 1967) *Crusading warfare.* Cambridge

TRAPP, GRAF O, tr. MANN, J.G. (1929) *The armoury of the castle of Churburg.* London

WARNER, P. (1968) *Sieges of the middle ages.* London

Science and technology

CROMBIE, A.C. (1961) *Augustine to Galileo,* 2 vols. London

DERRY, T.K. and WILLIAMS, T.I. (1960) *A short history of technology from the earliest times to* AD *1900.* Oxford

GILLE, B. (1966) *The Renaissance engineers.* London

MUMFORD, L. (1934) *Technics and civilization.* New York

PARTINGTON, J.R. (1960) *A history of Greek fire and gunpowder.* Cambridge

SINGER, C, HOLMYARD, E.J, HALL, A.R. and WILLIAMS, T.I. (1954-8) *A history of technology,* 5 vols, esp. vol. 2. Oxford

WHITE, L. (1962) *Medieval technology and social change.* Oxford

N.B.   More precise references from the titles listed above and from other books and articles are given below in the notes. It has not been possible for reasons of space to give a full account of all the works and guides available on the individual castles mentioned in the text. Finó (1967) contains a full and up-to-date bibliography of this nature for French castles (and some others) and I am particularly grateful for the help I have derived from this book; Tillman (1958-61) in Vol. 3 has a long bibliography for castles in German-speaking countries. For English castles see the National Trust Guides and the Ministry of Works HMSO guides which include many excellent individual accounts, only some of which are given below. For Spanish castles I have depended very much on Weissmüller (1967).

Notes

Abbreviations to the Notes below

A.E.A.C. = *Asociación española de amigos de los castillos*
Chat. Inst. Hist. = *Institut International des Châteaux historiques*
Hist. King's Works = Colvin, H.M. *et al* (1963) The History of the King's Works (see above)
C.A.F. = *Congrès archéologique française*
M.G.H. = *Monumenta Germaniae Historica*
Cam. Econ. Hist. = Cambridge Economic History of Europe

Preface

1 Quoted from W. H. Auden (1967) *About the house*, p. 73, published by Faber and Faber.

Introduction

1 This and the following figures are taken from *Bulletin No. 20, Chat. Inst. Hist.* (1966). Hotz (1965) p. 4 gives figures for German-speaking countries. He also quotes a figure of 40,000 castles formerly existing in France.

Chapter 1

1 See Coulborn (1956) for discussions of feudalism in non-European countries. The appearance of feudalism as the inevitable response to anarchy is a favourite theme in science fiction, in, for example, the books of Isaac Asimov, Poul Anderson, and in John Christopher's *The death of grass*.
2 See Porada, E. 'Battlements in the military architecture and in the symbolism of the ancient Near East' in *Essays in the history of architecture presented to Rudolf Wittkower* (1967) ed. Fraser, D, Hibbard, H. and Lewine, M.J. London.
3 See Oman, *Art of war*. Book I, Chapter 6, and also Drachmann, W. (1963) *The mechanical technology of the ancients*. Copenhagen.
4 Jones (1968) pp. 99-102.
5 See Alcock, L. and Ashe, G. 'Cadbury: is it Camelot?' in Ashe, ed. (1968) *The quest for Arthur's Britain*, London, pp. 155-88.
6 Jones (1968) p. 83.
7 Liutprand of Cremona, tr. Wright, F.A. (1930) *Works*, London, pp. 241-2.
8 Gibbon says: 'The vices of Byzantine armies were inherent, their victories accidental.' Vol. II, p. 382. See Oman, *Art of war*, Book IV, Chapter I, for a reasoned defence.
9 Ortiz Echagüe (1956) p. 9. For Baños see Sanz y Diaz, J. (1958) *La alcazaba de Baños*, Boletin A.E.A.C. No. 20, pp. 20-4.
10 Quoted from Oman (1924) *Art of war*, vol. I, p. 86, published by Methuen & Co.
11 Schuchhardt (1931) pp. 177-90, and also Von Uslar (1964) Chapter 6, p. 34.
12 Flodoard, ed. and tr. Lejeune, M. (1854) *Histoire de l'église de Reims*, 2 vols. Vol. I, pp. 341-5; Vol. II, pp. 17-8; Vol. I, pp. 308-9.
13 Lewis, A. R. (1958) p. 389, but see Oxenstierna (1966) pp. 103-41.
14 Abbon, ed. and tr. Waquet, H. (1942) *Le Siège de Paris par les Normands: poème du IXᵉ siècle*. Paris.
15 Lewis, A. R. (1958) p. 392.
16 Described in Meyer (1963) pp. 61-3, and Von Uslar (1964) pp. 68-70.
17 Gruszecki, A. 'Castles in Poland' in *Bulletin No. 19, Chat. Inst. Hist.* (1965).
18 Jones (1968) *The Vikings*, pp. 360-4.
19 Herrnbrodt, A. (1958) *Der Husterknupp*, Vol. 6. Bonn Jahrbuch. Cologne and Graz.
20 Eydoux (1969) p. 35 ff.
21 Pépin, E. (1925) *Chinon*. Paris, and Crozet, R. (1949) 'Chinon' *C.A.F. CVIᵉ session* (1948) Tours, pp. 342-51.
22 For the Rüdesheim castles see the entries in Tillmann (1958-61) vol. 2, and Hotz (1965) *Kleine Kunstgeschichte*, p. 18.
23 Quoted from Koebner, R, 'The settlement and colonization of Europe', *Cam. Econ. Hist*, vol. I, p. 61, published by Cambridge University Press.
24 See Strayer, J, 'Feudalism in Western Europe' in *Feudalism in history* (1956) ed. Coulborn, R, pp. 15-25.
25 *Raoul de Cambrai*. tr. Crosland, J. (1926) London, p. 105. The wars in this poem may be based on an incident shortly described by Flodoard in an entry for the year 943.
26 Bloch (1961) p. 313.
27 For what follows on Fulk Nerra see Halphen (1906), Southern (1953), and also Norgate (1887) vol. I.
28 For Langeais see Lesueur, F. (1949) 'Le château de Langeais', *C.A.F. CVIᵉ session* (1948) Tours, pp. 378-85.
29 Norgate (1887) pp. 165-6.
30 Halphen says of him: 'Ses violences sont grandes mais ses pénitences éclatantes', p. 130.

Chapter 2

1 See White, L. (1962) but also discussion of his theories by Hilton, R.H. and Sawyer, P.H. in *Past and Present*, **24** (1963) pp. 90-100, and by Bullough, D. (1965) *The age of Charlemagne*. London.
2 This dependence on the manor was shared by monasteries and secular residences as well as the castle. It does not mean that every manor had a castle attached to it.
3 A point made by Allen Brown, R. in *The Normans and the Norman Conquest*, p. 61.
4 Ordericus Vitalis, tr. Forester, T. (1853) *Ecclesiastical history of England and Normandy*, 4 vols, London, vol. II, p. 19.
5 *Anglo-Saxon Chronicle*, tr. Garmonsway, G.N. (1953) London, p. 200.
6 Beeler, John H. (1956) 'Castles and strategy in Norman and early Angevin England', *Speculum*, XXXI, pp. 581-601. This article is discussed in Hollister (1965) pp. 162-4.
7 Renn (1968) p. 14 and Map D.
8 *Current archaeology*, November 1967, which also contains descriptions of Bramber, South Mimms, and Penmaen. For Abinger see Hope-Taylor, B. (1956) 'The Norman motte at Abinger, Surrey and its wooden castle' in *Recent archaeological excavations in Britain*, ed. Bruce-Mitford, R.L.S, London, pp. 223-49. For general discussions of the motte-and-bailey castle see Allen Brown, R, *The Norman Conquest* (1969) and the same author's earlier *English medieval castles* and essay in *The Bayeux Tapestry*, ed. Stenton. For continental examples, see Herrnbrodt (1958) and Von Uslar (1964) pp. 102-8.
9 Lambert of Ardres, *Historia comitum Ghisnensium*, *M.G.H.* XXIV, pp. 589-90.
10 Quoted from Bloch (1961) p. 301.
11 Lambert of Ardres, *M.G.H.* XXIV, p. 624. This translation, which is a passage by Walter de Clusa incorporated in Lambert of Ardres, and the one following from John of Colmieu are taken from Armitage, E.S. (1912) *The early Norman castles of the British Isles*, pp. 89-90 and pp. 88-9 respectively, published by John Murray (Publishers) Ltd, London.
12 See *Hist. King's Works*, vol. I, pp. 28-32, vol. II, pp. 706-29, and also Allen Brown, R. in *The Bayeux Tapestry*, ed. Stenton.
13 Piper (1912) Chapter 6, p. 173, Schuchhardt (1931) pp. 224-5, and Meyer (1963) p. 80, all devote much space to the disputed etymology of this term. It seems, however, that it does not mean what it says, ie, the tower designed to keep peace on the mountain, but that it comes from a root common with the English belfrey, the French *beffroi*, and the Italian *beffredo*.
14 *Vita Bennonis Episcopi Osnabrugensis*. *M.G.H.* Scriptores XII (1856). Göttingen.
15 The translation from Bruno's *Liber Saxonici Belli* (ed. Lohmann, M.G.H.S.S. (1937) pp. 28-9) is taken here from Davis, R.H.C. (1957) *A history of medieval Europe from Constantine to St Louis*, pp. 249-50, published by the Longman Group Ltd, London.
16 *Annales*, ed. Holder-Egger, O. (1894) Hanover and Leipzig, pp. 286-7 and 292 for what follows on Canossa.

17 Bertolani del Rio (1959) pp. 65-8.

18 Translation from *A selection of the letters of Gregory VII*, tr. Emerton, E. (1932) pp. 111-2, Columbia University Press, New York.

19 For this Karlstein and Rothenburg see Meyer (1963) pp. 68-76.

20 For the importance of this siege see Harvey, J. 'The development of architecture' in Evans (1966) p. 112.

21 Ribéra, Julian, tr. and abridged by Hague, E. and Leffingwell, M. (1929) *Music in ancient Arabia and Spain, being La Música de las Cantigas*. Stanford.

22 For recent accounts see Weissmüller (1967) pp. 106-11 and Finó (1967) pp. 315-7.

Chapter 3

1 Runciman, Sir S. (1960) *The Sicilian Vespers*, p. 110.

2 For the importance of the stirrup see White, L. (1962) and the other references in note 1, Chapter 2.

3 See, for example, Liddell-Hart, Sir B. (1954) *Strategy: the indirect approach*–'the spirit of feudal chivalry was inimical to military art', p. 75, or the remark that Lot quotes with approval, saying that the European nobility 'sacrificed tactics and strategy for an impossible dream: to strike heavily at the enemy while remaining invulnerable to his returning blows', *Art Militaire*. vol. II, p. 429. But see Allen Brown (1969) pp. 49-51 for a defence of the Normans as soldiers.

4 Hohler, C. in Evans (1966) p. 166.

5 For the sieges of Le Puiset, see Suger, ed. and tr. Waquet, H. (1929) *Vie de Louis VI le gros.* Paris, esp. pp. 137-43 for the first siege.

6 Fedden and Thompson (1957) p. 59.

7 See *The history of Fulk Fitz-Warine* englished by Kemp-Welch, A. with an introduction by Brandin, L. (1904) London. See also Oman (1926), pp. 134-8.

8 Quoted in Powicke (1961) p. 199, published by Manchester University Press.

9 These examples are all taken from Smail (1967) pp. 201-3.

10 Painter, S. (1956) 'The Lords of Lusignan in the eleventh and twelfth centuries' in *Feudalism and liberty*, pp. 41-72.

11 Finó (1967) p. 27

12 See Mortet, V. and Deschamps, P. (1929) *Recueil des textes rélatifs a l'histoire de l'architecture.* vol. II, XIIe-XIIIe siècles, Paris, pp. 80-2.

13 William of Malmesbury, tr. Giles (1904) *Chronicle of the Kings of England*, London, p. 442.

14 This is shown by the following quotation from Lambert of Ardres, *M.G.H.* XXIV, pp. 640 ff. (The passage is also interesting as one of the few surviving to show the ambivalent attitude of the peasant to these fortifications: admiration equally balanced with fear.) Arnold II, count of Guisnes and Ardres, fortified Ardres against his enemy the count of Boulogne in about 1200. '. . . many oftentimes came together to see these great earthworks; for such poor folk as were not hired labourers forgot their penury in the joy of beholding this work; while the rich, both knights and burgesses and oftentimes priests or monks, came not daily only, but again and again every day, to refresh their bodies and see so marvellous a sight. For who but a man stupefied and deadened by age or cares, could have failed to rejoice in the sight of that Master Simon the Dyker, so learned in geometrical work, pacing with rod in hand, and with all a master's dignity, and setting out hither and thither, not so much with that actual rod as with the spiritual rod of his mind, the work which in imagination he had already conceived?– tearing down houses and granges, hewing to the ground orchards and trees covered with flowers or fruit, seeing to it with the utmost zeal and care that the streets should be cleared, on workdays even more than on holidays, for all convenience of traffic, digging up kitchen-gardens with crops of potherbs or of flax, treading down and destroying the crops to make straight the ways, even though some groaned in the indignation of their heart, and cursed him under their breath.' Translation from Lambert of Ardres in Coulton, G.G. *A medieval garner* (1910) p. 170, published by Constable and Co. Ltd, London.

15 Ordericus Vitalis, vol. III, p. 25.

16 See Partington (1960) for descriptions of these recipes and also Villena, L. 'Evolution of fortification and poliorcetics' in Bulletin No. 19, *Chat. Inst. Hist.* (1964).

17 White (1962) p. 128. For Petrus Peregrinus see Sarton, G. (1950) *Introduction to the history of science*, vol. II, Baltimore, pp. 1030-2. He wrote his letter on magnetism while at the siege of Lucera in 1269.

18 Translation from Alexander Neckam, taken from Holmes, V.T. *Daily living in the twelfth century* (1952) University of Wisconsin Press, pp. 183-4. In the course of this book Professor Holmes translates nearly the whole of Alexander Neckam's *De nominibus utensilium* from which this passage comes.

19 Giraldus Cambrensis, ed. and tr. Butler, H.E. (1937) *Autobiography*, London, p. 35.

20 Lambert of Ardres, *M.G.H.* XXIV, p. 629.

21 Translation by Scott Moncrieff, C. (1919) *The song of Roland*, London, lines 2375-84.

22 Translated from *Les Troubadours.* vol. II, ed. Lavaud and Nelli (1966) Paris, p. 260.

23 See *Arthurian romances.* tr. Comfort, W.W. (1913) London. This book does not include *Perceval*.

24 *Tristan* by Gottfried von Strassburg, tr. Hatto, A.T. (1960) Harmondsworth, p. 293.

25 *The high history of the Holy Grail*, tr. Evans, S, 2 vols (1898) London.

26 Hohler, C. in Evans (1966) p. 161.

27 For many other examples particularly concerning Cornwall see Jenner, H. (1915) 'Some possible Arthurian place-names in West Penwith' in *Journal of the Royal Institution of Cornwall* XIX, pp. 46-89. The author tells of how, in 1867, he heard of an old man who had seen the ghosts of King Arthur's soldiers drilling at Castle-an-Dinas (near St Columb) and 'remembered the glancing of the moonbeams *on their muskets!*'

28 Tr. Mustard, Helen M. and Passage, Charles E. (1961) New York.

29 Tr. Hatto, A.T. (1960) Harmondsworth. The same translator has also made a version of the *Nibelungenlied* (1964) Harmondsworth.

30 Tr. Merwin, W.S. (1959) London.

31 Tr. Bell, C.H. (1931) in *Peasant life in old German epics.* (Columbia Records) New York

Chapter 4

1 *Crusader castles* (1936) London.

2 For this and what follows see Smail (1967) especially Chapter VII.

3 Suger, ed. Waquet, *op. cit.* p. 39.

4 Poole (1951) p. 155.

5 Crosland, J. (1962) *William the Marshal*, London, p. 20. See also Painter, S. (1928) *William Marshal*.

6 For these three castles see Toy (1953) pp. 104-9 and Finó (1967) pp. 346-7, 367-70, and 406-10.

7 Described in Eydoux (1969) pp. 133-45.

8 See Poux (1925).

9 *Hist. King's Works.* (1963) vol. I, p. 67.

10 See Allen Brown, R. (1966) *Dover castle*, H.M.S.O. Guide, London, and the same author in *Hist. King's Works* (1963) vol. II, pp. 629-41.

11 Pépin (1925) and Crozet (1949). See note 21, Chapter 1 above.

12 Powicke (1961) p. 196, published by Manchester University Press.

13 Gébelin (1964) pp. 49-52.

14 See Dieulafoy, M. (1898) 'Le Château-Gaillard et l'architecture militaire au XIIIe siècle.' *Mémoires de l'Institut National de France (Académie des inscriptions et belles lettres)* **36**, 1st part, pp. 325-86.

15 See *Oeuvres de Rigord et de Guillaume le Breton*, ed. Delaborde, H.F. (1882) 2 vols, Paris. William le Breton described the siege not only in verse (*Phillipidos* Bk. VII, vol. II) but also in a prose chronicle (vol. I, pp. 212-20).

16 The buildings the French broke into at this point did not, it is thought, form part of Richard's original scheme, but were built during John's reign.

17 See Gébelin (1964) pp. 52-8, who describes at some length what he calls the 'Philip Augustus formula'.

18 Gille (1966) p. 50, but see the account in Finó (1967) pp. 333-7. There are excellent old photographs of the keep in Lefèvre-Pontalis, E. (1913) *Le château de Coucy*, Paris.

19 Translated from *La Chanson de la Croisade*, passages in *Les Troubadours*, vol. II, ed. Lavaud and Nelli (1966) Paris, lines 8680-98.
20 'To the excellent and illustrious lady, Blanche, by the Grace of God Queen of the French, Guillaume des Ormes, seneschal of Carcassonne, her humble, devoted, and faithful servant, greeting: Madam, these presents are to make known to your Excellency that the town of Carcassonne was besieged by the self-called Viscount and his accomplices, on Monday, September 17, 1240 . . .

'They began a mine against the barbican of the Narbonnaise gate; and forthwith we, having heard the noise of the work underground, made a countermine, and we made in the inside of the barbican a great and strong wall of stones laid dry, so that we could thereby protect the full half of the barbican; and then they set fire to the hole they were making, in such wise that the wood having been burnt, a portion of the front of the barbican fell down.

'They began to mine against another turret of the lists; we countermined and succeeded in taking possession of the chamber which they had formed. They began, thereupon, to run a mine between us and a certain wall and they destroyed two crenelles of the lists; but we set up there a good and strong paling between them and us.

'They undermined also the angle of the town wall, in the direction of the bishop's house, and by dint of mining they arrived under a certain Saracen wall, at the wall of the lists; but immediately as we perceived this, we made a good and strong paling between us and them, higher up in the lists, and we countermined. Thereupon they fired their mine and flung us to a distance of some ten fathoms from our crenelles. But we forthwith made a good and strong paling and thereon a good brattish (or breast-work) with good *archières*: so that none amongst them dared to come near us in this quarter.

'They began also, Madam, a mine against the barbican of the gate of Rhodez, and they kept beneath, because they wished to arrive at our walls, and they made a marvellous great passage; but we, having perceived it, forthwith made a great and strong paling both on one side and the other thereof; we countermined likewise, and having fallen in with them, we carried the chamber of their mine.

'Know also, Madam, that since the beginning of the siege they have never ceased to make assaults upon us; but we had such good cross-bows, and men animated with so true a desire to defend themselves, that it was in their assaults they suffered their heaviest losses.

'At last, on a certain Sunday, they called together all their men-at-arms, crossbow-men and others, and all together, assailed the barbican, at a point below the castle. We descended to the barbican, and hurled so many stones and bolts that we forced them to abandon the said assault, wherein several of them were killed and wounded.

'But the Sunday following, after the feast of St Michael, they made a very great assault on us; and we, thanks to God and our people, who showed great good will in defending themselves, repulsed them; several amongst them were killed and wounded; none of our men, thanks be to God, were either killed or received a mortal wound. But at last, on Monday, October 11, towards evening, they heard news that your people, Madam, were coming to our aid, and they set fire to the houses of the bourg of Carcassonne. They have destroyed wholly the houses of the Brothers Minors, and the houses of a monastery of the Blessed Virgin Mary, which were in the bourg, to obtain the wood wherewith they made their palisades. All those who were engaged in the said siege abandoned it secretly that same night, even those who were resident in the bourg.

'As for us, we were well prepared, to God be thanks, to await, Madam, your assistance, so much so that none of our people were in want of provisions, how poor soever they might be; nay more, Madam, we had in abundance corn and meat enough to enable us to wait during a long time, if so it was necessary for your succour. Know, Madam, that these evil doers killed, on the second day after their arrival, thirty-three priests and other clerks, whom they found on entering the bourg; know moreover, Madam, that the Seigneur Pierre du Voisin, your constable of Carcassonne, Raymond de Capendu, and Gerard d'Ermenville, have borne themselves very well in this affair. Nevertheless the constable by his vigilance, his valour, and his coolness, distinguished himself above all others. As for the other matters concerning these parts, we will be able, Madam, to speak the truth to you respecting them when we shall be in your presence. Know therefore, Madam, that they had begun to mine against us strongly in seven places. We have nearly everywhere countermined, and have not spared our pains. They began to mine from the inside of their houses, so that we knew nothing thereof until they arrived at our lists.

Done at Carcassonne, October 13, 1240.'
Taken from Viollet-le-Duc (1860) pp. 38-42.
21 Oldenbourg (1959) p. 333.
22 See Fliche, A. (1951) 'Aigues-Mortes', *C.A.F. CVIII^e session*, Montpellier (1950) pp. 90-103.
23 De Schryver, A. (1966) *Guide to the castle of the counts of Flanders*, Ghent.
24 Hindley (1968) pp. 159-68 and see also Pélichet, E. 'Le château de Chillon'. *C.A.F. CX^e session*, Suisse Romande (1952) pp. 270-82.
25 Quoted in Salzmann (1952) p. 382.
26 See Caiger-Smith (1963) p. 82.
27 See A.J. Taylor's essay 'The King's works in Wales 1377-1330' in *Hist. King's Works*, vol. I, pp. 293-395 and also the same author's H.M.S.O. guides *Caernarvon Castle and town walls* (1966) and *Conway Castle and town walls*
28 Edwards (1954) pp. 64-5.
29 Taylor, A.J. 'Military architecture' in *Medieval England*, ed. Poole, A.L, vol. I, p. 98.
30 Cruden (1960) pp. 22-6.
31 For a short survey of Irish castles see Le Clerc, P. in *Bulletin no. 13, Chat. Inst. Hist.* (1960). See Leask (1941) for Trim and Carrickfergus, pp. 27-34.
32 *De expugnatione Lvxbonensi*, ed. and tr. David, C.W. (1936) published by Columbia University Press, New York.
33 *Ibid*, pp. 161-3.
34 Thompson (1928) p. 555.
35 See the account in Weissmüller (1967) pp. 140-223.

Chapter 5

1 Otto of Freising and Rahewin, tr. Evans, A.P. and Knapp, P. (1928) *The Two Cities* (Columbia Records) New York, p. 45.
2 Barraclough (1966) p. 137.
3 Asche, S. (1954) *Die Wartburg und ihre Kunstwerke*. Eisenach.
4 Hotz, W. in *Burgen der Hohenstaufen in Schwaben. Franken und Hessen* by Wülfing, O.E. (1960) Düsseldorf, p. 142.
5 Hotz (1965) p. 105.
6 See Thompson, J.W. (1931) *Economic and social history of Europe in the later middle ages (1300-1530)* New York, p. 129.
7 For the castles mentioned here see Hotz (1965) pp. 100-5.
8 See Munz (1969) pp. 103-4.
9 See Hotz, W. in Wülfing (1960) above, p. 146.
10 See the charming little book by Walter Hotz, *Burg Wildenberg im Odenwald* (1963) Amorbach.
11 For Heidenreichstein see Piper, O. (1904) *Oesterreichische Burgen*, vol. III, pp. 46-60. For Rappottenstein see *ibid*. vol. IV pp. 129-36.
12 Wülfing (1960) p. 150 and Meyer (1963) pp. 122-4.
13 Quoted from Thompson (1928) p. 497.
14 Barraclough (1966) p. 245, n. 2.
15 Baethgen (1951).
16 Gerö, L. 'Hungary' in *Bulletin no. 14, Chat. Inst. Hist.* (1961).
17 Otto of Freising (see above) p. 128.
18 See Waley (1969) p. 20.
19 *Ibid*. p. 175.
20 Munz (1969) pp. 177-9.
21 For Frederick II's castles see the works listed above by Hahn (1961) Shearer (1935) Willemsen and Odenthal (1959). See also Gifuni, G. (1937) *Lucera*, 2nd edn, Urbino.
22 Gregorovius, F. (1889) in *Wanderjahre in Italien*, vol. 5, p. 174, Leipzig.
23 Munz (1969) Chapter 1 'The Kyffhäuser Legend' pp. 3-22.

Chapter 6

1 Ritter (1953) pp. 93-8 who points out that though Sicard de Lordat was in charge of Gaston-Phébus's artillery, he made no specific provisions against attack by enemy artillery in the designs of these castles.

2 Eydoux (1969) pp. 226-7.

3 Lot (1947) vol. I, p. 344-8, 359-64; vol. II, pp. 13-14, 484.

4 Smail, R.C. (1958) 'Art of War' in *Medieval England*, ed. Poole, A.L, vol. I, pp. 147-52. See also 'War and society 1300-1600' with papers by Macfarlane, K. B. and Hale, J. in *Past and Present* (1962), pp. 3-36.

5 Finó (1967) p. 254.

6 Warner (1968) p. 185.

7 The siege took place in 1338 when the earls of Salisbury and Arundel failed in their attempt partly because of the strong defence and partly because French provision boats could reach the castle. Agnes used to wear mail herself and her splendidly dressed maids would use white napkins to wipe away the dust on the battlements raised by the impact of missiles from the English machines. D.N.B. vol. XVI, p. 150.

8 Taken from Lord Berner's translation of Froissart's *Chronicles*, reprint of 1812, London, vol. I, p. 103.

9 See Keene (1965).

10 Trapp (1929) p. 19.

11 Rörig (1967) p. 168.

12 Quoted in Gille (1966) p. 108.

13 Derry and Williams (1960) pp. 139-41.

14 *Selections from the notebooks of Leonardo da Vinci*, ed. Richter, I.A. (1952) Oxford, pp. 294-6.

15 *Mémoires* of Olivier de la Marche, ed. Beaune, H. and d'Arbaumont, J. (1884) Paris, vol. 2, Chapter 29.

16 Huizinga (1937) p. 251.

17 William Mathews in his *The ill-framed knight* (1966) Berkeley and Los Angeles, especially Chapter 3.

Chapter 7

1 Pradel, P. (196?) *Avignon: le palais des Papes*. Paris.

2 Finó (1967) p. 262.

3 For the Hundred Years War and its background see the works by Perroy, Hay, Waley, and Fowler listed above.

4 Fowler (1967) pp. 123-4.

5 Bonnel, E. (1963) 'Le fort Saint-André a Villeneuve-lès-Avignon' *C.A.F. CXXI^e session*, Avignon et Comtat-Venaissin, pp. 202-5.

6 De Fossa, F. (1910) *Le château de Vincennes*. Paris. For more recent accounts see Finó (1967) pp. 428-31 and Gébelin (1964) pp. 76-9.

7 Grodecki, L. (1957) *Le château de Pierrefonds*. Paris.

8 Ritter (1953) p. 121, and Pressouyre, S. 'Le château de Tarascon' (1963) *C.A.F. CXXI^e session*, Avignon et Comtat-Venaissin, pp. 221-43.

9 Grand, R. (1919) 'Le château de Josselin'. *C.A.F. LXXXIe session*, Brest et Vannes (1914) pp. 302-22.

10 Lewis, P. (1968) p. 214.

11 Eydoux (1969) pp. 177-89.

12 Finó (1967) pp. 348-53.

13 *Ibid*. pp. 411-3.

14 Stym-Popper, S. (1955) 'Le château de Salses' *C.A.F. CXII^e session*. Le Roussillon (1954) pp. 406-24.

15 Quoted with spelling modernized from Lord Berners's translation of Froissart's *Chronicles*, 1812 edition, vol. II, p. 480. Berners calls Mérigot, Aymergot Marcel.

16 Allen Brown (1954) pp. 96 and 99.

17 *Hist. King's Works*, vol. II, pp. 793-804.

18 Wood, M. (1965) p. 171.

19 Simpson, W.D. (1965) *Bodiam Castle, Sussex*, National Trust Guide, London.

20 Finó, J.F. (1967) p. 259.

21 Fowler, K. (1967) p. 200.

22 Wood (1965) p. 166.

23 Wood (1965) p. 170.

24 Simpson (1969) p. 144.

25 Cruden (1960) pp. 131-6.

26 Wood, M. (1965) p. 168, calls the term 'pele tower' inaccurate and, drawing on the research of Dr R.W. Brunskill, points out that the pele was a temporary wooden fortification used by the English army against the Scots. The proper terms are 'tower house' for a stone tower of three or more storeys and 'bastel house' for the longer house of two storeys.

27 *Works*, ed. Skeat, p. 314, lines 321-35.

28 Caiger-Smith (1963) pp. 95-8.

29 Ortiz Echagüe (1956) p. 14 and Layna Serrano, F. (1960) *Castillos de Guadalajara*, Madrid, 2nd edn, pp. 505-16.

30 Sainz de Robles (1962) pp. 232-5.

31 Ortiz Echagüe, J. (1956) pp. 24-5.

32 de Almeida (1948) vol. III, p. 166.

33 *Ibid*. vol. III, pp. 25-8.

34 Weissmüller (1967) pp. 58-67.

395 Salses, France. A drawing by the Portuguese Francesco da Hollanda which shows well the new idea of concealing the castle in the landscape. *Madrid, Biblioteca Nacional*.

35 *Ibid*. pp. 75-80.

36 *Ibid* pp. 128-35. See also Dotor, A. (1957) '*Los castillos de Segovia*' in *A.E.A.C.* pp. 12-21.

37 *Ibid*. pp. 67-74.

38 *Ibid*. pp. 154-7.

Chapter 8

1 For the castles of the Teutonic Order see the works by Clasen, Schuchardt, and Piper in the bibliography. Many aspects of the Order are dealt with in Klemens Wieser, ed. (1967) *Acht Jahrhunderte deutscher Orden in Einzeldarstellungen*, Vol. I of *Quellen und Studien zur Geschichte des deutschen Ordens*, Bad Godesberg. Treitschke's *Das deutsche Ordensland Preussen* was translated in 1942 by Paul, E. and C. as *Treitschke's Origins of Prussianism (The Teutonic Knights)* London, and for more recent short accounts see the works by Hay (1966) and Baethgen (1951).

2 See Frankl (1962) and Harvey (1950) for the influence of the Gothic brick buildings of the north.

3 Clasen (1939) vol. I, p. 59.

4 The most recent full account of Marienburg is Schmid, B. (1955) *Die Marienburg*, Würzburg.

5 See Eichendorff's essay *Die Wiederherstellung des Schlosses der Deutschen Ordensritter zu Marienburg* in *Werke und Schriften*, vol. 4, pp. 951-1052. Stuttgart.

6 See Clasen (1931).

7 Tuulse (1958) p. 109.

8 See Jarrett, B. (1935) *Life of Charles IV*. London.

9 See Drováková, V. and Menclová, D. (1966) *Karlštejn*. Prague.

10 For the paintings at Karlštejn see Martindale (1967) pp. 225-30.

11 Quoted from Maček (1958) p. 37.

12 Heymann (1955) p. 103. For the castle of Kalich see *ibid*. pp. 218-9.

13 *Ibid.* p. 13.
14 For Pernštejn see Piper (1908) *Oesterreichische Burgen,* vol. 6, pp. 159-83 and Knox, B. (1965) *The architecture of Prague and Bohemia,* pp. 119-20.
15 See Meyer (1963) pp. 155-9 for reconstructions.
16 Barraclough (1966) p. 342.
17 Hotz (1956) p. 22.
18 Hotz (1965) p. 220.
19 See Meyer (1963) pp. 133-40 for reconstructions.
20 *Ibid.* p. 163-70.
21 Schlegel, R. rev. Klein, H. (1962) *Guide to the castle of Hohensalzburg.* Salzburg.
22 Michel, F. (1969) *Burg Eltz.* Munich.
23 Piper, O. (1904) *Oesterreichische Burgen,* vol. III, pp. 46-60.
24 Maedebach, H. (1969) *Veste Coburg. Kunstführer 871,* 2nd ed. Munich.

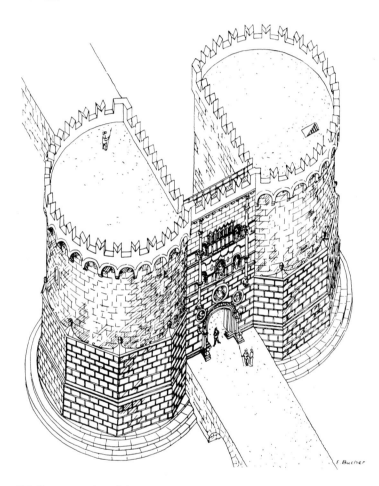

396 Reconstruction of the gateway to the Capua Bridge. This fortification built for the Emperor Frederick II *c* 1235 and mostly destroyed in the early sixteenth century was notable for many reasons. Drawing on classical inspiration especially in the style of the sculpture, it expressed his imperial ambitions. The octagonal bases to the drum towers reflect the fascination with this form that appears most completely in Castel del Monte.
The archway later provided an inspiration for Alfonso of Aragon's triumphal arch in the Castel Nuovo at Naples. (After Hotz)

25 Schellart, A.J.M. (1960) in Bulletin no. 13. *Chat. Inst. Hist.*
26 Gille (1966) Chapter 4, p. 79 ff.
27 Villani, ed. Zingarelli (1934) p. 93.
28 White, J. (1966) pp. 176-80.
29 *Ibid.* p. 330.
30 Filangieri, R. (1965) *Castel Nuovo: reggia angoina ed aragonese di Napoli.* Naples.
31 White, J. (1966) pp. 188-9 and Perogalli (1960) p. 199.
32 White, J. (1966) 331-3.
33 *Ibid.* p. 331.
34 *Ibid.* pp. 333-5.
35 Beltrami, L. (1894) *Il Castello di Milano.* Milan.
36 Rotondi, P. (1969) *The ducal palace of Urbino: its architecture and decoration.* London.

Chapter 9

1 Fowler (1967) p. 138.
2 Oman (1924) vol. 2, p. 212 accepts an earlier entry for Metz in 1324 but this is now considered doubtful.
3 Finó (1967) p. 277.
4 Derry and Williams (1960) p. 140.
5 White, L. (1962) p. 101.
6 Quoted in Cipolla (1965) p. 29.
7 Finó (1967) p. 283.
8 Cipolla (1965) p. 23.
9 By J.R. Hale in his essay 'The early development of the bastion; an Italian chronology, *c* 1450-*c* 1534,' in *Europe in the late middle ages,* ed. Hale, J.R, Highfield, R. and Smalley, B, p. 466 ff. on which what follows largely depends.
10 For the Sangallo family, see Gille (1966) pp. 115-20.

Chapter 10

1 Hill, C. (1958) 'The Norman Yoke' in *Puritanism and revolution,* London, pp. 50-122.
2 Not all the castles were held for King Charles. See Wallace Notestein's account of how Brilliana, Lady Harley, held the castle of Brampton Bryan with immense resource and courage for Parliament in *English folk: a book of characters* (1938) London, pp. 273-308.
3 Frankl (1962) p. 245. But see Sir John Summerson's admirable essay *English castles* (1940) for the views of someone who likes them positively.
4 Dehio (1923) vol. 2, p. 297.
5 *Faerie Queen,* Book II, Cant IX, xxi, xxii.
6 Dehio (1923) vol. 2, p. 299.
7 *The complete works of Saint Teresa of Jesus,* tr. and ed. Allison Peers, E. (1946) London, vol. II, p. 88.
8 See Whistler, L. (1938) *Sir John Vanbrugh: architect and dramatist 1664-1726.* London. As a young man, Vanbrugh was imprisoned for a time in the Bastille, an experience which had a deep influence on him. 'It seems,' says Whistler p. 50 'as if in some way haunted by the memory of imprisonment, he was for ever trying to escape from those phantom walls by rebuilding them in a happier context.'
9 *Childe Harold's Pilgrimage,* canto III.
10 In his essay 'The word "Romantic"' in *Poetic craft and principle,* London (1967) pp. 190-2.
11 Quoted from Runciman, Sir S. (1965) *The fall of Constantinople,* p. 149.

Index

Bold figures indicate illustrations

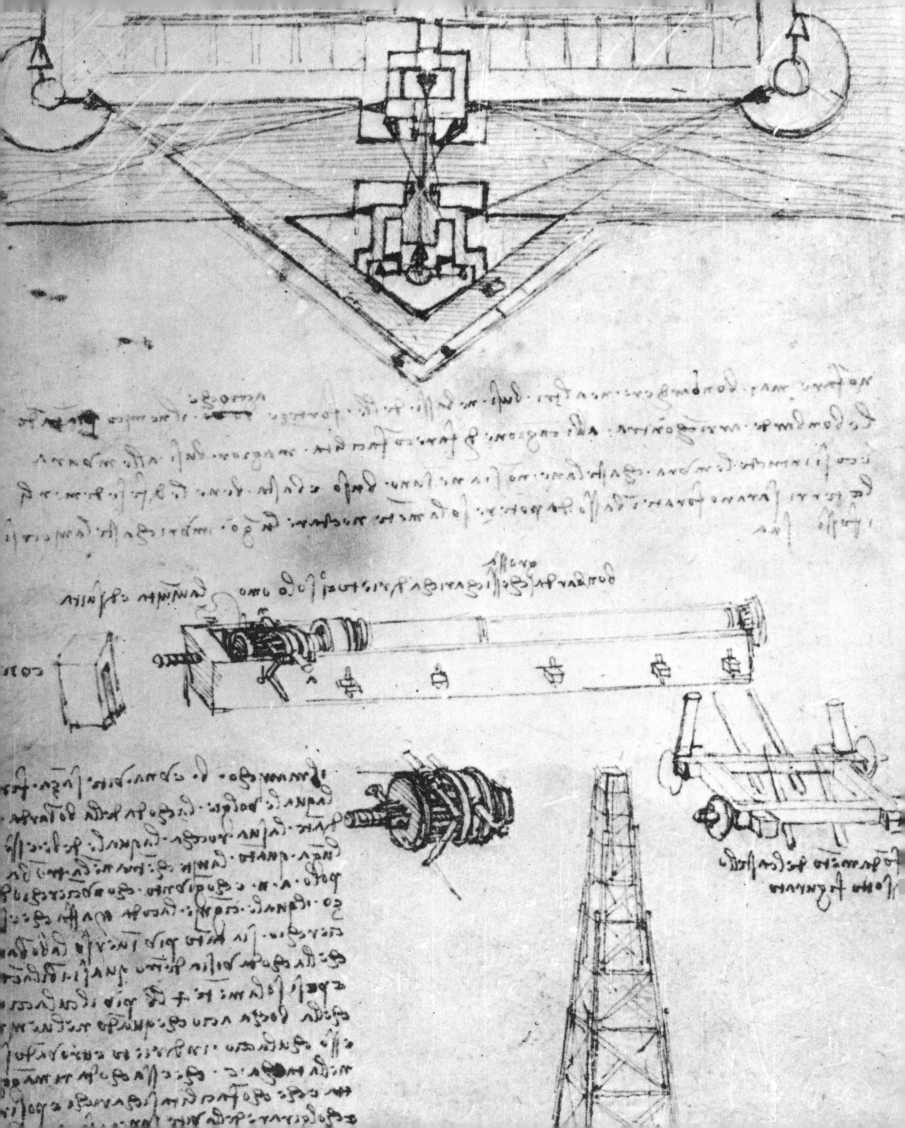